RELIGIOUS CONCEPTIONS

OF THE STONE AGE

and their influence upon European thought

RELIGIOUS CONCEPTIONS

HARPER TORCHBOOKS
The Cloister Library
HARPER & ROW, PUBLISHERS
NEW YORK AND EVANSTON

OF THE STONE AGE

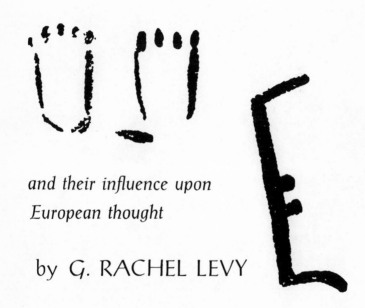

and their influence upon
European thought

by G. RACHEL LEVY

'*Sunt geminae somni portae, quarum altera fertur Cornea, qua veris facilis datur exitus umbris.*'

— Vergil, Aeneid VI. 893-4

To
T. E. L.
O lux Dardaniae . . .

RELIGIOUS CONCEPTIONS OF THE STONE AGE. *Printed in the United States of America.* First published in 1948 by Faber & Faber Limited, London, under the title THE GATE OF HORN and here reprinted by arrangement.

First HARPER TORCHBOOK edition published 1963 by Harper & Row, Publishers, Incorporated, *New York and Evanston.*

INTRODUCTION TO
THE TORCHBOOK EDITION[1]

Henri Frankfort

The value of Miss Levy's work lies in a combination of great
learning with intuitive insight. Its title[2]—*The Gate of Horn*—
can be understood in more ways than one, but, as an evoca-
tion of the final passage of the sixth book of the *Aeneid*, it orientates
the reader. For there Virgil describes the two Gates of Sleep: one
is of shining ivory, and through it false dreams are sent to the
world above; the other is of horn, and it allows passage to true
shades. The title, then, characterizes the work as a vision, for the
reality of shades is not susceptible to proof. Yet they are claimed
to be "true," and we ignore them at our cost. For if the historian
is a willing victim to contingency, resigned to the defects of his
sources, his image of the past suffers from his self-imposed limitations. To see that image completed by intuitive perception is a
challenge and an enrichment: it compels one to ask whether one
has gone to the limits of permissible interpretation; it may reveal
that one's understanding is deepened when these are passed.

Miss Levy presents us with "a study of the religious conceptions
of the Stone Age, and their influence upon European thought."
But her work was "not undertaken to prove a theory, but developed under the stimulus of continual surprise" (p. xiv). Hence
the procedure is descriptive and follows chronological sequence.
First the remains of the Old Stone Age are discussed and corre-
lated with "the religious ideas common to modern hunting
peoples." In this part (Part I), which is most illuminating, the
"cavern" is made the focal point. And its significance in the
Neolithic and Chalcolithic periods is indicated by the subtitle of
Part II: "The Cave as Temple and Tomb." Part III is entitled

---

[1] This Introduction originally appeared as a review article in *Journal of
Near Eastern Studies*, Volume IX, No. 1. It is reprinted with the permission of
The University of Chicago Press.

[2] Professor Frankfort refers to the title of the original edition.

"Ziggurat and Pyramid" and consists of three sections: "Culmination" (Egypt and Sumer), "Perversion" (Central America), and "Revolution" (Palestine). Part IV is called "Survival" and deals with "The City States of the Aegean Bronze Age." Part V is "Resurrection in Greece" and deals with the Greek mystery cults and with the intellectual development of philosophy and the drama.

But if the general arrangement of the book reflects the historical sequence, the articulation of the material, the emphasis, and especially the allusions—backward and forward—which impart to the narrative an exceptionally close texture, carry the argument unflaggingly through the wealth of descriptive detail.

The argument of the book agrees with the underlying assumption of all history, to wit: that the development of human culture is a continuous process. But Miss Levy undertakes to demonstrate this continuity in the field of religious imagination. At the end of her brilliant discussion of the Old Stone Age she remarks that its "declining peoples" are lost from view, "having bequeathed to all humanity a foundation of ideas upon which the mind could raise its structures" (p. 70). Her standpoint implies the monogenesis of culture, and thus she can say of the native civilizations of the New World that "the conditions of their development, separated in the early Neolithic phase from an Asiatic past, caused them to reject certain aspects of their Palaeolithic heritage which remained vital and enduring in the East" (p. 178). Her view certainly explains a number of facts which we are likely to pass over in silence: that figurines of naked, often pregnant, women are found in the Old Stone Age, as well as in the New, throughout Europe and western Asia; that figures with animal masks appear in the Old Stone Age, in Chalcolithic Egypt (Small Hierakonpolis palette) and in Bronze Age Mesopotamia (inlays on a harp from Ur; orthostats at Tell Halaf); that megalithic structures—in their richest development (at Malta) forming artificial caverns—are found all along the Atlantic and Baltic coasts, as well as in Palestine and India and Melanesia; and that the ritual erection of monoliths and dolmens in the latter region (at Malekula) at the present day elucidates the significance of ancient megaliths as strikingly as the ceremonies of the Australian black fellow explain the art of the French and Spanish caves and rock shelters. There is, then, an excellent prima facie case for Miss Levy's contention that she traces "the survival of a body of related ceremonial customs, which seem, however greatly their significance may have deepened and widened in the early civilisations upon which our own is founded, to have their sources at the very beginnings of discernible human institutions. There they appear, not as haphazard or isolated phenomena, but already organised into a coherent discipline, which may even merit the name of religion" (p. xiv).

The author is well aware of the lacunae in our evidence; she disclaims the possibility of offering "certain proof of development from a common source." But "the weight of the whole body of evidence accumulated here is offered as an expression of a living unity of belief and practice, which underlies the religious, artistic and social development of the ancient world before the revolutions of the Iron Age" (p. xiv).

The worst gap in the evidence lies between the Old and the New Stone Age. Braidwood has argued, in several papers and lectures, that we do not know as yet the earliest stage of the "village cultures." On the one hand, a great deal is known about the life of the hunters and food-gatherers of the Old and Middle Stone Age; on the other hand, early Neolithic settlements throughout the Old World confront us with the achievements of agriculture, domestication, pottery-making, and weaving. But Miss Levy's theme allows her to pass over in silence the problem of the origin of these arts, as long as she can make the continuity in religious thought and usage plausible. She sees

a continuous development of conceptions which survived because they held the seeds of all religion, which were to ripen through revolutionary changes in civilization [p. 87].

The religious thought of the great civilizations of the Near East was, in its turn,

the culmination of the Stone Age religion of reciprocity, in which, by ritua[1] attunement to the rhythm of seasonal change, man shared with divinity the responsibility for its maintenance, so that the ceremonies first introduced to guide the birth and death of the hunter's quarry, were replaced in natural succession by those considered necessary to assist the New Year to be born, the very sun to rise, the harvest to be cut down [p. 87].

At this point of Miss Levy's story, where the reader of this *Journal* will be most deeply interested, some of the evidence appears, unfortunately, to be forced. It is undeniable that our view on Egypt and Babylonia gains in depth in the impressive perspective in which it is made to appear. But the handling of the material is not so satisfactory and so reliable as elsewhere. This is in part the result of its peculiar and problematic nature. But even so the connection between early Iranian (p. 93) and predynastic Egyptian (p. 109) painted pottery, on the one hand, and "Capsian geometric conventions," on the other, seems contradictory. The nature of kingship in Egypt (p. 175) and in Babylonia (p. 171), respectively, is not entirely understood. If it is illuminating to see the "bent-axis approach" to the top of the earliest ziggurats and the spiraliform ascent to those of the first millennium B.C. as forms of the "labyrinthine" or "conditional" entry of the megalithic monuments and the earlier caves, it is (in this reviewer's opinion) hardly probable that the passages into the pyramids of Egypt can be interpreted in that way (p. 174). Or, if we admit, as we must, that the crowns of the rulers embody supernatural powers, it must be remembered that the divine crown is not shown on the head of any Mesopotamian ruler except Naramsin and that the filial relation between Pharaoh and his crown is more easily explained as a particular instance of Pharaoh's relation to any goddess than by means of an identification of crown and cavern (p. 176).

But some inaccuracies are bound to occur in a work of so wide a scope; they do not, in the book under review, affect the validity of the main argument which, as we have said already, does not pretend to present binding proofs. It is, for instance, of interest that the significance of cattle images in the religions of Egypt and Mesopotamia can be viewed as a Palaeolithic heritage (pp. 101 ff.). Such a distant common origin would also explain the curious fact that the attribute of the goddess of birth in both countries is the bicornate uterus of a heifer. It is equally interesting that Miss Levy finds in the totemism of the Old Stone Age the ancestor of Egyptian animal worship. The present reviewer has explained zoölatry in Egypt without reference to an anthropological concept which has been much abused and has been employed, especially by Moret, with a connotation "unknown to ethnographers" (Arnold van Gennep, *L'État actuel du problème totémique* [Paris, 1920], pp. 179–202). But the work under review suggests that such a rejection is too radical; perhaps a more ancient and more universal religious attitude did underlie Egyptian animal worship, and it was on it that the meaning we assigned could have been grafted. When we read that totemism implies that

a certain beast or other object of nature was believed to embody at the same time the abiding ancestral spirit perpetually incarnated within a particular group or clan; the willing sacrifice by which that group maintained its life....; the living force present in even greater potency within its manufactured image or symbol; and finally the soul latent in every member of the group, made effectual on initiation, which was the experience of individual unity with all of these [pp. 34–35] . . .

and when we read, further, the profound observations that this totem, as a manifold entity,

is an abstraction, contact with which affects the individuals of the species. That is why art is necessary to such a religion, and why approach of the forms and symbols is so strictly guarded, since they are nearer to reality than the separated lives [p. 39] . . .

then we must ask whether the spiritual life of the Egyptians expressed in their art and religion did not show a greater affinity to that of Palaeolithic man than we usually admit. The question is stimulating, even though it calls up at once such profound differences as the subsidiary, passive, role played by the mother-goddess in Egypt where, in contrast with Western Asia and Greece, all the creator-gods are male. When Miss Levy states that "the history of Asia is full of revolts against the Stone Age conception of unity, attained through embodiment in ritual, as an end in itself" (p. 196), the question arises whether Egypt, too, had moved away from this ideal in creating the royal mediator.

The revolution to which the author refers is specifically discussed in connection with the Hebrews, appearing when "a point is reached, in the mutual development of God's image and the human soul, when . . . as a result of [the] separation of the divine idea from its natural and animal affinities, the means of contact gradually becomes ethical" (p. 196). We cannot discuss this chapter in detail, nor the treatment of the Cretans, who "developed a religion unusually detached from formal bonds, but emotionally binding in its constant endeavour to establish communion with the elemental powers" (p. 214). The reviewer will merely add as a rider that he does not accept the Thisbe rings and the "Ring of Nestor" as genuine documents.

We must likewise refrain from discussing the final chapters in which the greatest achievements of Hellas, treated with boldness and penetration, are shown to comprise, in another sense than Rohde saw, dark elements of greatest antiquity.

We have defined the value of Miss Levy's work at the outset of this article. We might now describe it, in different words, as a total absence of the antiquarian attitude of mind. Throughout she treats religious thought as an actuality of which we cannot merely know the external manifestations but which we can understand in an imaginative experience. Hence she can end her description of the Near Eastern "religion inaugurated in the bucolic hut, in which the rites of fertility and of sacrifice were united" (p. 106) by saying that "its life-giving function was never forgotten through the rise and decay of the civilisations which it helped to found, was apparent when the present religious cycle was inaugurated for the West in the Cave-Byre of Bethlehem between the gentle beasts."

CONTENTS

CONTENTS

PART V

RESURRECTION IN GREECE

PREFACE

During a large part of the decade which preceded the second world war, I was attached to an expedition engaged in uncovering a group of archaeological sites in Iraq. Scattered among the journals available for discussion when each day's dust had been removed, were several articles by Mr. W. F. Jackson Knight, which dealt with the labyrinthine defences of legendary cities and tombs. There was also a series of investigations into the nature and origin of the mythical Labyrinth, published by Dr. F. Muller in current numbers of the Dutch journal *Mnemosyne*.

The work of these scholars appeared to offer scope for a fuller interpretation than had so far been possible, of protective rites discovered both in the vanished civilisation with which the expedition was concerned, and in the related cultures of neighbouring states.

Later, amid the resources of European libraries, it became apparent that any attempt to discover a general relationship among ceremonies designed for the defence of sacred buildings of the bronze age, must be taken back not only to the Neolithic cults upon which they appeared to be founded, but even across the immense chasm of climatic change and economic upheaval, which separated both cultural phases from the Palaeolithic social order.

At this point, a grant from the University of London enabled me to supplement the years of Middle Eastern travel with visits to the Megalithic sites of Malta and Southern Brittany, and to the Palaeolithic caves of south-west France and the Pyrenees. Then the war shut off further contacts, and after 1940 my access to foreign publications also ceased. Additions and revisions, made since then, are confined to notes, with the important exception of some fifteen pages of the Megalithic chapter in Part III, for which the publication, in 1943, of the first volume of John Layard's *Stone Men of Malekula*, supplied rich new material which greatly strengthened my argument, by its record, taken from the lips of a people still in a Megalithic stage of culture, of the meaning and purpose of rites performed in the author's presence, and of the monuments erected for their celebration. The following pages, however, were not undertaken to prove a theory, but developed under the stimulus of continual surprise. They deal with the survival of a body of related ceremonial customs, which seem, however greatly their significance may have deepened and widened in the early civilisations upon which our own is founded, to have their sources at the very beginnings of discernible human institutions. There they appear, not as haphazard or isolated phenomena, but already organised into a coherent discipline, which may even merit the name of religion.

No line of research into the distribution through time and space of individual rites or objects of cult, which may seem to bear a relation to the earliest known ceremonies, can offer certain proof of development from a common source, but the weight of the whole body of evidence accumulated here, is offered as the expression of a living unity of belief and practice, which underlies the religious, artistic and social development of the ancient world before the revolutions of the iron age.

The investigation is limited in scope to archaeological and literary remains embodying certain conceptions which directly influenced the development of European thought. It leaves out of account, for example, the enormous creative achievements of early India and China. It reaches forward in time only to the raising of prehellenic religious conceptions to an intellectual level in early Greek philosophy and drama, where their influence is potent still. The whole problem of Mithraism, which appears to share so many elements of the religion of the Stone Age, is therefore left untouched.

It is my hope, however, that the material assembled here forms an organic whole which betrays its relationship with other organisms, springing, it may be, from similar origins. The survival and lasting significance, through eras of unimaginable change, of such a body of coherent ideas, may afford some consolation at this catastrophic time.

I am glad of this opportunity to record my gratitude to the Senate of London University for the travelling grant which enabled me in 1938 to visit Stone-Age sites in South-Western Europe; to Professor Dorothy Garrod, who put her great knowledge at my disposal, read the palaeolithic chapters of this book,

PREFACE

and helped me in every possible manner; to Mr. Miles Burkitt, for kind criticism of the early chapters; to Professor Henri Frankfort for reading the Sumerian and Egyptian parts of the text and for unfailing practical help and advice in general from the time when he first suggested the writing of this book, and equally to Mrs. H. A. Frankfort, whose insight into problems of ancient art has been a continual inspiration.

I am deeply grateful to Dr. A. B. Cook and Dr. Gilbert Murray, whose criticism of the later chapters was a stimulus and encouragement, and to Mr. W. F. Jackson Knight for his *Cumaean Gates* and some very useful points of difference. I wish also to express my warm thanks to Dr. Fritz Saxl, Director of the Warburg Institute, for putting at my disposal the skill of his photographer, Dr. Fein; to my cousin Winifred Simon for lending me her cottage to work in; to Joan Joshua and Audrey Cohen for generous time given to checking references; to Miss D. M. Vaughan for compiling the index; and to Miss Mackenzie and Mrs. Titcombe for typing the text. Lastly I should like to thank my publishers for their consideration.

1946   G. RACHEL LEVY.

ACKNOWLEDGMENTS OF SOURCES
OF THE ILLUSTRATIONS

I am indebted to the Institut de Paléontologie humaine for the illustrations reproduced in Pl. I, and for many plans and drawings in the text, from the publications of the Prince of Monaco Foundation; to the Trustees of the British Museum for photographs reproduced in Pls. XXIV, XXV (a) and (b) and XXVI (c) from the Guide to the Maudslay Collection; to the British Museum and the University Museum of Pennsylvania for the reproductions in Pl. IX (a) and (b), and Pl. XI (e), of objects discovered by their joint expedition to Ur; to the University Museum of Pennsylvania also, for the photograph reproduced in Pl. XXV (b), and the illustration, in fig. 59, from *Museum Journal* XV; to the Controller of H.M. Stationery Office, for permission to reproduce, from the Official Guide to Stonehenge, the plan and diagram of Pl. XX (b) and fig. 78; to the Director and Librarian of the Museum at Valetta, for fine photographs of objects from the Maltese temples reproduced in Pl. XVI, XVII and XVIII; to the Curator of the Musée Miln-Le Rouzic at Carnac, for the reproduction in Pl. XIX, of two figures from Le Rouzic and Keller's *La Table des Marchands;* to the Directorate of Antiquities in Iraq for the reproduction of objects from the Iraq Museum in Pl. XI (b) and (c), and the Museum of Modern Art, New York, by whose courtesy Pl.III (b) is reproduced here from Frobenius' *Prehistoric Rock-Pictures.*

To the Archaeological Survey of India, for Pl. XII(c) and (d), to the Society of Antiquaries and the executors of the late Sir Arthur Evans, for fig. 92, reproduced from *Archaeologia,* vol. LXV; to the Egyptian Exploration Society, for Pl. VIII(c) and (d), and Pl. XIV (c); to the Hellenic Society for figs. 101, 104, 107, 109, 119, 120 and 123, all from the *Journal of Hellenic Studies,* to the Hispanic Society of America and Yale University Press, for Pl. VI (a) and figs. 40 and 48, and to Professor Mallowan and the British School in Iraq, for figs. 43 and 44, reproduced from *Iraq II.*

I am grateful to the Director of *L'Anthropologie,* for the reliefs

ACKNOWLEDGMENTS

from Lalanne's excavations reproduced in Pl. VII; to the Editor of *Antiquity*, for Pl. XV and Pl. XVI (*e*), reproduced from vol. IV, and Pl. XX (*a*) from vol. X; to the Hon. Editor of the *Wiltshire Archaeological and Natural History Magazine* for fig. 77; to L'Imprimerie Berger-Levrault, for eleven figures from Péquart and Le Rouzic's *Corpus des Signes Gravés des Monuments Mégalithiques du Morbihan;* to Editions Picard, for fig. 7, from Mainage, *Les Réligions de la Préhistoire;* to Sir Leonard Woolley and Librairie Geuthner, for Pl. VIII (*a*) and (*b*); to Librairie Grund, Paris, for Pl. XXVI (*b*), reproduced from Basler and Brummer's *L'Art Précolumbien;* to C.W.K. Gleerup Bokförlag, of Lund, for figs. 93 and 102 reproduced from Nilsson's *Minoan-Mycenaean Religion*, and fig. 118, reproduced from Persson's *The Royal Tombs at Dendra;* to the Oxford University Press and Mr. Charles Zammit, for Pls. XVII (*a*) and (*b*) and XVIII (*d*) and (*e*), reproduced from *Prehistoric Malta;* to Messrs. Chatto and Windus, for Pl. XXI, and figs. 79 to 85, reproduced from Layard's *Stone Men of Malekula;* to the Clarendon Press for the Bushman drawings after H. M. Tongue, reproduced in figs. 31 and 33; to Messrs. Macmillan and Co., Ltd., and the executors of the late Sir Arthur Evans, for nineteen figures reproduced from Evans' *Tree and Pillar Cult* and *The Palace of Minos*, to Messrs. Macmillan also, for three figs. from Sollas, *Ancient Hunters*, for plates from Spencer and Gillen's *Northern Tribes of Central Australia*, reproduced in Pls. III, IV and V, and for Pl. X (*b*), XXII (*a*), and XXIII (*d*), from Frankfort's, *Cylinder Seals;* to Messrs. Methuen and Co. Ltd., for fig. 57, taken from Budge's *Gods of the Egyptians*, vol. II; to Messrs. Longmans Green and Co. Ltd., for fig. 34, reproduced from Matthews, *Mazes and Labyrinths* after Cotton, and for fig. 68 from Parkyn, *Prehistoric Art;* to Messrs. Putnam and Co. Ltd., for Pl. IX (*d*) from Pl. XXXVIII of the English edition of *Tel Halaf*, by M. von Oppenheim; to Messrs. Rider for permission to reproduce fig. I from Whishaw's *Atlantis in Andalusia* in my Pl. XIII (*b*); to Messrs. Geo. Routledge and Sons, Ltd., and Messrs. Kegan, Paul, Trench, Trübner and Co., Ltd., for five reproductions from Childe's *The Dawn of European Civilization* and *New Light on the Most Ancient East*, and one each from Moret's *The Nile and Egyptian Civilization* and Davy and Moret's *From Tribe to Empire;* I wish also to express my gratitude to Prof. Dorothy Garrod, for her help with the map in fig. I; to Miss V. C. C. Collum, for the

ACKNOWLEDGMENTS

photo reproduced in Pl. XIX (*a*) from her book *The Tressé Monument;* to the Countess Bégouen for fig. 20, from *Revue Archéologique*, 1934; to Mr. Pierre Delougaz for the unpublished photo from Khafaje shown in Pl. XIII (*a*), and to Dr. Thorkild Jacobsen, Director of the Oriental Institute of Chicago, for allowing it to appear before the publication of the Official Report.

Lastly I must apologise to a few authors, publishers and institutions with whom I was prevented from making contact owing to difficulties of communication arising out of the war. I hope that they may accept my assurance that the discourtesy is unintentional, and thank them for the permission which would no doubt have been granted.

LIST OF PLATES

1. PALAEOLITHIC WALL PAINTINGS
facing page 16

(*a*) Palimpsest at Altamira.
(*b*) Crouching bison, Altamira.
(*c*) Silhouetted hands at Castillo.
(*d*) Procession at Font de Gaume.

2. PALAEOLITHIC RELIGIOUS, MAGIC, AND EVERYDAY REPRESENTATION
17

(*a*) Female diagram from Predmost (Obermaier after Kriz).
(*b*) Magician at Les Trois Frères (Breuil).
(*c*) Stylization at La Roche.
(*d*) Rock painting at Cogul (Breuil).
(*e*) Horse amulet from Isturitz (R. de Saint-Périer).

3. RELIGIOUS ART AND PRACTICE AMONG RECENT PRIMITIVES
32

(*a*) Australian cave painting (Bradshaw).
(*b*) The great Hand from Wadi Sora (Frobenius).
(*c*) The Path of the Rope (*Illustrated London News*, Aug. 1939).
(*d*) Wollunqa ground-drawing (Spencer & Gillen).

4. MODERN CEREMONIES
33

(*a*) The Duk-Duk dance in New Guinea (Obermaier).
(*b*) A North-American bear dancer (Catlin).
(*c*) Ground drawing of the Emu totem (Spencer & Gillen).
(*d*) An Emu dancer (Spencer & Gillen).

5. PALAEOLITHIC AND MODERN COMPARISONS
48

(*a*) Magdalenian 'ceremonial wand'.
(*b*) Churinga of the rain totem (Spencer & Gillen).
(*c*) Kurnai bull-roarer.
(*d*) Palaeolithic bull-roarer.

LIST OF PLATES

10. PASTORAL SUMER DEPICTED ON CYLINDER SEALS

11. SUMERIAN RITUAL SCENES   108

12. SUMER AND INDIA   109

13. COPPER AGE BURIALS   112

14. EGYPT—HATHOR AND THE EARLY KINGS 113

25. OLD EMPIRE MAYAN SCULPTURE

facing page 192

(*a*) Stele from Quiriguá.
(*b*) Divinity scattering seed from Piedras Negras (Photo, University Museum of Pennsylvania).
(*c*) The Night Sun. Monolith from Quiriguá, (British Museum).

26. NEW EMPIRE, MEXICO AND BOLIVIA 193

(*a*) Pyramid of Kukulcan at Chichen Itza.
(*b*) The Aztec Earth-Goddess (National Museum of Mexico).
(*c*) Toltec Serpent Column from Chichen Itza (British Museum).
(*d*) Decapitation in the ball-court. Frieze from Chichen Itza (*Illustrated London News*, July, 1937).
(*e*) Monolithic Gateway at Tiahuanacu.

27. MINOAN ART 208

(*a*) Part of Griffin fresco round the throne-room at Knossos (Evans).
(*b*) The 'Harvester' Vase from Haghia Triada (Savignone).

28. THE HAGHIA TRIADA SARCOPHAGUS 209

(*a*) Procession with offerings (Heraklion Museum).
(*b*) The Bull Sacrifice (Heraklion Museum).
(*c*) The Griffin. Detail from fresco at Knossos (Evans).
(*d*) Griffin chariot from the Sarcophagus (Bossert).

29. FUNERAL RINGS 240

(*a*) Procession of Genii before the Goddess. Signet from Tiryns (Karo).
(*b*) The 'Ring of Nestor' (Evans).
(*c*) The 'Ring of Minos' (Evans).

30. RELIEFS 241

(*a*) The Lion gate at Mycenæ.
(*b*) Masked Procession. Shell plaque from Phaestos.

LIST OF PLATES

31. GREEK NATURE RELIGION

facing page 256

(*a*) The Meeting of Apollo and Dionysos at Delphi (Hermitage).

(*b*) Satyrs awakening the Earth in Spring (Berlin).

(*c*) The Child as First Fruits (Stamboul Museum).

32. GREEK MYSTERIES   257

(*a*) Pinax of Ninnion from Eleusis (Rev. Internationale d'Archéologie, 1901).

(*b*) Relief from Eleusis (Nat. Mus. Athens).

FIGURES IN THE TEXT

FIGURES IN THE TEXT

PART ONE

PALÆOLITHIC—THE CAVE AS HABITATION AND SANCTUARY

CHAPTER I

THE CAVERNS

This story begins with the retreat of the icefields after the last and greatest period of cold ever known to these latitudes, when members of the first races belonging to our own lineage are believed to have moved across the bitter steppes of Eastern and Central Europe, to find security in caverns of the limestone cliffs and mountain sides of South-West France and North-West Spain. Here they have left records of the development of a system of beliefs and practices which, lost and reformed through the catastrophes of progressive or antithetical civilisations, may be shown to have influenced, to have helped to create, the spiritual and intellectual activities of to-day.

This is an endeavour to trace the growth, destruction and revival of that system at certain crises of the earliest history of Europe and its neighbours, which are perceptible in the sporadic light of archæological research, or of the monuments and literary remains that suggest the profound significance of the cave in the race-memory and traditions of more advanced peoples.

Its founders appear, on the evidence of their bones, to have belonged chiefly to the race called Crô-magnon after the locality in which it was first distinguished; a tall and well-proportioned people with a brain capacity of modern dimensions. Their stone implements (Aurignacian industry) are distributed across Europe and the Near East, the later phases of the culture being extended, in the present state of our knowledge, far into Siberia,[1] where hut-foundations have left traces suggestive of religious or magical beliefs connected with the chase or the

---

[1] *L'Anthropologie*, xliii, 1928, E. A. Golomshtok, 'Trois gisements du paléolithique supérieur russe et sibérien,' pp. 341–346. S. N. Zamiatnine in *Paleolit S.S.S.R.*, Moscow, 1935, pp. 78–124.

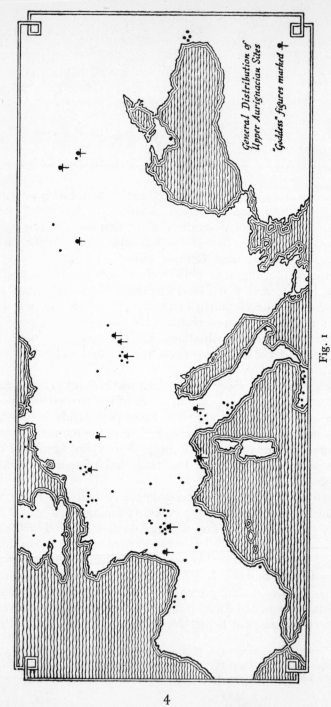

General Distribution of
Upper Aurignacian Sites

"Goddess" figures marked ⚲

Fig. 1

4

domestic hearth (fig. 1). A hunting people of kindred culture crossed into Eastern Spain at a rather later date from North Africa, where climatic conditions had long favoured the growth of open-air communities.[1] Much can be learnt from the paintings on their rock-shelters on both sides of the Mediterranean, of the activities of their daily life, but very little of religious beliefs. The building up of the elaborate organisation to be considered here, can only as yet be traced in the remote depths of the caves of Western Europe, where it survived the alien occupation of Solutré, to attain its perfection in the succeeding Magdalenian culture, intensified by isolation during a partial return of glacial conditions.

THE PRECURSORS

The Crô-magnon peoples were not the first to make their homes in caves. They dispossessed a race of ape-like beings, the Neanderthal Men, beside whose animal strength they must have resembled the ghostly waifs of their own later self portraiture on the cavern walls. These creatures, who had survived the prolonged rigours of the great glaciation, eventually perished in contact with the fragile superiority of true man; but before their extinction they may have bequeathed the art of life in shallow grottoes opening on to terraces which caught the sun, set well above some valley of accessible water, as they bequeathed the example of beautiful craftsmanship in their stone implements (Mousterian industry). They appear to have spread, in the warmer epoch, over a great part of the world; the final development of one of those sub-human races who in the passage of myriads of centuries have left no intelligible records beyond their fossil bones scattered at rare intervals in the open river drifts of the old world, their more numerous worked stone implements, and the ashes of fires.

It can no longer be assumed that the onset of Arctic conditions drove Neanderthal man to make his home in caves, for his kinsmen had lived in this manner amid the temperate

---

[1] See H. Obermaier, *Fossil Man in Spain*, 1924, and M. C. Burkitt, *Prehistory*, 2nd edition, 1925, for a general account of their culture.

fauna of Palestinian cliff-ledges.[1] And the remarkable fact is now long established that this creation of a home was not confined to the living family or group. The uncouth bodies of Mousterian men, who hardly walked upright, who seem never to have developed fully articulate speech, were buried in trenches laboriously excavated in the floors of their caves, under conditions which leave no doubt that the living believed in their continued existence, at a period long antecedent to the coming of the Crô-magnons into Europe. The careful sepulture of women and children, with implements and offerings, indicates the existence, if not of the family, at least of the group or clan, whose uniting bonds were felt to extend through time, for the animal bones found beside certain of these graves are too numerous to represent a funeral feast, and suggest continuous relationship.[2] There are even the first indications of art in cup-shaped depressions carved into the underside of the stone slabs laid upon one Neanderthal grave,[3] and the red ochre, now an indistinguishable suffusion of colour, which was occasionally painted on their bodies. There are sometimes signs of continued habitation above them; the bones in these shallow trenches would, in fact, have otherwise been dispersed by beasts in spite of the overlying stones. The frequent presence also, of fine weapons beside the men, points to a reliance on the protection of the dead, to the preponderance of affection over fear in the attitude of the survivors.

This is the earliest indication in Europe of belief in a nonphysical existence. But such people could not have inaugurated the religion of the cave, for which the development of art was essential. Skeletons of a very primitive type of Mousterian man have lately been discovered amid glacial deposits on Mt.

---

[1] F. Turville-Petre, *Researches in Prehistoric Galilee*, 1925–1926, and Sir A. Keith, *Report on the Galilee Skull, British School of Archæology at Jerusalem*, 1927; D. A. E. Garrod, 'The Near East as a Gateway of Prehistoric Migration', in G. G. MacCurdy, *Early Man*, 1937, p. 33 ff.; idem, *The Stone Age of Mt. Carmel*, vol. i, 1937, pp. 106, 113. Sir A. Keith and T. D. McCown, in MacCurdy, op. cit., p. 41 ff.

[2] G. H. Luquet, *The Art and Religion of Fossil Man*, 1930, p. 166. *L'Anthropologie*, xxiv, 1913, A. and J. Bouyssonie and L. Bardon, 'La Station Moustérienne de la "Bouffia" Bonneval,' pp. 629–632.

[3] L. Capitan and D. Peyrony, 'Découverte d'un sixième squelette mousterién à la Ferrassie, Dordogne,' *Revue anthropologique*, xxxi, 1921, p. 382 ff. See fig. 41 below.

Carmel in Palestine, in a cave adjacent to another containing the graves of a contemporary human community akin to the future Crô-magnons. Here the appearance of both types of implement in a single archæological stratum, reveals the possibility that the Neanderthal burial customs may have actually been acquired by a far earlier contact than was hitherto supposed, with human people who already, in a temperate climate, inhabited caves. For the burials on Mt. Carmel exhibit a similar careful disposal of the dead.[1]

LIFE AT THE CAVE-MOUTH

Apart from the proximity of such graves and possibly the presence of stone or ivory female figurines which are not at this time directly connected with cave-ritual, the hearths associated with the Aurignacian industry of the West show few indications of religious practice. The Crô-magnon dwellings were the shallow grottoes of their predecessors, or the entrance-halls of vast subterranean passage-ways always open to daylight; the shelters and workshops to which the hunting communities repaired after the chase. These were perhaps used intermittently, following the seasonal migrations of the herds, and occupied as an alternative to the huts known, from their existing foundations and the painted records, to have been constructed from an early period where climatic conditions allowed.[2]

The epoch of greatest cold had driven the mammoth and the reindeer southward, to wander in enormous herds, together with the woolly rhinoceros, the bison, fallow deer and saiga antelope, with various breeds of horse, over the grassy plains which gradually replaced the frozen tundra and stunted Arctic forests, right down to the valleys of Northern Spain. The

[1] Sir A. Keith and T. D. McCown; in MacCurdy, op. cit.; T. D. McCown, article 'Fossil Woman', in *The Times* of March 19th, 1937, pp. 17–18.

[2] Hut foundations were found, for example, in Palæolithic levels at Gagarino on the Don (E. A. Golomshtok, op. cit., in *L'Anthropologie*, xliii, 1928, pp. 334–336; S. N. Zamiatnine in *Paleolit S.S.S.R.*, pp. 26–27) and at Mal'ta in Siberia, *v.* note i, p. 3.

Reed or wattle huts appear to be represented on the cave walls of Altamira in Spain, and of La Mouthe in the Dordogne. (E. Cartailhac and H. Breuil—*La Caverne d'Altamira*, 1906, pp. 54–55, 88, and fig. 44; and Comte Bégouen, 'The Magic Origin of Prehistoric Art,' in *Antiquity*, 1929, p. 10.)

animals, to judge by the distribution of their bones and by symbols painted on the cavern walls, were driven into pits, over precipices; were trapped, stoned, and wounded with darts and javelins. Their comparatively puny hunters, whose continued existence was entirely dependent upon the great beasts, do not seem to have relied solely on physical or even on mental skill. At the cave mouth where they shaped their weapons of flint and bone, of mammoth-ivory and reindeer-horn, they also hollowed the shallow bowls occasionally found to-day, in which blazing moss must have floated on fat to guide their exploration of the interior halls. At the entrance, too, they struck off graving tools and ground colours out of mineral earths and charcoal, to be compressed into bone tubes and employed within (as it is hoped to show), to attain a relationship with their prospective benefactors and victims.

ACTIVITIES OF THE DEEPER RECESSES

It was formerly maintained that the animal shapes which illuminate with such startling beauty the solitude of remote chambers in these caverns, were the free expression, gradually perfected by the huntsman's exactitude of hand and eye, of delight in the vitality, strength or speed of his quarry, and indeed such personal joy and admiration is intensely present in these achievements (fig. 18, page 20). But the conditions of their portrayal, soon to be described, are deliberately unfavourable both to the exercise and the display of art for its own sake. They combine most significantly to support the conclusion, now strengthened by an accumulation, both of direct archæological evidence and of ethnological material from elsewhere, that they formed an essential part of ceremonies conducted in those recesses, which were removed, not only from the physical energies of the chase, but almost invariably also from the domestic life about the hearth, by natural barriers consisting of intricate and frequently dangerous passages, whose meanderings seem to have imparted their mystery to later legend.

For it is hoped to show first that these ceremonies were of a religious nature, as yet inseparable from art, magic, and social and economic experiment, and later that this religion, developed under very terrible physical conditions, was an integral

8

organism capable of communicating itself to the civilisations of a more clement time.

Let us now examine the environment in which these works are to be found. Figs. 2 and 3 show the distribution of the most important painted caverns discovered before 1940, among the steep cliffs above the river-valleys of the Dordogne, the Vézère and the Lot, fig. 4 their situation along the northern foothills

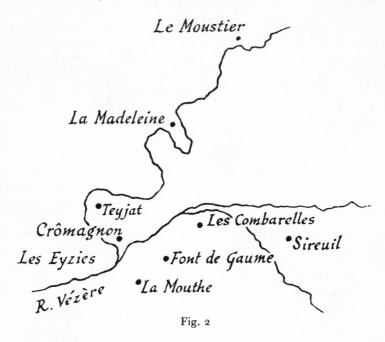

Fig. 2

of the Pyrenees and the Cantabrian Mountains. The great caves in all these regions display exactly the same general choice of conditions for the production of an art whose identity of style testifies to the distribution of a common culture on both sides of the mountain barrier.

INTERNAL CONDITIONS OF THE CAVES

Figs. 5, 6 and 7 (p. 12) reproduce plans of a few of these cave-systems which reveal the separation of the entrance chamber, with or without the vestiges of occupation, from the halls and

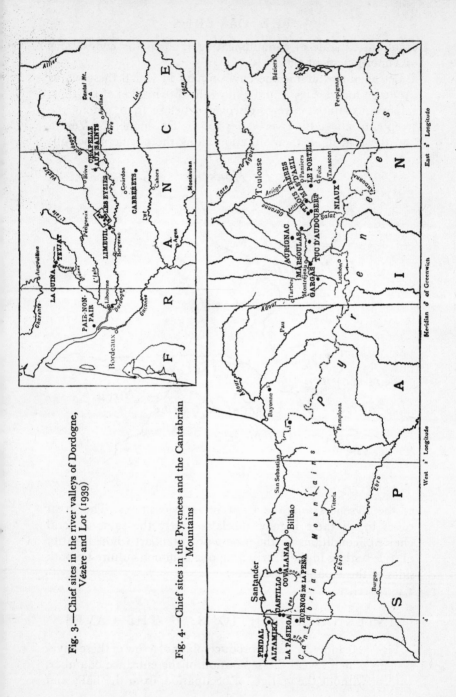

Fig. 3.—Chief sites in the river valleys of Dordogne, Vézère and Lot (1939)

Fig. 4.—Chief sites in the Pyrenees and the Cantabrian Mountains

passages in which paintings and engravings occur. It will probably be conceded from a glance at the plans alone, that 'No one would dream of hedging round a mere picture-gallery with such trying turnstiles',[1] but they give little indication of the formidable nature of these defences of twisting, often very narrow, always slippery corridors, along which the intruders groped their way, clinging to curtains of stalactite, descending into chasms, negotiating waterfalls or chimneys, into the gigantic darkness of halls such as those of Niaux, whose dimensions their tiny lamps could never have revealed (there are no signs of torch-blackening in the tunnels); where their freed footsteps sped silent over sand-hills left by the extinct river, and the dripping of distant water was terribly magnified to ears alert for the cave-lion or bear, and beyond these to desired recesses, which sometimes retain the impression of their hands and knees beneath the glaze of deposits from the roof. The entry to Pech-Merle has such narrows, such abysses, such sliding cataracts of stalactite,[2] the chamber of Clotilde must be approached on hands and knees.[3] Font-de-Gaume, as the plan reveals (fig. 5), once straitens to a tunnel through which a broad figure can only with difficulty be pressed, before advancing to the halls of frescoes. La Pasiega is reached through a man-hole below which a subterranean river hurls itself against precipices above whose most perilous ascents are painted signs and animals. It leads by 'a labyrinth of sometimes dangerous, always narrow galleries, above an inaccessible rock-face', to the painted hall with its rock-cut 'throne', 'a mystery desired and sought,' as its discoverers describe it, 'in an arcanum forbidden to the profane.'[4]

At Montespan three hours are required to overcome the obstacles of 'un dédale de galéries superposées', whose only signs of previous occupation are the tracks of great beasts in the clay, to a natural stairway leading up to one small gallery, where the moulded figures remain above a floor covered with ruined reliefs. Tuc d'Audoubert, approached like Montespan

---

[1] R. R. Marett, *The Threshold of Religion*, second edition, 1914, p. 218.

[2] A. Lemozi, *La Grotte-Temple du Pech-Merle*, 1929, chaps, 2, 3, 4.

[3] *L'Anthropologie*, xv (1904), p. 643; xvi (1905), p. 440. E. Cartailhac and H. Breuil, *Peintures et gravures murales des cavernes pyrénéennes*.

[4] H. Breuil, H. Obermaier and H. Alcalde del Rio, *Peintures et gravures murales des cavernes paléolithiques: La Pasiega*, Monaco, 1913, p. 54.

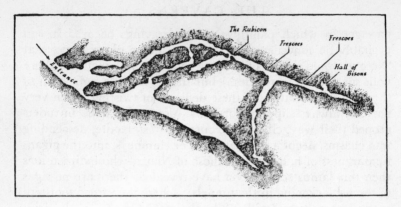

Fig. 5

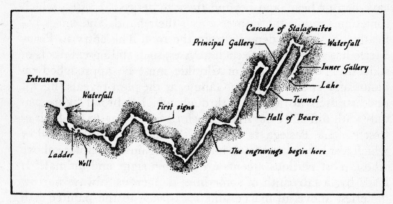

Fig. 6

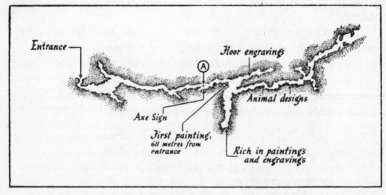

Fig. 7

by means of a sunken river, requires a climb by ladders and pegs, then a crawl through corridors to the prints of dancing feet and the modelled bisons beyond.[1] Les Trois Frères needs half an hour's walk through a succession of corridors to the chamber whose principal figure is wholly visible[2] only after the crawl through a pipe-like tunnel and negotiation of a rock-chimney, with a foot on either side of the chasm.[3]

The descent to Labastide is a vertical pit. The cave opens from its side, a hundred feet down, into another pit that leaves only a narrow ledge by which passage can be made to vast corridors. Beyond these a grand lion's head snarls above herds of horses.[4]

The eyes of the first human explorers, in the few poor representations to be found here and elsewhere among the splendid animals forms, have the unfocused stare of owls or night-prowling beasts. They must have come to distinguish darkness from deeper dark, if only to avoid crushing their skulls against the pendant stalactites. But the poise of their prey in the outer snow-light could never have been discerned with the sharpness essential to huntsman and artist alike, if their lives between hunts had been passed in total gloom. Indeed, the signs of daily activities which abound in the archæological levels of the entrance chambers and open caverns are strikingly absent here. Apart from an occasional graving tool, lamp or fallen fragment of colour (their palettes may have been of skins, like those of the Eskimos), there remain only their sparse footprints and the designs on walls, ceilings, pillars of stalagmite, or mud-laid floor, comprising abstract symbols or natural forms, painted in coloured earths or drawn with soot or charcoal mixed with fat, engraved and sometimes modelled in clay, ranging from the first tentative lines of the earliest Aurignacians to the complex masterpieces with chiaroscuro and

[1] *L'Anthropologie*, xxiii (1912), pp. 657–658, Comte Bégouen, 'Les statues d'argile de la caverne du Tuc d'Audoubert (Ariège).'

[2] The figure is painted and engraved. Only the painted parts are visible from below.

[3] *Revue Anthropologique*, 1934, pp. 115–119, Comte Bégouen and H. Breuil, 'De quelques figures hybrides de la caverne des Trois-Frères (Ariège).' Also 'Un dessin relevé dans la caverne des Trois Frères', *Comptes rendus de l'Ac. des Inscr. et Belles Lettres*, 1920, p. 303.

[4] N. Casteret, *Ten Years under the Earth*, 1939, pp. 23–25.

some perspective, of late Magdalenian culture.[1] Throughout the long florescence of this art, the same preference is manifest for remote interstices or niches, which look like side-chapels, generally furnished with a natural platform, and decorated, often crowded, like the little 'hall of the bisons' at Font-de-Gaume or the procession in the long gallery (pl. I*d*), with a medley of animal shapes depicted from every angle of vision, one often effacing another, through generations which reveal many developments of style, as at Altamira (fig. 8 and pl. I*a*).

Fig. 8

Such painted recesses, frequently occurring in the neighbourhood of spacious, smooth, easily accessible wall-spaces, could only have been utilised with the greatest difficulty by men crouched sideways or lying on their backs or completely doubled up, scarcely able to spare, from supporting their own weight, a hand to steady the feeble lamp, still less to trace the bold, firm shapes of their vision. Many of these require of the spectator an equally restricted position, others a struggle through the narrow apertures of some hidden cul-de-sac leading from a hall empty of art, like the birds in the secret corridor of El Pendo.[2] Other figures are set high, to be reached by artist or spectator after a perilous climb, as in the Galérie des Chouettes at Les Trois Frères, or the ascent to the six oxen engraved at La Loja on the summit of a pyramid of stalagmite,

[1] H. Breuil and H. Obermaier, *The Cave of Altamira*, 1935 (Hispanic Society of America, etc.). Chap. vi, 'Relative Chronology of Paintings and Engravings in French Caves.'

[2] H. Alcalde del Rio, H. Breuil and L. Sierra, *Les cavernes de la Région Cantabrique*, 1911, pp. 36–38.

where the face and body of the beholder are pressed against the decorated surface.[1]

Long rods must have been used for the painting of signs on the overhanging walls of Santián or Pech-Merle, or on the roof at Bolao Llanes,[2] arched above one of those sunless lakes whose prehistoric existence may be presumed from the absence of stalagmites in their beds. It is difficult to imagine that certain of these signs could ever have been visible from below.

Apart from the choice of remote areas of the inner halls as the setting of these works,[3] and their difficult approaches, it will be noticed that a considerable space has generally to be traversed before the first forms or symbols appear, and it has sometimes been suggested that changes in the outer atmosphere through this immense passage of time, may have destroyed paintings which once reached to the cave mouth. But such climatic instability would not have obliterated engravings, nor those figures which became varnished with stalagmite; nor would its influence have been likely to extend through the vicissitudes of half a mile of tortuous passages to the first sign on the walls of Niaux, Trois Frères or Tuc d'Audoubert. The famous polychrome bisons of Altamira, which do lie near the present entrance, their bright colours long protected by a landslide, are of later date than the hearths at the cave mouth; that is to say, they were worked after the cave had ceased to be inhabited.[4] Nor could motives of security from the great beasts who shared their cave-life have interposed such barricades between the homes of Crô-magnon men and the works of art beyond, for the huge skulls of the cave-bear are common in the chambers, for example, of Gargas and Pech-Merle. Their footprints at Tuc d'Audoubert accompany the tracks of human feet on narrow ledges above some chasm or morass; the grooves of their claw-sharpenings may be discerned above and below a single series of painted signs at Castillo;[5] the tunnelled walls are

[1] H. Alcalde del Rio, H. Breuil and L. Sierra, op. cit., pp. 55–56.

[2] M. C. Burkitt, *Prehistory*, second edition, 1925, p. 202.

[3] In the recently discovered cave at Lascaux near Montignac, paintings are found close to the entrance. But this cave, into which the intruder drops twenty feet through a narrow chasm, was never inhabited. It was presumably only used for ceremonies (see p. 21, note 1, below).

[4] H. Obermaier, *Fossil Man in Spain*, 1924, p. 260.

[5] H. Alcalde del Rio, H. Breuil and L. Sierra, op. cit., fig. 104.

smooth in places from the passage of their enormous bodies. Their bones were often crushed by rocks, presumably aimed from above. The feet of the cave lion, too, have stumbled on slippery footholds which retain their pressure on the clay. Until these monsters were extinguished in the mortal cold of the partial glacial return,[1] the cave-entrance would have been the region least disturbed by alarms. The choice of the cave depths must have another origin.

THE RECORDS

It is now time to examine the works depicted upon the cavern walls, to note the peculiar qualities and limitations of their style.

They may be classified under three groups according to subject: (a) abstract signs, (b) animal forms, (c) human representations.

THE SIGNS

The signs range from 'macaroni' or mæanders traced with rod or finger upon the clay which coated the ceilings, usually of vestibules, to the elaborate 'tectiforms', considered to be huts or traps, painted in red or black, grouped upon the wall face or laid upon the body of a beast.

The mæanders, which belong to the most primitive art of the caves, sometimes appear in a form resembling a pathway or plan, which may possibly, at Niaux for example, serve as a chart of entry to the inner halls. La Pileta has instances of enclosures which may represent the cave itself (fig. 9, p. 17), approached by dotted lines resembling footprints, and one like a corral in which double tracks occur among the heads of beasts (fig. 10, p. 17). A similar function may be attributed to the great bear tracks engraved upon the floor of Niaux. There are also the zig-zags, along which a feline beast prowls, leading to the pictured hut-roof at La Mouthe. La Pasiega has one very remarkable enclosure approached by such footprints (fig. 11, p. 18) divided into partitions in two of which rudimentary animals were later drawn. Its entrance is closed by the Aurignacian triangular symbol of female fertility to be discussed later. The same par-

[1] See N. Casteret, op. cit., pp. 76, 77.

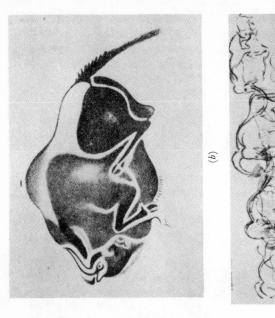

(a)

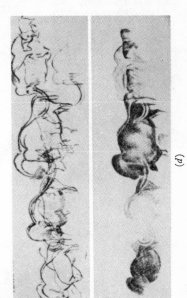

(b)

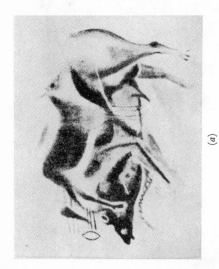

(c)

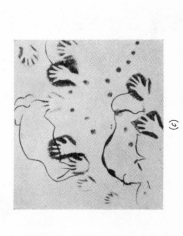

(d)

Plate 1. PALAEOLITHIC ART

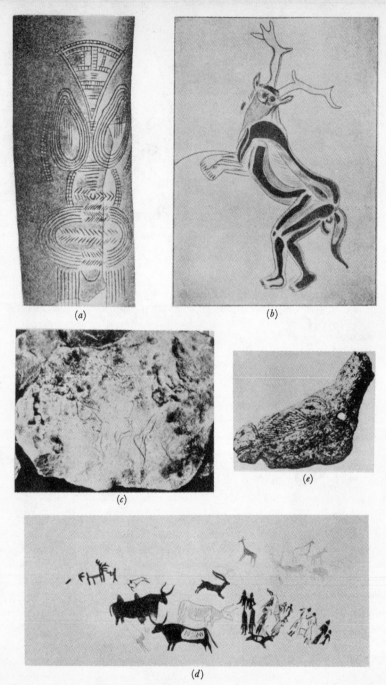

(a)

(b)

(c)

(e)

(d)

Plate 2. PALAEOLITHIC RELIGIOUS, MAGIC AND EVERYDAY
REPRESENTATIONS

titioned enclosure occurs again in this cave, guarded by the same symbol, but empty (fig. 12, p. 18). It is at a height above the entrance to the hidden chambers of La Pasiega that the strange group of symbols occurs, which seems to represent the entry of human feet to the mysteries of the interior (fig. 13, p. 18).

Another primitive class of signs is to be found in the positive and negative impressions of hands, either grouped in a particular spot, as at Gargas or Castillo (pl. I*c*), or placed, at Pech-Merle, above the forms of animals, or actually engraved, at Montespan, upon the shoulder of a horse. The negative impressions, produced by painting or blowing colour on to the

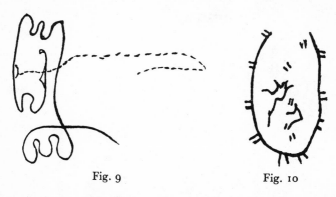

Fig. 9   Fig. 10

rock surface round the flattened member, are generally of the left hand; the positive records of the paint-covered palm and fingers are chiefly of the right. As even Mousterian skeletons are right-handed, it appears that a desired contact or prerogative is expressed, rather than a dedication of the instrument of hunter or artist. Private ownership or achievement would hardly be understood at this stage of social development. The famous impressions of mutilated hands, whether actual or feigned, occur only at Gargas. No incomplete fingers are found in Palæolithic graves, so there could have been no general custom, like that observed, for instance, among the Hottentots, of the sacrifice of fingers for mourning or other religious purposes.

The 'pectiform' signs sometimes depicted above or upon the forms of animals, are probably conventionalised hands (fig. 14).

A number of signs (the 'claviforms') seem to represent weapons, darts, boomerangs, harpoons, or axes, like the symbol

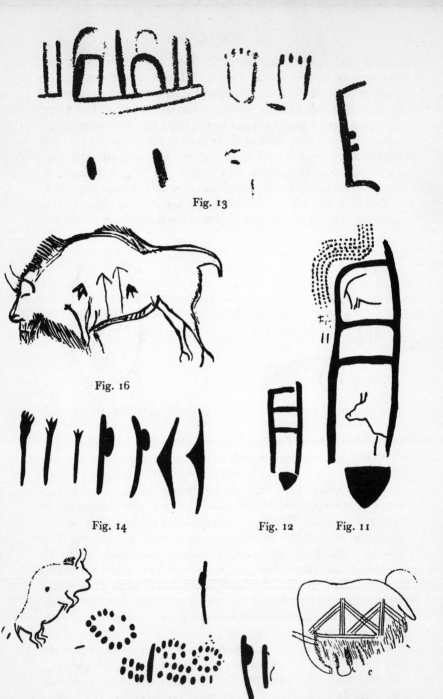

Fig. 13

Fig. 16

Fig. 14

Fig. 12

Fig. 11

Fig. 15

Fig. 17

so impressively occupying an empty wall at the approach to the painted chambers of Niaux. At Santián a group of these signs occurs together with stylised hands and arms (fig. 14, p. 18). They appear to serve the same purpose. Rows of small discs surrounding an apparent victim may be stones, like those beside the collapsing bison at Niaux (fig. 15, p. 18), or around and upon a bear at Montespan from whose mouth blood issues. Darts and arrows are commonly seen fixed in the bodies of mammoth and bison (fig. 16, p. 18).

The 'tectiforms' are probably to be interpreted as traps rather than huts,[1] since these too are often found upon the figures of the greater beasts (fig. 17, p. 18). Such a symbol imposed upon a mammoth at Font-de-Gaume has the central stake broken as if beneath his weight.[2]

The clay statues of the cave lion and bear at Montespan were ceremonially pierced, but not those of the male and female bison at Tuc d'Audoubert, where fertility and not death was desired.

In general, if the above interpretations are correct, it is obvious that the signs had a magical intent, some as at Pasiega, devised for the increase of the herds, others for their destruction. Even the 'ground-plans' would constitute symbolic charts or entry-permits, rather than guides to the actual route.

THE ANIMALS

We come now to the chief glory of cave art, the beasts whose portrayal at its best has rarely been equalled in any subsequent culture. The intensity of the remembered image, the inward realisation of animal life, were due in part of course to the hunter's training, upon which existence depended as never afterwards in these latitudes; while the vivid recognition of beauty in harmonious relation, the rejection of non-essentials, combined with the sure and sensitive movement of contours over rough surfaces, are undoubtedly the expression of developed artistic power, and have a direct appeal before which the intervening millennia are forgotten (pl. I and fig. 18, p. 20).

We have seen that the artist's choice of locality makes it impossible that he worked for delight alone; the enumeration

[1] Comte Bégouen, in *Antiquity*, 1929, the 'Magic Origin of Prehistoric Art', p. 10, considers those at La Mouthe to be certainly huts. They are very late.
[2] Bégouen, op. cit., p. 10.

of painted signs just given, will have exposed an intent of magic compulsion. But such conquest would not require this beauty; symbols would have sufficed as they did with the instruments of death—and symbols were known to them long before they had achieved artistic mastery. It is hoped in the course of these chapters to show that reciprocity was their aim, a participation in the splendour of the beasts which was of the nature of religion itself, and so required this elaborate separation from

Fig. 18

normal activities; that the perfected forms which flowered in the pitch-dark solitudes were types by which ritual called up the species; that exactitude was desired for the sake of closer attunement, so that brown bear is still distinguishable from cave bear, and three breeds of horses can be recognised,[1] and the pyramidal stance of the mammoth has been verified in the Siberian ice-bogs. For this reason the animal figures almost invariably occur singly, without foreground, sometimes appearing vertically or upside down. Their individual isolation is not due to ignorance of composition, though naturally, with such an object in view, the narrative side of this art remained undeveloped in comparison with the brilliant achievements of those kinsmen in East Spain and Africa, who were concerned

[1] Bégouen, op. cit., pp. 14–15.

to depict upon their rock-shelters the actual hunt or battle.[1] But certain designs engraved upon the Magdalenian implements presently to be described, show that the relation of groups in action was understood by the cave-dwellers. Only in the ritual of the cave it seems to have been out of place, except very rarely where butting males appear together, or male and female, or a hind with young.

The sanctity of the animal image seems to have received additional force from the consecration of a given spot. The custom

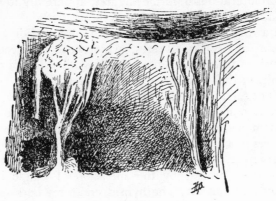

Fig. 19

of utilising natural formations of the rock or stalagmite deposit in the horse at Font-de-Gaume (fig. 19, above) and some of the bisons of Altamira (pl. I*b*), or the stag's horns added to a skull-shaped

---

[1] Again Lascaux appears at first sight exceptional, in possessing a possible hunting scene. See H. Breuil, 'Una Altamira Francesca. La Caverna de Lascaux en Montignac (Dordoña).' *Archivo Español de Arquelogia*, No. 44, Madrid, 1941; plate 23. Breuil compares it (p. 382) with an engraving on a flat stone found at Péchialet, representing two men attacked by bears, and suggests that some early influence may be visible at Lascaux from East Spanish Art, which may have disappeared in South Western France with the return of the glaciers. But hunting scenes on movable objects are by no means uncommon. In such scenes the hunter wears no mask (p. 25). The man with outstretched arms and stiff legs at Lascaux may be no corpse gored by the bison who faces him on the cave wall. His birdlike mask and his attitude may be related to the bird on a pole (if such it is) which is placed beside him. If one could imagine a hunting scene depicted in the depths of a cave, it would surely represent success and not defeat. The disembowelled bison as a separate figure would follow a fairly common precedent.

depression at Niaux, suggest that the cave itself was considered the repository of mystic influence, that the animal 'souls' were conceived to exist already in such localities. The crowding of paintings on to the walls of 'chapels' will also be recalled (most of them with a natural platform below), and the use of a single spot where figures have been imposed one above the other, through long periods of stylistic development; those below conceivably adding to the holiness of later arrivals, the whole constituting an island amid surrounding emptiness. There are, too, the occasional alterations of former figures, apparently to ensure a fresh relationship (perhaps before a hunt), without the necessity of drawing a new design. The lion engraved on stalactite in a cranny of Les Trois Frères,[1] whose head has been drawn three times in different positions and the tail twice, or the boar of Altamira with four running and four standing legs, are good examples of such a practice. They have been called monsters, but these retouchings are in complete contrast to the one example of monstrous imagination found in this same cave of Trois Frères in a unique composition (fig. 20, p. 24) of over-ripe Magdalenian style, where, as we shall see, the integrity of the animal idea is broken by the intrusion of magic into the domain of religious art. The hybrid creatures here depicted, as well as the being (pl. II*b*) who dominates them from above, are conceptions born of masked ceremonial.[2]

HUMAN FIGURES

Men are represented very sparsely, very timidly, in striking contrast to the bold certainty of animal design. This poverty has been ascribed to lack of practice, but in the representations of birds and fishes, which are also of rare occurrence in cave art, no such hesitancy is found. The stooping attitudes also, which for all their general lack of style, leave a deep impression of humility and awe (figs. 21, 22, pp. 25, 24), have been attributed to the

[1] Bégouen, op. cit., p. 12.

[2] Since this was written, the discovery of the painted cave of Lascaux has produced a new 'monster' (Breuil, op. cit., pl. I, and p. 368). The reproduction shows plainly that this is a masked man or woman, a 'sorcerer' taking animal attributes. The emergence of human or half-human limbs from beneath the dappled skin is clearly visible. The head covered with an animal mask is held at a human angle, giving an equivocal expression which never occurs in representations of beasts.

inexperience of draughtsmen accustomed to depicting animals. But in the art found outside the cavern depths; the statuettes, the reliefs, the engravings on weapons; an upright posture is almost invariable. The face, again, is usually more tentative even than the body, and when clearly shown almost always wears an animal mask (fig. 22 below). It can only be concluded that men and women are introduced into cave art solely in the act of ritual, in the masked dances practised by all primitives to obtain communion with a worshipped being. Certain figures engraved on small objects (figs. 24, 25, p. 24) greatly strengthen

Fig. 22

this conclusion, and the 'sorcerer' of Trois Frères (pl. IIb), though he may represent a being of another order, is a type created in the image of a masked man.

The skeletons in their graves are those of upstanding intelligent men and women, the outcome of a very long physical development in unknown regions, and potentially too great for their primitive environment. They quite naturally felt themselves inferior to the perfected species who were at home in it, being still at an early stage of their journey and their very deficiencies due to the budding of interior powers. The qualities which impelled them under such conditions to elaborate the rites in which, as will be seen, so many of the arts had their origin, in which social coherence was founded, which contained the germs of nearly every religious conception to be developed in later civilisations; qualities which helped them, no doubt, to outlive the physically powerful Neanderthal races, gave them a vision of achievement which the animals alone fulfilled. Thus they appeared worthy to be shown in company with the animal images, only in a disguise which imitated them.

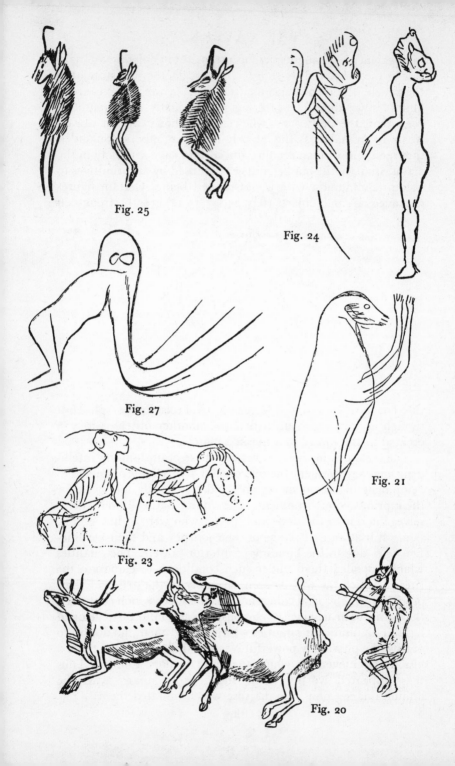

Fig. 25

Fig. 24

Fig. 27

Fig. 21

Fig. 23

Fig. 20

THE CAVERNS

The so-called erotic scene engraved in the little chapel at Les Combarelles seems an example of such a ritual dance; the stooping man and woman being palpably clothed in skins and wearing tails.[1] The heads of both, now obliterated by stalactite, would have worn masks, for scenes of daily life have never yet been found upon the walls. A fairly well-preserved single masked figure is the Mammoth Dancer from this cave (fig. 27, p. 24), and a few other delineations of men and women remain with masks clearly shown. There is also a type of stylised female figure depicted here, at Pech-Merle and La Roche, which is evidently derived from the statuettes of the domestic hearths presently to be described, and though nearly always headless, shows artistic felicity because it represents an idea rather than a human being (pl. IIc).

THE MOVABLE ART

The movable objects found at the cave mouth are of two classes, each connected more or less directly with the ritual of the interior. The javelins, harpoons, boomerangs, arrow-straighteners or ceremonial staffs, recovered from the vicinity of Magdalenian hearths, were carved out of tusk, horn or bone into animal forms (fig. 26, p. 26) or groups which often utilised, as cave formations had been used, the original shape of scapula or antler (fig. 28, p. 26), or they were engraved with figures of the animals as on the cavern walls. Upon these weapons the tectiforms and similar signs are naturally absent, but compositions of animal and human figures in action are rather more common, as we saw, and appear usually to illustrate ritual connected with the hunt (figs. 29 and 30, p. 26). Occasionally the hunters themselves, or the masked dancers, are seen. It is worthy of note that such hunters are never themselves shown in disguise, so there is little likelihood, even apart from their weaponless postures, that the figures of masked men and women on the cave walls were disguised for hunting, like the Bushmen.

The carving of the animal images and of the above scenes on

---

[1] L. Capitan, etc., *Peintures et gravures murales des cavernes paléolithiques. Les Combarelles aux Eyzies*, 1924, plate vi. A torch held sideways clearly brings out engraved lines of fur on the bodies.

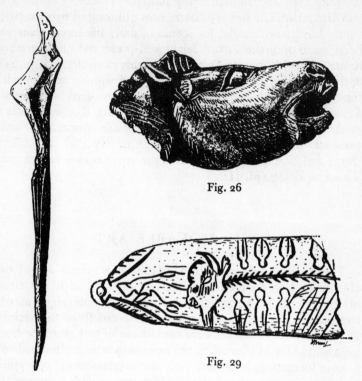

Fig. 26

Fig. 28

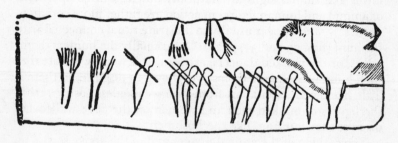

Fig. 29

Fig. 30

Magdalenian weapons was probably due, as will be seen, to the desire to attract the prey by this means. That is, it had a magical intent.

These people also carved amulets, like the pierced horse-heads cut from the bones of horses at Isturitz and Laugerie Basse (pl. II*e*). Inscribed stones are common, and probably (as it is hoped to show) of great ritual significance. Flat stones are also engraved with animal figures, often superimposed as in the palimpsests of the cave niches. Engraved blocks of an early date had been laid face downwards at La Ferrassie,[1] many of them displaying the triangular female symbols; at Labastide they lay in this position, bearing animal designs, within artificial stone circles in the cavern depths.[2] This makes it possible that the Solutrean coloured animal reliefs, mostly of gravid females, found on their faces at Le Roc,[3] were not thrown down from the wall by later comers, but that some significance was attached, even before the discovery of agriculture, to contact with the earth; that the cave was already a Mother. It may even be that the great 'fallen' reliefs of Laussel,[4] also found face-downwards, had thus been laid, their subjects showing them to be vehicles of female potency, the great subject of Aurignacian sculpture, as will be subsequently described. The Azilian painted stones of Birseck and Mas d'Azil belong to a late group bearing signs believed to have been derived from the East Spanish figures of men.[5] The former had all been intentionally broken.

In general it appears that stones inscribed, perhaps at one period also sculptured, with figures or signs, were retained in the caves as objects of sanctity.

The Aurignacian statuettes in ivory and stone are only found in a domestic context, or apart from cave life. Their great importance will be considered in a later chapter.

[1] L. Capitan and D. Peyrony, *Revue anthropologique*, xxxi, 1921, pp. 92–112, 'Les origines de l'art à l'Aurignacien moyen. Nouvelles découvertes à la Ferrassie,' figs. 6, 11, 18.

[2] N. Casteret, op. cit., pp. 28–29.

[3] H. Martin, 'The Solutrean sculptures of Le Roc,' *Antiquity*, 1929, pp. 45–48.

[4] G. Lalanne, *L'Anthropologie*, xxiii, 1912, pp. 129–149. 'Bas-Reliefs à figuration humaine de l'abri sous Roche de "Laussel".'

[5] See tables of comparison in H. Obermaier—*Fossil Man in Spain*, 1924, plates xxi a and b.

CAVE AS DWELLING AND SANCTUARY

ELUCIDATION OF THE IDEAS INVOLVED

It has been wisely postulated that every interpretation of prehistoric religious phenomena should be accompanied by an archæological document.[1] Here such illustrations are richly present from the very nature of the system under discussion, and constitute the primary source of our knowledge. But the only explanation of Palæolithic records, especially of those found in the cavern depths, which satisfactorily accounts both for their qualities and their limitations, is supplied by the investigations conducted at the end of the last century, into the mentality, the social and religious customs, of the dying races who had remained until recent times in a similar phase of culture; whose methods of livelihood, art and ceremonial, bear the same interrelation, and are largely bound up with the sanctity of caves.

It is now necessary to consider these cultures in relation to the material that has been described.

[1] Th. Mainage, *Les Religions de la préhistoire*, 1921, pp. 124–127 (note 55).

CHAPTER II

THE RELIGIOUS IDEAS
COMMON TO
MODERN HUNTING PEOPLES

T he races of hunters who still use implements of a Palæolithic character, are fast dying under the impact of a
developed mentality, as the Neanderthals died with the
coming of Aurignacian culture. Some are spiritually dead as
communities in the artificial existence of reservations.

The Tasmanians vanished before any investigation had been
conducted into the beliefs and customs which maintained the
vitality of the race. They belonged physically to some lost
archaic type; their stone weapons are said to have had Mousterian affinities; they used windscreens in the open, and also
caves.[1] They still made the rafts in which they had reached their
island, probably in the European Ice Age (Pleistocene), before
it became isolated by the widening of the straits. Nothing is
known of their religious customs, but a visitor to their island
a hundred years ago, has recorded that an old woman showed
him flat stones about two inches wide, marked in various directions with red and black lines, which, she said, were friends
'plenty long way off'.[2]

The Australians may also have reached their continent in
late Pleistocene times, for a fossil cranium found at those
levels is said to be identical with the modern type.[3] They must
also have crossed in rafts or canoes (for the fauna of the continent is distinct), and must have arrived in the South after the

[1] James Backhouse, *Narrative of a Visit to the Australian Colonies*, 1843, p.
104; W. J. Sollas, *Ancient Hunters*, 3rd edition, 1924, fig. 44.

[2] H. Ling Roth, 'Cave Shelters and the Aborigines of Tasmania,'
Nature (1899), lx, p. 545, quoted by Sollas, op. cit., p. 109.

[3] S. A. Smith, 'The Fossil Human Skull found at Talgai, Queensland,' in
Philosophical Transactions of the Royal Society of London, Series B, vol. 208, 1918,
pp. 351–387; M. Boule, *Fossil Men*, 1923, p. 370.

isolation of Tasmania, which they never reached, though they seem to have dispossessed and mingled with Tasmanians on the mainland.[1] Pleistocene traces have been discovered, of their passage along the southern coasts of Asia.[2] Their stone implements are of almost all known Palæolithic types, with some intrusion of Neolithic polished weapons probably brought by traders from the islands. Canoes, too, exist in the north and east, and rafts in the north-west, but no kind of vessel along the south-west coast. Nor did they ever experience the great economic revolution which follows the establishment of agriculture. They used huts as temporary dwellings and caves and rock-shelters as centres of social life. They knew the throwing-stick but not the bow, struck off stone knives and axes, and shaped spear-throwers, boomerangs, harpoons and pins somewhat resembling the Magdalenian.[3] The investigations conducted at the end of the last century into the elaborate religious and social customs, found to differ only in detail over all those parts of the continent where life was still maintained intact from external influence, was a revelation of primitive mentality—primitive indeed only in a comparative sense, since the great complexity and high organisation of the system pointed to a long previous development.[4] It constituted a kind of spiritual culture in a people at the lowest stage of material civilisation, and one of the strangest things about it was the close resemblance, even identity, with systems already known, generally in a decadent or fragmentary form, in other hemispheres. Its existence in so complete a form throughout Australia, whose Palæolithic culture had received so few accretions from without, does in itself suggest a very remote, if not a Pleistocene origin for this system, while its distribution over all those parts of the globe where succeeding civilisations have left the least mark, points in the same direction. In some of these localities there are also to be found cultural, if not racial, vestiges of Palæolithic relationship.

The *Bushmen* of South Africa, like the Australians, were hunters who made implements of a Palæolithic, especially of an

[1] Sollas, op. cit., p. 125.

[2] M. Boule, *Fossil Men*, 1923. D. S. Davidson, 'The Antiquity of Man in the Pacific,' in G. G. MacCurdy, *Early Man*, 1937, pp. 269–276.

[3] Sollas, op. cit., p. 110.

[4] R. Verneau, *Les Grottes de Grimaldi*, ii, fasc. 1, 1906, p. 125 ff.

Aurignacian, type, and never learnt the science of agriculture. In their case a racial link has been suggested by means of the rare Negroid skeletons found in Aurignacian graves, a gradual degeneration being presumed to have occurred during the millennial pursuit of game southwards through Africa.[1] Their art shows the closest affinities with rock paintings of North Africa and Eastern Spain, but there is also a cave art, whose meaning, though said to be religious, can no longer be interpreted by the straggling survivors of the war of extermination, which drove them from their hunting grounds into the half-life of the Kalahari desert. The last to be killed in that war was a painter in whose belt were found twelve horn tubes of colour resembling the Aurignacian paint-tubes already described.[2] The painters are said to have formed an initiated caste, distinct from that of the sculptors who made the rock engravings of the south. They lived, it is stated, chiefly in small caves, while the sculptors used huts grouped round the greater caverns which were their permanent rallying-places. It has also been considered probable that the sculptors followed a more easterly route southwards, leaving traces of their work by the way.[3] If these are indeed their work, such migrations might reflect the cultural distinction between those Aurignacians of Central Europe and Russia who inhabited huts and made stone and ivory statuettes, and the cave-dwellers who inaugurated painting in the West and might have entered Africa from Spain. A southward movement of these or other races may be assumed from paintings found in former Bushman territory, and appropriately within caves, with Franco-Cantabrian affinities, but certainly influenced also by the hunting scenes of East Spanish and North African Capsian rock-shelters.[4] Other compositions show masked ceremonies performed by men and women whose

---

[1] Anthropological evidence of their Northern origin seems now forthcoming. See Sir A. Smith Woodward, 'A fossil skull of an Ancestral Bushman from the Anglo-Egyptian Sudan,' *Antiquity*, xii, 1938, pp. 190–195, which, he finds, agrees very closely with the fossil Boskop skull discovered in the Transvaal (*J.R.A.I.*, 1925, lv, 179); also S. H. Haughton, 'Prelim. Note on the ancient human skull-remains from the Transvaal,' *Trans. R. Soc. S. Africa*, 1917, vi, 1–13.

[2] Sollas, op. cit., p. 489.

[3] G. W. Stow, *The Native Races of S. Africa*, 1905, pp. 12–14.

[4] L. Frobenius, *Prehistoric Rock Pictures*, 1937, fig. 145.

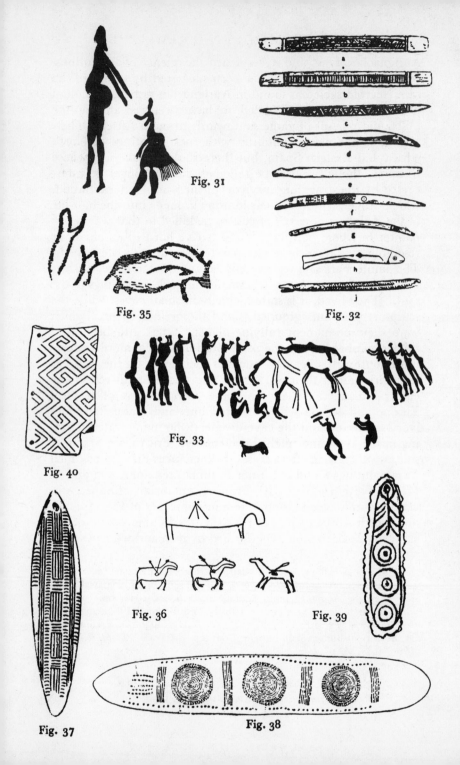

Fig. 31

Fig. 35

Fig. 32

Fig. 40

Fig. 33

Fig. 37

Fig. 36

Fig. 39

Fig. 38

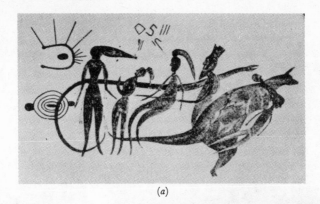

(a)

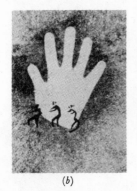

(b)

(c)

(d)

Plate 3. RELIGIOUS ART AND PRACTICE AMONG RECENT
PRIMITIVES

(a)

(b)

(c)

(d)

Plate 4. MODERN CEREMONIES

physical type and clothing can often be exactly paralleled in East Spanish paintings or Aurignacian sculpture (fig. 31, p. 32).

The rock engravings, however, are not composed, and often occur as palimpsests. Like the cave paintings they are sometimes of very fine quality, in formal beauty comparable to European productions, though never quite attaining the self-identification of the artist with his subject which makes the inward life of the animal apparent in even the more humble Palæolithic works. The poverty of the anthropological material is in this case, therefore, considerably supplemented by the language of an accomplished art. What is known from these sources of their religious and social customs, is in accordance, like those of several other races scattered over Africa, with the system under consideration.[1]

The *Eskimos* share with these the manufacture of weapons of a Palæolithic type, in their case chiefly Magdalenian. The resemblance is especially close in their implements of ivory or bone, such as spear-throwers and shaft-straighteners, chisels and rods, as may be observed from a comparison between the shapes and decoration of the two groups of tools in fig. 32, p. 32. There are again the stone saucer-lamps which the Eskimos, too, fill with fat upon which shredded moss burns without smoke.[2] Magdalenian examples of kindred shape have been found, and these must, as we saw, have been kindled in a similar manner, since no smoke has stained the low ceilings or walls of the inner caves.

The illustration shows how the Eskimos share with the Magdalenians the custom of carving upon implements or weapons the image of the prey, but there are no examples of this art previous to the arrival of Europeans in the seventeenth century.[3] A definite racial inheritance has been postulated on the evidence of a type of skull, first found in a Magdalenian grave at Chancelade, whose measurements correspond very exactly with Eskimo proportions.[4] It is thought that remnants

[1] See pp. 38, 39 below.

[2] Sollas, op. cit., pp. 575–576, quoting Hans Egede: *A Description of Greenland*, London, 1745, p. 117.

[3] E. Cartailhac and H. Breuil, *La Caverne d'Altamira*, 1906, p. 149, quoting Hoffman, 'The Graphic Art of the Eskimos,' *Smithsonian Institution Annual Report*, 1895, Pt. ii, pp. 739–968.

[4] Testut, 'Recherches anthropologiques sur le squelette quaternaire de Chancelade, Dordogne.' *Bull. de la Soc. d'Anthr. de Lyon*, viii, 1889, pp. 131–246.

of Magdalenian people of the short Chancelade type may have followed the reindeer northward at the onset of a warmer climate, until, finally reaching the remote North-west, they found conditions in which they were at home. No traces of such a passage have been discovered—in fact, it is possible that Iceland and Greenland were then already seabound. If so, the Eskimos must have entered the American continent by way of Siberia, like the tall Red Indian races who followed them; but Magdalenian culture is in the present state of knowledge centred in Western Europe. The route of their migration must therefore remain conjectural.

Their religious conceptions have long been modified by contact with Christian peoples. Of these, as of their art, no earlier record survives. What is known, however, of their relationship to the herds of caribou (reindeer), the seals and walruses upon which their existence depends, resembles that of their highly organised hunting neighbours to the south.[1] The social and religious system of these Northern American tribes bears in its turn the closest relation to the elaborate organisations of the Australian continent.

The above examples demonstrate the possibilities of Palæolithic cultural, and even racial, migrations to each of the continental regions which have remained isolated from the succession of later civilisations. It is hoped to show that the records of religious ideas which they appear to have held in common, and fragments of which have been found in other remote regions, are precisely those which can be illustrated from Palæolithic evidence, and can, conversely, alone explain that evidence in a coherent and comprehensive manner.

It may be imagined that the elaborate discipline now known to have been based upon a relationship of which the animal was the focal point, arose out of the organisation of the hunt at a period when the prey was rare and greatly prized. In the form existing in recent times under the name of totemism, a certain beast or other object of nature was believed to embody at the same time the abiding ancestral spirit perpetually incarnated within a particular group or clan; the willing sacrifice by which that group maintained its life (even when eaten but sparingly or in ceremonies, or only by the opposite group from

---

[1] L. Lévy-Bruhl, *The 'Soul' of the Primitive*, 1928, p. 65.

which the former drew its wives); the living force present in even greater potency within its manufactured image or symbol; and finally the soul latent in every member of the group, made effectual on initiation, which was the experience of individual unity with all of these. As we saw in the case of the Crô-magnon peoples,[1] it is easily conceivable that the perfected animal species should be an object of emulation among human beings whose desires so far surpassed their achievements. What is remarkable in the beliefs of comparatively savage races such as the Australians and the rather more advanced Neolithic peoples of Melanesia and North America, is the spiritual and truly religious conception of a connection originally based upon the need for food, and sufficiently effective to hold the group in social and economic cohesion. It is equally surprising that art should hold so integral a position in this unity, as to render the image or emblem more sacred than the actual entity; that magic, though intrinsically important as a means of action, should be only an instrument of mutual creation.[2] The primary group-relationship known to us was not that of blood, but of a willed participation in a life both physical and non-physical, which stretched through time to include the dead and the unborn.[3]

The existing form must have had a long development. The true primitive could not so far have detached himself as a conscious individual, that recurrent ceremonies were necessary for closer communion with his fellows, in the invocation of the potency by which they lived and moved. The disintegration experienced in the first stirrings of separate identity would itself have clamoured for such an orientation, but long experiment must have preceded the discovery that power could be isolated by the inhibition of personal desires, and preserved for use at a certain time and place—the separation of sacred and profane in the rhythm necessary for creation.

[1] See p. 23 above.

[2] Magic may be defined as the imposition of non-physical power to attain a specified end. Religion is the maintenance of abiding relationship.

[3] The results of the investigations of ethnologists into the spiritual ideas current among dying primitive peoples have been summarised among others by Sir J. G. Frazer in *Totemism and Exogamy*, 1910. E. Durkheim, *Elementary Forms of Religious Life*, 1915. L. Lévy-Bruhl in *Les Fonctions mentales dans les sociétés inférieures*, 1910.

Such a system could conceivably have beeen perfected by the Crô-magnon race, which possessed a brain-capacity so far from savage as to make it potentially the equal of modern man. It will be well therefore to turn now to those expressions of ideas held in common by recent 'primitives' which seem to be shared with the cave-dwellers of post-glacial time; noting their social correlatives for which no Palæolithic evidence exists, and distinguishing finally the Pleistocene religious material not characteristic of existing totemic communities, but of outstanding importance, on the other hand, in the succeeding Neolithic civilisations of Asia and the Mediterranean coasts.

THE CAVES

During the performance of religious ceremonies in Central Australia, a procession is usually formed to fetch sacred objects from some cave or crevice in the rocks which is regarded as their inviolable sanctuary. The palms of the initiated tribesman may first be placed over the entrance to establish their right of entry,[1] a custom which perhaps explains the impressions of hands found upon Australian rock-walls as upon those on either side of the Pyrenees.[2]

The procession takes a winding path, in memory, they say, of the first endeavours of the divine ancestor to reach the earth. Thus in the well-known ceremony for the propagation of the witchetty-grub, the winding march is taken to ten sacred caves in which stones have been deposited to represent this insect and her eggs. After contact has been established, first between the stones and their own persons, later with the sacred rock by throwing against it both the egg-pebbles and the churingas ('spirit houses') of the group,[3] they return to enter the cave-like 'chrysalis' which has meanwhile been constructed at the camp, while the onlookers remain silent and prostrate round it. From this they emerge singing the re-born grub.[4]

[1] B. Spencer and F. J. Gillen, *The Northern Tribes of Central Australia*, 1904, p. 267. [Hereafter quoted as *Nor. Tr.*]

[2] See fig. 14 and pl. Ic.   [3] See fig. 37.

[4] B. Spencer and F. J. Gillen, *The Native Tribes of Central Australia*, 1899, pp. 170–179. [Hereafter quoted as *Nat. Tr.*]

In general, the actual dances took place on consecrated ground in the open; and symbols both of the object of worship and of its journeys were traced upon the soil and the bodies of the celebrants. This applies equally to the initiation ceremonies of the boys and girls, whose period of seclusion seems to have been passed in the bush, with the exception of novice magicians, who repaired to a cave for their sleep of death and rebirth.[1] The churingas, however, of the central tribes, those incised or painted objects of wood or stone which were believed to hold in union divinity, animal and man[2]—including the recent dead and those awaiting incarnation—and were shown to every initiate at the moment of his passage from boyhood to membership of the clan, were guarded in caves from secular contagion.[3]

There is here a striking resemblance to the rites for rebirth practised by civilised races who succeeded the Palæolithic, but little that could be definitely associated with the European cave-dwellers. In the territories to the West, however, occupied by the Karadjeri who cherish the mythical Rainbow Serpent, a number of caves have been found to contain paintings made or retouched by initiates of each totemic division, on the particular chamber or passage wall allotted to that group, to promote the increase, they said, of the totemic species, by the power which brought the rain. It was considered sufficient, moreover, that their chief should dream of a visit to the cave-galleries, for rain to fall.[4] The souls of the unborn were intimately related to the image of the Rainbow Serpent upon the walls, and the chamber or gallery, with the waterhole which was his point of access to this world. A man's connection with his mythical ancestors was maintained by means of the paintings on the chamber-wall of his group, the site of their 'spirit houses'.[5]

---

[1] B. Spencer and F. J. Gillen, *Nor. Tr.*, pp. 480–484; *Nat. Tr.*, pp. 524–525.

[2] See pp. 46 and 47.

[3] C. Strehlow, *Die Aranda und Loritja-Stämme in Zentral-Australien*, ii, 1902, p. 78.

[4] A. P. Elkin, 'Totemism in N.W. Australia; ii, The Tribes of Dampier Land,' in *Oceania*, vol. iii, No. 4 (1933), pp. 461 ff., quoted by Sir J. G. Frazer, *Totemica*, 1937, p. 102.

[5] P. M. Kaberry, 'The Forrest River and Lyne River Tribes of N.W. Australia,' in *Oceania*, vol. v (1935), No. 4, pp. 431–432, quoted by Frazer, op. cit., pp. 114–115.

These sacred localities of the West seem thus to correspond with the churingas of the central tribes, the one group using portable emblems, the other the images in the consecrated place. All of this is strictly reminiscent of Palæolithic conditions, even down to the signs which represented to the Australians the point of contact between the worlds (pl. IIIa). In these caves as in the Palæolithic (on the evidence of footprints and engravings) women took part in the rites, and hither, in contrast to the general custom among savages, bones of dead initiates were sometimes brought from their tree shelter, to be laid beneath the wall-paintings, the bones being covered with red ochre 'to keep them clean'.[1]

The Bushmen of South Africa asserted, as we saw,[2] that the paintings on their cavern ceilings and walls, as distinct from the scenes of 'East Spanish' Capsian type on open rock faces, were of religious origin, though their meaning was forgotten. They stated also that the masked ceremonial dances so often depicted in the caves, had been actually performed there (fig. 33, p. 32). In these dances women are frequently and conspicuously portrayed.[3] Like the Karadjeri caves described above, the Domboshowa painted cave of Southern Rhodesia was used to promote rainfall and was a place of pilgrimage. The Makumbi painted cave in the same region is too far removed from water for continuous habitation, and unsuited to any purpose but a religious one.[4] It is not known if initiations were conducted in South African caverns, but many remained into modern times as centres of communal life among the scattered kraals or cave shelters, and were often the official dwellings of chiefs and named after the animal emblem of the clan.[5]

Caves have been found in former Bushman territory which contained the ashes of hearths, and stone implements, and also skeletons buried under flagstones, in accordance with Palæolithic habit but contrary to the customs of modern primi-

[1] E. P. Elkin, 'Rock-Paintings of N.W. Australia,' in *Oceania*, vol. i, No. 3 (1930), pp. 257–279, quoted by Frazer, op. cit. pp. 129–145, of which see pp. 129 and 144.

[2] See pp. 30–33 above.

[3] See, for instance, fig. 31.

[4] M. C. Burkitt, *South Africa's Past in stone and paint*, 1928, pp. 158–159.

[5] S. S. Dornan, 'Notes on the Bushmen of Basuto Land,' *Trans. S. African Phil. Soc.*, 1909, xviii, pp. 437–450, quoted by Sollas, op. cit., p. 471.

tives. In one of these, flat stones were painted with human and animal figures.[1]

This evidence, though so meagre, affords ground for the opinion that caves were used in South Africa down to recent times for purposes resembling Palæolithic practices.

For the mimetic dances of the inhabitants of the North American plains, a sacred cabin whose walls were decorated with paintings, seems usually to have replaced the cave.[2] In New Mexico figures of the totemic animal were carried at the New Year from their guarded repository to a chamber where rites were performed for success in the hunt.[3]

A common belief among North American aborigines, shared also by the vanished civilised races of Central America, concerned the primal emergence of their ancestors from caverns in or under the earth[4] (fig. 34, p. 51).

RELATION TO THE ANIMAL WORLD

The Totem, as we saw, is a manifold entity, a focus of the life-energy of a group embodied in the immortal ancestor. It is generally conceived as human, but able to assume an animal form—also immortal—for maintaining the earthly life of its descendants who are incarnations of its spirit. This form is an abstraction, contact with which affects the individuals of the species. That is why art is necessary to such a religion, and why approach to the forms or symbols is so strictly guarded, since they are nearer to reality than the separated lives. For this reason ceremonies are required to raise the human group to a state of such intensity of shared action and emotion, that it can create a commensurate power.

[1] L. Péringuey, 'The Stone Ages of South Africa as represented in the collection of the South African Museum,' *Ann. S. Afr. Mus.*, viii, pp. 1–218. A photograph of one of these stones, painted with figures of dancing women, is reproduced in Burkitt, op. cit., fig. xx, (1).

[2] E. Cartailhac and H. Breuil, *La Caverne d'Altamira*, pl. xxxiii, 2, after F. Boas, 'The Social Organisation and the Secret Society of the Kwatinkl Indians,' pl. xxxvi, *Smithsonian Institution Annual Report*, 1895, pt. ii, pp. 311–738.

[3] *Twenty-third Annual Report, Bureau of Ethnology*, Washington, 1904, ii. F. H. Cushing, *Zuñi Fetishes*, quoted by Sollas, op. cit., p. 424.

[4] See below Part iii, p. 187.

It is a tremendous conception, too great, it would seem, to have been discovered by any one of its humble adherents among the vanishing primitives of to-day.

The rites may be classified as follows:

REPRESENTATION

Representation in art, that is the re-creation of the abiding form upon which power depends. Through this, by mutual consent as we shall see, members of the species may be dedicated for fertility or death. Thus Catlin's paintings were welcomed by the Mandan Indians 'because they brought the bisons',[1] and the seasonal retouchings of painted figures in the cave-chambers of the Karadjeri were believed to aid the reproduction of the totemic species.[2] So too the Cora Indians deposited clay images of the required beasts in a mountain cave to ensure their increase.[3] The grandly modelled bison pair of Magdalenian Tuc-d'Audoubert[4] must have been created for a similar purpose; there are no symbols of weapons upon or around them, nor symbolic wounds. Further, the Karadjeri galleries of the Female Rainbow Snake were associated with human birth. To touch up her image caused the going forth of the spirit children to be found by the fathers and incarnated in the mothers.[5] The female symbols of La Ferrassie will be remembered, and the female beasts of Le Roc, both laid to face the ground. We may also recall the stylised images of the 'Mother Goddess' engraved on the cave walls and ceilings of Pech-Merle, La Roche and Les Combarelles.[6] Retouchings, so familiar in the Palæolithic caves, were considered by the West Australian tribes to preserve continuity with the first paintings of mythical age.[7]

[1] G. Catlin, *Illustrations of the Manners, Customs and Condition of the North American Indians*, 9th edition, vol. i, 1857, p. 105 ff. They classed him as a medicine-man because of his paintings.

[2] Frazer, op. cit., p. 102.

[3] C. Lumholtz, *Unknown Mexico*, 1903, vol. i, p. 485 ff.; Mainage, op. cit., pp. 235–236, note 52.

[4] See p. 19 above.

[5] A. P. Elkin, 'Rock Paintings of N.W. Australia,' *Oceania*, vol. i, no. 3 (1930), pp. 257–279, quoted by Frazer, op. cit., pp. 129–145, of which see p. 143.

[6] See pl. II*c*.   [7] A. P. Elkin, op. cit., pp. 273–279.

Such fertility rites belonged rather to magic than to religion, that is to say, they were conducted to effect contact through the image for a specific purpose; and this is equally the case with those figures of beasts in which arrows and javelins are found, which are seen falling into traps or smitten with stones, as we saw them at Niaux and Montespan. In India, too, there are rock paintings of animals in Palæolithic style with arrows in their sides (fig. 35, p. 32). These symbolic wounds are very prevalent in the rock drawings of the Ojibwa Indians (fig. 36, p. 32) and in the cave-paintings of the Bushmen. The Zuni Indians of New Mexico make stone images of their mountain lion, to which they bind a flint arrow head near the heart. They like to use for these images a piece of stone already resembling the creature of their devotion.[1] This reminds one of the Magdalenian choice of natural formations at Niaux and Font-de-Gaume.

With such objects in view, and with such conceptions concerning the real models of these portraits, it will be understood why the animals of the prehistoric cave painters usually appear unrelated to each other. The customs of the Karadjeri might explain the retouchings as intended to preserve continuity with the past while making contact for specific purposes, and also their immediate restriction to certain areas as the prerogative of certain groups for the conservation of sanctity. Both of these might account for the Palæolithic palimpsests with their evidence of age-long succession. These last are, moreover, a feature of Bushmen cave-art. The survivors of that race say that new figures were only superimposed after the death of a former initiated artist.

The magic intent in the art of all these peoples would in no way impede the endeavour after perfect accomplishment, for even among the Australians of the central deserts, to whom naturalism is impossible, careful finish and unfailing accuracy is achieved in the production of the symbolic ground drawings.[2] On the contrary, realism and ritual exactitude would equally conduce to perfect attunement. In the Palæolithic style the hunter's and artist's knowledge was combined, while the weight of the united faith of his group (if modern analogies are taken

[1] Sollas, op. cit., p. 424, quoting *Rep. Bur. of Ethnol.*, Washington, of various dates.

[2] See pl. V*c*.

into account), must have strengthened the draughtsman's vision till that in its turn affected the observers to an exaltation of the ideal species unattainable by individual experience. For though specifically magic in aim, these works cannot be separated from the whole body of ritual, which was a harmonious aggrandisement of the theme: divine power, animal, man. One branch of art, indeed, still practised in totemic America, suggests that even in representation some reciprocal relationship was thought to be established between the hunter and his prey. This is the habit of carving the image of the desired victim upon the hunter's weapon,[1] already familiar to the reader as a custom of the Magdalenians, who seem here also to have sought the added sanctity of resemblance in the natural forms of antler or shoulder-blade.[2]

The former tribesmen of British Columbia held that no animal could be killed against his wish or will.[3] The Eskimos attributed the dwindling of the caribou herds, after too zealous hunting, to reluctance for incarnation on the part of the archetypal caribou.[4] When a member of the species is struck down the One is wounded; so the Indian of the plains carves that image on his weapon to demonstrate his kinship and claim from it the privilege of sacrifice. The totemic form naturally attracts the individual bear or buffalo, and thus the hunter feels himself especially gifted for the pursuit of his own totem.[5] This is a religious conception in which both participants act through their essential union.

PARTICIPATION

The masked dances of all these peoples were a deliberate means of approach to the animal nature and therefore to the divine. 'They are to us what prayers are to you,' explained an old Bushman.[6] Head-dress, tails, skins, posture, were outward

---

[1] E. Cartailhac and H. Breuil, *La Caverne d'Altamira*, p. 152, quoting Murdoch, *Ethnological Results of the Point Barrow Expedition*, pp. 180, 209, 247, 403, etc.

[2] See fig. 28.   [3] *J.R.A.I.*, xxxv, 1905, p. 136.

[4] L. Lévy-Bruhl, *The 'Soul' of the Primitive*, p. 65.

[5] Hill Tout, 'Ethn. Rep. on the Stseelis and Skaulits Tribes,' *J.R.A.I.* xxxiv, 1904, p. 324, quoted by E. Durkheim, *Elementary Forms of Religious Life*, 1915, p. 159.

[6] Sollas, op. cit., p. 484.

aids to an inward assimilation; united action heightened their sense of power to the level of effective energy, for they believed that the food-producing totem needed their help in procreation as they must ask his own for destruction. As sanctity was increased by the separation and reservation of locality, so it could be stored by limitation in time to certain occasions of prescribed action. Such were the buffalo-dance of the Mandans,[1] the Bear dance of the Sioux with lifted paws[2] like the seemingly postulant hands at Altamira (fig. 21, p. 24), the New Guinea masked dancers of pl. IVa, who so closely resemble the chamoismen of the Teyjat engraving,[3] the Mantis dance of the Bushman,[4] the Emu dance in Central Australia (pl. IVd). Thus even Magdalenian men and women are occasionally depicted in the sacred galleries, though still very timidly, when masked in the exaltation of similar rites. The disguised performer, as we saw, who enchants the two humanised beasts, one for fertility, the other for death, in the passage of Les Trois Frères,[5] is not a religious participant but a sorcerer.[6]

In most modern instances the animal dances were connected with designs painted on the walls of cave or cabin, or made for the occasion, like the Australian ground-drawings which symbolise the totem and its wanderings.[7] In the Pyrenean cave of Tuc d'Audoubert there are prints of perhaps a similar dance, performed apparently on the heels, under a low ceiling which would have necessitated a stooping posture.[8] Winding tracks connect the footprints, and these possibly indicate, like the ground drawings of Australasian dances, the journey of the holy being. Since several Palæolithic engravings exist of a masked man and woman together,[9] it is possible that a 'sacred

---

[1] Catlin, op. cit., p. 157 and plate 67. In this dance the men clad in bisons' skins carried the lance or bow with which they hunted them. They spoke of the ceremony as 'an expedient which never failed' on occasions when the bison herd left the locality.

[2] G. Catlin, op. cit., pp. 245–246, plates 19 and 102. (Cf. pl. IVb.)

[3] Fig. 25.   [4] Fig. 33.   [5] Fig. 20.

[6] See p. 22 above. He has assumed the attributes of several animals in place of identity with one.

[7] B. Spencer and F. J. Gillen, *Nor. Tr.*, pp. 239–247, and pp. 737–742 (Ground Drawings of the Wollunqa Totem).

[8] Comte Bégouen, *L'Anthropologie*, xxiii (1912), pp. 657–665, 'Les statues d'argile de la caverne de Tuc d'Audoubert (Ariège).'

[9] See fig. 23.

marriage' was performed on behalf of the beasts.[1] Bone pipes and whistles seem to have existed in quaternary times and are perhaps illustrated in fig. 20, p. 25. Thus the repetition of sounds in time may have been recognised, though a repeated pattern is rare in the visual art; the movements of the heavens having no specific significance to men whose life habits centre in the caves. So the rhythmic intermittence, by which energy was conserved for creation among recent primitives, may at this stage have been only the pauses between hunting expeditions, or between breeding seasons. A certain discipline, for the conservation of power, is nevertheless indicated here.

COMMUNION

Among those Central Australian tribes in which the totemic system was purest, the food-giving totem was eaten sparingly, at ceremonies, or in times of want, or in immature condition, or only by the contrary and corresponding moiety of the clan.[2] The famous Intichiuma rites, by which the fertility of the species was assured, ended in a fast after which the chief was compelled to taste the totemic food and share it with the elders of the clan.[3] In some cases the men of an alien totem killed and brought the meat to the chief, who said: 'I made this for you; eat freely,' but himself abstained.[4] In the spring rite for the increase of the kangaroo, a portion of the fat was offered to the totem itself, as recorded in an extant hymn.[5] It appears therefore that in some instances at least, the life-energy of the natural animal was intended to be conveyed to the divine power as well as to his celebrants; that the eating was in fact a sacrament. The myths of these tribes show the ancestors partaking of the sacred flesh, and for this reason, and also because of the great variation of the restrictions both here and in Africa and America, it has been conjectured that the sacred animal

---

[1] G. Catlin, op. cit., p. 168, seems to describe the performance of such a rite, during the bison dance which was part of the great initiation ceremonies among the Mandan Indians.

[2] B. Spencer and F. J. Gillen, *Nat. Tr.*, pp. 202, 204; A. W. Howitt, *The Native Tribes of South-East Australia*, 1904, pp. 145, 147.

[3] B. Spencer and F. J. Gillen, *Nor. Tr.*, p. 173; *Nat. Tr.*, p. 204.

[4] B. Spencer and J. Gillen, *Nor. Tr.*, pp. 308–309.

[5] C. Strehlow, op. cit., iii, 1, 1910, p. 12.

was once the food of the clan, partaken in common, and, because it was sacred, ceremonially—still further tightening the
intricate bond of life.[1]

Since the cults hitherto discussed were addressed to the
image or symbol rather than the individual animal, such eating
would appear natural, and in Palæolithic conditions almost
inevitable. Nevertheless, a discrepancy has been noted in certain cases between the animals portrayed on quaternary cavern
walls and the bones among the hearths. At Marsoulas, for example, there are no paintings of reindeer, but their bones are
very numerous in the ashes; in the earlier designs of Altamira,
ibexes are common, and are followed later by the rare figures
of stags. But both these species are found in very considerable
numbers in the *late* deposits.[2] Either painting was not practised
when game was abundant, or the 'totemic' animal was not
himself eaten, in some localities at least, where choice was
possible.

Again there is the frequent occurrence of immature bones in
the open caves. Of course the young of the herds would be
most easily trapped or run down, but there is also the possibility that the full-grown animal was avoided as more sacred, in
accordance with the customs of some modern tribes.

On the whole there is no positive evidence of ceremonial or
sacrificial consumption in Palæolithic times. We can only say
that it would harmonise with other customs which reveal the
primitive relations with animal life then and now. The last of
these is:

EXPIATION

As we noted in the case of the caribou decimated by the
Esquimos, the immortal power behind the species must be propitiated by avowal of kinship when a member is struck down.[3]
The Canadian tribesmen fasted and prayed to the beasts before
they started in pursuit;[4] the Cherokees abstained from food

---

[1] See R. Briffault, *The Mothers*, 1927, vol. ii, p. 471.

[2] H. Alcalde del Rio, H. Breuil and L. Sierra, *Les Cavernes de la région
cantabrique*, 1911, p. 214; H. Obermaier, *Fossil Man in Spain*, 1924, pp. 239,
260.

[3] Above, p. 42.

[4] P. F. X. de Charlevoix, *Journal d'un voyage dans l'Amérique septentrionale*,
1744, vol. iii, pp. 115-116; (Lévy-Bruhl, *Fonctions mentales*, pp. 266-267.)

on every day of a hunt.[1] The Ainu condoled with their bear.[2]

When the animal had been killed, in Canada as in Africa, the concluding rites of the cycle had to be repeated in order to preserve continuity. The hunter's intention was to stultify vengeance and to restore harmony both with the dead animal and the soul which persisted through the multiplicity of lives and deaths. In Mexico he strokes the dead deer, saying 'Rest, elder brother'.[3]

It appears possible that the scene engraved on a bone from Raymonden and depicted in fig. 29, p. 26, representing as it does a solemn concourse surrounding the dismembered corpse of a bison, is a deprecatory rite of this nature, and that the processional group found at La Madeleine (fig. 30, p. 26) illustrates the previous religious dedication before the hunt. In neither of these cases do the devotees wear masks.

THE SYMBOLIC OBJECTS

It is once more the aborigines of Australia whose possessions of a sacred nature resemble most nearly the stones, bearing figures and symbols, which are known to have been intentionally placed in certain Palæolithic caves. The churingas of the central tribes were slabs of wood or stone within which the spiritual body of the 'eternal uncreated' ancestor had been distributed when he touched the earth. They contained the souls of the unborn, and their presence in the water-hole, rock or tree, which was the point of divine entry to this world, caused passing women to conceive.[4] The belief in this method of incarnation was held alike by the tribes who recognised or did not recognise the fact of paternity. It was independent of the physical relation, and thus resembled the ideas of conception from the souls of dead children current in North America and in Ancient Britain.[5] The churinga of the newly-born was in

---

[1] J. Mooney, 'The sacred formulas of the Cherokees,' *Bureau of Ethnology*, Washington, Rep. vii, pp. 342, 370, 372; Lévy-Bruhl, op. cit., p. 268.

[2] Mainage, op. cit., p. 345, quoting Tylor, *Primitive Civilisation*, i, p. 544.

[3] Or, for a doe, 'Sister.' See Lumholtz, *Unknown Mexico*, ii, p. 45; Lévy-Bruhl, op. cit., p. 275.

[4] C. Strehlow, op. cit., i, 1907, pp. 2–5; ii, pp. 4, 52–53.

[5] Briffault, op. cit., vol. ii, pp. 448–449.

some cases 'discovered' by the father, but became an integral possession only at the 'second birth' of the initiation ceremonies of adolescence, when the boy, after various purifications, was shown the emblem with the words, 'This is yourself.' He was told that it was also the secret body of the immanent and transcendent ancestor,[1] as well as of the animal or other natural phenomenon which was his link with physical life. It was thus the most sacred of tangible objects and was guarded, as we saw, in a cave or rock-crevice, except during solemnities, when it was pressed against the body as a medium of contact with the unseen.[2] The churinga was often inscribed with geometric patterns of concentric circles or spirals, or waving lines like that of the rain-totem in pl. Vb, which were said by its possessors to represent both the ancestor (whether or not in animal form), and his wanderings to the places of entry into this world.[3] The churinga of a wild-cat man (shown in fig. 38, p. 32) was said to represent the actual dance of the men of the totem round the sacred spots of contact.[4] As these dances mimed the ancestral journey, the symbolism is the same.

The flat stones of La Ferrassie will be called to mind, inscribed with Aurignacian symbols and figures, and laid face downwards in the cave, and the engraved stones placed within circles of rocks in the recesses of Labastide. So will the famous collection of stones at Mas d'Azil painted with symbols,[5] some of them apparently a stylised degradation of the human form, identical with the figures of late East Spanish rock painting.[6] These were long ago related by scholars to the churingas.[7]

A similar câche of painted pebbles came to light at Birseck, deliberately crushed as if by an enemy.[8] It seems likely that the

---

[1] C. Strehlow, op. cit., ii, pp. 75–77.

[2] B. Spencer and F. J. Gillen, *Nor. Tr.*, p. 261.

[3] B. Spencer and F. J. Gillen, ibid., pp. 730–737.

[4] B. Spencer and F. J. Gillen, Id., *Nat. Tr.*, p. 148, fig. C.

[5] See p. 27 above.

[6] H. Obermaier, *Fossil Man in Spain*, pls. xxia, xxib.

[7] Prof. A. B. Cook was the first to demonstrate the connection in 'Les Galets peints du Mas d'Azil', *L'Anthropologie*, xiv, 1903, pp. 655–660; F. Sarasin stated his agreement in 1912. (See note 8.)

[8] F. Sarasin, 'Les Galets coloriés de la Grotte de Birseck près Bâle.' *Comptes Rendus, Congrès International d'Anthr.*, Geneva (1912), i, 1913, p. 566 et seq.

conventionalised figures, used with no apparent religious intent by the rock painters of Libya and Eastern Spain, were applied by their neighbours to the cave ritual. Curiously, some of the Australian geometric figures have also been traced to earlier zoomorphic forms,[1] but in any case, as we have seen, they symbolised moving animate beings. There is also, it will be re-called, the assertion that geometrically painted stones, in size and shape resembling the Azilian, represented the 'far-off' people of Tasmania.[2]

A special implement of the churinga type is the Bull-Roarer, which produced the voice of divinity to terrify the candidate and the distant women and children during the earlier ordeals of initiation.[3] This was generally made of wood and pierced for whirling. Several similar objects appear among the Mag-dalenian finds, of which pl. V*d* gives an excellent example. They are indistinguishable in general form and decoration from Australian specimens, but their purpose is of course un-known. The bull-roarer, however, was used in the mysteries of the succeeding civilisations of Europe, sometimes retaining its Magdalenian pattern.[4] Its whirling movement was connected in Australia with the spiral or whirlwind of passage between the worlds.[5]

Spirals, it may be noted, are the most frequent decorative motif of the Magdalenian 'ceremonial wands' (pl. V*a*).

THE SIGNS

The signs painted or incised on the walls of the Pleistocene caverns, found their counterparts, as we saw, in cases where wounds were designated, among the animal representations of most hunting communities. The paintings of the Bushmen fur-nish examples also of the zig-zags, rows of discs, and enclosures (pl. V*f*), which may have been expected to draw the prey to-wards snares or stockades, or merely into the hunter's spell. One Australian cave has conventionalised boomerangs and

---

[1] P. Wernert, 'Representaciones de antepasados en el arte paleolitico.' *Comisión de Investigaciones Paleontológicas y prehistóricas, Memoria 12,* Madrid, 1916.

[2] See p. 29.   [3] A. W. Howitt, op. cit., p. 627 ff., and other authorities.

[4] A. B. Cook, op. cit.   [5] B. Spencer and F. J. Gillen, *Nor. Tr.,* p. 373.

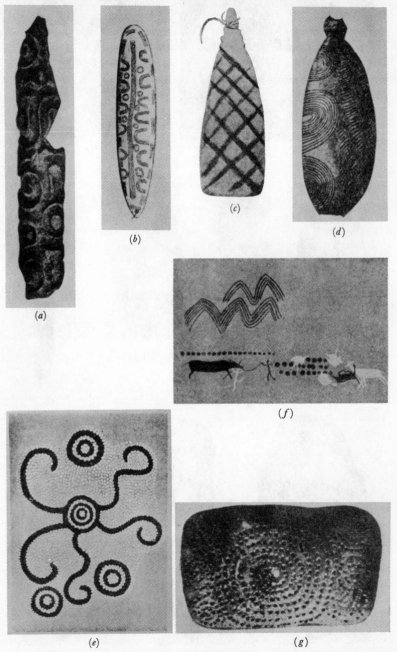

Plate 5. PALAEOLITHIC AND MODERN COMPARISONS

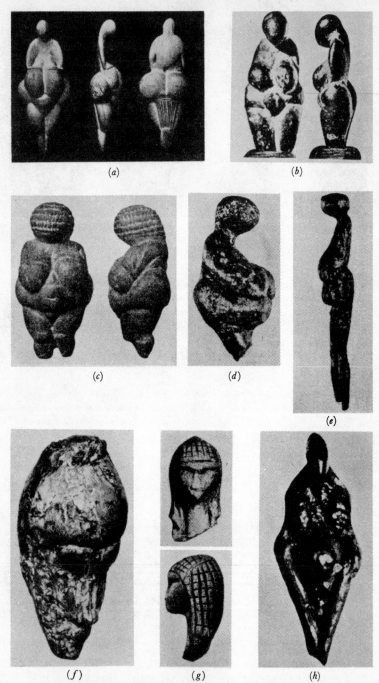

(a)

(b)

(c)

(d)

(e)

(f)

(g)

(h)

Plate 6. AURIGNACIAN FEMALE FIGURINES

other weapons together with human hands and arms which can be paralleled at Santián (fig. 14, p. 18). Impressed hands are common in Australia, and occur on rock-faces in California, in Peru (together with animal figures), and in Africa.[1] It will be remembered that the hands of initiates were laid above the cave opening when churingas had to be removed for ceremonies, 'to let the spirits know,' they said.[2] In New Mexico a boy leaves the impression of his left hand in the shrine. After marriage he returns and impresses the right hand beside it.[3] With these examples in view, it may be conjectured that the hand-impressions of Palæolithic cavern walls—including the left-hand negatives—connoted not merely power over the prey nor even the consecretion of the instrument of hunter and artist, but a testimony of their presence in a sacred place. The mutilation of the fingers, of which the impressions on the cave of Gargas afford the sole examples,[4] was customary until recently in South Africa, America, in the Pacific Islands, and in India, for mourning, dedication and sacrifice. Feigned or symbolic mutilation is also known.[5] No sign of this practice has appeared, it will be remembered, among Aurignacian skeletons, yet the amputations of Gargas do seem a little to strengthen the link which binds them to the Bushmen.

There are also certain other designs of hands which differ from the above by their great size in relation to adjacent human figures. The two pairs on the engraving of fig. 30, p. 26, seem to belong to this group, as possibly the African examples (pl. IIIb). Such a great hand appears in the Australian ground drawing of the Emu totem among the Wiradthuri,[6] but the evidence is at present too meagre for any definite religious significance to be assigned to these figures.

[1] Sollas, op. cit., p. 417.   [2] *Nor. Tr.*, p. 267. See p. 36 above.
[3] M. C. Burkitt, *Prehistory*, 2nd ed., 1925, p. 308.   [4] See p. 17.
[5] Sollas, op. cit., p. 416; Frazer, *The Dying God*, p. 219.
[6] R. H. Mathews, *J.A.I.*, xxv (1895); 1896, pp. 295–318, and xxvii, 1898, pp. 532–541; Mainage, op. cit., p. 230.

THE PATHWAYS

A further symbolic design occurs, it will be remembered, usually at the entrance of some group of chambers of the Palæolithic caves. This is the 'macaroni', once, at Gargas, forming a beast's head, and once his body;[1] sometimes taking the appearance of a plan, as at Niaux. Similar designs, also resembling plans, appear on the rocks of North Africa. Among movable objects we saw them on Magdalenian 'bull-roarers' and staffs, and in Eastern Europe a regular mæander has been found incised on ivory, and an elaborate decoration of spirals punctuated on a flat stone in Aurignacian Siberia (fig. 40, p. 32 and pl. V*g*).[2]

The ground drawings still made in modern times for Australian ceremonies represent, like the figures on the churingas, either the totemic ancestor himself, in his capacity of food-producer (as in the design of the Emu's entrails and eggs in pl. V*c*), or his wanderings, searches, and place of arrival or contact or rest, in the earth. In general, concentric circles indicate 'stopping places', waving lines mean 'searchings'[3] (pl. V*e*); a ground-drawing of the Wollunqua totem, made amid deep emotion to the accompaniment of chants, represents this strife and cessation.[4] The pathways between the worlds are also trodden by his human adherents in the dances by which they assimilate themselves with his life-force—and the waving track still discernible between the dancer's footprints round a ground-symbol at Montespan, will not be forgotten.[5] So a human companion sometimes accompanies the divine being on his journey, as in pl. III*d*, another symbolic drawing of the Wollunqua, where a man's footprints are marked along the winding path, and his embracing arms in the horn-like projection

---

[1] G. H. Luquet, *The Art and Religion of Fossil Man*, 1930, fig. 85.

[2] The geometrical tendency of these Eastern examples as compared with the vague and irregular lines of W. Europe and Africa, show them to be possible prototypes of the style described in Part ii, chap. i.

[3] B. Spencer and F. J. Gillen, *Nor. Tr.*, p. 740.

[4] B. Spencer and F. J. Gillen, ibid., fig. 309, pp. 240 ff.

[5] Page 43.

above the central circle where he aided the mythical snake to his final descent into the earth. The other circles are previous resting places where he left the spirit children of the clan. The journey and transformations of this beast are themselves described as ceremonies.[1]

Similarly, among the Pima Indians of Arizona a spiral sand-drawing (fig. 34, below), illustrated in a Spanish manuscript of the eighteenth century, was said to represent the emergence of their ancestors into the physical world, and spirals of a like nature have been inscribed on a stone wall in the Pimal country.[2] So among the Dakota, trees and animals are described as the spots

Fig. 34

'at which the god has stopped'.[3] We have already noted the sense of participation perceived by such peoples between an object and its locality. These drawings, which symbolise the divinity and his path in one, show that motion is similarly conceived. It has been pointed out that such movements are of the nature of causality,[4] so that the roads taken by the divine power are themselves currents of energy. 'I am the Way and the Life.'

This is well though crudely illustrated in the ceremony of the Dog totem in Northern Australia, where a winding path is cut through the bush (pl. IIIc) for a processional march, which represents at the same time the flounderings of the ancestral beast

[1] B. Spencer and F. J. Gillen, *Nor. Tr.*, p. 743.

[2] W. H. Matthews, *Mazes and Labyrinths*, 1922, pp. 153, 154, and fig. 131.

[3] Alice G. Fletcher, *Rep. Peabody Mus.*, iii, p. 276, n.

[4] J. N. B. Hewitt, *American Anthropologist*, 1902, pp. 35–36. Quoted by Durkheim, op. cit., p. 203.

through the primeval mud, and also the rope by which it was drawn on to dry land by the human 'companion'.[1]

Both the winding path, and the rope or clue, appear in European tales of entry into an actual or subjective spiral maze,[2] and with these savage analogies before us it does not seem unreasonable to connect such a pathway between the two worlds, both with the winding entrance signs of the Palæolithic caves, and with the choice of intricate and difficult passages to their inner sanctuaries.

WHERE NO CONNECTION CAN BE FOUND

Of the social organisation so integrally bound up with the religious systems of the hunting peoples who survived till yesterday, we can discover no trace in the records of post-glacial time. Some of the Australian tribesmen say that exogamy is more recent than their primal totemism, which appropriately goes back here and elsewhere to the mythical origin of the race, yet the fact that this elaborate relation between the totemic groups of a clan existed also on the other continents, does point to a common source.[3] Of the initiation ceremonies which linked the religious and social aspects of group solidarity, we have again, with the very problematical exception of the 'bull-roarer', no direct evidence of Pleistocene inheritance. This spiritual rebirth of the individual was often associated in central Australia with the Intichiuma ceremonies for the reproduction of the totemic species,[4] which, as we saw, is likely to have had some prehistoric prototype. Among the ordeals customary in Australian and other primitive communities, was the knocking out of a tooth, and the epipalæolithic skeletons of the

---

[1] *Illustrated London News*, Aug. 12th, 1939, pp. 277–279; D. F. Thomson, 'Proof of Indonesian influence upon the Aborigines of North Australia.'

[2] Compare the kitten who unwinds the ball of wool before Alice penetrates the looking-glass, and the fatal spindle of the Sleeping Beauty.

For an interesting investigation of the whole subject see W. F. J. Knight, *Cumæan Gates*, 1936.

[3] Frazer, *Totemism and Exogamy*, 1910, i, 350 ff.

[4] B. Spencer and F. J. Gillen, *Nor. Tr.*, p. 178; Strehlow, *Die Aranda*, iii, 1, pp. 1–2. The latter remarks that the initiation festivals reproduce the regular (Intichiuma) rites, but for a different end.

Natufian women of Shukbah and Mt. Carmel show signs of such a practice.[1] Like the mutilations of Gargas, a resemblance of custom confined to a single locality cannot safely be considered as evidence of connection.

We do not know if the Bushmen were initiated in caves. Among the Australians these rites were performed in the bush, apart from the camp of the clan, except in the case of the medicine-men, whose novices, as we saw, repaired to a cave for their death-sleep and rebirth.[2]

Later civilised races, however, did perform such ceremonies in caves or crypts, and considered the cave as the mother from whom they were born again. And these rites, as will be seen, were similar in action and intent, though modified with developed mentality, to those seemingly shared between the vanished and the existing peoples in the hunting stage of culture. That is to say, they aimed at renewal through union with divinity.

[1] Sir Arthur Keith, *Proceedings of the First International Congress of Prehistoric and Protohistoric Sciences* (1932), 1934, p. 46.

[2] See p. 37.

CHAPTER III

THE MOTHER GODDESS
AND THE DEAD

In considering the documents of their beliefs left behind by the races of glacial and post-glacial time, one artistic type confronts us which is absent from the culture, whether sacred or profane, of recent hunting peoples. The Aurignacian female images are distributed through a region (fig. 1, p. 4) which stretches from Siberia to Southern France, and are most numerous on the Eastern sites. Sculpture was a mode of expression peculiar to Aurignacian art. The Solutreans of Le Roc may have learnt to use or produce reliefs of animals during their short-lived intrusion; but the Magdalenians who inherited the Aurignacian traditions of draughtsmanship and are responsible for the magnificent frieze of horses and other beasts cut in high relief at Cap Blanc,[1] confined themselves chiefly to the carving of tools and weapons. The production, however, of feminine statuettes, was maintained in the Eastern sites which kept their Aurignacian culture through the various periods of change in the west.[2] It is very notable that South Eastern Europe and Western Asia were precisely the localities in which succeeding civilisations developed their religious type of the Mother Goddess, in the stylised form characteristic of East European art generally, and also of the latest Palæolithic art. The possibilities of cultural inheritance will be discussed in a later chapter.

There is a slight indication of a cult of the Mother Goddess among the forebears of modern 'primitives'. Figurines of this class have come to light, for instance, beneath volcanic débris

[1] G. Lalanne and H. Breuil, *L'Anthropologie*, xxii, 1911, pp. 385–402.

[2] H. Obermaier, *Fossil Man in Spain*, 1924, p. 222; T. Volkow, 'Nouvelles découvertes dans la station paléolithique de Mézine,' *Congr. intern. d'anthr. et d'archéol. préhist.*, sess. xiv., Geneva, 1912; C. Absolon, *I.L.N.*, Nov. 30th, 1929, p. 936.

in Mexico,[1] but the warlike tendency of the prehistoric Amer-
can communities eventually brought the male element into
dominance. The Bushmen, in whose ceremonial paintings
women are prominent, often wearing the fringed back-apron
of certain Aurignacian statuettes,[2] confined their rock carvings
to animal forms. If such figures existed in more perishable
material, they have long vanished. The ancestral myths of the
Australians allow women, as we saw, an important place. According to these, they once took the divine journeys, which
would give them a part in ceremonies, such as they retained
until recently in Western Australia.[3] But here and throughout
the continent the concentration of creative energy must at some
period have required the separation of the sexes during the performance of the most solemn rites. It does appear possible, indeed, that on all the continents where later civilisations did not
influence her development, the 'Mother Goddess' disappeared
from the religious system, as her images disappeared from the
Magdalenian hearths. In South Eastern Europe, on the other
hand, in the North African hinterland and Western Asia, the
great discoveries of the succeeding eras, especially the domestication of animals and the cultivation of corn, imparted to this
conception an increasingly deep significance.

The burial rites have a similar history. Primitive groups or
families usually remove themselves from the vicinity of a kinsman's corpse—whether the relationship be of blood or of other
communion—at least until after the 'second death' presently to
be described. Their dead remain powerful to help or harm. In
Australia, for instance, they guard the children, before initiation
opens to these the solidarity of the clan.[4] But only when relationship is no longer personal, when they have become a part
of the ancestral spirit, are they objects of sanctity in any sense
differing from the sanctity of living members in union with the
whole.

The Palæolithic dead, as we saw, were usually buried in the
habitations of the living. They still had a personal place in the
group for there are signs that they received offerings.[5] This was

[1] H. J. Spinden, *Ancient Civilisations of Mexico and Central America*, chap. i.
[2] See fig. 31.   [3] See p. 38 above.
[4] C. Strehlow, *Die Aranda*, ii, p. 7. V. Stefansson found a similar conception among the Eskimos: *My Life with the Eskimo*, 1913, pp. 397–400.
[5] Page 6 above, and pp. 65–70 below.

the second conception to become all-important in the Neolithic religion, and through that to the great civilisations whose influence is still felt within our own.

It is therefore necessary to consider what little is known of both these aspects of religious cult, and to try to recover the ideas which may have related them to the animal ceremonies in the caves.

THE MOTHER GODDESS

THE STATUETTES

The little statues of mammoth ivory, stone or conglomerate, represent in general an upright woman with small featureless bent head and feeble arms usually laid upon her huge breasts, with very wide or deep hips, loins and abdomen, and legs dwindling to small or non-existent feet. The great width or depth of the central portion may have been partly determined by the formal limitations of the tusk from which many of the images were carved, but it occurs also in the stone figures and is there undoubtedly due to a psychological rather than a technical cause. As was noted in an earlier chapter, these were found in Aurignacian levels of habitation, not in the separated recesses presumably devoted to cave rites, though stylised figures evidently derived from the statuettes are drawn or incised on the ceilings or walls of the inner chambers of Pech-Merle, La Roche[1] or Les Combarelles, with none of the hesitation and lack of artistry so marked in the portrayal of purely human creatures.[2] At Gagarino on the Don a number of these images were distributed within, and close beside, the circle of stones which marked a hut-formation.[3] Their milieu is definitely domestic, and they are never found among the furniture of burials. Some cult of human fertility is indicated, which was brought into touch with the rites for animal reproduction in the caves. This cult appears, on the evidence of the statuettes, to have originated among the Aurignacians of Eastern Europe

[1] See pl. IIc.   [2] See p. 23 above.

[3] E. A. Golomshtok, *L'Anthropologie*, xliii, 1933, pp. 334–336; S. N. Zamiatnine in *Paleolit S.S.S.R.*, pp. 26–77; *Gagarino, Ac. de l'hist. de la culture matérielle*, Moscow, 1934, pp. 29 ff.

and spread westward, where the figures are found in smaller numbers, occasionally (pl. VI*a*) possessing great formal artistry. A small immature torso and a poor specimen carved from a horse's tooth seem to be Magdalenian survivals. They do not appear in the Capsian of Africa.

A tall and a squat type are found in Aurignacian levels from the Don to the Northern shore of the Mediterranean, and may correspond to a general division into long-legged and short, noted among the graves.[1] The short-legged examples are obese, and always naturalistic in style, like the famous 'Venus' of Willendorf (pl. VI*c*) and her sister from Russian Gagarino (pl. VI*d*). The taller figures throughout the region of distribution are slender, even elegant, except for a central width or depth. They differ as a class from the former type in showing a tendency to abstraction, most complete in the figure from Lespugue (pl. VI*a*), where the geometric forms combine in a creation of great artistic stability. The vestige of clothing in the back-apron (similar to that worn by women of the Bushmen and found again in Aurignacian figurines from Mal'ta in Siberia)[2] does not break this abstraction; is indeed most skilfully used to oppose the lateral rotundities by prolonging the direction of vertical back, and hair falling from the featureless head, bowed as if above an unseen child. The exaggeration of the central area is not steatopygous; this particular figure was cut along the width of the tusk, and is therefore broader than its depth. But the volume is certainly intentional and reminiscent, at least to modern eyes, of the profundities and pendent stalactites of the caves. A steatite figure from Grimaldi resembles it closely (pl. VI*b*), giving the same impression of brooding maternity. The drooped head of conglomerate found in Moravia may have belonged to such a figure,[3] though here as in the ivory head from Brassempouy (pl. VI, *f* and *g*) the eyes and nose are indicated and there is the suggestion of a mouth. Although the decay of the material may partly account for its subtlety, this head is of an elevated type, and accords with neighbouring burials.[4]

The general unimportance among the statues of face, hands and feet may have originated in fears of magic dangers, but is

[1] See p. 33 above.
[2] M. M. Gerasimov in *Paleolit. S.S.S.R.*, 1935, pp. 78–124.
[3] C. Absolon in *I.L.N.*, Oct. 2nd, 1937.
[4] Sir A. Keith in *I.L.N.*, Oct. 2nd, 1937, Absolon's article.

far more likely, if these were religious abstractions, to be due simply to concentration on the regions of fertility. Steatopygy is infrequent, though it does occur, either by accident or intention, in the stone figure from Savignano[1] and another from Grimaldi.[2] Since the condition is an artificial acquirement, this would not racially connect the Aurignacians of North Italy with the Bushmen.[3] It may have been admired by the taller race, while obesity was perhaps cultivated, as it still is in many primitive tribes,[4] among the short-limbed people of the Chancelade type.[5] Or perhaps it was merely deemed appropriate to a 'Goddess' of fruitfulness, for the Magdalenian scrawls of women are slender.[6] Among images of normal proportions which belong to neither of the two groups, are the bone figurines, with hands joined before their breasts, from Mal'ta in Siberia,[7] and a young crouched or kneeling torso from Sireuil.[8]

It has often been suggested that these statuettes served an erotic purpose.[9] But apart from the fact that nothing in their attitude warrants such an assumption, there is that absence of the personal factor in the art of similar peoples, to which, it appears from all other records, the races of the Aurignacian and Magdalenian cultures conformed. It must also be remembered that they do not occur among personal possessions in graves. On the positive side there is the stylised representation of these images in the sacred precincts of the caves, where the fostering

[1] P. Graziosi, 'Su di una statuetta steatopigica preistorica rinvenuta a Savignano sul Panaro, in Prov. di Modena,' *Arch. per l'Antropologia e la Etnologia*, liv., 1924; Florence, 1926, pp. 165-167.

[2] 'La Polichinelle,' see L. Passemard: *Les statuettes féminines dites Vénus stéatopyges*, Nîmes, 1938; plate iii, figs. 1 and 2.

[3] R. Briffault, *The Mothers*, 1927, vol. ii, p. 163; T. Zammit and C. Singer, *J.R.A.I.*, liv, 1924, pp. 67-100, 'Neolithic Representations of the Human Form from the Islands of Malta and Gozo.' L. Passemard, op. cit., discusses the figures so far known from this standpoint, and comes to a negative conclusion.

[4] R. Briffault, op. cit., ii, p. 162.

[5] See p. 33 above.   [6] See chap. i, fig. 24.

[7] See M. M. Gerasimov, op. cit., p. 83, fig. 3. The slender proportions, as Prof. Garrod has pointed out to me, are in this case probably due to the fact that the figures are carved from bone.

[8] See L. Passemard, op. cit., pl. ii, fig. 8.

[9] For instance, by L. Passemard, op. cit., pp. 121, 122, and especially G. H. Luquet, 'The Art and Religion of Fossil Man,' 1930, pp. 109-111.

of individual passion is unthinkable if the last chapter holds any truth, since it would have impeded the unity of creative energy directed to a common end. Male representations again are never thus dehumanised on the walls, though there is the rare appearance of a slender hunter's torso among Aurignacian statuettes,[1] and fragments of a unique example in ivory, with no evidence of religious significance, from a grave at Brünn.[2]

The engravings on the chapel wall at Les Combarelles[3] have been frequently called erotic. They occur in one of those recesses which seem to have been dedicated over a long period to a particular purpose, and have a natural platform or altar. There are traces on its apse-like wall of several human forms. The two clearest have their faces obliterated by stalagmite, and these are always restored as human, but the woman stooping in the animal posture of the dance and the stooping man who follows, appear, as we saw, to have short tails and also the signs of skins visible on their bodies in certain lights. It is only reasonable therefore to conclude that they were masked, and engaged in mimetic ritual for the fertility of the wild herds, like the Mandan buffalo dance described by Catlin.[4] A somewhat similar scene of bent figures in horse masks is engraved on a bone from Abri-Murat (fig. 23, p. 24).

The famous sculptured reliefs from Laussel[5] have also been proffered as evidence that the statuettes were images of personal desire. The most notable of these is the fine relief of a woman of the short type lifting a bison's horn (pl. VIIa); the horn through whose point, in later religious cults, the creative force of the beast was thought to be expelled. The rough mass of her hair, cut like that of the ivory from Brassempouy (pl. VIg), was formerly thought to be a huge and prognathous head, which supported the evidence of negroid racial connection afforded by the Grimaldi skeletons and a few others in Central Europe. Her face, however, egg-shaped and featureless as

---

[1] For example, the beautiful relief from Laussel (pl. VIIb), G. Lalanne, *l'Anthr.*, xxiii, 1912, pp. 129 ff.), and a torso from Brassempouy (E. Piette, *L'Anthropologie*).

[2] A. Makovsky, 'Der diluviale Mensch im Loess von Brünn,' *Mitt. der Anthr. Gesell. in Wien*, Bd. xxii, 1892, pp. 82–83.

[3] See chap. i, p. 25.   [4] See p. 44, note 1.

[5] G. Lalanne, *L'Anthropologie*, xxii, 1911, pp. 257–260, and xxiii, 1912 pp. 129–149.

usual, looks over the right shoulder towards the horn which she is perhaps about to blow. She was once coloured red. Several other less accomplished reliefs of women were found fallen or placed upon the ground, two of them also carrying horns to which their heads are turned.[1] There was also the slender torso of a huntsman (pl. VII*b*) apparently discharging an arrow or dart.[2] It has recently been suggested that the women with horns were believed to assist the hunt, in accordance with savage analogies, by emitting the magic force.[3]

But there is a fourth woman among the reliefs whose arms rest along her sides like those of certain of the statuettes.[4] The lower half of this figure is much damaged (pl. VII*d*). Its discoverer saw it as 'lying' on its background, and considered a circular area at the lower end to be the head of a second figure, either of a child during birth or a man whose body below the chest was hidden by hers. It is thus restored in some handbooks.[5] On the unsatisfactory evidence of a photograph,[6] this woman appears to stand upright like the others in the rockshelter, and to be of the tall type, the 'forked beard' of the supposed male head being the remains of her two legs ending in feet set together, as they are elsewhere in the few cases in which they are represented. A suggested restoration is appended on these lines (pl. VII*c*) for comparison with pl. VI*h* from Grimaldi. This doubtful 'group' has been produced as the crowning proof of the erotic nature of the statues.[7]

[1] See the restoration by S. N. Zamiatnine, op. cit., fig. 24; and in *Paleolit. S.S.S.R.*, 1935, plate 26.

[2] G. Lalanne, *L'Anthr.*, xxiii, loc. cit.; R. de Saint-Périer, *L'Art préhistorique*, 1932, pl. viii, 1. The figure of a hind is said to have been discovered on a neighbouring slab of stone.

[3] By S. N. Zamiatnine, op. cit., pp. 81–82. L. Frobenius, *African Genesis*, 1938, shows in fig. 4 masked men lifting a rhinoceros by the magic power of their horns, on a rock-engraving in the Fezzan. Frobenius also shows in *Das Unbekannte Afrika*, p. 23, a rock drawing of a hunting-scene in which the archer bending his bow is connected by a magic line with the figure of a woman who raises her arms.

[4] G. Lalanne, *L'Anthropologie*, xxii, loc. cit., fig. 1. The author mentions that the lower 'head' was unpolished, showing that the surface is damaged.

[5] S. Reinach in *Répertoire de l'art quaternaire*, 1913, p. 120, gives a restoration on these lines.

[6] The original is, or was before the war, in the possession of Mme. Lalanne at Bordeaux.

[7] By G. H. Luquet, op. cit., p. 110.

The engraved symbols on the overturned stone slabs of La Ferrassie will not be forgotten.[1] Among these were outlines of animal heads and 'cupolas' in relief.[2] One of these last has been carved by a flint implement in the interior of Pech-Merle.[3] Neolithic tomb-symbolism, which many thousands of years later retained the cup-holes, mazes, stylised weapons, and feet, shaped such cupolas deliberately as maternal breasts, but the Aurignacian cupolas are not always in pairs. The interpretation is doubtful, but worth noting. There was also the triangular

Fig. 42

symbol, already described as occurring twice before enclosures painted on the walls of Pasiega,[4] which is incised, too, in position, on stylised figurines from Mezin.[5]

The symbols of La Ferrassie come very early in cave ritual.[6] They are probably middle-Aurignacian, going back, that is to say, to a period before the art of animal drawing had reached its maturity. The statuettes, as we saw, extend through upper Aurignacian, and continue in a stylised form in the East (fig. 42, above), through the Magdalenian and Azilian ages of the

[1] See above, p. 27.

[2] L. Capitan and D. Peyrony, 'Les Origines de l'art à l'aurignacien moyen,' *Revue Anthropologique*, xxxi, 1921, pp. 92–112.

[3] A. Lemozi, *La Grotte-Temple de Pech-Merle*, pp. 99–107.

[4] See figs. 11 and 12.

[5] H. Obermaier, op. cit., p. 222, quoting T. Volkow, 'Nouvelles découvertes dans la station paléolithique de Mézine,' *Congr. Intern. d'Anthr. et d'Archéol. préhist.*, *sess*, 14, Geneva, 1912, t. i.

[6] L. Capitan and D. Peyrony, op. cit.

West, where a general conventionalism eventually signified the decay of animal art.

That the later assimilation of caverns to the body of a Mother of Rebirth may have had some prototype in the days when the cave was both home and sanctuary, is suggested by the Aurignacian engraving on ivory from Predmost (pl. IIa). This, as the illustration shows, is of the nature of the Australian ground drawings and the 'macaroni' animals of Gargas[1]; an ivory 'bull-roarer', ornamented with the concentric curving lines of the churingas, comes from the same site (pl. Vd). Such patterns represented to the Australians and others, as we saw,[2] pathways of the divine force and also its embodiment,[3] a twofold conception familiar in savage America.[4] The feminine design of pl. IIa seems to be emblematic of a similar causality.[5]

So we come to the enquiry as to the position of the female figures in the religious system sketched in the last two chapters.

THE RELIGIOUS CONCEPTION

Peoples such as the Melanesians and North Americans who are advancing from pure totemism, and locally and partially the Australians also, have distinguished the spiritual substance, in which all are one and holy, as a dynamic force well known under the names of Mana and Wakanda. This creative motion may be considered as masculine.

Now the animal rites of the caves were certainly instituted by the Aurignacians, and the female images, though never present in these sanctuaries, are as certainly an expression in the outside world of a power which also had its place within[6]—hence the stylised wall engravings and the inscribed and painted symbols. It seems reasonable to imagine that the makers of those statuettes had also passed beyond the stage of localised relationship with the archetypal beasts, to the conception of a pervading principle, not in this case their own creative power, but a life-substance through which that power could act, conceived already in the human form of maternal fecundity.

[1] See p. 50.   [2] See pp. 51, 52.
[3] See p. 51.   [4] See p. 51, fig. 34.
[5] Professor Obermaier was the first to recognise it as a female figure.
[6] See p. 25, and pl. IIc.

THE MOTHER GODDESS AND THE DEAD

The need for unity recognised by the institution of ceremonies is the first acknowledgment of a sense of separation;[1]
the isolation of the uniting potency a first step in the establishment of relationship—no mere participation—between the
human group and the One. This anthropomorphic shape
marks a further stage in the clarifying of human personality,
for before men can raise themselves above the animals they
must perceive the divine in human form.

The fact that their underlying principle was feminine would
eventually bring the perception of duality, so that when their
successors had established superiority over the beasts by domestication, and this all-receptive Maternity had become the
Earth-Mother in whom their corn was sown, a son might be
born to that Mother out of the aspiration of man.[2] There is no
evidence that their own rare figures of a young hunter were the
objects of a cult.[3]

BURIAL RITES

AMONG MODERN PRIMITIVES

In the totemic systems, as we saw, physical birth is not sufficient to make the child a member of his clan—that is, completely living. A rebirth is necessary, sometimes described as
the moment when he receives his soul.

Similarly, the death of the body leaves its occupant still a
kinsman of the living until his true death is celebrated after a
certain period has elapsed. From that point of time he is
usually considered, at least in Australasia, to have no personal
existence, but to form part of the life of his totemic ancestors,
awaiting rebirth. His limited survival is thus the arc of a continuous cycle which binds the clan through time. Its stages
have been classified as follows:[4]

[1] The acknowledgment being not necessarily a conscious one, since
artistic expression comes from a deeper level.

[2] See Part ii for archæological evidence that the Neolithic and Chalcolithic
male deity was a derivation from the Mother, not an independent conception of the worshipper.

[3] See, for instance, p. 60 above.

[4] Lévy-Bruhl, *Fonctions Mentales*, 1910, pp. 360–361.

(1) Death to funeral.

(2) Funeral to end of mourning (the severing of relations).

(3) Awaiting reincarnation.

(4) Birth to naming.

(5) Between naming and initiation.

(6) Initiation to death.

The first funeral almost always necessitates a removal of the living from the neighbourhood of the corpse. Among peoples with so firm a sense of communal solidarity, death is naturally feared as contagious. Then, too, the dead man might attempt to bring someone he cherished to his side, or be envious of those left behind. Thus the Bushmen would move their kraal from the vicinity of a new grave, which was often a rock-shelter; fearing no malice, for they left the dead his bow and staff and painted him with ochre to simulate life, but asking his pardon, none the less, for their own continuance among the living.[1] So in Australia, as in North America, the corpse might be exposed on a distant tree-platform, or be buried or partly burnt or even eaten by the community in preliminary funeral rites which always included self-wounding, because blood was the physical counterpart of the mystic life-union. It was probably represented in the red ochre sometimes painted over the sacred bone, when that was brought to its later resting-place in the final funeral rites, which were usually celebrated with great solemnity after an interval of a year or more, when the flesh had disappeared.[2]

This second funeral may be considered to set the man free to join his clan among the dead, for separation from these would be a disorientation as catastrophic as the excommunication of the living from the tribal ceremonies. The surviving kinsmen, therefore, whose grief was usually very real, deliberately severed personal relations, though the dead remained present at communal celebrations by means of the churingas,[3] and were thought in many cases to guard or inhabit the immature. Among the Arunta of central Australia a depression was made in the final burial mound, facing the direction of the clan camping ground in the Alcheringa, that is, the region of the mythical

[1] D. Livingstone, *Missionary travels and researches in South Africa*, 1857, p. 165, quoted by Sollas, op. cit., p. 478.

[2] B. Spencer and F. J. Gillen, *Nor. Tr. of Central Australia*, pp. 530–543.

[3] Ibid., p. 261.

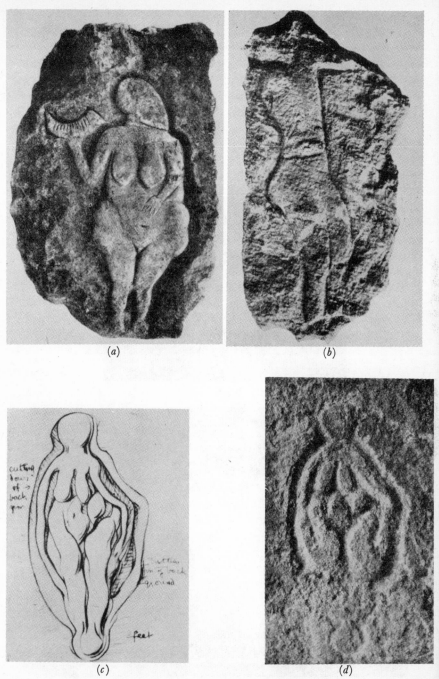

(a)

(b)

(c)

(d)

Plate 7. AURIGNACIAN RELIEFS

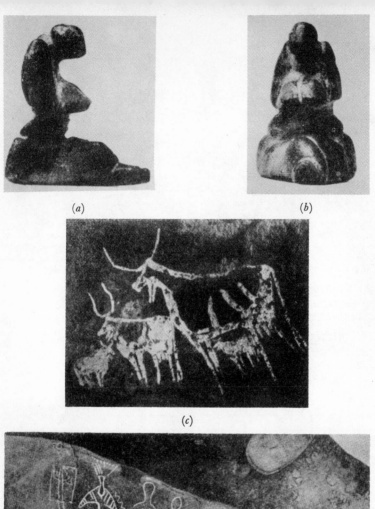

(a)　　　　　　　　　　　　　　(b)

(c)

(d)

Plate 8. TRANSITION

ancestors.[1] The Warramunga made beside the grave of the Bone, a ground-drawing of the entry to earth of their totemic snake, and covered each with a stone called by the same name.[2] The North West American Indians painted his totem upon the body of the dead.[3]

Amid the great variety of customs natural where death is considered as continuous with life, a general body of beliefs may be distinguished to which these conform, even where they differ from, or contradict, one another. These may be summarised as totemic cohesion in space and time.

PALÆOLITHIC

The burial customs of the primeval cave-dwellers reveal a similar consensus of general beliefs beneath much variety of detail, though no cyclic system comparable to the above can be inferred from their remains. A desire, on the contrary, to preserve the actual corpse of the kinsman in their midst, is evinced until the period of cultural decline. We saw in the first chapter how even the early denizens of the caves on Mt. Carmel carefully buried their dead with offerings of food,[4] and how the barely human Neanderthals of Europe laid them in the cave-earth with their weapons and ornaments. In the burial below the Mousterian rock-shelter of La Ferrassie, the man lay within a natural recess, the woman in an artificially deepened cavity, with the children in trenches near them. Protecting stones were laid above, and it was on the lower face of one of these that cup-holes (fig. 41, p. 66) were discovered turned towards the earth and the dead.[5] Their meaning to Neanderthal man cannot be conjectured, but throughout their prolonged history they are connected with funeral rites. Other examples were found on stones among the Aurignacian deposits at l'Abri Blanchard,[6] and similar depressions are cut into the rock before that cliff-

---

[1] Ibid, p. 506.   [2] Ibid., fig. 152.

[3] F. Boas, 'First General Report on the Indians of British Columbia in Fifth Report of the Committee on the North-Western Tribes of the Dominion of Canada,' *Report of the 59th Meeting of the British Association for the Advancement of Science* (1889), 1890, p. 537. Quoted by E. Durkheim, op. cit., p. 119.

[4] See chap. i, p. 6.   [5] See chap. i, p. 6.

[6] W. J. Sollas, op. cit., fig. 121 (2 and 3).

terrace on Mt. Carmel where the excavators found the Natufian dead still recumbent in their coronals of shells.[1]

In front of the children's graves at La Ferrassie a ditch had been dug which contained animal bones and cinders.[2] The presence of many such bones and a bison horn in the pit dug at the entrance of the burial cave of La Chapelle aux Saints, shows this to have been a Mousterian custom, and the latter gives the impression of offerings or feasts partaken through a long period.[3] Since no used weapons were found, with the exception of flints

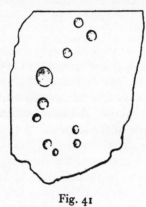

Fig. 41

whose points were mostly broken at the tip as if in the splitting of bones, and since the cave roof was very low, it is just possible that these are vestiges of a cult.[4]

Neanderthal skeletons were usually buried in the attitude of sleep, but the male corpse of La Ferrassie, whose head had been severed after death, showed signs of the bandaging occasionally practised at a later epoch.[5] His is a special case; and perhaps he was considered dangerous.

Aurignacian and Magdalenian burials, on the other hand, display much variety of posture, the corpse being extended in

[1] D. A. E. Garrod, *The Stone-Age of Mt. Carmel*, 1937, vol. i, pp. 10–13 (depressions in the Lower Natufian pavement); pp. 17–19 (shell-chaplets).

[2] *L'Anthr.*, xxiv, p. 633, n. 1; xxxi, p. 344 (Breuil). G. H. Luquet, op. cit., p. 165.

[3] *L'Anthr.*, xxiv, pp. 627–633; Luquet, op. cit., pp. 165–166, 169.

[4] *L'Anthr.*, xxiv, pp. 632–633; G. H. Luquet, op. cit., pp. 166–167.

[5] L. Capitan and D. Peyrony, *Revue anthropologique*, xxxi, pp. 382–388.

the noble Crô-magnon fashion of Western Aurignacian levels,[1] curved sideways in a manner reminiscent of Mousterian practice,[2] or again in the closely flexed position[3] common among modern primitives in Africa, America and Australia, and almost universal in the Neolithic burials of Europe and North Africa; whether from fear of ghostly activities or to simulate an expectation of birth—if indeed the pre-natal posture was known. The motive could not have been lack of space, as such examples of binding before death occur in widely-hollowed graves, chiefly Magdalenian, and perhaps represent a revival of the tradition exemplified at La Ferrassie.[4]

The corpses sometimes clasp a joint of meat,[5] and occasionally horns or tusks lie near them, like the Mousterian bison-horn of La Chapelle. A whole mammoth skull with its tusks was found beside the human remains in the Welsh Paviland cave,[6] and a mammoth tusk above the skeleton at Brünn.[7] It appears that the magic property of such defences as a fountain of energy—of which the Laussel reliefs probably furnish an illustration[8]—was also made available to the dead, a custom analogous to the placing of bulls' horns upon modern grave mounds in the Nile Valley,[9] and to the long continued attachment of horned gates and altars to sepulchres of the Neolithic and Bronze Age Mediterranean, later to be described.

Down to Azilian times no special orientation was observed. Throughout this period women were buried as individuals, with ornaments and offerings, and sometimes carefully pro-

[1] For example, the male skeleton of the Grotte des Enfants at Grimaldi (*Les Grottes de Grimaldi*, ii, fasc. 1, pl. 1).

[2] Like the two negroes of the same Grotto. (R. Verneau, *L'Anthr.*, xiii, p. 567, fig. 2.)

[3] As at Chancelade. (Hardy, *La Station quaternaire de Raymonden*, 1891, p. 49.) G. H. Luquet, op. cit., fig. 109.

[4] G. H. Luquet, op. cit., p. 170.

[5] For example, the tallest skeleton of the cemetery of Mughâret es Skhul on Mt. Carmel (see article 'Fossil Woman', by T. D. McCown in *The Times* of March 19th, 1937, pp. 17–18) held against his chest the fossil jaw of a boar.

[6] W. Buckland, *Reliquiæ Diluvianæ*, 1823, pp. 82, et seq.

[7] H. Obermaier, 'Der Mensch der Vorzeit' (Bd. i, of *Der Mensch aller Zeiten*), p. 298.   [8] See p. 59 above.

[9] A. B. Cook, *Zeus* i, p. 508 ff. See also G. Catlin, *N. American Indians*, vol. i, plate 48, where a pair of horned bison skulls (male and female) are set above a mound of secondary burial; an invariable custom, he says.

tected like the men by horizontal and vertical slabs of stone, forming the rudiments of a tomb.[1] The grave of the Negroid youth at Grimaldi was reopened at a later date to receive the body of an aged wife or mother.[2] Children also wore elaborate ornaments such as the necklace, pendants and ring-diadem found upon the skeleton of a three-year-old child, who had been buried under an Aurignacian hut-foundation at Mal'ta in Siberia, with his tiny implements around him.[3]

In addition to such stone implements, often especially well-wrought and always intact, and the bone tools and ornaments such as hairpins, shells are very frequently strewn over the corpse in large numbers, in the position of a former cap or kilt,[4] or are heaped on the ground in its neighbourhood, like the tomb-offerings of the Ægean bronze age. Beads too are common, cut from mammoth tusks or shaped from the teeth of stag, horse or bear. These, like the shells, had doubtless an amuletic value, and in Magdalenian times were sometimes engraved.[5] Some of them displayed, in their undisturbed state, a noticeable beginning of that rhythmic and symmetrical arrangement which was to become characteristic of the art of their successors who lived under the sky.[6]

Implements and ornaments are often covered, like the body itself, with the red ochre which recent primitives employed to simulate blood or the life-energy of which it was the physical counterpart. The red ochre sometimes lies round them in cakes, and steeps all the vicinity with its colour, so that all the surrounding objects, it may be supposed, may keep their living quality in the other world.

In conformity with the general desire to preserve a physical continuity, which is apparent in all these graves, Palæolithic

[1] G. H. Luquet, op. cit., pp. 155–156, quoting Grimaldi ii, pp. 22, 23, 277.

[2] *L'Anthr.*, xiii, pp. 566–567; *Grimaldi*, ii, pp. 25, 27, 260; G. H. Luquet, op. cit., p. 178.

[3] M. M. Gerasimov in *Paleolit S.S.S.R.*, 1935, p. 119, fig. 36.

[4] G. H. Luquet, op. cit., p. 42; *Grimaldi*, ii, fasc. 1, pp. 29–32, 298, 299; E. Rivière, *De l'Antiquité de l'homme dans les Alpes Maritimes*, 1877, p. 119 and pl. xiii; D. A. E. Garrod, op. cit., pp. 17–19.

[5] M. Boule, *Les Hommes fossiles*, 2nd ed., 1923, p. 266; Luquet, op. cit., pp. 45–46.

[6] Especially the necklace from the triple sepulchre of Barma Grande (Luquet, fig. 35, after R. Verneau) and a fine Natufian example from Mt. Carmel (D. A. E. Garrod, op. cit., p. 18).

skeletons are usually found intact, so carefully have they been respected by those who passed their daily lives above them. The male skeleton at La Ferrassie was exceptional, as we saw, in suffering decapitation after death, and in Magdalenian levels also there are rare cases of displaced bones, or of completely separate arms, feet or skulls, surrounded by offerings and coloured red.[1] The former conditions may conceivably be due to the depredations of animals, but the latter does suggest an occasional custom of secondary burial. There is also the Pyrenean fragment of a human jaw containing a few teeth, deeply reddened and pierced for suspension, the relic of a friend (one may judge from the colour) retained for contact with his soul.[2] Possibly analogous with these are the cup-skulls of Placard.[3]

But later, in the epipalæolithic Natufian of Palestine there is definite evidence of the collection of the bones after death for a common reburial.[4] At Ofnet in Bavaria,[5] also late in the post-Magdalenian deposits, the famous nests of skulls, in one case numbering twenty-seven specimens, had been severed after death, and laid in their places through a considerable period to face the West, those of the women and children being richly ornamented. These, together with a single skull, found in a similar level near Lierheim,[6] strongly suggest that towards the end of this civilisation some form of secondary burial may have become a practice with its accompanying ideas, of which memories were afterwards preserved among the backward races. Such collections of the skulls of revered persons, laid close together like these, are objects of pilgrimage in New Caledonia.[7] The mythology of certain islands of the New Hebrides describes events related to a similar practice.[8]

The impregnation with red ochre of so many skeletons of the

[1] R. Verneau, *Grimaldi*, ii, fasc. 1, p. 298; H. Breuil and H. Obermaier, *L'Anthr.*, xx, p. 211.

[2] In Comte Bégouen's private Museum at the Château of Pujol.

[3] H. Breuil and H. Obermaier, *L'Anthr.*, xx, pp. 523 f.

[4] D. A. E. Garrod, op. cit., pp. 14, 15, 18, 19.

[5] R. R. Schmidt, *Die diluviale Vorzeit Deutschlands*, 1912.

[6] F. Birkner, 'Der paläolithische Mensch im Bayerischen Ries.' (*Wiener prähist. Zeitschr.*, Bd. 1, Vienna, 1914.)

[7] F. Sarasin, 'Streiflichter aus der Ergologie der Neu-Caledonier und Loyalty-Insulaner auf die europäische Prähistorie,' *Verhandl. d. natur. Gesell. in Basel*, Bd. xxviii, Heft, 2, Basle 1917, pp. 3–27.

[8] See below, p. 157.

preceding periods has also been taken as evidence of interment after the flesh had been removed. But it seems far more likely that the colour was painted on to the skin, perhaps in the form of symbols like the American totem-painting upon the dead,[1] or perhaps simply coating it. The ochre would have soaked through to the bones as it has soaked into the surrounding soil. It appears therefore that before the Palæolithic decline, secondary burial was unknown or extremely rare, marking a consistent divergence from modern primitive custom, the divergence which would naturally follow a difference of conception to which habitual sepulture below the hearths of the living already bears witness. That is to say, the rich Palæolithic material of Europe and Asia combines to demonstrate a belief that the dead remained a part of the family or group, that they kept their association with the grave and its furniture, that their presence, if at all feared (the red ochre and unbroken weapons testify to the contrary), was still more strongly desired, and sometimes at least retained by cult; that the attitude, in short, of the living towards the dead, bore less resemblance to the beliefs of recent primitives, than to those of the Neolithic and Bronze Age civilisations, which regarded the body and its tomb as a continuous link between the two phases of existence.

Thus the later history of Palæolithic burial customs resembles that of the images of the Mother Goddess. These two aspects of religious observance in the open cave, not directly associated with the ritual of the interior, were passed on to the immediate cultural successors, among whom, as we shall see, cave memories persisted. Outward led to inward, when these came to excavate or construct their first monuments after its pattern; and because the whole tomb was a cave, they could unite the two conceptions as their creators had never done. There is some fragmentary evidence, soon to be considered, that the Neolithic invaders of the temperate epoch may have established contact, in several localities, with the declining peoples of the old Stone Age, after the herds upon which their spiritual and physical existence depended, had died or fled northwards, and the forests, which their axes could not sever, were invading the plains, and they themselves, perhaps, were racially exhausted, having bequeathed to all humanity a foundation of ideas upon which the mind could raise its structures.

[1] See p. 6 for the great age of this custom.

PART TWO

NEOLITHIC—THE CAVE AS
TEMPLE AND TOMB

CHAPTER I

TRANSITION

CLIMATIC CHANGE—PASTURAGE
AND NOMADISM

While the hunting peoples of Europe and Asia were developing their culture amid the fauna of a semi-arctic world, the regions surrounding the enormous rivers, along which the first civilised states were to arise, consisted of grassy parklands still plentifully watered by the rains which have long since left them to desiccation. With the retreat of the northern ice-cap their richness was already fading, and perhaps for that reason groups of immigrants began to appear at this period among the forests and swamps of the newly-temperate Europe which had defeated Palæolithic man. The new-comers, racially various like their predecessors, prospered in this landscape partly because their ground axes could keep back the trees from the clearings, and raise huts above the level of the marsh, but chiefly because they were now independent of the great herds which had vanished into the Northern tundra, having elsewhere achieved the revolution which is comparable to the modern capture of energy by machines. They could breed animals and cultivate plants for their needs.

Other important discoveries, such as the crafts of weaving, pottery, and boat-building, mark the influx of a fresh mentality, but the economic change to food-production, with its necessary concentration on cyclic recurrence, was at the root of all these creations of balance and symmetry.

The territories from which, on archæological evidence, they must have arrived, are just those in which the wild species are found from which cattle, sheep and cereals have been developed. Only in Western and Central Asia, for instance, could the three species of wild sheep which gave rise to the domestic breeds, have been taken, on present evidence, under the protection of man, who might presumably have followed their changes of pasture through a long period, keeping off the beasts of prey, till both could live side by side.[1] On those plains the ewe is still milked like a cow.

North America, too, possesses a wild sheep, but the pre-Columbian inhabitants never tamed it. In Europe the moufflon is native to Corsica and Sardinia, but remained wild to a comparatively late period. It now appears certain that the dog shared the miserable hearths of the declining Palæolithic peoples in Northern and Western Europe,[2] but the bones of the domesticated descendant of the long-tailed Asiatic sheep, the Urial, are first found among the kitchen middens of Denmark, and the lake-dwellings of Switzerland, at the very beginning of Neolithic phase of culture.[3]

No indigenous wild sheep now exists in Africa, and the oldest bones found in Egypt are said to belong to an Asiatic variety.[4] For cattle-breeding, however, the evidence so far available points in the contrary direction. The parklands of North Africa had, as we saw, a long Palæolithic history before the withdrawal of the rains drove its men and beasts to the oases and the river valleys—which means that here we can draw upon the testimony of art.

Indeed, the mountain-tribes above the Nile Valley, who may have also made animal rock-drawings in the great pleistocene tradition,[5] themselves appear to have kept cows.[6] Perhaps they

---

[1] M. Hilzheimer, 'Sheep' in *Antiquity* for June, 1936, p. 195 ff.; V. Gordon Childe, *New Light on the Most Ancient East*, 1934, pp. 46–47.

[2] His bones have been found in Azilian hearths in England and in the Maglemose culture of Mullerup in Zealand. (H. Obermaier, *Fossil Man in Spain*, 1924, pp. 344 and 363–364.)

[3] M. Hilzheimer, op. cit.

[4] M. Hilzheimer, Africa (*J. Internat. Inst. African Lang. and Cult.*, vol. iii), 1930, p. 474.

[5] H. A. Winkler, *Rock Drawings of Southern Upper Egypt*, i; *Sir R. Mond Desert Exp.*, 1938, p. 20 and pls. xvii and xviii. The Eastern branch of these people, to whom the Nile at that period presented no political barrier, were also responsible, according to Winkler, for the drawings of his plates xx and xxi, but these seem by their style more likely to have been left by a people of Aurignacian affinities, possibly the ancestors of the Bushmen. See also R. F. Peel, 'The Painted Caves of Wadi Sora,' *Antiquity*, vol. xiii.

[6] H. A. Winkler, op. cit., i, p. 20. He says the artificial deformation of the horns, and the care taken in representing the udder, show domestication to be contemporaneous with the presence of elephant and giraffe in these regions.

had learnt to do so from their Capsian neighbours of the Western Desert, whose paintings are identical, as we have seen, with those of the East Spanish rock-shelters both in style and in the habits and costumes displayed. The cows shown in their desert pictures suggest a gradual emergence of those grasslands from the Palæolithic economic stage (pl. VIII*c*). Their breed of small oxen seems roughly contemporary with the petroglyphs of the extinct giant buffalo; but the ram, later so important in this region, does not appear. Cattle, but no sheep, are similarly to be found in the East Spanish rock-paintings of the late type, as also in the Bushman scenes which so closely resemble them.

Thus in spite of the fact that archæological discoveries from the earliest levels show that domestic cattle had a very long and very important history in Western Asia also, it appears likely that a sheep-breeding branch of the Neolithic peoples entered Europe from the East, while a cattle-breeding branch from Africa kept contact with Spain. Before considering the changes which they effected, it is necessary to examine the second factor of the economic revolution; namely, the cultivation of plants for the service of man.

CYCLIC CHANGE—THE SOWING OF THE CROPS

The same general region, which bred the ancestors of the domestic animals, possesses also the uncultivated grasses from which our present cereals are derived. Wild barley is found from Afghanistan to Palestine, and during the pluvial period must have flourished in Northern Africa. The emmer wheat, too, is native to Western Asia,[1] but seems to have been early cultivated in the vicinity of the Nile Valley and Abyssinia.[2] As in the case of the domestic animals, there appear to have been several centres of distribution over a great area in cultural contact.

[1] H. J. E. Peake, *J.R.A.I.*, lvii, 1927, p. 22 ff.; A. E. Watkins, 'The Origin of Cultivated Plants,' *Antiquity*, vii, p. 73 ff.; V. G. Childe, op. cit., pp. 44–45.

[2] N. I. Vavilov, *Studies on the Origin of Cultivated Plants*, Leningrad, 1926, p. 163.

The Natufians of epipalæolithic Palestine used bone handles with a groove into which a row of little flints were fixed to form a sickle, as teeth are set in a jaw.[1] The Capsians of North Africa, to whom the Natufians appear to have been racially allied,[2] used stone querns for the grinding of some kind of grain.[3] This does not entail the settled life of the agriculturist, for tribesmen wandering to-day across semi-desert plains may till their plots in hollows left moist by winter storms, moving them when the soil becomes exhausted, as they move their camels or sheep in pursuit of the scanty pasturage of spring.

Again, nomadic hunting tribes such as the Hadendoa, who frequented the Upper Nile Valley in recent times, scatter millet seeds in the mud left by the inundation and remain to reap their crop.[4] The drying of the opulent plains after the pluvial epoch, may have driven the hunters thus to utilise the floods of many streams. It cannot therefore be asserted that the deliberate control of the periodic overflow was first undertaken by the predecessors of the Egyptians. A contemporary economy seems to have been imposed under similar conditions along the banks of the Euphrates and perhaps the Indus also; but archæological discoveries in Egypt give the clearest picture of the whole process from the time when Palæolithic hunters, forced by drought from the surrounding uplands, occupied the terraces above the marshy valleys of the Nile and its yet flowing tributaries.[5] They may have come to utilise the flood deposits like the Hadendoa—the earliest graves in fact hold tokens of this double mode of life[6]—till they learned to dig canals, and at

[1] D. A. E. Garrod, *J.R.A.I.*, lxii, 1932, pp. 257–269; F. Turville-Petre, *ibid.*, pp. 271–276.

[2] Sir Arthur Keith, 'The Late Palæolithic Inhabitants of Palestine,' *Proc. of the First International Congress of Prehist. and Protohist. Sciences* (1932), 1934, p. 46.

[3] *L'Anthropologie*, xlii, p. 429.

[4] V. G. Childe, op. cit., p. 51.

[5] *Oriental Institute Publications*, Chicago, vol, xvii, 'Prehistoric Survey of Egypt and Western Asia,' ii, 1933, by K. S. Sandford and W. J. Arkell, vol. xviii, idem., iii, 1934, by K. S. Sandford; *Vignard Bull. soc. préhist. française*, xxv, 1928, p. 200 ff., 'Une nouvelle industrie lithique: le Sebilien.'

[6] This may be affirmed of all the purely Neolithic settlements. Hunting was to remain a ritual duty even among the Pharaohs.

length, because of the need for co-operative irrigation, organised their scattered units into a single state.[1]

Similarly, the need to clear their terraces of the great trees which still cloaked the valley, may have first induced such men to grind their stone axes to the required fineness, instead of merely striking out their shape with a view to strength and balance; but the age of the earliest ground axes of the Delta is doubtful, and the isolation inherent in the new mode of life, which tied a community to its parcel of land beside the stream, does not alter the fact that this was a civilisation whose great inventions in their earliest stages were common property over an immense area. We saw how widespread were the Palæolithic industries, and even, to an extent more racially limited, their art; but the creators of Neolithic civilisation were scientists, whose discoveries, therefore, like those of to-day, were available to anyone who mastered their technique. For this reason also there are comparatively few records in which changes of style can be traced with certainty. Only changes of culture are evident, as in the great developments of pottery or architecture.

Thus their whole history must remain considerably telescoped; there are only the parallel achievements, in domestication, in irrigation, in pottery, in building, radiating from the two cultural provinces, already distinct in Palæolithic times: the provinces of North Africa and Asia. The two were certainly in communication, though only at the end did they betray evidence of direct interrelation.

We saw in the last chapter that certain religious conceptions survived the tremendous, indeed antithetical, changes of mentality which had created, and were derived from, the new mode of life. The evidence of actual continuance is very fragmentary, but it does exist in both these centres, along with some slight but precious testimony of contacts in Europe.

[1] See A. Moret, *The Nile and Egyptian Civilisation*, 1927, pp. 33–37. Prof. Arnold Toynbee, in his *Study of History*, vol. i, p. 305 ff., draws a tragic picture, on Anderson's and Garstin's evidence, of hardships suffered in the reclaiming of the Nile banks. 'These heroic pioneers . . . plunged into the jungle swamps of the valley bottoms' developed, he believes, in their struggle to survive, the qualities necessary for civilisation, along with the irrigators of the Euphrates and other great rivers farther East.

POINTS OF CONTACT

In Asia the evidence is at present slightest of all. At Arpachiyeh near Nineveh[1] a flourishing Neolithic civilisation has been traced through a number of occupation levels, whose pottery, made in local kilns, bears witness to a common culture which once stretched to the Mediterranean coast, and later to the islands. Amid spindle whorls, corn, and the bones of domestic animals, were numbers of clay figurines, female and headless, in the squatting posture probably of childbirth (fig. 43, p. 80). There is a somewhat later painted type showing a rudimentary bent head and hanging breasts (fig. 45, p. 80). The style of this last example in particular, is strikingly different from later convention. 'No doubt,' says their discoverer, 'that we are in direct line with a tradition that goes back to . . . Brassempouy, Lespugue, Willendorf, and Wisternitz.'[2] But a far more definite approximation in style, technique, size and material, is to be found in a stone figurine from an unknown site in North Syria,[3] which is reproduced in pl. VIII*a* and *b*. Here is the unmistakable Aurignacian featureless bent head above huge breasts upon which the forearms appear to repose (compare pl. VI*a* and *c*, Part I), so different from the upright neck (and head where this remains) of purely Neolithic statuettes (fig. 44*a* and *b*, p. 80). But there is one surprising link with these: the seated posture which is unknown to Aurignacian sculpture, but seems characteristic of the Neolithic Middle East. This single cultural link is important because of the later predominance of the Mother Goddess in Western Asia, as also in Bronze Age Crete, whose well-known religious emblems already appear as motifs of this Neolithic painted pottery.[4] Its Northern locality suggests a possible descent from the Aurignacian of the Russian river-shores, or even of Siberia.

[1] M. E. L. Mallowan and J. Cruikshank Rose in *Iraq*, ii, part i, 1935; 'Excavations at Tall Arpachiyeh, 1933.'

[2] Mallowan and Rose, op. cit., p. 87.

[3] Published by C. L. Woolley, in *Mélanges Syriens offerts à R. Dussaud*, Paris, 1939, p. 135 ff. It was acquired from a peasant in the North Syrian plain, and its provenance is otherwise unknown.

[4] Bucrania and double axes—see fig. 50 and Part iv, 1, below.

The Natufian serrated sickles are found in Central Asia, in a curved form reminiscent of the true jaw-bone; and the first human figures on the painted pottery of North Syria and Susa are of the Late Capsian geometric and wasp-waisted type, with the feathered head-dress, which also survives in Neolithic Egypt (fig. 46, p. 80).

In Africa, on the other hand, there is definite testimony of the penetration into the last Capsian paintings of Neolithic ideas.[1] The conventionalism which appeared in the West with the late Magdalenian loss of creative power, and had always been a positive factor in the art of Eastern Europe, had increased in the Azilian phase of culture under Capsian influence, paving the way for the Neolithic abstract vision, until the conventions derived from human and other natural forms became standardised into a kind of sign-language, and probably formed one ingredient of the subsequent Mediterranean alphabetic script.[2] This means that the artistic change, like the religious, was partly a matter of evolution, and not entirely due to foreign elements.

Even the implements tended to become geometrical, a step towards the mechanical perfection of Neolithic, and the Capsian convention for the female form may have had its share in the subsequent predilection, over a wide area, for violin-shaped amulets of the Mother Goddess (figs. 48 and 49, p. 80).

Among the Sahara rock paintings of this transitional period of cattle-breeding, a 'Mother Goddess' also appears carved in relief or incised (pl. VIII*d*); slender above, with a tiny head and enormous middle parts clothed in a bell skirt. She is sometimes depicted naturalistically with waving locks, and woven or tatooed decoration, but passes through many stages of stylisation. It is interesting, in view of the possibilities mentioned in the previous chapter, to find her image stylised within cup-depressions in the rocks.[3] Another link with the past in these deserts west of the Nile Valley, is the presence of 'macaroni'—waving lines connecting persons and groups—the lines of jour-

[1] See below, p. 81, notes 3 and 4.

[2] Prof. Gilbert Murray here reminds me that the first letter of the alphabet in Phœnician and Græco-Roman scripts, is in name and shape a bull's or ox's head.

[3] H. A. Winkler, op. cit., ii, 1939, pp. 28–29 (pls. xliii (2) and xliv): 'I conclude that these drawings do not represent real women but statuettes.'

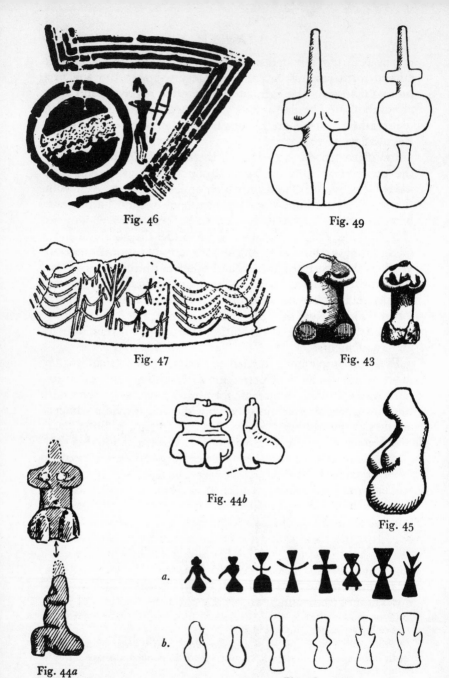

Fig. 46

Fig. 49

Fig. 47

Fig. 43

Fig. 44*b*

Fig. 45

Fig. 44*a*

a.

b.

Fig. 48

neys, as their discoverer truly observes, or of connection between the hunter and his prey.[1] Women, it is to be noted, are numerous, wearing the bell-skirts of Spanish Cogul, and there is at least one child who resembles the so-called 'idol' of that painting (pl. II*d*). All this suggests that the women in the painting at Cogul are grouped in no religious dance as has been supposed; they are perhaps watching beasts, like those painted over the probably tame oxen to their left, with the small man above them leading (not pursued by) a bull. The 'idol' would be one of their children, his big sheath and fringed knee-bands being merely reminiscent of African costume.[2] A male God has not yet appeared.

Several other Spanish rock-shelters show this mingling of cultures. Sierra Morena has paintings in late Capsian style shewing people leading beasts; La Pileta has late Palæolithic naturalistic animals in association with geometric forms; and there are numerous other examples of the introduction into paintings, whose style had descended from those flourishing in Magdalenian times, of later motifs, which in one case include a metal dagger and a dolmenic image of the Mother Goddess—the work of Megalithic builders.[3] On Chalcolithic vases from Los Millares, the formalised animals of the rock-shelters appear with the double-triangular sign derived from the female figure of Capsian art (fig. 48, p. 80), probably to signify the presence of the Mother Goddess[4] (fig. 47, p. 80).

In North Italy there is even a trace of the meeting between the old cave-dwelling population and the carriers of the future civilisation, who were buried in caves with red ochre and other signs of the old rites. In certain localities, such as the Veronese and Gargano, Palæolithic implements are mingled with their

---

[1] H. A. Winkler, op. cit., ii, p. 32, plates lviii–lxi, 1.

[2] This scene has frequently been adduced in evidence of a supposed phallic cult, or, together with a formless patch of paint on the extended arm of a bell-skirted woman from another East Spanish rock-painting at Alpera (fig. 110 of H. Obermaier, *Fossil Man in Spain*) of idol worship. The various subjects of the Cogul picture are said by the Abbé Breuil to belong to several periods, but in none of these do religious scenes appear to be represented in East Spanish art.

[3] M. C. Burkitt, *Prehistory*, 1921 and 1925, eds. pl. xxxvi, p. 404. The last is from Peña Tu in Cantabria.

[4] V. G. Childe, *Dawn of European Civilisation*, 1925, fig. 1, d (and, less well shown, in 3rd ed. 1939, fig. 126, 3).

pottery. This culture was not brought by the new-comers, for many of their other sites, especially in Liguria, have no mixture of industries.[1] Such contacts may account for the subsequent importance along the Mediterranean shores of rock-cut tombs and those constructed to resemble cave-burials, as also for their special elaboration of the rites of the dead, however profoundly these may have been enriched by the influence of religious developments in the East.

Throughout the Europe of this intermediary period, under the continuous rains which heralded the approach of temperate conditions, dwindling communities existed on the shores of rivers, lakes, or sea, by harpooning fish or collecting molluscs, of whose discarded shells huge mounds yet remain.[2] The creators of the Maglemose industry had some knowledge of basket work and raft-making, and had domesticated the dog.[3] The Lyngby culture of Scandinavia included axe-like weapons whose distribution suggests a southern origin, possibly in the mammoth ribs, pierced for hafting, and the celt-like ivory implements which may have fitted them, found in Vistonice and Predmost.[4]

Such industries are already reaching forward to the weaving, the watercraft, and the polished axe of the Neolithic Age, and their art shares the geometric tendency now common to East and West alike, in its general detachment from the animals of cave ritual; but in Poland and Northern Hungary, where no cave-dwellings were maintained after the extinction of the reindeer, epipalæolithic Tardenoisian microliths are frequently found among the sand-dunes, which must have been welcomed as oases in the midst of encroaching forests. These flints are mingled, as in Italy, with pottery, and with the new triangular arrow-heads.[5] There are a few similar traces, in sandy districts of South-West Germany, of an encounter between encampments of surviving hunters and those who were to succeed them. 'These scattered families, if they took to food-production,

[1] T. E. Peet, *The Stone and Bronze Ages in Italy and Sicily*, 1909, p. 181 ff.

[2] H. Obermaier, *Fossil Man in Spain*, pp. 324–326; V. H. Childe, op.cit., chap. i.

[3] For dogs, see above, note 2; for rafts, V. G. Childe, *The Dawn of European Civilisation*, 1925, p. 8; *The Danube in Prehistory*, 1929, p. 21.

[4] V. Gordon Childe, *The Danube in Prehistory*, 1929, p. 13.

[5] Childe, op. cit., pp. 18–21.

when they came in contact with the Neolithic peoples in the subboreal phase, would multiply rapidly and exercise a decisive influence on the subsequent development of civilisation.'[1]

If their teachers brought the sheep and barley out of the Asian plains, they were probably conveyed in light craft up the Danube, for Vinca, a natural port above the Iron Gates, has preserved their first pit-dwellings with female clay figurines, and pottery, ornamented with the spirals and mæanders of Palæolithic Eastern Europe, and with 'script' signs like the Capsian. From the earliest levels this culture is saturated with Ægean elements, and may represent the Northern branch of a common migration,[2] but only in the North could it have found survivors of the old order.

THE NEW MENTALITY

Thus the invaders might have discovered, at various points, new-comers who could revive the memories and traditions of their own past in the East and South, giving to European Neolithic a peculiar quality, especially strong in its links with the cave. But the Neolithic revolutions were all accomplished elsewhere, and were opposed in their essential nature to the conceptions of the past.

The hunting peoples had organised their powers into a religious and social economy through the medium of art, based (it has been suggested above) upon the recognition of a single life-giving principle conserved in the changeless stability of the cave.

Movement in time could not, therefore, be intelligibly apprehended until the reaping of wild corn was replaced by the punctual recurrence of seed-time and harvest in the ground prepared by seasonal inundation, until the first shepherds had learned to reckon the period of increase by the moon's phases and the pathways of the stars.

This concentration upon the cycles of seasonal advance and retrogression must have called their attention to the interplay of opposing forces, and their regularity. The rudiments of all

---

[1] Ibid., pp. 20–21.   [2] Ibid., pp. 66–67.

the arts were discovered in the Stone Age, but those which depended upon numerical relation could not have existed till now.
The Magdalenian mimetic dances, their whistles and pipes of
birds' wings,[1] opened the way towards music and poetry, of
whose existence there is no warrant until written records appear. The Aurignacian huts of wattle, upon their rude foundation of stones, were not yet architecture, which can be traced in
Neolithic Mesopotamia from the period when the first hand-
shaped lumps of mud, sun-dried, became brick units of definite
size and form, to be repeated in arithmetical proportion. These
were later refined in the constructions of stone, whose sacred
associations were retained, as will be seen, in the rock-bound
countries to the West. The arch was an early discovery, made
perhaps while imitating, in the balanced order of the new
units, the Sumerian vaulted huts of reeds.[2]

The same perception of balance must have converted the
crude rafts, which may have had a very long previous history,[3]
into boats shaped for cutting the waters, and perfected till sails
became useful for inter-communication. These were their first,
and for long their only, vehicles of transport, and held a special
place in the religious imagination of their own civilisation and
its immediate successors.[4]

Rough clay bowls were found in the Magdalenian cave of
Montespan, and hollowed stone lamps elsewhere; baskets, too,
were woven in epipalæolithic times,[5] and gourds and skin con-

[1] See above, p. 44.

[2] The true arch is found in the king's grave (PG. 789) of the 'Royal
Tombs' at Ur; C. L. Woolley, *Ur Exc.*, vol, ii; *The Royal Cemetery*, 1934,
pp. 232–237. Above ground it occurs in the Akkadian level at Eshnunna
(Oriental Institute Communications, no. 17, 1934; *Iraq. Exc.*, 1932–1933,
p. 15 and figs. 10–12).

[3] The Straits of Gibraltar, for instance, were at least partly open in
Palæolithic times, but the North African and East Spanish cultures were
practically identical.

[4] Models of boats occur in a Stone Age environment in the graves of
Africa and Asia. Later legends of the voyage of the newly dead are frequently set among Stone Age conceptions. See, for instance, p. 56 of chap. iii
below.

[5] Impressions of fine matting were found among the shell-mounds of
Rhinluch in Brandenburg (Childe, op. cit., p. 24). Baskets seem to be represented on the East Spanish rock painting of Saltadora (*Fossil Man in
Spain*, fig. 56), and in the famous honey-gathering scene (*Fossil Man in Spain*,
fig. 116).

tainers probably carried water to the home. All these may have had their part in the invention of pottery, but only a people who conceived of motion returning on itself could build up a shape round emptiness, in place of carving it from some bone or stone which already seemed to bear its image, and revolve it in their hands to a cyclic symmetry which eventually demanded the wheel. Its hardening in the fire involved no alteration of form, for which the older religious and magic experience might have prepared its makers, but the willed transformation of the nature of its material must have required a mental revolution.

So, too, the patterns of incised or painted decoration, which acquiesced in the turning surface through an unending flow of alternating forms, were a natural manner of expression for those who had watched the 'perpetual revolution of configured stars', and in particular, for the wandering shepherds of Asia. The Aurignacian religious experience, which gave such importance to the image, had laid the foundations of all later symbolism, but the abstract art of the pastoral peoples, because it arose directly from the Neolithic vision of life, which was concerned with principles, was spiritually antithetic to the conventionalised productions of the Palæolithic decadence. Yet æsthetic limitations induced them to employ Palæolithic conventions, and thus the geometric human and animal figures of late Capsian hunting scenes found their proper artistic environment on the pottery of Susa.[1]

The rhythm of these patterns over a curved surface was perhaps based on the vertical and horizontal alternations of the loom, a yet more perfect expression, both of that duality which now possessed their imagination, and of their delight in mechanical contrivance. So inventive were they that traces of copper occur fairly early in most Neolithic habitation levels which were occupied over any considerable period. This did not replace the use of stone till far later in the history of civilisation, nor did it alter the Stone Age conceptions of men, whose former pre-occupation with formal changes in a single existence which incorporated divinity, stone, animal and man, might have prepared them for the transformation produced by running metal into a mould. Even the polished stone axe is thought to have been based upon a copper prototype, though it has

[1] See fig. 46 above.

now come to light in a purely Neolithic context at Mersin.[1]

The polished axe, which was to become the emblem of the gentle life of cleared forest and reaped harvest, as also of the sacrifice of the peaceful beasts who like their wild predecessors had a portion in divinity—the axe which was the successor of the painted sign upon the cavern walls of France and Spain, and a forerunner of the Cross[2]—bound the Neolithic religion with the progressive civilisations of the Bronze Age.

It also bound together, as will be shown in later chapters, the two aspects of that religion as developed in East and West, the one concerned with promoting seasonal fertility by rites analogous with those once invented to assist animal and human reproduction, the other developing the symbolism of stone, to become the abode of divinity in the altar and especially in the tomb, the cave-like habitation of the dead.

The Mother Goddess presided over both. With the accomplishment of domination over the admired beasts, man might be expected at last to give his own form to divinity, but there is full evidence that his relation with his sheep and kine maintained its inherited reciprocity. Service was still regarded as mutual and sacrifice as voluntary, for the Goddess wore the Cow's horns in Asia and Africa alike. Domestication, indeed, must have imparted a new tenderness to the ancient bonds of kinship, well attested when the art of the succeeding era came to replace, in both centres of civilisation, the crudities of Neolithic attempts at naturalism (see pl. X*b* below).

In the growing consciousness of duality, the Mother retained her former abiding and fundamental status as the earth into which men return and out of which all birth emanates, the 'provident field' whose grain, that constantly springs up and is again cut down, shares the nature of man himself.[3] But no cult of a male divinity is discoverable in Neolithic archæology; though we shall find, in the articulate religious systems of the states which were developed out of the village communities of the Stone Age, a young God who dies

---

[1] M. C. Burkitt, *Explorations in Cilicia*, part ii, 'The Earlier Cultures of Mersin,' *Liverpool Annals of Archæology and Anthropology*, xxvi, 1939, nos. 1–2, pp. 68, 71, 72, pl. xxxix, 10.

[2] See below, pp. 142 and 146.

[3] C. G. Jung, *Contributions to Analytical Psychology*, 1928, p. 124 (Mind and the Earth).

and is reborn with the year's flowering and decay, and is invariably said to have introduced the knowledge of agriculture. The tales must be true, since Neolithic mentality, as we have seen, was concerned with recurrent change and the force inherent in movement; and since all life was still interrelated in divinity, the rites, established to assist nature in her courses, now required his presence as distinct from the static fecundity which sends him forth and once again receives him. It seems likely, on the archæological evidence, that the Neolithic peoples had not the power to create a new artistic type—and for them such representation was no longer essential—so that the young God, though doubtless embodied in man, in the male beasts, and in all vegetation, could leave no contemporary record of his cult. There are, however, architectural hints of his presence, as we shall see.

When the eyes of men were eventually turned from the fertility of earth to the causes of seasonal change in the heavens, and the deity of the sun drew to himself the cyclic rites of the vegetation divinity,[1] the young God whom he had supplanted remained to enact especially his night or winter sojourn below the earth. Tales of their battles for supremacy point back to the power of a Dying God through the voiceless past. He was, indeed, never overcome, being like his Mother an authentic immortal evoked by fundamental human experience.

Thus his assimilation with the higher power involved no break with the old order, but stood to the Neolithic religious achievement as that did to the religion of the cave; a continuous development of conceptions which survived because they held the seeds of all religion, which were to ripen through revolutionary changes of civilisation. This was to be the culmination of the Stone Age religion of reciprocity, in which, by ritual attunement to the rhythm of seasonal change, man shared with divinity the responsibility for its maintenance, so that the ceremonies first introduced to guide the birth and death of the hunter's quarry, were replaced in natural succession by those considered necessary to assist the New Year to be born, the very sun to rise, the harvest to be cut down.

This relationship was also understood conversely, so that early written documents record that the rising of the Young God from his winter sleep of death in the subterranean chambers, held a hope for the resurrection of man.[1] Such a belief would seem to have been naturally transmitted from the primitive ideas concerning the cave as mother of rebirth, now reinforced by the lesson of the seeds, through the Neolithic ceremonies in which the sense of mutual causality was so compelling. It is demonstrated in the monuments of the dead.[2]

The history of both series of rites must now be traced in greater detail.

[1] See below, p. 175, note 5.
[2] See below, figs. 64 and 68.

CHAPTER II

THE CATTLE-BYRE
AND
THE MILK-YIELDING TREE

WESTERN ASIA

In the present state of our knowledge, a region stretching westwards across the mountains of Iran, the plains and foot-hills of Northern Iraq and North Syria, to Anatolia and the Cilician coast, bears remains of the earliest Neolithic towns, already planned constructions of brick and stone.[1] They seem to hold an intermediary position between the religious builders of the Mediterranean Chalcolithic, and the communities of shepherds and herdsmen along the southern river-valleys, whose religious conceptions so profoundly affected that culture. Excavation, however, has so far uncovered in these cities no more trace of the symbolism of stones than of the ritual of tillage and the pastures. They are spiritually inexpressive.

Since the people of Al 'Ubaid culture who succeeded them were also the first settlers to raise their reed huts above the marshes of the future Sumer,[2] the development and religious organisation of the city states of southern Mesopotamia could not have passed, in that region, as in Egypt, through all the phases of emergence from Palæolithic; indeed, their country was not old enough for such a history; they created it themselves from the silt of the two rivers. But their religion always remembered its hills and its mountain beasts, and raised an artificial mountain for communion with divinity. The importers

[1] For example, Arpachiyeh near Nineveh—excavated by the British School in Iraq (Gertrude Bell Foundation). Brak and Tell Halaf on the Khabur, excavated by the British School in Iraq and by Baron von Oppenheim. Alishar Huyuk in Anatolia, by the Oriental Institute of the University of Chicago, Mersin in Cilicia by the Neilson expedition.

[2] *Vierter Bericht uber Uruk, Abhandl. Preuss. Akad. Wissen. Phil. Hist. Kl.,* 1932, Nr. 6.

of the Chalcolithic culture, first recognised at Al 'Ubaid near Ur,[1] had demonstrably supplanted, in the North, peoples of a long Neolithic tradition, which was later strengthened by contacts with Iran; and because most of our knowledge of the religious ideas of this epoch can only be won by tracing a path backwards from the monuments of a more artistically communicative era, the Northern cities, with their lengthy series of occupation levels incontestably underlying the first signs of the use of metal, must be examined for any corroboration they may reveal of the link between Palæolithic conceptions and the succeeding religious symbolism, so deeply tinged with presumably inherited ideas, for which the contemporary evidence has hitherto scarcely existed.

Crouched female figurines of Palæolithic type were, it will be remembered,[2] unearthed at Arpachiyeh (fig. 45, p. 80). From Tell Halaf on the Khabur comes an obese stone statuette 'reminding us greatly of the Palæolithic Venus figures',[3] and also painted squatting female images similar to those at Arpachiyeh (fig. 43, p. 80) which are again found at Tell Chagar Bazar in the same region, and are stylistically connected with the standing Chalcolithic figurines of Al 'Ubaid and Ur. In the Northern type the head is practically non-existent, in the Southern it is emphasised, because masked or animal-headed, a characteristic repeated even in the child sometimes carried in the arms (pl. IX*a*).

Tell Halaf has also two damaged reliefs in stone (said to be contemporary with its Chalcolithic pottery), representing the first Asiatic animal musicians. On the better preserved of these, the lion is seated and plays the harp, the other beasts, among whom the ass is most prominent, dancing before him, or performing with other instruments, all in human attitudes (pl. IX*d*). In these blurred contours there is no indication of disguised men, but on the Copper Age shell plaque which used to stand between the legs of the divine bull in the 'king's' grave at Ur, such beasts again appear, this time in good preservation, as musicians and dancers (pl. IX*c*). Here the ass plucks the strings of his harp with human fingers, and below him the scorpion-man lifts his arms in the attitude of the sacred reptile. In the upper register the lion and his companion this time imitate the

[1] H. R. Hall and C. L. Woolley, *Ur Excavations*, 1, *Al 'Ubaid*, 1927.

[2] Page 78 above.

[3] Baron Max von Oppenheim, *Tell Halaf*, English edition, 1933, p. 214.

functions of priestly ministrants bearing the paraphernalia of sacrifice and libation, and below the skin of the lion's fore-paw his human hand provides the clue to these strange appearances.[1] A contemporary seal-impression from Ur shows the lion again seated and raising a ceremonial goblet before his attendants, among whom are three asses, making music upon various instruments.[2] Another such impression comes from Fara,[3] and yet another from Sargonid Eshnunna, where the lion and ass face each other in human posture, drawing from ceremonial tubes the communion beverage of the symposium so often illustrated on temple plaques.[4] The Ur inlay suggests in all these a continuing inheritance from the masked dances of the Palæolithic votaries who combined the offices of dancer and priest, and a hint of their succession in the lion-priests of the Babylonian funeral plaque,[5] or the fish-clothed ministrants of Assyrian reliefs.

In the animal orchestra of Tell Halaf and the roughly contemporary performing jackal from Hierakonpolis in Egypt,[6] the functions of the masked dancers are artistically transposed to the beasts with whom they were assimilated, just as in later times the Minoan or Assyrian ministers of divinity sometimes represented human votaries in palpable disguise, sometimes dæmonic beings emblematic of the triple nature—animal, man, deity. The Tell Halaf relief cannot be considered as comic, since all its later counterparts in Sumer show definite religious affinities. Sumerian legend affirmed (according to its Greek interpreter) that a being, of human form but cloaked in the body of a fish, had risen from the primeval waters to teach them civilisation, 'after which nothing further was invented;' perhaps the record of a religious debt to the past.[7] The epic figure of the

---

[1] C. J. Gadd, *History and Monuments of Ur*, 1929, pp. 35–37, was the first to recognise these as disguised human beings.

[2] L. Legrain, *Ur Excavations III. Archaic Seal Impressions, 1936*, no. 384; H. Frankfort, *Cylinder Seals*, 1939, text fig. 28.

[3] E. Heinrich, *Fara*, 1931, pl. 65 *d-g*.

[4] H. Frankfort, *Cylinder Seals*, 1939, text fig. 30.

[5] A. B. Cook, 'Animal Worship in the Mycenæan Age,' in *Journal of Hellenic Studies*, xiv, 1894, fig. 13.

[6] J. E. Quibell and F. W. Green, *Hierakonpolis*, ii, 1902, pl. xxviii.

[7] Berossus, quoted by C. J. Gadd, op. cit., pp. 7–8, and note i; I. P. Cory's *Ancient Fragments*, 1828, p. 24 ff.

half-animal Enkidu, and the bull-man who perhaps represented him in art, may be other such records.

Here, then, are two Palæolithic links first discernible in the North, but it was also in these towns that the typically Neolithic arts of architecture and decorated pottery reached their first perfection. On several sites, in fact, the earlier levels (though not the earliest of all, which are very primitive) show a high development not afterwards maintained, expressive of the first flush of delight in measured achievement.[1] While the rocky lands of North-West Syria and Anatolia were natural cradles for experiments in stone construction, the kilns of Arpachiyeh show that the painted ware common to nearly all that region was manufactured beside the Tigris,[2] and along such river banks, it may be conjectured, lumps of mud—the pisé of primitive construction—were first shaped to the accurate proportions of bricks used in the construction of the planned towns of the Khabur with their massive defending walls upon stone foundations. At Mersin in Cilicia, below similar walls of sun-dried brick (which even possessed windows), were stone-built houses whose corners were of ashlar masonry.[3] The main street of Arpachiyeh was raised above the winter mud by a surface of pebbles from the Khosr and the Tigris. This important pottery centre had no defences, nor were any weapons found there. Perhaps the vicinity of Nineveh afforded protection, but it may also have been a religious site, bearing to the Nineveh of this era a relation similar to that which Al 'Ubaid was to bear to Ur. The more massive of its ten circular foundations of stone probably supported corbelled or radiating courses of brick faced with plaster,[4] exactly like those which still form the high domes of the 'bee-hive' villages of modern Syria, the spring of whose arch starts like these (to judge by the one remaining example) almost from ground level.[5] The 'foreign' domes of an Assyrian relief from Nineveh are of exactly this form, and provide a use-

---

[1] At Mersin, for instance, see note 3 below.

[2] Mallowan and Rose, *Iraq*, ii, 1, 1935, 'Excavations at Tall Arpachiyeh, 1933,' p. 5.

[3] J. Garstang in *Liverpool Annals of Archæology and Anthropology*, xxvi, 1-2, 1939; *Expl. in Cilicia*, p. 59.

[4] Mallowan and Rose, op. cit., p. 28, figs. 7-12.

[5] Seton Lloyd in *The Architect*, June, 1935, p. 399.

ful link between the two.[1] The Neolithic examples are, however, provided with a rectangular antechamber, the whole curiously anticipating the bee-hive tombs with rectangular entrances of the Eastern Mediterranean Bronze Age. One example at Arpachiyeh, standing outside the central group, was indeed subterranean, and this had its antechamber at right angles to the main axis, like the side chamber of some of the Mycenæan tholoi. These structures had been continually rebuilt, and were completely looted in antiquity—but figurines of the Mother Goddess, with her domestic animals, and fine pottery fragments, are numerous in the adjoining rubbish heaps. The graveyards which clustered round them and were used by the succeeding race, do suggest the presence of a possible cave-like sanctuary or tomb, but of this there is no direct evidence.[2]

A house of this period which may have been a shrine with adjacent workshop, such as was afterwards common in Mesopotamia, contained a large stone figure of the Goddess with a small attendant carrying a vase; with these were five stone fingers and one human finger bone, like those found severed in the graves.[3] This impels a backward glance to the feigned and actual mutilations of recent primitives and the hand-impressions on the cavern wall of Gargas. There was also a painter's stone palette and set of bone tubes, with much pottery decorated with the polychrome patterns on a light ground, in flowing but formal brush-strokes, of the type called Tell Halaf, and now found over all this area to the sea.[4] Its importance to this enquiry lies partly in its connection with Iranian decorative types with their human and animal figures allied with late Capsian geometric conventions, but chiefly in its stylised heads of moufflons and especially of oxen, with emphasis on the horns (fig. 50, p. 94), which together with the 'double-axe' motif of meeting triangles, looks forward both in style and subject to the Bronze Age Mediterranean. The presence in the adjoining chamber of the Mother Goddess and her 'dove' (to which the bird faces of the subsequent Al 'Ubaid figurines to the south

[1] Mallowan and Rose, op. cit., p. 33, fig. 22.

[2] Ibid., op. cit., p. 34.

[3] Mallowan and Rose, op. cit., p. 99.

[4] On the sites of the later Hittite towns of Carchemish, for instance, and Sakjegeuzi on the Euphrates, and of Atchana near Antioch, and eastward into Iran.

may possibly owe their appearance),[1] suggests that these already had a connection with her cult as in Minoan Crete (whose population came mainly from Western Asia). In this building there are even Neolithic forerunners of the double-axe, in the form of small stone amulets. Not that there is any trace of the cult of pillar or tree, or of the horned altar. The North was perhaps too busy with material achievements to have elaborated such a system in its entirety.

The Chalcolithic Iranian culture was also centred in small towns, though we saw that the beautiful vases and bowls of Susa made their geometric human figures of the feathered hunting type, and their favourite beast is the ibex. Baluchistan

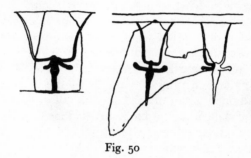

Fig. 50

painted pottery is analogous in style[2] and the culture is now known in Northern India near the Afghan frontier, where figurines are found with painted crossbands as in the Khabur, or cone-shaped as at Susa and at Alishar in Anatolia, or bearing the incised triangle of Al 'Ubaid which was to characterise the female clay figures of Western Asia in the Bronze Age.[3]

But when we come to the first indications in Sumer of religious beliefs which can be interpreted by later texts and later art, the above fragmentary links between past and future fall into their places as corroborative only. For here the deep conceptions were in infancy, which became the very foundations of the kingdoms of the Copper Age and from them have shed their influence upon the religions of civilisation.

As already noted, those foundations were pastoral and agricultural. At Al 'Ubaid, on the Euphrates, the first graves to be

---

[1] See pl. IX*a* and *b*.   [2] *Memoris of the Arch. Survey of India*, passim.

[3] Simone Corbiau, 'New finds in the Indus Valley,' *Iraq*, iv, pp. 1–9, fig. 2.

identified as belonging to the race which raised the early settlements of reed huts above the waters of the retreating Persian Gulf, were grouped, several miles outside their already important town of Ur, round the temple subsequently known as that of the Goddess Ninkhursag. At the period of these later rebuildings her worshippers continued to bury their dead above the forgotten bodies of the pioneers, and the cemetery was the property of the temple. In this age there is no trace of a settlement, so that the dead must have been brought from Ur, probably by water, since the model of a boat is common among the furniture of Sumerian burials.[1]

The name of this local personality of the Mother Goddess 'who was worshipped with little variation of doctrine and rite, in all the cities of Sumer', means Lady of the Mountain, another mark of the nostalgia of the immigrants into the marshy plains, who yet in imagination lifted their eyes to the hills.[2]

But the Mountain was in later days the tomb of the Young God in his winter death, as illustrated by ritual scenes upon the seals,[3] and by the Greek text and Assyrian inscription which speak of the Ziggurat of Babylon as the grave of Marduk.[4] It has also been suggested that those who stood in the court of the Temple of the Moon God at Ur facing the Ziggurat—the temple-tower erected, according to custom, in the West, where the Land of the Dead was located—would have the cemetery of Al 'Ubaid directly behind it.[5] The Ziggurat had, of course, a far higher significance (as will later be seen), in which this chthonic aspect would play a minor part, but it does appear probable that the Goddess still received the dead into her mountain as she may be said to have done in the days of the cave-dwellers. There is also a Sumerian mythological text which says that first among the divinities who mourn the Dying God is 'Geshar (=Nin)khursagga thy Mother'.[5]

[1] Hall and Woolley, op. cit., p. 149 ff., especially p. 153.

[2] See C. J. Gadd's account of the Goddess in Hall and Woolley, op. cit., pp. 141–146 ff.

[3] H. Frankfort, 'Gods and Myths on Sargonid Seals,' in *Iraq*, i, part i, 1934, and *Cylinder Seals*, pp. 117–118.

[4] Diodorus, ii, 7. 'Semiramis built . . . the grave of Belos.' Strabo and Aelian also refer to the Ziggurat of Babylon in this manner. See also Sidney Smith on a Brick Inscription of Assurbanipal, *J.R.A.S.*, 1925, pp. 52–53.

[5] Gadd, in Hall and Woolley, op. cit., p. 146 and note ii.

The Great Goddess is also called Nintinugga, 'She who gives life to the Dead', and a closely allied personality is Ereshkigal who gave Tammuz, the Semitic embodiment of the Young God, back to the living world, and is nevertheless mistress of the 'Land without Return'.

It is noteworthy too that the dead of Al 'Ubaid were interred in the 'embryonic' attitude, while their contemporaries at Ur were all extended for burial.

All this is valuable in linking her with the Goddess of the Megalithic tomb-stones,[1] as also for its undertones discernible in her motherhood, now marvellously transferred to the byre and the fold.

The people who built her temple had left behind them in the East a highland culture which still fought for existence with the wild beasts, as seal impressions on both sides of the ranges bear witness, and there the masked dances seem to have retained their importance, for animal-headed human figures or beasts in human attitudes are very frequently represented. They still loved also to portray the ibex or moufflon amid the flora of the rocky clefts.[2]

But even the first-comers who drained the swamps, did not depend for their livelihood on spearing the wild pig among the rushes, or snaring the water fowl, for rude querns are found in the earliest habitations, and clay sickles of the jaw-bone type, along with flint hoes for tilling the reclaimed fields. Only the dung with which their reed huts were plastered and mud images, apparently of cattle, suggest that the expanses beyond, today whirling with dust or disoriented in the vibration of mirage, were beginning to present the peaceful picture of flocks and herds moving slowly across the verdure of enormous plains, which is still to be observed after winter rain-storms in the North. In ancient days the calm must have been frequently shattered by attacks of wild beasts who had descended from the mountain barrier. It will be seen that the Mistress of the Mountain of the Dead became, in her other aspect of guardian of the fecundity of the deep pastures, the very enclosure which protected the kine, and especially the door of entry, like her triangular symbol which closes the gate of the magic corral on the walls of Pasiega in Palæolithic Spain (figs. 11 and 12, p. 18), Such enclosures are common on the seals across the border,

[1] See p. 131.   [2] See Frankfort, *Cylinder Seals*, pl. iv, *j* and *l*.

where the actual taming may have taken place. They would represent the intermediary stage. But the seals and stone vases of the people who re-built the temple at Al 'Ubaid, at a time when copper was still rare, continually repeat a single subject, which is partially illustrated in the frieze of shell and limestone inlay that once decorated the walls of the temple itself (fig. 51, below). The sacred herd, such as is known to have supplied the temple dairy farm with 'the holy milk of Ninkhursag' at

Fig. 51

Lagash,[1] is returning from pasture, to be met by the young calves who spring from their byre exactly as Homer describes: 'At the sight of their mothers the calves skip so wildly that their pens can no longer hold them; they break loose, lowing all the while and gambolling.'[2] The religious intention of the scene (fig. 51, above) becomes clearer when it is remembered that all through historic times the infancy of kings and priests was nourished on this milk, that even an Assyrian text refers to it in these words:[3]

> '*Little wast thou, Assurbanipal, when I delivered thee to the Queen of Nineveh,*
> *Weak wast thou, when thou didst sit upon her knees,*
> *Four teats were set in thy mouth.*'

Thus the Goddess of the pastures was herself the Cow, and is in fact so designated in an incantation for the help of women in travail.[4] It is the old reciprocal symbolism of the totemic

[1] Gadd, in Hall and Woolley, op. cit., pp. 142–143.

[2] Odyssey X, 410–414. (Trans. T. E. Shaw, *The Odyssey of Homer*, 1932, p. 146.)

[3] Gadd, in Hall and Woolley, op. cit., p. 142, quoting Craig, *Religious Texts*, 1, p. 6 ff.

[4] The beautiful cow to whom the Moon God in the form of a strong bull sent healing oils. Ibid., p. 143, note 2. Quoting Ebeling, *Keilschrifttexte aus Assur relig. Inhalts*, no. 196, rev. 10 ff.

religious phase, transferred to the tamed beasts who now more than ever may be thought willingly to minister to man. The temple frieze shows all the stages in the preparation of her milk, by men whose shorn heads mark them as priests, and it is to the Goddess that the calves rush for nourishment at the entrance of the shrine. But the seals and carved reliefs afford ample evidence that the reed-woven shed itself betokens her presence. Indeed the little 'hut' amulets with surmounting reed-bundles which became common throughout Iraq, are also found at Brak[1] in the North in the form of a stylised woman, sometimes even with a hut-shaped child upon her breast (fig. 52, below), in a convention also used in the Sahara[2] (fig. 53, below).

Fig. 52

Fig. 53

Whether in the dairy frieze or the smaller representations of return to the calves, the byre is always the central feature, and especially its gate, the beasts issuing from the side-doors only. The byre, or the gate alone, is commonly flanked by pillars of a peculiar form which have been identified as bundles of reeds bound at intervals and rolled above to allow a rope or pole to pass through them for the suspension of a mat-curtain to act as door.[3] It is noteworthy that when stone replaced reed-construction in Egypt as brick replaced it in Sumer, a cylindrical lintel still represented such a mat rolled on its rod, among the square-cut features of the doorway[4] (fig. 54, p. 99). Reed-bundles

[1] M. E. L. Mallowan in *Illustrated London News* of Oct. 15th, 1938. Mr. Mallowan does not believe, with Prof. Andrae, that these figures are formally derived from hut-amulets.

[2] L. Frobenius, *Das unbekannte Afrika*, 1923, p. 127.

[3] By W. Andrae, *Die Ionische Säule, Bauform oder Symbol?* 1933.

[4] W. Andrae, *Das Gotteshaus und die Urformen des Bauens im alten Orient*, 1930, fig. 48*b*.

like these are bent today by the marsh-Arabs of Southern Iraq
for the construction of their vaulted huts, and were doubtless
so employed by the earliest settlers, when these curving pillars
were still rooted and alive. In the Uruk and Jemdet Nasr
cultures of Sumer they are no longer a constructive feature,
but stand apart from the door of the byre like the sacred pillars
of Syria in later days. They are often seen as a standard upon
its roof (pl. X*a*). They may even appear with no building at
all, in pairs or singly, before the flocks or herds.[1] It is evident
that they have become a symbol, which is indeed employed
after the invention of writing as the ideogram of the Mother
Goddess Inanna.[2] It has also been found as an ornament or

Fig. 54

amulet in clay, and this exactly resembles the sacred knot of
the Minoan Bronze Age of Europe (pl. IX*e*, *f*, *g*). The reed-
columns appear in a secondary form as a looped pole, perhaps
a palm-trunk, in exactly the same relation to hut or door, that
is, as part of its construction (fig. 51, p. 97), as separate
flanking pillar (pl. XI*b*) or as a standard upon its roof (pl. X*b*).
Like the rolled bundle it has also been found in amuletic form,[3]
and appears in later scenes with no adjacent building, to mark
an invisible gate or shrine.

As an artistic motif at least, and almost certainly as a religious one also, this pole, the counterpart of the reed-pillar,
whose loops may be multiplied as the illustrations show, became the sacred tree,[4] the interchange of whose significance
with the pillar of stone will hereafter be demonstrated. In this
connection three points are of great importance:

[1] See pl. X*c* below.
[2] A. Deimel, *Sumerisches Lexikon*, 1925, Bd. 1, Nr. 103, 1.
[3] In copper at Tello.   [4] W. Andrae, *Die Ionische Säule*, p. 55 ff.

1. The reed-bundle and therefore the looped-post, both fashioned for the insertion of a closing or binding feature to guard the tamed beasts, is the certain symbol of the Mother Goddess as the Gate of a sanctuary which is in itself (to judge by the hut-amulets) conceived as her body ('He the Lamb and I the fold'), an idea already perhaps formed in the mind of Palæolithic man.[1] The bundle or post may itself symbolise the Gate, or be set beyond it as an extension of its power, like the pillars later to be described, which guarded the temple gates in Syria and Palestine, and the sacred city gates of Troy.[2]

2. The connecting rope or pole, as in the temple dairy frieze, sometimes takes the shape of a crescent. This might be thought to represent a slack rope, which would be sufficient to hold the door of matting across the opening of a small hut. But on the stone bowls of green steatite common towards the end of this period (pl. XIIe), and found also in contemporary India, a substantial shrine takes the place of the hut, with the same crescent above the doorway. This crescent evidently represents the Moon-God of Ur, the Bull, who was also a fertility God, the spouse of Ninkhursag.[3] It occurs once on the forehead of a cow in the temple frieze. This very primitive forerunner of the celestial symbolism of the stone lintels of Megalithic construction, is again most significant.

3. The curved outward-turned reed-cluster is formally connected with the ram's horns, which like those of the bull, and of the Palæolithic bison at Laussel, but especially by reason of their spiral form,[4] would be thought of as springs of creative energy. This volute is also later associated in art with the downward curled palm-fronds of the Tree of Life, and as such takes its place in Anatolian column-capitals as ancestor of the Ionic order, and of the volutes of Attic tombstones with their hint of renewed existence.[5] The ram's horns appear as an artistic embellishment of altars in the same region. They may have been one factor in the creation of the Horned Altar of sacrifice to the Goddess in the Mediterranean Bronze Age, and if so, would be its earliest link with the Horned Gate be-

[1] To judge by the Pasiega enclosures, above, figs. 11 and 12.

[2] H. G. G. Payne, quoting C. Blegen, *Journal of Hellenic Studies*, liii, 1933, p. 298; W. F. J. Knight, *J.H.S.*, liv, 1934, p. 210.

[3] Gadd's suggestion in Hall and Woolley, op. cit., p. 143.

[4] Compare pp. 162 and 163.   [5] W. Andrae, *Die Ionische Säule*, p. 59 ff.

(a)

(b)

(c)

(d)

(e)

(f)

(g)

Plate 9. EARLY WESTERN ASIA

(a)

(b)

(c)

(d)

Plate 10. PASTORAL SUMER

tween day and night, between life and death, human and divine, to which we shall need to return with the coming of the Sun-God.

For the cow-heads of the Sumerian Copper Age, like the sacred calf of Egypt, had a triangle between the horns inlaid in mother of pearl (pl. XI*d*); that triangle which afterwards stood as an upright cone or little mountain between the horns of Syrian altars.[1] The Ziggurat itself, the architectural Mountain, was furnished with horns at Susa and in Babylon.[2] Of this form also is the Horned Crown later worn by all deities and divine kings, itself an altar and a Gate between heaven and earth like the summit of the temple-tower.[3] Our earliest portrait of the Goddess of the byre and sheep-fold already wears it (pl. XI*c*), as she stands before her Gate to receive the horned beasts and the corn-sheaves brought for sacrifice—herself to herself. 'The problem of what went on in the temple is here quite simply and clearly answered: it was the communion of man with God through oblations drawn from the whole realm of nature.'[4] A later seal-impression from Ur illustrates the same scene, perhaps before this very temple beyond the town (pl. XI*e*). For not only does the bent reed-pillar recall the cow-byre, but over the lintel is Imgidud the lion-bird of earth and sky, whose still extant cast in bronze[5] once grasped his wide-antlered victims upon the outer wall of Ninkhursag's temple at Al 'Ubaid, probably above its gate. The Lion-headed eagle, a conception already familiar in the Uruk period of close connection with the monsters of Elamite imagination, was an appropriate emblem of the fertility God, husband of the Great Goddess, in its double capacity of mortal-immortal, and especially fitted to be set above the Door. Its spread wings appear again in the winged Gate of Early Dynastic seals below which the Goddess holds the Bull a captive for sacrifice. The Bull's horns were early assimilated with the Moon's crescent by a

---

[1] A. E. Evans, *Tree and Pillar Cult*, fig. 21.

[2] See passage in Assurbanipal's narrative of the sack of Susa quoted by Sidney Smith, 'Assyriological Notes,' *Journal of the Royal Asiatic Society*, Oct., 1928, p. 858; *Babylon, Epic of Creation*, vi, 49.

[3] See Part. iii, chap. i, 'The Crowns'.

[4] W. Andrae, *Antiquity*, 1936, p. 146, quoted by Frankfort, *Cylinder Seals*, p. 18.

[5] Now in the British Museum.

people whose manner of life induced them to consult the changes of the sky.[1]

'All analogy would lead to the belief' that once a year Ninkhursag celebrated her divine nuptials with the Moon-God of Ur. At Ninkarrak of Isin the Goddess sailed along the river to the meeting at Nippur with her spouse. 'Before her face' says the hymn which celebrated that voyage, 'goes the divine emblem.'[2] Perhaps in early days it was the God who journeyed to her along the stream, on his return from sojourn in the lower world, and possibly the seal of Uruk date found far to the North at Tell Billeh,[3] illustrates such a meeting (pl. XIb). 'Before her face' is borne her necklace,[4] which she was forced to relinquish while seeking the God's liberation in the world of death. Behind her appears the rolled mat upon its pole, which is to join the pillars of the Gate, and is possibly a forerunner of that ceremonial link which was to hang between the sacred columns of Minoan Crete. The looped reed pillars are here visible on either side of her shrine, to which a barque approaches, bearing a male figure between blooming plant stems, like the 'bough' carried to the temple of the Goddess in later legends of the West by those who crossed the waters of death. So may the seal of the same stylistic period seen in pl. XIa portray the same God in a boat with blossoming prow and stern, his bull-epiphany before him bearing the shrine or altar or couch of the Goddess, for her symbols stand above it. He appears in identical posture on yet a third seal of the period (pl. Xc) grasping flowering boughs between rampant horned sheep beside the reed-pillars of the Goddess which surround a calf. His successor in Semitic days was Lord both of vegetation and of the sheep-folds.[5]

[1] L. Legrain, 'The Art of the oldest civilisation of the Euphrates Valley,' *Museum Journal (Philadelphia)*, xv, 3, 1924, pp. 157–160.

[2] Gadd, in Hall and Woolley, op. cit., p. 143.

[3] A kilted female figurine belonging to the succeeding cultural epoch, has recently been found at Khafaje, see *I.L.N.* Sept. 26th, 1936, figs. 4 and 5.

[4] The necklace of the Goddess still remains on Megalithic tomb-stones of Western Europe when nearly all her other features have disappeared. See fig. 68 below.

[5] Frankfort, in *Cylinder Seals*, p. 114, quotes from Langdon's *Tammuz and Ishtar*, where Tammuz is first said to be 'grown great in the submerged grain' (p. 15), and later as 'leading goat of the land . . . bearing the shepherd's staff' (p. 35).

CATTLE-BYRE AND MILK-YIELDING TREE

The ceremony seems to have taken place in a booth or hut such as is commonly depicted at this time (as we saw) upon vessels of dark green steatite, fragments of which have also appeared in Northern India (pl. XII*d*). It probably recalls the farm, being usually hung with mats or skins, or imitating wattle (pl. XII*e*). The crescent drop above the doorway is always retained. Part of such a sculptured vase recently found at Tell Agrab in the Diyala region east of the Tigris, shows a humped Indian bull standing within the shrine (pl. XII*b*). A fragment which must have faced it retains the upper head and torso of a seemingly female figure enthroned, with a kneeling or floating ministrant above her shoulder (pl. XII*a*). A frieze of cow heads runs below the roof of this building, like those round the temple at Al 'Ubaid. The bull resembles very closely the beast incised with written signs on seals of Mohenjodaro in the Indus Valley. In the art of that region too a horned Goddess appears (pl. XII*c*). The tie between Sumer and Northern India may go back to the first settlers among the marshes, for beads probably from the Nilgharry Hills were found in their graves,[1] and the early images of the Goddess, of common type, will be remembered. This religion, then, had a wide provenance.

It is stranger still to recall that, several thousand years later in civilised Athens, the annual symbolic marriage of the wife of the king archon with Dionysus was celebrated in a building called the cattle-shed.[2] A link between East and West is probably to be found in Minoan Crete, since the Greek legend of Queen Pasiphae, who was enclosed in the wooden image of a cow for union with a sacred bull, must perpetuate the memory of a similar rite. We may ourselves glance backward to the engravings on the chapel wall of Les Combarelles.

But the booth had a long life in Babylonia.[3] The earliest

[1] C. L. Woolley, *Antiquaries' Journal*, x, 1930, pp. 327–341.

[2] Aristotle, *de Rep. Ath.*, iii, 5; J. E. Harrison, *Prolegomena to the Study of Greek Religion*, 1903, p. 537. 'The conjecture lies near to hand that in bygone days there was a marriage to a sacred bull.'

In Pekin the 'ox shed' for the performance of a sacred marriage is still to be seen in the field where the Chinese Emperor, up to the year 1911, regularly performed the ritual of ploughing to initiate the year. See E. A. Armstrong, 'The Triple-furrowed Field,' in *Class. Rev.*, lvii, I, p. 4.

[3] Its history as a tent has been studied by Count Alexander zu Eltz in *Bull. of the American Inst. for Iranian Art and Arch.*, v, 2, 1937, pp. 63–69, 'Nomadic tradition in the prehistoric Near East.'

sacred sites, as the excavation of Erech has revealed, consisted of a temenos with its gate—the 'pure enclosure' assigned to Ninkhursag in an inscription from Tello[1]—containing only a hut of wattle and clay, to which the rough clay beginnings of a terraced tower were added at a subsequent period. This may be one reason why the Gate or merely its pillars sufficed, then and later, to indicate in art the presence of a shrine.

A foundation tablet of the third millennium B.C., dedicated to Ninkhursag by the ruler of Ur, still calls her temple 'Kesh', which means a protection or sanctuary. It is also described as 'the solid reed-construction' and 'the brilliant grove',[1] though by that time brick building had reached a high state of perfection.

Again, the earliest edifices found within the temenos of Erech (=Uruk, the modern Warka), had recessed walls upon which the pattern of reed matting was perpetuated by the insertion of nail-heads of various-coloured clay; such plaited mats as today line the clay walls of huts in southern Iraq. 'It was then the traditional sacred hut that was given this permanent form.'[2] The recessed style, therefore, of the great brick temples and palaces of the Imperial age look back to very humble beginnings —to the byre itself, since our earliest representations of hut-shrines bear the emblem of the Goddess.

But throughout the millennia of monumental building a tent-like or wattled hut was itself retained for rites of just that dual character compatible with the lethal and the fruitful personalities of the Goddess. The *gigunu* of historic texts is sometimes described as a booth at the summit of the Ziggurat (Herodotus' 'chapel of the bed'), made green with leafy boughs when the sacred marriage was consummated between the priestess and the God during the manifestation of the 'oracle'; sometimes as a tent standing in the temple enclosure, but often again as a tomb or cavern, the 'dark and secret place' of chthonic ritual, which might celebrate the meeting in the underworld of the Goddess with her spouse, later hymned as the descent of Ishtar.[3]

The Royal Tombs at Ur, like those at Kish, suggest that, in one period at least (the culmination, it is true, of an era of close connection with Egypt), these two aspects were combined, for

---

[1] Legrain, op. cit., pp. 153–154.

[2] W. Andrae, *Antiquity*, x, 38 (1936). 'The Story of Uruk,' p. 141.

[3] Sidney Smith, *Journal of the Royal Asiatic Society*, Oct., 1928, pp. 850–854.

the Queen was found alone in her splendid apparel, surrounded only by her women, the car and oxen that had brought them, and the harp-player who had accompanied the procession; while the 'King' was interred with his fighting men higher up the shaft without.[1] The chaplet, which lay upon the couch beside the Queen's body, included among other amulets the rare images of stags, like those in the copper grasp of Imgidud on the walls of Al 'Ubaid, and is paralleled by a cluster of amulets found in a temple chamber of the period at Eshnunna (Tell Asmar), upon a similar band of white dust which had presumably once been leather.[2] Among these were three images of Imgidud, the emblem (as we saw) of the fertility God, whose name is inscribed upon a bowl in the câche of copper vessels from the same building, which exactly match the gold and silver services of Ur.[3] Stags are mentioned in the later texts as the customary victims to be sacrificed at a sacred marriage ceremony,[4] and in the same temple of Eshnunna, in which the jewels and ritual vessels had been hidden, a limestone tablet and a seal were found, which represent the actual rites. Here the flowering boughs reappear upon the wall (they were also affixed in coloured limestone to the walls of Al 'Ubaid), the couch is spread with skins, and its legs are shaped like the fore and hindquarters of a bull.[5]

On certain occasions, therefore, the *gigunu* would have been the scene of human sacrifice, which is likely to have replaced or accompanied that of the animals when the God became anthropomorphic. Being connected with fertility rites performed for the community, it may have been considered as voluntary and reciprocal between votary and God. Certainly no signs of violence are present in the tombs of Ur. That such rites had a Chalcolithic, even a Neolithic, origin is curiously attested by the Cave of the Bats in Spain,[6] which in its rude cultural setting of the Stone Age, presented, on its discovery

---

[1] Cf. C. L. Woolley, *Ur Excavations*, ii, 'The Royal Cemetery,' p. 37 ff.; S. Langdon, *Excavations at Kish*, vol. iv, 1934, ch. ii.

[2] *Oriental Institute Communications*, 17, Iraq Exp., 1932–1933, 1934, figs. 28, 29.

[3] *O.I.C.* 17, pp. 35–39.   [4] Sidney Smith, op. cit., pp. 859–860.

[5] *O.I.C.*, op. cit., figs. 40, 42; Frankfort, *Cylinder Seals*, pl. xv, 1.

[6] Don Manuel de Gongora y Martinez, *Antigüedades prehistoricas de Andalucia*, 1868, pp. 1–58.

eighty years ago, a scene exactly resembling the spectacle of Ur. That is to say, the skeleton of a 'queen' in robes of skins, with necklace and diadem of teeth and shells, reclined in the inner chamber before a semi-circle of clothed and adorned women's bones with the feet towards her. All had carried beautifully woven baskets of grain and poppy seeds, the latter being possibly the cause of their quiet deaths (pl. XIII*b*). In the passage without lay soldiers bearing flint weapons, and among them a man who wore the only fragment of metal found in the cave—a gold headband of a kind common in early Sumer. The cave had been sealed and its entrance marked by a Megalithic stone.

This then is the darker aspect of the religion inaugurated in the bucolic hut, in which the rites of fertility and of sacrifice were united, probably by association with the sowing and reaping of the corn. That its life-giving function was never forgotten through the rise and decay of the civilisations which it helped to found, was apparent when the present religious cycle was inaugurated for the West, in the Cave-Byre of Bethlehem between the gentle beasts.[1]

EGYPT

It will be remembered that in the Nile Valley alone is it possible to trace the continuous growth of a civilised state from its epipalæolithic beginnings. The records are scanty enough even here, but sufficient, it is hoped, to relate the Mother Goddess in her several personalities, together with the animal-headed Gods of later polytheism, to religious elements of the Stone Age, as well as to place the Dying God well back in the pre-dynastic era. The religion of Egypt throughout its long history, was especially concerned with the relation between the rites of reproduction and of death. She exemplifies more directly than Sumer, for reasons that will be explicit when we come to the Monuments, the Chalcolithic pre-occupation with the cave-tomb as a means of rebirth, which was inherited by Megalithic Europe. It is therefore especially important to

[1] 'O magnum mysterium et admirabile sacramentum, ut animalia viderent Deum natum jacentem in præsepio.' (Antiphon in the office of the Roman Church for Christmas morning.)

consider the creation of Egypt from the first tentative settlements, and the sources outside the valley upon which she drew
at intervals for the enrichment of her individuality, made strict
by the desert cliffs which rigorously limited the abounding
fertility of the reclaimed river-shores.

THE NEOLITHIC SETTLERS

In the Upper Nile Valley tribes physically and linguistically
allied with the earliest Egyptians have been found in modern
times to be grouped in autonomous totemic clans, the Dinka
being ruled by magicians, and the rather less primitive Shilluk
by divine kings of animal ancestry.[1] The Egyptians of history
may have evolved from such beginnings.

The Hadendoa too will be remembered, who in recent times
appeared each year from their hunting-grounds in the Eastern
desert, to scatter seeds in the mud left by the periodic inundation, and remained to reap their crop.[2] The earliest burials of
Tasa in Middle Egypt indicate a similar mode of life. They are
widely dispersed, as if belonging to nomads, but contain, as
we saw, grain-rubbers and ground axes, for felling trees above
the swamps. These people made excellent pots, derived from
basket ware, and wove linen robes.[3]

The first settlers in the Fayum reaped their wheat and barley
with serrated flint sickles, and used bone harpoons like the epipalæolithic Natufians; but they also kept domestic animals.[4]

Allied to these two were the Merimdians, who lived on the
edge of the Western Delta in huts or windscreens probably
descended from Palæolithic habitations, and like them buried
the dead among their dwellings, in the attitude of sleep.[5] But

[1] C. G. Seligman, *J.R.A.I.*, 43, 1913, 'Some Aspects of the Hamitic
Problem in the Anglo-Egyptian Sudan,' p. 598 ff.; V. G. Childe, *New
Light on the Most Ancient East*, 1934, p. 10.

[2] See above, p. 76.

[3] G. Brunton, *Antiquity*, iii, 1929, 'The Beginnings of Egyptian Civilisation,' p. 465 ff.

[4] G. Caton-Thomson, *J.R.A.I.*, lvi (1926), 'The Neolithic Industry of
the Northern Fayum Desert,' p. 309 ff.; Childe, op. cit., p. 56.

[5] H. Junker, 'Vorläufige Berichte über die Grabungen der Akademie der
Wissenschaften in Wien auf der neolithischen Siedlung von Merimde-
Benisalame,' in *Anzeiger der Akad. d. Wiss. Wien. phil. hist. Kl.*, 1929, 1930,
1932, 1933; 1930–1934; Childe, op. cit., p. 58 ff.

these people already used the polished axe as an amulet, and in spite of their Capsian proclivities, the finely developed Neolithic crafts of all the above tribes had already strong affinities with those of Western Europe, and of Neolithic Crete and Anatolia, as may be recognised in their dark-faced pottery, polished axes, mace heads or clay ladles.

None of these settlers shows signs of political cohesion, for they could still combine their wandering hunter's life with periodic crop-raising. After their time, however, a degenerate craftsmanship and a layer of sterile sand suggest the drying of their water-courses.[1] Possibly they migrated.

The Badarians, newcomers with south-eastern affinities, elaborated their culture in Middle Egypt, perhaps driven at last by the increasing drought to inaugurate the control of the floods. Rare signs of copper appear, but their flint industry is poor and does not include weapons of war. They made a fine burnished pottery, and female figurines occur in their graves, which are furnished like houses with pillows, eye-paint and its palettes, and clay models of boats, and are sometimes lined with matting. The crouched bodies generally faced West, and ceremonial burials of cattle and sheep are also found.[2] They were, in fact, the cultural ancestors of the Egyptians.

The Amratians of Upper Egypt[3] were closely allied to the Libyans, a people who clung to Capsian culture down to historic times, their religious chiefs retaining the tailed belt and feathered head-dress and knee-fringes, and their highly-regarded[4] women the bell-skirts of East Spanish and African rock paintings.[5] It has been suggested that the Amratians were nomads from the drying grasslands of the Libyan region who mingled with the Badarian farmers, and that the clash of their divergent cultures inspired the sudden progress of the early pre-dynastic civilisation.[6] They were still, it seems, organised into totemic clans, who lived in round huts grouped in auto-

[1] Junker, op. cit., 1929.

[2] G. Brunton and G. Caton-Thompson, *The Badarian Civilisation*, 1928.

[3] W. F. Petrie, *Prehistoric Egypt*, 1920, passim; Childe, op. cit., pp. 69–84.

[4] G. D. Hornblower, 'Predynastic Figures of Women and their Successors,' *Journal of Egyptian Archæology*, xv, 1929, p. 29ff.

[5] See O. Bates, *The Eastern Libyans*, 1914, for a comprehensive account of their culture.

[6] Childe, op. cit., p. 84.

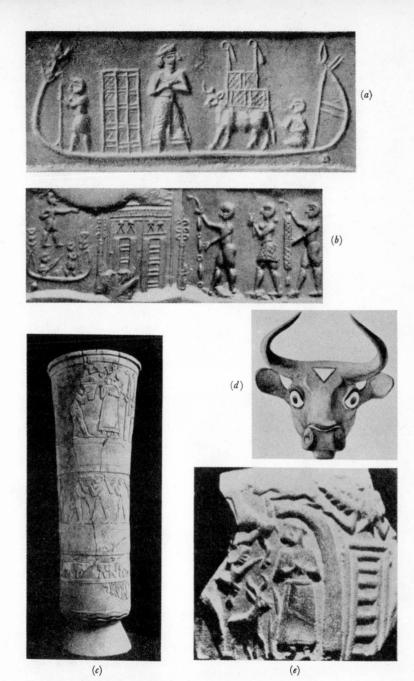

Plate 11. SUMERIAN RITUAL SCENES

(a)

(b)

(c)

(d)

(e)

Plate 12. SUMER AND INDIA

nomous villages, for emblems appear which later represented clan ensigns, and later still, local deities. A rudimentary script of Capsian affinities is now used for pot-marks on their vases, all the vessels in a single grave being marked by the same sign.[1] The scenes painted upon their funerary vases (which make free use of Capsian conventions) or carved on their slate palettes, serve the purpose of the later tomb-paintings, and are evidently religious and magical like those.[2] Statuettes of women are of the faceless type with the huge lumbar expansion, familiar from Palæolithic times, and nowhere existing among the well-preserved skeletons of these graves; but their arms are raised in the ritual attitude of the vase paintings and rock-drawings in the Western desert.[3] There are also male figures allied in style to those of Stone Age Crete. Their pottery is somewhat inferior to Badarian, but their flint weapons are of incomparable beauty.

The high civilisation which followed, with its strongly-marked Asiatic affinities, may have started in the Delta, where the need of protection against floods required the same kind of co-operation as in contemporary Sumer, but its remains are only preserved in the dry south. Gerzean painting is far more explicit than its forerunners, though the austere stylisation of the Chalcolithic East now replaces the Capsian convention to which it had always been akin.[4] Only the already developing Egyptian formal vision, which was averse to unending motion, kept an axial arrangement in its scenes of the despatch of the funeral barque and the mourning on the shore. Vases and implements in the tombs are now often purposely broken.[5] This cannot have been done with the object of disarming the deceased. They must have been sacrificed for his continued use, and suggest the intrusion of foreign conceptions.

The clay and ivory figurines give place at this stage to the animal amulets of Sumer and Elam, but the subjects of some of these, notably the falcon, the cow's head and the bee,

---

[1] Childe, op. cit., pp. 72–73, 'whose origin is ultimately to be sought in Palæolithic marks.'

[2] J. Capart, *Les Débuts de l'art en Égypte*, 1904, p. 212.

[3] H. A. Winkler, 'Rock Drawings of Southern Upper Egypt' (*Sir Robert Mond Desert Exp.*), i, 1938, pl. xxxv, 29, 30. Also xxxvi, 36 and 37 from Weigall *Travels*, pl. xxix, 4 and 5 (Wadi 'Abbad).

[4] See examples in Petrie, *Prehistoric Egypt*.   [5] Childe, op. cit., p. 94.

suggest their application to local totemic cults. Copper is still rare, as in contemporary Asia, but the indigenous flint-flaking reaches a new perfection in changed forms. It is typical of Egypt that the Asiatic mud-bricks, which appear at the end of this period, are used not for the erection of temples, of which no certain traces exist, but for the graves of chiefs, and that the first Egyptian wall-paintings reproduce the style and subjects of the funerary vases. High-prowed Sumerian vessels here encounter their own river-craft.[1]

The ensigns set above the native boats which are painted on these vases, suggest that certain villages are now on their way to becoming the chief towns of their districts, the 'nome capitals' of later days. When two or more of these ships appear together, their ensigns are always those later recorded as belonging to contiguous nomes.[2]

Again, the processions of animals on the ivory knife-handles believed to date from this period, though Asiatic in style and found at the termination of caravan routes from the East, seem to record Nilotic clan conflicts, for they are always grouped in the same order, with the elephant of the first nome of Upper Egypt at their head.[3]

But most of all the slate palettes of the late pre-dynastic age, which depict by the symbolic use of the ensigns the struggles which immediately preceded the political union of Egypt,[4] throw light back upon the gradual formation of the Egyptian state under Chalcolithic conditions, which point to a continuous interweaving of social and religious life (pl. XIV*a*).

AGRICULTURAL FOUNDATION OF THE EGYPTIAN STATE

The civilisations of the Nile, Euphrates and Indus, are seen working along parallel lines and in communication, once their political coherence is established; but the union of Egypt under a single government is the only one which can so far be traced

[1] Childe, op. cit., pp. 121–122, fig. 51.

[2] P. E. Newberry, 'The Petty-Kingdom of the Harpoon and Egypt's Earliest Mediterranean Port,' *Liverpool Annals of Archæology and Anthropology*, i, 1908, p. 18; idem., 'Some Cults of Prehistoric Egypt,' op. cit., v. 1912, p. 134.

[3] G. Bénédite, 'The Carnarvon Ivory,' *Journal of Egyptian Archæology*, v, 1 (1918), p. 225 ff.   [4] See below.

directly to the social and political units of the Stone Age, by the vestiges of known facts which are precious because they are all that is available.

The necessity then, of bringing the phenomenon of the annual inundation of the Nile into the service of agriculture, forced the groups or clans, who may be conceived (to judge by the present backward survivors of those regions) as united in some form of self-contained totemic coherence, to a co-operation of continuous effort based upon locality. Each basin of irrigation would have formed an agricultural district, the future nome, dependent upon the efforts of its neighbours who controlled their own portion of the river, and itself responsible for the existence of those down-stream, as the water was passed on through the length of the land. For this reason a reciprocal discipline was incumbent upon all the nomes, and eventually a central authority would be required to see that it was maintained.[1] Here, as in Mesopotamia, good government entailed the keeping open of the canals.

The ethnic survival of the clan divisions is attested long before historic records begin, by the ensigns on the pottery and the schist palettes;[2] their territorial grouping was to be preserved throughout Egyptian history, the clans becoming provinces and the clan-divinities, who are symbolised by the ensigns, the half-animal Gods of Egyptian polytheism.

The written script shows the first towns to have been crossways surrounded by a circular defence, to which the labourers in the fields would have returned along the raised paths at nightfall, a cluster of huts, byres and workshops round the house of wattle which may be later recognised in the palace sign,[3] the abiding place of that divinity who gave to the district the name which it was always afterwards to retain, whose visible image was its ensign, who was now presumably incarnate in the person of its chief.[4]

For among such centripetal settlements, made necessary by agricultural conditions, the life formerly shared by all members of the communistic hunting clan seems to have become concentrated in a single being to whom obedience was rendered

[1] See A. Moret, *The Nile and Egyptian Civilisation*, 1927, p. 33 ff., and A. Moret and G. Davy, *From Tribe to Empire*, 1926, pp. 124–125, 148.

[2] A. Moret, *Mystères égyptiens*, 1913, p. 143 ff.

[3] Id., *The Nile*, p. 41 ff., fig. 6.   [4] Id., *The Nile*, p. 42.

because he represented that life by inheriting or incarnating its protecting divinity. He was thus the mouthpiece of its relations with its neighbours, advised no doubt by a Council of Elders whose early existence is recorded in the texts.[1] The first portraits of such chiefs show the clan ensigns which form their hieroglyphic name, endowed with life to support them in action (fig. 55, p. 118); the written characters retaining the potency of totemic designs.

Secondary towns would spring up with a growing population, the head-men being subject to the ruler of the district capital. The lists of later days show their organisation to be definitely religious, appending to each nome the title of its God, its priests, sacred barque and tree, its protecting serpent and prohibited food.

Concerning this last, penalties for the slaughter of members of a particular species were only imposed in its own nome, and their ceremonial burial seems to have been similarly localised, to judge by the mummies so far discovered.[2]

Again, the old clan ensigns, some of which can be traced back, as we saw, to the Amratian settlers, are known to have been retained for about half the emblems of historical nomes. For the other half no evidence remains.[3]

The Gods of the nome capitals show on the whole a similar origin. There are first those indisputably connected with the ensigns, showing that the city has kept the deity of the original group, but, in its new mental concentration and partial withdrawal from the fields, requires for it a human shape. An embodiment of that amalgamation is ready to hand in the masked dancers, as still depicted at this period both in Asia and Africa. So the figures of the Egyptian Gods wear their original animal or other emblem as a mask. That is to say, it is the aspect of themselves by which they communicate with their earthly representatives. Such are the Falcon and Ibis of the 2nd and 15th nomes. Then come those Gods of the capital who are distinct from its ensign. The 6th nome of Upper Egypt, for example, whose ensign is the crocodile, belongs to the Cow Hathor. Such represent almost certainly a political conquest.

---

[1] Id., *C. R. Acad. des Inscr.* 1916, p. 378; *Pyramid of Pepi II*, 1930 ed. Sethe para. 1041.

[2] Herodotus, ii, 67, 69; A. Moret, *The Nile*, p. 365.

[3] A. Moret, op. cit., p. 46.

(a)

(b)

Plate 13. COPPER AGE BURIALS

(a)

(b)

(c)

Plate 14. EGYPT: HATHOR AND THE EARLY KINGS

The God of the nome is in these cases a defeated divinity who has yielded his territorial overlordship to a successor, but retained his traditional presence in the ethnic group. There is evidence of such strife and assimilation in some of the nome emblems—the 16th nome, for instance (fig. 56, p. 118), has an oryx on whose back perches the victorious falcon of Horus; in Upper Egypt the crocodile of the 6th, who has yielded preeminence to Hathor, has a dagger in its eye, which could hardly at this stage be the attribute of a totemic emblem, but would rather symbolise defeat, since deities do not die, but are absorbed by their conquerors. Thus also certain Gods came to preside each over several capitals, the sign of the political concentrations of the nomes into confederacies or kingdoms; the schist palettes especially show that already in the prehistoric period Horus was patron of many clans.[1]

Again there is the case of cities later built on virgin territory reclaimed from the Nile, with no Stone Age past. Such were Memphis and Thebes, which were taken under the protection of Gods who reigned nearby.

In general, the transformation of totemic clans into agricultural communities on a territorial basis, seems to have constituted the permanent foundation upon which the Egyptian state was fused into unity, the pre-dynastic schist palettes, together with the funerary vases, bearing witness that political life was inseparably linked with religion from its beginning. The title of *isag*, 'tenant-farmer of God' proudly borne by Sumerian kings,[2] suggests a similar basis of empire.

CHALCOLITHIC UNION OF EGYPT

The texts of historic times refer to three periods of Egyptian prehistory, beginning with the cosmic Gods, who were at first without form (name), until fused with the deities of the animal and other emblems, who reigned of course on earth. They were succeeded by their sons, the kings of the North and the South; the Delta and the Valley, and the earliest history that emerges is that of the antagonisms and sufferings of these Gods, at once cosmic and agricultural—that is local—as emblematic of the conflicts of the kings.

[1] A. Moret, op. cit., pp. 50–53.
[2] C. J. Gadd, *History and Monuments of Ur*, 1929, p. 4.

The political grouping and organisation of the territorial regions can in fact only be deduced, as we have already seen, from the religious relations.

First then, the texts based on older legends reveal the early greatness of the Western Delta, where contact with the Libyans greatly influenced the future of Egypt. The Western group of nomes retained in historic times the hunting emblems derived from that common past, and the hieroglyphic sign of the West included the Libyan ostrich feather. Their Goddess Neith retained her individuality.

Climatic conditions have destroyed the archæological evidence of early civilisation in the Delta, but an Eastern confederacy must have paralleled the organisation of the Western nomes, and must have also been subject to foreign influences. Its emblem in later days was an object resembling a cone between horns or mountains, like the crown of Western Asia and the Syrian altar.[1] The living ensigns of the East and West led processions at the coronations of Egyptian kings.

The 9th nome of the Eastern confederation had possessed the only ensign that was anthropomorphic, a figure with feathered crest, bearing a shepherd's crook and an ox-goad or flail.[2] His humanity fitted the typical religious creation of the agricultural era, Osiris, the God whose worship was to become universal because it represented all human experience, who now took over his attributes[3] and his province, calling the nome capital Busiris, and becoming chief over the Eastern nomes. Later he absorbed the Western nomes into his kingdom, and their originally independent divinities became his fellow-workers, the Rulers of the North.[4]

The religious myth ascribes his defeat to the God of the

---

[1] P. E. Newberry ('Two Cults of the Old Kingdom', *Liv. An. Arch. and Anthrop.*, i, 1908, pp. 24–29), who says that the emblem of the double (or cleft) mountain which appears on Neolithic pottery was called Ha in the Pyramid texts, and that the nome God Ha gave his name to the district which became merged with that of the Bull. Later he became Lord of the West.

[2] Anzti., fig. 20 of A. Moret, *The Nile*, pp. 78–80, 85–87, quoting *Pyramid Texts*. The 'Children' of the 18th and 19th nomes are considered late.

[3] 'Horus has made thee to live in this Thy name of Anzti' (*Pyr.*, para. 614). In *Pyr.*, 648, he is said to preside over the West. (A. Moret, op. cit., p. 80, n. i).

[4] A. Moret, op. cit., p. 86.

Southern Desert. The vengeance of his son Horus the Falcon, who was assimilated with the Cosmic Horus of the warfare between Light and Darkness, became symbolic of the long struggle for supremacy of the Followers of Horus, which is illustrated in the schist palettes found at Hierakonpolis, and was finally resolved in the union of North and South under the Falcon ensign, with Upper Egypt as the centre of Government.

The kings of the period of struggle are already depicted bearing the shepherd's crook and the ox-goad of Osiris, the mythical founder of the Neolithic civilisation of Egypt and the world, but they have not discarded the animal's tail of Palæolithic ritual (pl. XIV*a* and *b*). The palette which illustrates the victories of Narmer is ornamented with heads of the Mother-Goddess Hathor—the 'House of Horus'—between her cow-horns, and similar heads hang as amulets from his girdle. The Falcon itself leads the symbolic reed-stems of his Northern prisoners, and his personal ideogram, the Fish Nar, from whom he takes his name is, as we saw, alive, and fights on his behalf (fig. 55 p. 118). On the under side of the palette he is shown in bull-form as son of the Cow-Goddess, overturning a fortress. The scene found on the same side which depicts his royal festival of periodic rebirth, includes the horned beasts in their symbolic enclosure.[1] We are still in a Stone Age milieu.

Similarly with the Scorpion king (pl. XIV*b*), whose name-sign lends its power to the mattock with which he overthrows the hostile town, while above him the Birds who figuratively represent the Rekhit people (Egyptians) and the Bows of the clansmen of the Bow, are hanged beneath the four ensigns of his confederacy.

These records coming from the Southern kingdom naturally illustrate the victories of the Valley, but some kind of co-ordination must be presumed, for Narmer at times wears the red cap of the North instead of the white mitre of Upper Egypt. The crowns were regarded as protective Goddesses, or forms of the Mother Goddess, embodying in the one case the serpent Wazet of Buto the Northern capital, which had Waz the papyrus for 'speaking arms', and whose chiefs had for title Biti the Bee, in the other the vulture Nekheb, which gave its

[1] See fig. 86 below. The animal enclosure or trap even appears on the tomb-painting of Hierakonpolis.

name to the southern capital Hierakonpolis, whose speaking blazon was the Lily or Rose.[1]

When the king of united Egypt, himself incarnate falcon, at last wore both crowns in one, he took these four emblems as his official titles: Lily, Bee, Vulture, and Uræus snake, presided over by the Falcon's divine sign. And because names were, as we saw, living entities, it follows that he absorbed into himself the emblematic divinities of the confederacies who themselves comprehended the totemic embodiments of the clans settled round the nome capitals.[2] By this means the king, naturally and not by mere imposition of power from without, drew into himself the life of the nation, which was thus truly one.

THE MOTHER GODDESS AND THE DYING GOD

One of the clan-ensigns of the Chalcolithic age had been the uplifted arms so commonly depicted as a human gesture on funerary vases or clay figurines or the rock-paintings of the desert, a gesture perhaps expressive of the invocation or reception of divine force. In the days of written texts this was the symbol of the Ka, the single life-energy once diffused through the totemic group, and like that both individual and collective, so that the king, by concentrating into himself the living emblems of all the regions, expressed the life of a whole people. 'Thou art the Ka of all the Gods,' says a Pyramid text of the Supreme Being.[3] Thus the quantity of this potentiality held by each divinity, determined his rank in the hierarchy, and thus the polytheism which recognised every local totem could continue to exist beside those deities of fertility and death who received their 'names' in the Egypt of the Stone Age, as once their animal archetypes had existed beside the Mother Goddess.

It was possibly under the influence of the peoples of the Western Desert, who had domesticated cattle in epipalæolithic times, that the Great Goddess was first conceived as a cow. The Libyan Goddess Neith, whose earliest shield emblem bore crossed mesolithic arrow-heads,[4] always retained her connection

---

[1] A. Moret and G. Davy, *From Tribe to Empire*, pp. 131–132, pp. 141–142.

[2] A. Moret, op. cit., pp. 140–142.

[3] A. Moret, *The Nile*, p. 358, quoting *Pyramid Texts*, para. 1609.

[4] A. J. Evans, 'The Early Nilotic, Libyan and Egyptian Relations with Minoan Crete,' *J.R.A.I.*, lv (1925), fig. 22, p. 220.

with the North-West, and a personality distinct from that of Hathor. Yet she too was a primeval cow; the flesh of whose animal embodiment was taboo to the Libyans throughout their history[1]—and even today they sacrifice a cow to bring rain. Her festivals, indeed, show her to have been also a divinity of vegetation, the fertility of her land being assured by a mock-battle of virgins, a dance of clashing shields, perhaps, like that performed in the Bronze Age to awaken the spring on shields of her pattern, which in Crete at least were of bulls' hides.[2]

Several extant inscriptions of a later age name her as Mother (or Cow) whose fruit is the sun, who began to bring forth before being born,[3] an exalted perception of primal matter which could not have been formulated at this time, but might nevertheless represent a development of the early worship of fundamental maternity.

As first material cause she is always a virgin Mother: 'I am all that has been, is, and shall be; no mortal has ever lifted my garment,' was inscribed in classical times above the door-way of her shrine.[4]

Hathor, her counterpart of the Eastern Delta, emerges from the Stone Age as horned Mother Goddess of the Followers of Horus, the Dwelling of the God, as her name signifies, by which he was incarnate on earth. The North-East, it will be remembered, was in touch with Western Asia, and here as in Sumer we find in Chalcolithic times a divinity who is both the protecting enclosure of the young God and the body from which he emerges, whether in human or animal form. Neith too is called in funerary texts the house and body of Osiris[5]—probably by assimilation with Hathor, for the child Horus is but the resurrected or immortal aspect of the dying Osiris; the Son of

[1] O. Bates, *The Eastern Libyans*, p. 96, note 9, quoting both classical and modern authorities, and p. 177.

[2] See below, p. 232.

[3] In this form on a statue now in the Vatican, described by H. Brugsch in *Thes. Inscr. Aeg.*, p. 637, i, 8. (O. Bates, op. cit., p. 205, note 7.)

[4] Plutarch, *de Iside et Osiride*, 10. Proclus, *In Timæum*, i, 30, repeats this with the addition: 'The fruit which I brought forth was the Sun;' O. Bates, op. cit., p. 205, notes 8 and 9.

[5] In the 'Lamentations of Isis and Nephthys', Osiris is called Son of Neith (D. Mallet, *Le Culte de Neit à Saïs*, 1888, pp. 7–8). In Chap. clxiii of the Book of the Dead, 'The Osiris N. is with the perfected spirit, he is the soul of the great body which is at Saïs: Neit' (Idem., op. cit., p. 6).

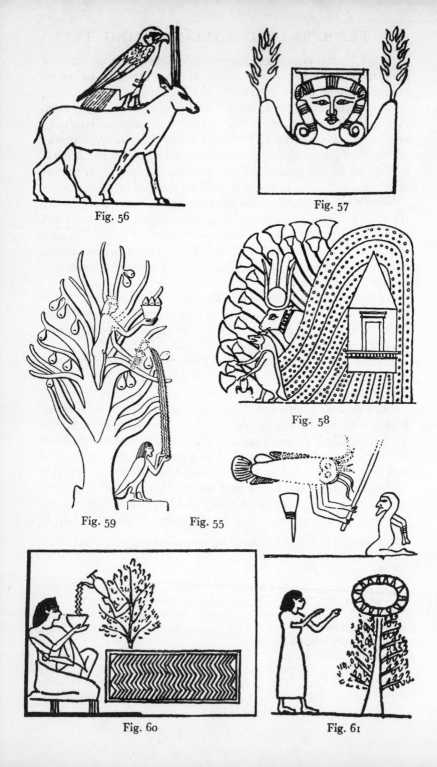

Fig. 56

Fig. 57

Fig. 58

Fig. 59   Fig. 55

Fig. 60   Fig. 61

the Goddess of the Stone Age being a single entity, like his Mother, whether she bears the name or personality of Neith or Hathor, or Isis, who later wore Hathor's horns which held the moon's disc, or Nut the Sky-Goddess, who every day produced like Neith the milk-calf of the sun.[1]

Thus the conception may have grown in each locality, by contributary images passed to and fro, from a far-off idea common to that part of the world in Palæolithic times. We saw how in Sumer it underlay the construction of the earliest temples. Similarly in Egypt, when, by assimilation with the Sky-Goddess, Hathor became the Celestial Cow, bearing the moon between her horns and spangled with stars, her legs were called the four pillars of heaven,[2] and kings of later days are portrayed between her forelegs as if within a Gate, above which the moon-disc is raised upon her horned crown (pl. XIV*c*). The crescent uplifted between the reed-pillars of the Sumerian sacred hut will not be forgotten, nor the likeness of those pillars to horns; Hathor indeed is sometimes herself a pillar with horned head as capital.[3] She is also to be seen between cleft mountains, the horned Gate that divides the death-sleep and waking of the sun (fig. 57, p. 119), and is herself that mountain enclosing its cave-tomb (fig. 58, p. 119). For equally with the Sumerian Mother Goddess she has her chthonic aspect, her shrine within the necropolis of Thebes.[4] Since she received the dead into her keeping, she was also conceived as the lion-headed Sekhmet.[5] The Babylonian Ishtar too had her lions, and the Great Goddess of Phrygia is carved on the door of the tomb flanked by the same beasts.[6] In the person of Kali this ferocious aspect of the Great Mother was to remain important among the Hindus. A lion guards the passage to the other world on the

[1] *Pyramid Texts*, para. 27.

[2] Lacau xx, Rec. 27, 221–226, quoted by J. H. Breasted, *Development of Religion and Thought in Ancient Egypt*, 1912, p. 279.

[3] Well illustrated in H. Schäfer, *Von ägyptischer Kunst*, 1930, p. 37, fig. 3.

[4] C. J. Gadd, in Hall and Woolley, *Ur Excavations*, i, Al 'Ubaid, 1927, p. 146.

[5] Ra used against the enemy his eye in the form of Hathor, who, drunk with blood, became Sekhmet. A. Moret, *The Nile*, p. 372 and note 2. 'Death's Lion-Roar and gust of nostril Flame;' J. E. Flecker, *The Burial in England*, 1915.

[6] See below, fig. 101.

Minoan Ring of Nestor,[1] but the tree whose branches there enclose the whole region brings us back to the more august function of the Egyptian Cow-Goddess beyond the grave— she suckled the child-like souls of the newly dead. 'Seek the cow-mother!' is the adjuration of the texts upon the walls of the tombs of early kings.[2] Below the earth, however, she is imagined no longer in the form of the benign beast, but as the Tree whose fruits are cast into the ground for renewal of life (figs. 59 and 60, p. 118). The sycamore of the South was regarded as the living body of Hathor, and the nomes dedicated to herself and to Nut were called conjointly the Land of the Sycamore.[3] The fruit of this tree, which grows directly from the stem, exudes a white fluid which was fed in later days to Greek infants, and beneath its boughs the Roman Twins were suckled on the Tiber bank.[4] The images of the Ephesian Artemis present the same Tree in human form with multiple breasts like milk-bearing figs above the stiff trunk. Artemis, as her Latin name implies,[5] was another Goddess of the Gate, and presided over birth.

A basket of these figs again seems to have been an early hieroglyphic sign for woman, Goddess or Mother.[6] On Minoan seals the young ministrant plucks or crushes their fruit in the Paradise of the Goddess (pl. XXIX*c*), and on the Asiatic side, cuneiform texts from Sumerian to Assyrian times describe the kishkanu tree of the underworld, with fruit of lapis-lazuli, 'beneath whose shadow are Shamash and Tammuz,'[7] that is, the Sun in his night or winter sleep, with whom the dying fertility God was made one (pl. X*d*).

[1] See below, pl. XXIX*b*.

[2] Cf. *Pyr. Ut.*, 387: 'Ho mother cows yonder! Ho sucking mothers yonder,' in the ascent of Osiris from the tomb. J. H. Breasted, op. cit., p. 149.

[3] G. Maspéro, *The Dawn of Civilisation*, 5th ed., 1910, p. 122.

[4] L. Siret, 'La Dame de l'érable,' in *L'Anthropologie*, xxx, 1920, p. 235 ff.

[5] i.e. Diana as the female counterpart of the double-headed Janus. See A. B. Cook, *Zeus*, ii, 1, pp. 392–422.

[6] Sir G. Elliot Smith, *The Evolution of the Dragon*, 1919, fig. 6*b*, p. 179, quoting Sir J. G. Wilkinson, *The Ancient Egyptians*, 1878, vol. iii, p. 149, and F. Ll. Griffith, *Hieroglyphics*, 1898, p. 34.

[7] S. Langdon, 'The Legend of the Kishkanu,' in *J.R.A.S.*, 1928, pp. 845–848. Two Akkadian seal-engravers, who show the Goddess rescuing Tammuz from his mountain tomb, have designed his prison in the form of a bent tree, clearly tapering from the root upwards. That is, the tomb was itself the body of the Mother, from which he would be born anew.

CATTLE-BYRE AND MILK-YIELDING TREE

The fruit of Hathor's tree in its human form was Osiris, whose corpse was scattered like the seeds after he had been persuaded to enter a chest—the cave or tomb of earth. In the myth of the wanderings of Isis, which corresponds with the search of Ishtar for the dead Tammuz in Asia, she finds the last and fruitful part of his body within a tree in Syria, which is then cut down to form a pillar of the king's house. The texts inscribed upon the tomb walls of the early Pharaohs call that tree the sycamore 'which enfolds Osiris'.[1]

The Egyptian pre-occupation with death would not permit to Osiris a new existence on earth; so Isis, hovering above his re-integrated body (on the bird wings of the Mother of the Falcon), conceives Horus who, born in secret among the reeds, takes his father's place like the sprouting of next year's vegetation. The lopped tree-trunk that had hidden him was set up by each king as chief act of the ceremony by which he periodically renewed his kingship. But it is clear that this tree is first the Goddess, the material body in which he becomes incarnate, the sycamore which gives milk to the dead, the tree of life of which he is the fruit.[2] So in mediæval manuscripts the Virgin is represented as the burning bush;[3] the lopped tree became the symbol of Osiris as did the crucifix of Christ.

Its pillar-aspect must also be observed; that assimilation of pillar and tree which seems to belong to the Syrian region and was so profoundly to influence Megalithic architecture, in fact all the monumental building which was founded upon Stone Age conceptions. The pillar-support of heaven, like the cow-legs

---

[1] A. Moret, *The Nile*, p. 89, note 2 (*Pyr. texts*, para. 1485).

[2] 'This is her throne; Leafy is its name,' says a Mandæan text, used in modern Iraq of Simat Hiia, 'the mother of all that has breath.' See E. S. Drower, 'Mandæan Writings,' in *Iraq*, i, 1934, p. 176. See also her fig. 5, 'The tree which nourishes with milky fruit sucklings that have died in infancy,' with the crescent- or horn-shaped upper branches. A Mexican codex shows such a tree upon which the souls of children feed, but it is, of course, connected with no cow-goddess. A remarkable seal from the Indus Valley shows the Bull led towards a horned Goddess standing within a tree which encloses her between branches curved like a pair of horns (see pl. XII*c*).

[3] And at the Renaissance also. See *Journal of the Warburg Institute*, vol. i, 4, 1938, p. 281 ff., and pls. 41, 42; *Mary in the Burning Bush*, by E. Harris. Also vol. ii, no. 1, 1938, pp. 69–70, note by A. Watson. Perhaps it is not too fanciful to see a survival of this conception in the Fairy Queen above the lighted Christmas Tree.

of Hathor by which the dead Pharaoh climbed; like the reed-pillars of the Sumerian byre which held the moon's crescent at their summit, represented the change, at the end of the Stone Age, from preoccupation with earth's fertility and decay, to observance of the faithful regularity of the heavenly cycles, which marked the culmination of Neolithic endeavour. So in fig. 61, p. 118 the Tree gives birth to the Sun itself.[1]

The river-journey of the body of Osiris to its sepulchre at Abydos was repeated in the funeral processions of his worshippers. That too must have a Stone Age origin, for clay models of barges containing corpse and mourners appear in early pre-dynastic graves and are commonly depicted on contemporary pottery.[2] Sometimes the grave itself is shaped like a boat, both here and in Sumer,[3] where model boats also appear in early dynastic graves such as the 'king's' grave at Ur,[4] or beside a child's body at Khafaje[5] (pl. XIIIa). The Pyramid texts show that a voyage by water was compulsory for the dead Pharaoh, and that his boat was a Goddess—the grave itself.[6]

Pillar, tree, ship, and horned gate will all reappear in Megalithic tomb-architecture and legends, East and West.

---

[1] On Assyrian reliefs and seals the sun hovers above the head of the Tree. See Frankfort, *Cylinder Seals*, pl. xxxii d, xxxiii a.c.h.

[2] Petrie, *Prehistoric Egypt*, pl. vii.

[3] W. B. Emery found such a grave at Sakkara under a Second Dynasty Mastaba. See *I.L.N.*, Feb. 12th, 1938, p. 249.

A. Parrot, in *Rev. Assyriologique*, vol. xxix, no. 11, 1932; 'Fouilles de Tello, 1931–1932,' p. 49, fig. 1, shows boat-shaped Hypogea of the patesis Ur-Ningirsu and Ugme.

[4] Woolley, *Ur Excavations*, i, *The Royal Cemetery*, pl. 20a.

[5] To be published in an O.I.P., *Houses and Graves of the Diyala Region*, by P. Delougaz.

[6] *Pyramid Texts*, par. 1201, quoted by A. Moret, op. cit., p. 178.

CHAPTER III

MEGALITHIC

MEDITERRANEAN

SACRED STONES AND TREES

Meanwhile the emblematic stones of Maz d'Azil and Birseck, of La Ferrassie and Labastide, which appeared as cultural ancestors of the Australian wood and stone churingas—those Palæolithic 'spirit houses' which may also have been regarded as concentrations of cavern sanctity—seem to have acquired a characteristic development in the Neolithic culture as extensions of the Earth's fertility. Its source is probably to be looked for in regions adjacent to the Eastern Mediterranean, a land of rock and isolated groves. This development is intimately connected with the beginnings of stone architecture.

Even today the peasants of Anatolia and Syria have their sacred trees, and in Arabia the anointing and circumambulation of monolithic stones were practised until fairly recently.[1] This is also true of modern India and the Far East, and indeed of many localities of Western Europe where the stones set up for ancient rites still stand and are still tended. The ritual appears to have radiated from a single centre, and is described in the art and literature of South-Western Asia in all its stages from the most primitive.[2] It was also assiduously practised during the European Bronze Age by the Minoans of Crete, the main body of whom had migrated in Neolithic times from Anatolia. It seems reasonable, therefore, to look to

---

[1] W. Robertson Smith, *Lectures on the Religion of the Semites*, 3rd (1927) edition, p. 210, note 1. At Okaz Doughty found these three stones still regarded as very sacred (C. M. Doughty, *Arabia Deserta ii*, 1921 ed., pp. 515–517).

[2] See below, Part iii, chap. iii, and Part iv, chap. i.

those regions for the revolution by which the earlier conception
of stones that possessed a spirit (afterwards retained in miniature as amulets) was developed into the setting up of stones for
the habitation of a spirit, or rather a place, kept sacred, to
which he can be summoned by rites. So Jacob first found that
his stone pillow was holy because of his dream, and then set it
up as a permanent Beth-El—a House of God.[1]

Such a stone was in itself an altar, because the presence of
the worshipper was necessary for the divine apparition; and
their communication was affected by some physical medium
such as oil or blood, oil being a refinement of the tree's fertility,
and blood a sharing of life.[2] Where no stone exists, the blood
of a slaughtered beast is still spilled by the Arabs upon the
earth, of which a stone (as we shall see) represents the upward
extension. Even the 'Palæolithic' Australians smeared their
blood upon the rocks of entry of the mythic ancestors to this
world, rocks which were considered to be a permanent treasury
of divine life.

Water too would be poured as a rain-maker over the rough
pillar or cairn, as it was later poured over the carved pillars of
the Ægean Bronze Age, for which the ancient cairn was sometimes used as a substitute; but in neither age was the fire-
sacrifice a part of this ritual of communication, for which direct
contact was necessary. Even a touch might suffice, like the
kissing of stones by modern pilgrims.[3] So classical authors could
speak of the Arabian 'Gods of Stone',[4] though they had no
statues; and could call their altar an idol.[5] But when images
were forbidden by Islam as an arrogation to humanity of God's
creative power (since the form, as in Egypt, would produce or
summon the deity), the standing stones retained their worshippers until modern times, because they assured a manifes-

[1] Genesis, xxviii, 18.

[2] Robertson Smith, op. cit., p. 386, considers that the fire sacrifice
originated in the burning of the fat and other special parts as too holy to
be consumed by worshippers.

[3] The Canaanite alignments at Gezer are polished by contact (R. A. S.
Macalister, *The Excavation of Gezer*, 1912, ii, 388) like the Wailing Wall at
Jerusalem to-day. See also W. Robertson Smith, op. cit., p. 80, on the
Kaaba at Mecca.

[4] Ibn Sa'd, no. 118, quoted by Robertson Smith, op. cit., p. 205, n. 3.

[5] Porphyry *de Abst.*, ii, 56.

tation of the divine only by mutual consent. 'Not merely were they a token that the place is frequented by a God, but a permanent pledge that in this place he consents to enter into stated relations with men.'[1] The injunction given to Moses against the dressing of the altar-stone must have reference to such observances, and so must the prohibition of steps, which would remove the stone from direct contact with the earth.[2]

Thus, in the Neolithic attitude to stones, man's will has entered to make a covenant with an unseen power, for whom he has taken the first step to provide a habitation, and indeed the pillar of rough-worked stone remained as an indispensable adjunct in a place dedicated to worship, even after the building of shrines had become a custom. The Arabian circuits still performed in modern times to mark off the boundary between sacred and profane, and to keep the pillar within holy ground, suggest that temples may have long been unnecessary. The first physical embodiment of this circumambulation would be stone circles, of which numbers survive in Transjordan, together with dolmens cupped for offerings,[3] though Palestine has been bereft of them by the reformatory zeal of the Maccabees.

The seals and gems, which illustrate the survival of stone-worship in the Eastern Mediterranean of the Bronze Age, show cairn, pillar, table-altar or tree, as interchangeable objects of libation (figs. 99, 100, 113, all on p. 224, and pl. XIX*a*). In that time and place, however, there was no taboo against the substitution of an anthropomorphic divinity, who often appears above or beside, or actually replaces, the form of tree or stone. The absence of the fire-sacrifice shows that the stone altar was still itself a place of sojourn of the deity.

These scenes strongly confirm the antiquity of the primitive customs still existing on the Eastern mainland, and connect them with the Neolithic architectural remains of Southern Europe.

They share with Syria and Arabia the association both of pillars and trees in isolated groups. Doughty saw at Medain

---

[1] Robertson Smith, op. cit., p. 207.

[2] Exodus xx, 25, 26.

[3] G. Perrot and C. Chipiez, *History of Art in Sardinia, Judæa, Syria and Asia Minor*, 1890, p. 292; C. R. Conder, *Syrian Stone-Lore*, new ed., 1896, p. 42 ff.

Saleh niches carved with triple pillars, a horned altar, and a single pillar, several times described in Nabatsean characters as the house of the God Aera or Auda;[1] and Herodotus mentions a congregation of seven stones which together represented two Arabian deities.[2] There are again, the double 'pillars of Hercules' set up by the Phœnicians over an enormous area of the ancient world. It is possible that the sanctity of groves of trees first led to multiplication of pillars, though the Syrian triplicities appear from their portrayal on late reliefs to have been related to the moon's phases. The threefold divinity of trees may be paralleled in the triple vision of Abraham beneath the Mamre oak,[3] or the three crosses set up by the Armenians to receive the Trinity.[4]

Late Mycenæan vase paintings sometimes show groups of five sacred columns with (at this period) celestial relations.[5] In Egypt the fertility God Min has his groups of two, three and five cypress trees.[6]

It is conceivable that one of the two unhewn pillars was at some time laid upon the other to make a table-altar for the reception of offerings or libations, its contact with the earth being kept by the vertical support. The pair may even have been considered bi-sexed like the Khasi dissoliths described below.[7] The triads again may have been arranged at some later time in the position of a dolmen, which was at once a table of offering and an earth-covered gateway to the world of the dead,[8] and such a disposition may have led finally to the grand conception of the trilithon, before it became the doorway of pillars and lintel to Megalithic temples or tombs, from which, like the pair of columns, it often remains detached.[9] In Sumer, as we saw, the Gate had always a special importance as controlling access to the enclosure which separated sacred and profane, its supports being duplicated as unattached guardians

---

[1] C. M. Doughty, *Arabia Deserta*, 1921, vol. i, figs. 1 to 5, facing p. 121 (the passage of the Diwan at el Hejr near Medain Saleh). No. 4 is a horned altar. Also p. 187 (Note on Medain Saleh by Philippe Berger, Sous-Bibliothécaire de l'Institut).

[2] Herodotus, iii, 8.   [3] Genesis, xviii.

[4] A. J. Evans, *The Mycenæan Tree and Pillar Cult*, 1901, p. 42.

[5] Evans, op. cit., fig. 23.   [6] Ibid., pp. 44 and 45, fig. 26.

[7] See pp. 152 and 153 at end of this chapter.

[8] See p. 153 at end of this chapter.   [9] See p. 133.

of the threshold.[1] The two masts before Egyptian pylons may have answered the same purpose. So with the Gate formed by three monoliths; when it became the doorway of a temple, a second gate isolated or intensified its peculiar attributes, like the horned gateway of China and Japan, which warns the pilgrim, perhaps a mile in advance, of the approach to a shrine. The Gate again, in the Bronze Age illustrations of this ritual, often stands, as in Sumer, for the sanctuary itself.[2]

Now the cult pillar of Ægean civilisation appears to receive added sanctity as an architectural member, for base, capital and architrave may be affixed to the shaft set up between worshipping dæmons or emblematic beasts (pl. XXXa). Such a conception may underlie the creation of stone architecture (which we now know to date, in Anatolia, for example, from Neolithic times),[3] as successive to the excavation of rock sepulchres with roofs vaulted in memory of the cave. Such stone-cut chambers might themselves be regarded as holy— the cavern-form of the Mother Goddess. These, on Minoan analogies, might then become shrines of a pillar, a concentration of chthonic energy like the stalagmite whose contemporary sanctity is attested in offerings found in actual caves.[4] Later the pillar itself became the support of the capstone of the vault. The tapering column-shafts of Malta and Crete may owe their shape to such a support of diminishing stones below a subterranean corbelled roof like those discovered in the Western Mediterranean.[5] The waisted altar, too, of these regions, may be reminiscent of the meeting of stalactite with stalagmite.

It is interesting to observe, in view of the two types of monument in which the dual nature of the Mother Goddess found new expression, that her lion is associated with the structural pillar or its substitute the Mountain, or carved upon the doorslab of a tomb (figs. 100 and 101 of Part IV, Chap. I below), whereas her horned beasts are set in heraldic devotion on either side of foliate pillars or trees, as in Chalcolithic Asia (fig. 113, p. 224, of Part IV, Chap. I below).

[1] Pl. XIc. [2] Pl. Xc.

[3] See above, p. 92. A similar series of Neolithic building levels has recently been found at Tell Hassuna in Northern Mesopotamia.

[4] See pp. 214, 215 below. [5] Evans, op. cit., pp. 89, 90, figs. 61, 62.

CAVE AS TEMPLE AND TOMB

STONE-AGE ARCHITECTURE OF THE MEDITERRANEAN

Whether the architecture of the islands of Southern Europe, which combined the monoliths, hewn or unhewn, of Asian stone-worship, with dressed ashlar-masonry, was a deterioration of the monumental tombs of Egypt, which repeated with match-less precision the simplicities of trilithic doorway or dolmen with holed orthostats and antechamber; or whether it repre-sented a development of the stone pillar-groups, tables, and circles, of more primitive peoples, is beside the point in this investigation, since the principles underlying both types of con-struction may be traced to a common source. But the civilisa-tions of the great river-valleys show less evidence of a primitive stone-worship than is found elsewhere—their pastoral and agri-cultural aspirations constituted a revolt from the cave. The countries adjacent to Egypt abound in rude stone monuments, but in the Nile Valley itself these are almost totally absent.

Dressed ashlar masonry, on the other hand, has been found in Cilicia, as we saw,[1] in a definitely Neolithic context, well below the first copper implements, and again there are the Neolithic bee-hive tholoi of Northern Syria and Iraq. Whether or not these were ever used for burials (and one at Arpachiyeh at least appears to have been subterranean), their construction, complete with corbelled vaulting and passage-way, reminiscent of hut or cave, seems at some time to have been taken over by the cave-loving Europeans of the South as an improvement on their rock-cut tombs.

The circular plan of Megalithic masonry, whether above or below ground, is also foreign to Egyptian proclivities, but not to the primitive circles of rough monoliths, nor to the Asiatic tholoi.

The contents of the Mediterranean shrines and burials, even in a purely Neolithic milieu, show them to be generally con-temporary with the Eastern kingdoms of the Copper Age, with which they must have had trade relations that left their stone civilisation unimpaired. It appears as if the Megalithic archi-tectural style was slowly carried by sea westward, with lesser modifications moving in both directions, as it is known to have travelled slowly along the coasts and islands of Southern Asia to the Far East; reaching both Atlantic and Pacific long after

[1] P. 92 above.

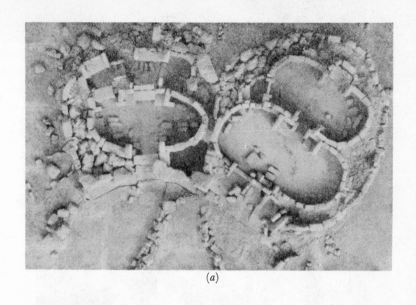

(a)

(b)

Plate 15. MALTESE MEGALITHIC TEMPLES

(a)

(b)

(c)

Plate 16. MALTESE RELIGIOUS ARCHITECTURE

the culture of its centre of origin had been superseded or overlaid.

The burials of this period found on the islands of Sicily and Sardinia, show for all their local peculiarities a very definite relationship with the East. Some of the rock-hewn tombs of Anghelu Ruzu on the latter island have pillars left in the centre of the excavated chamber, carved with the heads of bulls or cows, and with reliefs of high-prowed ships.[1] The probably contemporary tombs of the Giants,[2] built of Megalithic orthostats and overlaid with earth—a common cave-memorial of this culture—have one feature which is distributed in a less distinctive fashion over all the Neolithic and Chalcolithic Mediterranean. The crescent or horned gateway of Western Asiatic shrines is here a part of the architectural plan (fig. 62a, p. 130), extended like embracing arms before the entrance to the tomb. This crescent is invariable at the opening of the great Maltese shrines, and a frontal semicircle of stones is also found before tombs at Los Millares in South Eastern Spain.[3] The type reaches far into the North West, where its original meaning may have been effaced, for the cairns of Caithness show a rudimentary second pair of horns at the rear.[4] A rude stone circle remains in Sardinia, of which the two stones that may be supposed to mark the entrance are shaped like horns (fig. 63, p. 130). A cave-byre connection appears to be constant throughout the Megalithic West.

Pillars, again, with pairs of breast-like 'cupolas', sometimes stand before or within the Sardinian horned tombs;[5] undoubtedly the visible form of the Mother Goddess, an upward extension of Earth's fertility as nourisher of the dead, and the stone counterpart of the milk-bearing tree. These too are common among the Western tombs.[6]

[1] *Monumenti antichi pub. per cura della Accad. dei Lincei*, Rome, xxv (1918), p. 868 ff.; V. G. Childe, *Dawn of European Civilisation*, 3rd ed. (1939), fig. 120.

[2] Duncan Mackenzie, 'The Tombs of the Giants and the Nuraghi of Sardinia in their West-European Relations,' in *Memnon*, ii, 3, pp. 180–210, Leipzig, 1909.

[3] Duncan Mackenzie, op. cit., fig. 22.

[4] Duncan Mackenzie, op. cit., figs. 26 and 27.

[5] Childe, op. cit., 1st ed. (1925), p. 106, citing G. Pinza, in *Monum. ant.*, xi (1901), figs. 139, 140; *Notizie degli scavi di antichità*, Rome, 1915, p. 117.

[6] See two late examples in V. C. C. Collum, *The Tressé Iron-Age Megalithic Monument* (Sir Robert Mond's Excavation), 1935, plate xxi, and my pl. xixa.

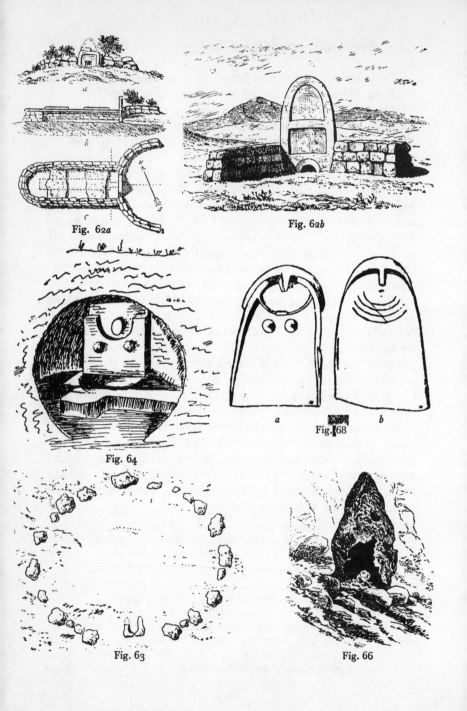

Fig. 62a

Fig. 62b

Fig. 64

Fig. 68

Fig. 63

Fig. 66

MEGALITHIC

Certain objects found in the early Sicilian graves point to specific connections with Anatolia.[1] There are also votive horns of clay.[2] These tombs have a holed doorway for offerings or other communication with the dead, and some door blocks are carved with cones from which roll the spiral volutes of guarded entry.[3] One very interesting tomb is closed by a pair of slabs which combine to form a conventionalised image of the Goddess (fig. 64, p. 130), the anterior stone bearing the shape of the Mediterranean horned altar. She appears in fact as rising through her Gate of Horn before the entrance to the grave. There can be no doubt of her position among these islands as Receiver of the Dead.

Malta at this period assumes great importance as a holy island, thronged with temples, whose majestic ruins constitute the most complete surviving expression in stone of Neolithic abstract vision. Those among them which have been scientifically excavated, are found definitely to antedate the use of metal on the island, but small objects from the graves, as well as certain stylistic indications, show them to have been contemporary with the copper-using kingdoms of the East.[4] The Mediterranean individuality of Malta was however strictly maintained, and the stylistic borrowings only applied where they chimed with her own formal vision. And since Neolithic religious ideas underlie the creative zenith of the Eastern states, there would be a common basis of understanding. But between them lay the region of stone, and these signs of contact

[1] Notably the bone plaque with sculptured bosses from Castelluccio (Childe, op. cit., 3rd ed. (1939), fig. 111), a type which occurs at Troy.

[2] These Mediterranean clay horns suggest the possibility that the clay 'bent nails' used in Chalcolithic Mesopotamia for the strengthening of clay and wattle walls of sacred buildings may have taken an added significance from their horn-like shape, and may, in fact, have originated as votive horns, since the first temple there was the cattle byre.

[3] At Castelluccio. *Bullettino di Paleontologia Italiana*, xviii (1892), pl. vi; (P. Orsi, *La necropoli Sicula di Castelluccio (Siracusa)*, pp. 67–84).

[4] At Hal Tarxien, a layer of sterile soil divided the temple floors, upon which no trace of metal occurred, from the Bronze Age graves lying above them. (Sir T. Zammit, *Prehistoric Malta*, 1930, p. 80.) Hal Saflieni must have been frequented for many hundreds of years, for the bones of several thousands of persons had, it is considered, been introduced at a period subsequent to its use as a shrine. No metal has been found in any of these burials. (Sir T. Zammit, *The Neolithic Hypogeum at Hal Saflieni*, Malta, 1935, p. 16.)

with the external world serve to throw into relief Malta's spiritual insularity, maintained apparently during a very long period of rebuilding and at least one influx of immigrants.[1]

No mines of flint or metal could have attracted a population to the island, for these do not exist there. Among the hundreds of Neolithic burials beside the rock-cut shrine of Hal Saflieni, no weapons are found. The polished green axes are, it is true, extremely common, but in a form too small and blunt for use.[2] They were amulets, buried as in Western Megalithic tombs, as emblems of sacrifice, and it may be, of resurrection. They are chiefly of chrysolite, which is found on the Italian mainland. Apart from pilgrims, the artistic remains bring to mind a population of herdsmen and fishermen, of quarry workers and craftsmen, who also terraced the stony hillsides for the sowing of scanty crops (there are few signs of agriculture), transporting their soil, and stones for building, in wheeled carts, whose tracks, deep-cut in the coralline limestone, occasionally run out to some cliff-edge, and are continued on a neighbouring island.[3] They would all be temple-servants, for no towns seem to have existed. Huge water cisterns were cut with stone tools in the vicinity of the temples of Mnaidra and Hagiar Kim,[4] and the cavern sanctuary of Hal Saflieni. Caves were still used as dwellings.[5]

The temples themselves, of which four groups now (1939) stand as fairly complete structures above ground, and a fifth is excavated from the rock beneath an inhabited street, while the plans of a number of others may be reconstructed from their ruins, are of a unique and remarkable character, which does not hide their stylistic ancestry in the pillar and the cave; in the rough stone 'Bethel', and the corbelled courses and rect-

[1] If such is the explanation of the late Neolithic burials above Hal Saflieni.

[2] Sir T. Zammit, *Hal Saflieni*, fig. 4.
The modern islanders have legends of a migration from Axe-land, apparently situated in Africa, where water was poured upon pillars of salt to turn them into men and women. See R. N. Bradley, *Malta and the Mediterranean Race*, 1912, pp. 251–252.

[3] R. N. Bradley, op. cit., pp. 261–262; Sir T. Zammit, 'Prehistoric Cart-tracks in Malta,' in *Antiquity*, ii, 5 (March, 1928), pp. 18–25.

[4] Sir T. Zammit, 'Prehistoric Remains of the Maltese Islands,' in *Antiquity*, iv, 13 (March, 1930), p. 74.

[5] Bradley, op. cit., p. 108.

angular passages of the tholoi. A glance at pl. XVa and b will reveal the customary concave or 'horned' shape of the entrance to the temenos, which usually enclosed two structures of unequal size, each with its own trilithic gate. This always gave access to a long passage-way of orthostats, once roofed with flat slabs, which passed between two pairs of semicircular apses of ashlar masonry supported upon a foundation of gigantic megaliths, in diminishing courses that presuppose a vault; or roofed by a true arch, whose spring is in a few cases preserved.[1]

The long central passage, sometimes widening into courts, eventually terminates in a raised platform like a chancel, beyond which is a cavern-like apsidal extension, usually approached by a trilithic doorway, preceded by a pair of guardian pillars, and itself enshrining a single pillar (pl. XVIb).

It will be noted that the orthostatic central corridor which extends from gate to inner shrine through the whole length of the building, is straight, like the usual passage-way of dolmenic tombs; but before the lateral apses or chapels of Hal Tarxien, and across the doorway of the ultimate apsidal sanctuary, are raised sills or thresholds (pl. XVIb), elaborately decorated with very precise and finished reliefs (further accentuated by the punctuation of their background), of geometric spirals, which often sprout or bud like the foliage of plants. A sill from Hagiar Kim, which shows two perfect spirals revolving from a central cone, and carvings still visible upon the huge threshold blocks at Gigantea on the neighbouring islet of Gozo, suggest that such decorated sills may have been universal. The spirally painted and incised pottery vessels found in the temples, show a corresponding perfection of craftsmanship and design, with all the Neolithic love of rhythmic sequence.

The monolithic columns that flank the chapel entrances are pierced for the insertion of curtain rods or other barriers, and the carefully wrought spirals on the raised thresholds which partly bar these entrances, must surely represent, beyond the strictly axial corridor, the old winding path of conditional entry, which appears here, and on the ritual bowls and vases, to be assimilated to the sacred tree (pl. XVIId). Within the entrance of the upper Temple at Mnaidra, a small elevation of a building has been carved in relief, with pillars and domed roof, a variant

[1] At Hal Tarxien, for instance (Sir T. Zammit, *Prehistoric Malta*, p. 31).

perhaps of the plans of the interior passages often depicted at the threshold of Stone Age tombs or caves.[1]

The dolmenic approach, and the setting of pillar tables and altars within cave-like recesses, of course resemble tomb-architecture, but no burials ever took place during the Neolithic occupation of these sanctuaries, whose pillars often taper abruptly downwards, or show the waisted form of the meeting of stalagmite with stalactite, or carry tables, sometimes superimposed (pl. XVIc), as if representing the upper and lower worlds.[2] Within the niches of their walls are often found the bones of horned victims of sacrifice, slaughtered apparently in the courts, and sometimes small votive figures or parts of bodies which suggest a healing cult, probably connected with the oracular chambers of curious acoustic properties found in four at least of the extant temples.[3] A pair of bull's horns lay before the entrance of a shrine at Hal Tarxien,[4] and two ram's horns were found buried in a hemispherical excavation in the stone floor before a sanctuary of Hal Saflieni,[5] and within the latest of the Tarxien temples several conventional and lifeless friezes of horned beasts occur.[6] This latest temple was a building of the decadence; but such reliefs still confirm the evidence of other Maltese monuments, that their excellence was abstract and intellectual, the shared consciousness of animal life being no longer a subject of immediate interest.

The combination of the ritual of the Asiatic stone altar with the cave-nostalgia of Mediterranean burials would sufficiently account for this tomb architecture of public ceremonial, which contained no corpse. It may possibly embody the cult of a Mother Goddess and young 'Dying' God, for a constant duality is perceptible in the plans of pl. XVa and b. There are pairs of temples behind their common concave boundary

---

[1] Sir T. Zammit, *The Neolithic Temples of Hajar Kim and Mnaidra*, Valetta, 1927, p. 24. A tiny stone model of a similar building was found at Ta Hajrat, with trilithic entrance, orthostatic curved walls, and vaulted roof. Another such model was discovered at Hal Tarxien (Sir T. Zammit, *Pre-historic Malta*, pl. xxiii, 8).

[2] Compare the Minoan shrines described on p. 217 below.

[3] See below p. 136.

[4] Sir T. Zammit, *Prehistoric Malta*, pl. vi, 2.

[5] Sir T. Zammit, *Hal Saflieni*, p. 38.

[6] Sir T. Zammit, *Prehistoric Malta*, pl. iii, 3.

wall—the number being increased only where re-building has taken place; there are pairs of apses and of flanking pillars before the doors, and the pairs of spiral mæanders, to which may be added pairs of double conical cup-holes.

The dual temples have other peculiarities: one for instance is always smaller than the other, and the plans (pl. XV*a* and *b*) reveal a strange feature, which must have been yet more perceptible when the apses retained their domes—unless indeed the covering earth concealed their shape under a tumulus[1]— the fact that each temple resembles a seated figure, with head at the axial dolmenic shrine, and shoulders and knees formed by the pairs of lateral apses. The enormous, nearly always monolithic, threshold-stone then resembles the base of a statue, and the whole calls to mind the small seated marble figures found before the altar of Hagiar Kim (pl. XVIII*a*). It seems possible therefore that these edifices were erected as bodies of the Gods, their habitation in the Egyptian sense, by which the form called up the divinity.[2] The smaller temple might then embody a young male God.[3]

The lack of chosen orientation strengthens the impression that these perpetually curved walls, and domed and vaulted roofs, are reminders of the cave sanctuaries of former ritual, and conversely the great Hypogeum of Hal Saflieni, excavated from the rock by immense labour with stone picks, so that its many chambers reproduce or extend the natural convolutions of a cave, reveals the most careful and finished imitation, at the entrances to these halls, of column, lintel and architrave (pl. XVI*a*), all approached through a pair of detached pillars, the rock-cut domes being carved or painted to imitate corbelled masonry. Here the sacred character of familiar temple construction is artificially imposed to intensify the sanctity of the cave, just as cave sanctity is invoked by the structural forms above ground.

The ceilings of two of the subterranean chambers of Hal

---

[1] The covering earth does not appear to have hidden the structure, to judge from extant small stone models.

[2] As the chancel of Breton churches, for example, is set at an angle to the nave, to represent the bent head upon the cross.

[3] Since the Mediterranean religion of the Stone Age appears from the monuments to have been matriarchal, like that of Bronze Age Crete, which was contemporary and in contact with the Maltese civilisation.

Saflieni are painted with designs of fruiting spirals, the geometric emblem breaking into life as the sacred tree.[1] Except
for such embellishments, vegetation is normally absent from
Maltese Neolithic art, but the tree itself rises up the length of
the columnar pedestal of an altar (pl. XVIIc), which formerly
stood in the temple of Hagiar Kim, the down-curving fronds
or volutes of Asia being conspicuous at its base.[2]

One hall of the hypogeum is surrounded by small cells or
cubicles (pl. XVIIa), which were probably used for incubation
—the practice of sleeping beside a holy stone or tomb or chasm
in order to obtain a revelation, which is best known from its
survival into classical times, but is constantly found in a Stone
Age milieu.[3] The presence of an aperture of peculiar acoustic
properties between this and the adjoining chamber, and its
repetition, in slightly varying forms, in side chambers of the
temples, at Hal Tarxien, Hagiar Kim, and Mnaidra, reveal the
device by which the oracle was imparted, and we may even
recognise two applicants for revelation in a pair of recumbent
clay figures discovered in the repository below (pl. XVIIb). It
will be noticed that the sleeping woman here illustrated wears
the bell skirt of Capsian times in the elaborate style retained in
Minoan Crete; and incidentally, that obesity may have its
own grace.

A quantity of models of parts of the body and crude but
realistic clay figures, apparently of diseased pilgrims, found
here, at Hal Tarxien, and in one apse at Mnaidra, makes it
likely, as we saw, that these oracles were healing shrines[4] like
the Temple of Asclepius at Epidaurus, where incubation was
practised in later days, and many similar votive offerings were
left behind.

Subsequently, it is believed, to the construction of the inner
halls, but still in a purely Neolithic environment, several caves
within the original entrance were filled with red earth, and an
enormous number of secondary burials introduced over a long
period,[5] probably for the sake of their proximity to the shrine.
It is here that the polished axe amulets were found in such

[1] Prof. Sayce made this comparison. Zammit relates it to Kings I, vi, 29;
(*Hal Saflieni*, p. 33).

[2] P. 100 above.   [3] As in Indonesia, below p. 153, or Bethel.

[4] Sir T. Zammit and C. Singer, *J.R.A.I.*, liv (1924), pp. 67–100.

[5] Sir T. Zammit, *Hal Saflieni*, p. 11.

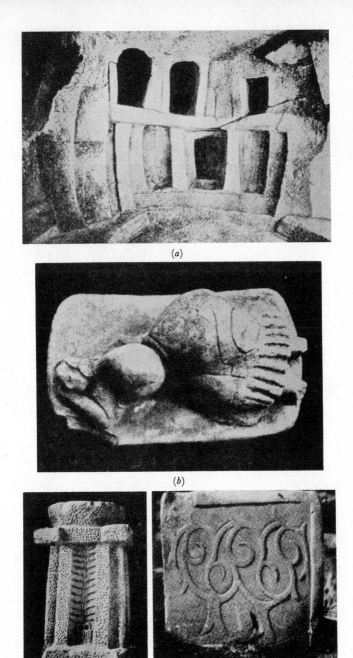

(a)

(b)

(c)   (d)

Plate 17. EXAMPLES OF MALTESE RELIGIOUS ART
AND PRACTICE

(a)

(b)

(c)

(d)

(e)

(f)

(g)

Plate 18. CARVED FIGURES FROM MALTESE TEMPLES

Plate 19. MEGALITHIC BRITTANY

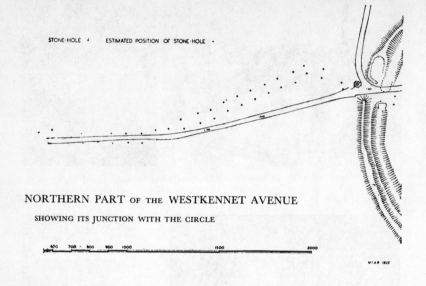

NORTHERN PART OF THE WESTKENNET AVENUE

SHOWING ITS JUNCTION WITH THE CIRCLE

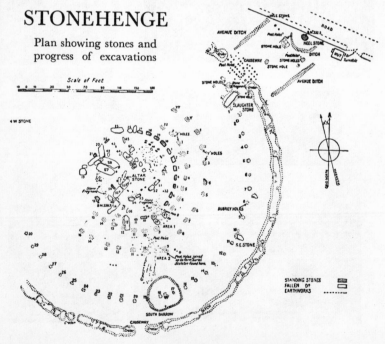

STONEHENGE

Plan showing stones and progress of excavations

Scale of Feet

Plate 20. MEGALITHIC WILTSHIRE

numbers; but figures of divinities are absent from these cave
interments as they are absent from the Palæolithic graves.
They have been found in the temples themselves, below and
above ground, seven of them seated before the tree-carved
altar of Hagiar Kim; one standing upright (pl. XVIII*g*)
within the trilithic entrance gate of Hal Saflieni, and two
others in a lower chamber. Another series, much broken, was
mingled with the débris of Hal Tarxien.[1] These are of fine
marble, well finished, originally coloured red in the ancient
fashion; and they show the sensitive conjunction of weight with
formal simplicity apparent in all Maltese abstract art. For
these statuettes belong æsthetically to a far different category
from the small naturalistic votive figures.

One or two of these last reveal, together with Palæolithic
affinities, some appreciation of living form (pl. XVIII*b*), but
they have not the selective mastery of the abstract images,
which seem to represent the ideal shapes of divinity (pl. XVIII*a*
and *g*).

It will be remembered that Aurignacian statuettes make
exactly the same distinction between the realistic type, which
finds its most perfect expression in the stone figure from Willendorf (pl. VI*c* above), and the abstract conception best represented in the ivory woman of Lespugue (pl. VI*a* above); and
it is remarkable that this divergence should reappear in the
Neolithic Mediterranean.

The peculiar obesity of the Maltese ideal figures, which
conceals any obvious difference of sex, their huge forearms
and thighs neatly tapering to tiny hands and feet, is perhaps
pathological,[2] and may have been adopted from living examples to express that passionless calm only to be paralleled
in Northern Buddhist art, which employs spherical forms for
the same purpose. Probably the love of convexity—which may
subtly modify even the lintel of a trilithon[3]—influenced their
conception of the Gods, whose forms we saw to be repeated in
the temple buildings themselves. In the present state of our
knowledge these figures are a unique achievement, which
relates to divine humanity the Neolithic abstract aspiration.
Since all but two are now headless, and pierced for attachment

[1] Sir T. Zammit, *Prehistoric Malta*, pp. 80–82, pl. xxii.

[2] Sir T. Zammit and C. Singer, *J.R.A.I.*, liv, p. 77.

[3] For instance, a lintel from Hagiar Kim now in the Valetta Museum.

at the neck, it may be presumed that a priesthood represented them in the temple ritual, the heads being accordingly changed from time to time. There is also, however, a third class of image, of such close affinities with Early Dynastic Sumerian sculpture that West Asiatic influence must be postulated here (pl. XVIII*c* to *f*). The conical vision of Mesopotamia would be more readily acceptable than Egyptian cubes; in fact examples of the cone itself have been found buried at temple gateways in Malta, just as in Babylonia.[1] On this island of stone they even modelled the large statuettes (of Sumerian early Dynastic dimensions) in unbaked clay, so that a group of them found together in a side chamber of Hal Tarxien, is almost disintegrated.[2] Like their prototypes they appear to represent votaries, but the lower part of a huge stone figure, otherwise quarried away, which stands in the entrance court of the latest temple at Hal Tarxien,[3] and a few other fragments of statues and reliefs found there and at Hagiar Kim, show that this style may have come into use generally for images of the Gods, a circumstance also paralleled in Sumer.[4]

Taken as a whole, however, the sacred island kept its artistic integrity, in spite of the foreign ships. In pitting their intellect against the weight of giant stones, her builders obtained a grandeur which was not merely dependent on size. But it must never be forgotten that the architectural elements so impressively assembled in these temples, were the stone circles, trilithons and dolmens, of the primitive Megalithic rites. The oracular dream cures took place in side chapels, and are chiefly of interest because of their later recurrence in Greece and Crete, but we must pass beyond the more barbaric, but equally grand stone structures of Western Europe, to the rude monuments still set up in certain Pacific islands, before light can be shed upon the central ceremony at the dolmens and the superstructures, above the raised sills of the inner shrine.[5]

---

[1] Sir T. Zammit, *The Neolithic Temples of Hajar Kim and Mnaidra*, pp. 26–28. He notes the Chaldæan analogy.

[2] Sir T. Zammit, *Prehistoric Malta*, pp. 96–97.

[3] Sir T. Zammit, op. cit., pl. i, 2.

[4] H. Frankfort in *Illustrated London News* of May, 1934. *Oriental Institute Communications* [or *O.I.C.*] No. 19, 1935, figs. 63 and 64.

[5] See last section below.

THE ATLANTIC SEABOARD

The Iberian peninsula, whose Palæolithic civilisations showed such vitality, must have enjoyed a rich culture in the later Stone Age, so numerous and varied are the remains of its rock-cut and stone-constructed tombs, and of the Megalithic monuments which pass on the Atlantic seaboard through all stages of development at a very early epoch of their culture.[1]

It will be remembered that Spain kept alive through an immense period the traditions of Capsian rock-painting, until the picture of a Megalithic tombstone, roughly carved or painted in the image of the Mother Goddess, actually appears, together with a riveted copper dagger-blade, among the degenerate epipalæolithic conventions of Peña Tu (note 3, p. 81 above). There is also the Chalcolithic pottery of Los Millares (fig. 47, p. 80), with its late Capsian animals, and punctured symbols, presumably of the Mother Goddess, derived from Caspian conventions for the female form.[2] The painted signs, therefore, which are to be found on the stone faces of Megalithic tombs in Spain and Portugal,[3] may be regarded as a transitional practice which helps to explain those other signs so frequently engraved on the dolmens of Brittany, in which emblems of the new religion are mingled with those inherited from the old.

This influence of the Palæolithic tradition of Eastern Spain upon the Megalithic tomb construction, which flourished and developed on the Western coast, was probably the result of a mingling of cultures beneath a wave of oriental influence, which enfolded the peninsula, while it was still, like Malta, in the Neolithic phase. This seems to have broken the barriers maintained between East and West in Spain from Palæolithic times, so that the developed Megalithic culture of the Atlantic shores spread throughout the peninsula, and probably beyond it, in

[1] Childe, op. cit., 1st ed. (1925), pp. 109–124; 3rd ed. (1939), pp. 250–266; E. T. Leeds, 'The Dolmens and Megalithic Tombs of Spain and Portugal,' *Archæologia*, London, lxx, (1920), pp. 201–232.

[2] Above, pp. 79, 80, and fig. 47.

[3] Childe, op. cit., 1st ed. (1925), p. 111; cf. 3rd ed. (1939), 'Painted signs of ritual significance and possibly Palæolithic descent.'

a backwash that passed over the islands,[1] while the construction
of Mediterranean corbel-vaulted tombs was extended conversely into Spain and Portugal, some of them with the holed
stone at the entrance and single central pillar.[2] The horned
gate now appears at Los Millares (fig. 65, below). The

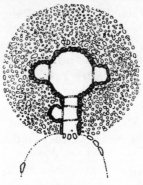

Fig. 65

'labyrinths' engraved on rock faces[3] may have arrived by this
route, but seem more probably to have been inherited from
the Capsian of Africa.

The strange scene in the cave of the Bats near Granada
(Part II, pl. XIII*b* above) will not have been forgotten.
There a Neolithic ritual was revealed, seemingly identical in
its main features with Early Dynastic burial rites at Ur and
Kish in Mesopotamia, the chief male participant wearing a
gold diadem of Sumerian type which is the sole fragment of
metal discovered in the array of stone weapons, fixed to their
shafts or handles with Asiatic bitumen. A Megalithic stone
pillar, the curious memorial of a fusion between two branches
of tradition derived from Neolithic beliefs, stands at a little
distance upon the desolate mountain path leading to the once
sealed cave. It is carved with a breast 'cupola' of the Mother
Goddess (fig. 66, p. 130).

[1] E. T. Leeds, 'Problems of Megalithic architecture in the Western
Mediterranean,' *Liverpool Annals*, ix, 1922, p. 29 ff.

[2] H. Obermaier, *El Dolmen de Matarrubilla*, 1919.

[3] L. Frobenius, *Prehistoric Rock Pictures*, 1937. Plate unnumbered, but
probably No. 60 of the Catalogue at the end of the volume: 'Rock engraving, San Jorge de Mogor. Labyrinth.' See also p. 36.

At this period of Oriental influence, when violin-shaped amulets, and objects of hippopotamus ivory or ostrich shell, appear in South-eastern Spain, together with a form of the ded-pillar, and with schist 'croziers' (which may possibly derive their form from the loop of the Goddess, but are certainly

Fig. 67

prototypes of the 'lituus' commonly engraved on Megalithic tombs), a flint industry, fine and elaborate enough to have emanated from Egypt, suddenly replaces the rather poor polished implements of Neolithic Spain. At the same time graves everywhere, whether rock-cut, corbelled, or Megalithic, contain examples of a unique image of the Mother Goddess engraved upon animal bones, stone cylinders, and schist plaques.[1] The comparison of fig. 67 with late tombstones in France (fig. 68, p. 130) shows that the Iberian objects represent the head of the deity above that necklace which had such ritual importance in Western Asia.[2]

Such emblems may well have found their way into France from the Iberian peninsula, for it was apparently from Spanish harbours that voyagers 'into the undared ocean swung north their prow', to plant Megalithic settlements along the shores of Western and finally of Northern Europe. Their object is unknown, and outside the scope of this enquiry; it can only be affirmed that isolated communities guarded, like the Jews of the Diaspora, the legacy of an ancient faith, for several thousand years into the Bronze Age and beyond. They do not appear to

[1] L. Siret, 'La Dame de l'érable.' *L'Anthropologie*, xxx, 1920, p. 235 ff.; id., *Questions de chronologie et d'ethnographie ibériques*, 1913.

[2] See p. 102 above.

have created a new civilisation, but they must have taught their religion to later peoples, to judge by the round barrows of the bronze-using immigrants which congregate round Stonehenge, and especially, by the tomb architecture of Northern France (fig. 68, p. 130), with its 'Goddess' doorways, its labyrinths, and most of all the dedication of the axe itself, the inscriptions of Roman date declaring that the dead lay under its protection.[1]

The Megalithic monuments never stand very far from the sea. On the wind-tormented point of Finistère, and about the shores and islands of the Gulf of Morbihan, the gigantic circles and alignments betray the energy born of terrible adventures. There are no sudden changes of style to mark the passage of successive phases from Neolithic down to Roman days, and each cultural period must have lasted longer in these remote outposts than in the centres of interchange. A long infiltration from without seems to have caused the gradual replacement of one industry by another in the graves of the faithful, but the ceremonial monuments continued to preserve their Stone Age traditions. In sepulchral types alone is there any variety of construction, the dolmen beneath a tumulus, with corbelled vault and passage-way, appearing, as in the South, along with the polished axe, towards the end of the Neolithic; the passage then gradually becoming important, with rude engravings, on its walls and roof, of the current religious symbols.[2]

The figure of the Mother Goddess is carved, as we saw, upon grave-stones of a late period in France. She is there only just anthropomorphic, sometimes a hewn stone with breasts and necklace only, or with breasts alone (fig. 68, p. 130 and pl. XIX*a*). This type may have been imported by another route, for the seafarers who set up the great dolmens along the coast of South Brittany were concerned exclusively with abstract symbolism.

The primeval maze of entry to the divine world is the subject most frequently repeated among these barbarous designs produced by percussion upon cap-stones or passage walls, as the polished axe, unused and votive only, is by far the most common offering among the stone implements, pottery, and

---

[1] J. Déchelette, *Manuel d'archéologie préhistorique, celtique, et gallo-romaine*, i, 1908, p. 398 ff.

[2] Z. Le Rouzic, 'Morphologie et chronologie des sepultures préhistoriques du Morbihan,' in *L'Anthropologie*, xliii (1933), pp. 225–265.

beads, found beside the bones of the collective burials within.[1]
The maze is no doubt indicative of the soul's wanderings, a
chart like that before the Cave of Malekula,[2] like those engraved
upon two stones in the Megalithic tomb of Bryn Celli Ddu in
Wales, and repeated in the actual passage of entry.[3] Fig. 69,
p. 144, from the covered way of Pierres Plates at Locmariaquer,
shows this to have been sometimes conceived as serpentine; and
fig. 70, p. 144, from the passage of Luffang, shows a development by which the single road inward leads to another figure,
possibly a crude representation of the Mother Goddess.[4]

The great stones of the dolmen on the island of Gavr'inis
(pl. XIXc) are carved all over with these convolutions in the
utmost elaboration, which is only approached at New Grange
in Ireland, where the tomb is of the early vaulted type. Both
these examples show the intricacies as sometimes leading to a
central triangle or cone, but several of the Gavr'inis stones
depict numbers of votive axes in the midst of the winding ways,
which seem to be implements of sacrificial fertility like those
flung into Cretan caves or struck into stalagmites (fig. 71, p.
144 and p. 215 below).

Again, at the summit of the ascent of Petit Mont, on the
opposite peninsula of Arvon, is a table-stone, impressively engraved with a pair of feet in the centre of the maze (fig. 72),
which strangely recalls the two feet among the group of symbols
at La Pasiega (fig. 13, p. 18). The mæanders are sometimes
replaced by a plan of chambers and passages (fig. 73, p. 144),
as they seem to be at Niaux.[5] At Pierres Plates again, the symbols of concentric curves and circles are arranged just like the
'pathways' and 'stopping places' of divine journeys on the Australian churingas (fig. 74, p. 144). Another kind of plan is shown
in fig. 75, p. 145, where the axe is seen beside an enclosure
shaped like a tombstone, and a cleft cone, of 'horned altar' type.
The cone or tombstone with almost anthropomorphic head and
arms (fig. 76, p. 145) is also seen emanating rays of divine

[1] Id., *The Megalithic Monuments of Carnac and Locmariaquer*, 1908, p. 26 ff.

[2] P. 156 below.

[3] W. J. Hemp, 'The Chambered Cairn of Bryn Celli Ddu' in *Archæologia*
(London), lxxx, 1930, pp. 179–214. He shows (1) that the tomb has a spiral
plan, (2) that this spiral is represented on stones. There is now a model in
the British Museum.

[4] Cf. fig. 81.   [5] See p. 16 above.

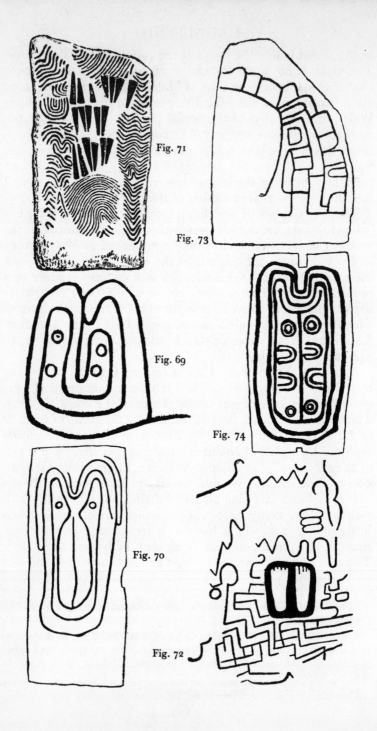

Fig. 71

Fig. 73

Fig. 69

Fig. 74

Fig. 70

Fig. 72

power. An emblem with handle fitted showing a pillar and cone and again reminiscent of Pasiega (fig. 13, p. 18), is repeated on a tomb re-used in Roman times with sexual embellishments.

The plough (pl. XIX*d*) is a common symbol upon these stones, another sacrificial instrument for breaking the earth for fertility, a development of the axe, and like it emblematic of the whole Neolithic civilisation. It lies on the enormous table-stone of the Table des Marchands at Locmariaquer, and it has been suggested that the rows of bent stems on the conical

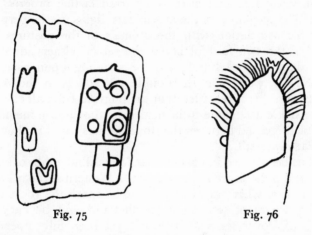

Fig. 75   Fig. 76

headstone which support it represent growing corn (pl. XIX*b*).[1] If this were so, the symbolism of the Eleusinian mysteries would here find a barbaric parallel.

The alignments or avenues of frequently huge, undressed monoliths, composed of local granite broken by the primeval glaciers, stretch across the plains round Carnac sometimes for a mile, leading in ten, eleven, even thirteen, lines, to some cromlech or stone circle, before reaching which they often change their angle of direction (pl. XIX*f*).[2] Here once again is the old pathway, the marked road to the sacred threshold of the circular temple, a 'processional way greater than imagination', of which the guiding stones in this case are themselves divine. It is said that their conjunction with the cromlechs is

[1] Z. Le Rouzic, *La Table des Marchands* (*Locmariaquer*), 3rd ed., 1936, p. 13 ff., gives a most interesting reconstruction of the half-effaced symbols.

[2] The alignments of Kerzehro, for instance; see Le Rouzic, *The Megalithic Monuments of Carnac and Locmariaquer*, p. 20, and of Carnac itself (p. 16).

orientated to the sun's path, showing that Ménec and St. Pierre Quiberon were frequented at the summer solstice, and Kermario then and at the equinoxes.[1] A few alignments have also, it is interesting to note, been placed as ceremonial pathways to tombs.

This locality is still a place of gathering for the annual *pardon* celebrated at the Church of S. Cornély. The legend of this saint's arrival in the vicinity, after his flight from the Roman soldiery on the backs of two oxen, and his transformation of the pursuing army, when the sea barred farther progress, into the ranked megaliths of the alignments, lights up the perpetual Neolithic association with the animals of the pastures. The horns of the two faithful beasts are set on either side of the West door of the church, a cross standing upon each pair (pl. XIX*e*), exactly as the double axe stands in the Ægean Bronze Age.[2] It is recorded that the pilgrims from all countries whose sick cattle came to be healed by the saint in memory of his rescue 'passed between the stone soldiers'; that is, they used the Pathways still.[3]

It has been noted in passing that Megalithic tombs of several types and periods are found along the Western seaboard of the British Isles, where menhirs and circles mark the route of recurring waves of settlement to Shetland and beyond. The Straits of Dover seem to have not yet been fully opened to these voyagers, for sailing round Scotland they arrived, very late in their history (to judge by the types of excavated tombs), on the Scandinavian shores, and in Holland and Germany, amid the fine bronze culture of Northern Europe.

In Scotland milk was still poured in recent times upon the cup-holes.[4] When a flowering branch of the elder which grows beside the king-post of the Rollright circle in Oxfordshire is cut on Midsummer Eve, the stone is still seen to nod his head,[5]

[1] Z. Le Rouzic, op. cit., p. 31, quoting MM. H. du Cleuziou and F. Gaillard.

[2] See fig. 108.

[3] Z. Le Rouzic, op. cit., pp. 31–33. Also his 'Carnac', 4th ed., 1928, pp. 17–18. He mentions the local belief: 'souvent la nuit des revenants se promènent dans ces allées.'

[4] Donald A. Mackenzie, *Ancient Man in Britain*, 3rd edition, 1932, p. 148, quoting records of Dingwall Presbytery 1649 to 1678.

[5] A. J. (later *Sir* A. J.) Evans in *Folk-Lore Journal*, 1895, p. 20: 'The Rollright Stones and their Folk-Lore.'

and numerous legends in the West keep alive the memories of the stone and tree cults suppressed by a law of Canute.[1]

But the two great temples of the chalk uplands of Southern England have something beyond a local importance. In the age of the Megalithic builders this region must still have been sprinkled with huge blocks of the sea-laid sandstone which once formed a sheet over the Wiltshire downs and Salisbury Plain, and which now lie as 'Grey Wethers' in a few remote valleys. The presence of these Sarsen stones, in the clean down-land raised well above the miasma of the swamps, but accessible by river from the little harbours, may have determined the choice of this region as a centre of religious life, at about the period when the beaker-using people, who brought across the shallows of the Straits the bronze industry of Central Europe, were beginning to travel along the Ridgeway from Kent. Judging by their round barrows, which lie around Avebury and cluster in hundreds about Stonehenge, these immigrants adopted the religion of the Megalithic builders, just as the creators of the Bronze Age civilisation of the Eastern Mediterranean had retained and developed the surrounding Neolithic beliefs.[2] Even at Malta burials of the Bronze Age were found to be grouped above the sterile layer of earth which overlay the floors of Hal Tarxien,[3] as if the later inhabitants, after the passage of many centuries, still desired that their dead might receive protection from a vanished ritual.

But the tremendous monoliths of the English circles were shaped by stone instruments, and their earthworks raised by picks of deer-horn.[4] Only one fragment of stone-filling at Stonehenge, the later of the two monuments, is slightly stained with copper.[5] But archæological research is scarcely needed to confirm this ultimate architectural expression of traditions already so old.

The grandeur of Avebury is independent of its size, though it is the largest stone circle in existence, composed of giant

[1] Donald A. Mackenzie, op. cit., p. 147.

[2] See Part iv., chap. i.

[3] See Zammit, *Prehistoric Malta*, p. 45.

[4] M. E. Cunnington, *Avebury*, 2nd ed., 1931, p. 14; F. Stevens, *Stonehenge*, 1933, figure on p. 39.

[5] E. H. Goddard, 'List of Prehistoric Antiquities in Wilts,' in *Wiltshire Archæological Magazine*, vol. 38 (1914), p. 172.

Sarsen monoliths, whose natural forms are only slightly shaped[1] to a proportion which does not destroy their appearance of primeval forces newly emerged from chaos. It resembles the structures of Neolithic Malta in a certain dualism expressed in the setting of two circles, one rather larger than the other, within a common circular boundary, and in the shaping of megaliths along the double line which forms its Avenue into two types roughly suggesting the Pillar and the Cone, and probably representing a difference of sex, some of them bearing double cup-stones surrounded by circular incisions.[2] This processional way runs for nearly two miles to the Sanctuary on Overton Hill, where concentric circles of stones were still erect two hundred years ago, and were supplemented by six circles of depressions which must have once held timber uprights,[3] preserving the old connection of stone pillar with tree. Round this, it is recorded, were many burials, the skeletons forming an outer circle with feet towards the central shrine.[4] The Avenue takes a bend (fig. 77, p. 149) before reaching the Sanctuary, and if this change of direction might have here been imposed by the contour of the hill, no such reason exists for the sudden sharp angle by which at its other extremity it meets the chalk causeway marking the original passage across the boundary rampart and ditch of Avebury (pl. XXa). A similar angle, it may be remembered, is turned by several of the great alignments near Carnac before they reach the cromlech, and seems to have existed, to judge by the depressions left by stones which once crossed its earthern Avenue (pl. XXb) at the entrance to Stonehenge also. This suggests a long-continued memory of the winding path of entry, which accounts for the name of 'Serpent' or 'Serpentine' Temples bestowed by Stukely and by Blake.[5] Burials of the round-barrow people are found against the standing stones of the Avebury processional road, but these

[1] A. Keiller and S. Piggott, 'The Recent Excavations at Avebury,' in *Antiquity*, x, 40 (December, 1936), p. 420.

[2] A. Keiller and S. Piggott, op. cit., fig. 7.

[3] M. E. Cunnington, 'The "Sanctuary" on Overton Hill, near Avebury,' *Wilts. Arch. Mag.*, vol. xlv (1932), p. 306.

[4] M. E. Cunnington, *Wilts Archæological Magazine*, vol. xlv (1932), pp. 300–335.

[5] For Blake's reconstruction, see p. 100 of *Jerusalem* (Keynes' one volume edition).

stones were allowed to fall in Celtic times, and the ploughs of
the Iron Age, which respected Stonehenge, have passed over
them.[1]

The existence of Woodhenge, a miniature Stonehenge of tree
trunks, whose positions were only discovered from the air,[2] and
of the Sanctuary on Overton Hill, suggest that concentric
circles of wood and stone were frequently established in this
region. The primitive use of such circles to designate, like the

Fig. 77

spirals, the path of entry between worlds, and the pacing or
dancing of such designs in imitation of the journeys of the Gods,
offers a perfect explanation of these structures.[3] The circular
plan would appear to have a chthonic rather than a solar
origin, for Avebury has no definite orientation, and that of
Stonehenge, like the Breton cromlechs, depends upon factors
outside its circles; that is to say, the 'altar' stone (which may
once have stood upright) is axial, not to the causeway which

[1] A. Keiller and S. Piggott, op. cit., p. 426.

[2] M. E. Cunnington, 'Prehistoric Timber Circles,' in *Antiquity*, i, 1
(March, 1927), pp. 92–95; O. C. Crawford, Editorial Notes, in *Antiquity*,
iii, 11 (September, 1929), pp. 257–259;

[3] Cf. p. 153 below.

marks the original entrance across the surrounding earthworks, but to an unhewn stone, set between the earthen banks of the Avenue, and outside its central axis, to mark the moment of sunrise at the summer solstice.[1] Two other stones, also unworked and of local Sarsen, stand without the circle at the North West and South East to define the equinoxes.[2] They may all have been so placed to determine the date of seasonal festivals.

The outer circle of Sarsen stones with carefully fitted lintels must once have been surrounded by an enclosure of possibly

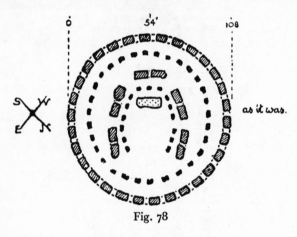

Fig. 78

wooden uprights, which have left depressions at regular intervals in the chalk soil.[3] The trilithons themselves enclose another circle of blue stones, foreign to that region, which have been traced to a locality in the hills of Pembrokeshire where several Megalithic circles survive.[4] It therefore seems likely that the builders of Stonehenge brought out of the West, with incredible labour, stones already sanctified by use. Within this circle five lofty trilithons of Sarsen stones, very nobly shaped, stood in a semicircle whose ends were prolonged—the now familiar Horned Gate (fig. 78, p. 150). The subtlety of their workmanship

[1] Stevens, op. cit., pp. 6, 26 and 63. See pl. xx*b*. Astronomical calculations based on this orientation would place the setting up of the Hele stone at about 1700 B.C. with a possible error of 200 years on either side.

[2] Stevens, op. cit., p. 25. [3] Stevens, op. cit., p. 34.

[4] They have been identified by Dr. Thomas of the Geological Survey as belonging to a limited area in the Prescelley Range.

atones, in the decadence of the Stone Age, for their loss of function as actual gateways, and takes the mind back to the isolated
trilithons of Phrygian worship, which opened into no temple
made with hands. At Stonehenge they enclosed an inner horse-
shoe of the smaller blue Welsh monoliths, so that both embraced
the central stone of the whole monument, the 'altar' already
mentioned, of fine micaceous sandstone, from another district
of Wales.[1] They formed, in fact, a kind of apsidal shrine around
it like the apses in which the cult-stones of Malta were set. Thus
the complete structure, like its very different neighbour at Avebury, is full of reminiscences of the South and East of perhaps
a thousand years before, which were strong enough to kindle,
on this remote island, the sombre splendour of its Neolithic
decline.

MELANESIA

The westward voyages of the Megalithic missionaries, exiles,
or explorers, have left no data but their monuments, upon
which to base, with some small help from the records of their
more civilised contemporaries, any conjectural religious system. But the Megalithic culture also spread eastward from its
still undiscovered starting point, travelling probably during
many centuries, even millennia, along the southern shores of
Asia and up its north-eastern coasts to Alaska and Japan. At a
fairly late period of its history, it seems to have crossed the
ocean to the highlands of Bolivia,[2] where the Spaniards eventually destroyed such vestiges of monumental ritual as the
Incas may have tolerated, or absorbed.

In the islands of the South West Pacific alone, a complete
Megalithic religion is alive today, among semi-barbarous communities practising occasional cannibalism and using polished
stone implements.[3] These gardeners and breeders of swine are
united in a strict and elaborate social discipline, by rites which
are intricately bound up with their rude stone monuments, but

[1] Dr. Thomas gives the neighbourhood of Milford Haven as the provenance of the 'Altar' Stone.

[2] See below, pp. 190, 191.

[3] A. Bernard Deacon, *Malekula, A vanishing People in the New Hebrides*,
1934.

betray, nevertheless, unquestionable links with the religious and social organisations of the food-gathering peoples of the Palæolithic level of culture. The publication of recent investigations in Malekula and other small islands belonging to the New Hebrides,[1] is of the utmost value here, because it discloses from the lips of the worshippers themselves, as related to a number of enquirers of diverse mental attitudes, a complete system of beliefs connected with the communal raising of great stones in similar arrangements to those which yet stand beside the Mediterranean and Atlantic shores. The system is everywhere corroborative, with modifications due to local circumstance, of the continuity and development of the religion of the Stone Age as described in the previous chapters.[2]

The inhabitants of Malekula say that hardly a single element of their culture is indigenous.[3] Its immediate origin is Indonesian, the two levels of culture now apparent on the island recalling two out of many migrations by that route out of Asia.[4] The so-called indigenous inhabitants of some of the Indonesian islands are known to believe in a common soul substance and animal ancestry,[5] while farther East the people of Papuan Kiwai practise agriculture and keep large stone axes (whose practical use is forgotten) as fertility charms,[6] yet hold initiation ceremonies in the communal 'Long House', with feigned death and rebirth, at sowing-time and harvest.[7] They even call their bull-roarer the yam-mother, and show the carved statuette of a woman at the harvest festival from which women and children are excluded. Here the hunters' rites for promoting animal fertility and destruction, have obviously been extended to assist the oscillation of the seasons, and on this island at least, which has not lost all memory of Asia (as the Australians have done), the Mother Goddess retains some vestige of both her powers.[8]

But the more recently arrived Khasi of Indonesia are said

---

[1] J. Layard, *Stone Men of Malekula, Vao*, 1942, passim.

[2] Layard's book was published after they were written.

[3] Layard, op. cit., p. 15.   [4] Layard, op. cit., p. 20.

[5] W. J. Perry, *The Megalithic Culture of Indonesia*, 1918; chapters xix and xx, quoting A. Kruijt, 'De legenden der Posso-Alfuren aangaande de eerste menschen,' in *Mededeelingen van wege het Nederlandsch Zendeling-genootschap*, xxxviii, 1894.

[6] W. N. Beaver, *Unexplored New Guinea*, 1920, p. 187.

[7] Beaver, op. cit., pp. 185–187.   [8] Ibid., p. 176.

to found their settlements round two stones, identified, like Jacob's Bethel, by dreams. They place them together, the male upright, the female horizontally.[1] As the latter receives most of offerings, the horizontal stone becomes a table or altar. It is called 'The first grandmother', and the other 'The first maternal uncle'.[2] These most primitive elements of Megalithic architecture are thus specifically regarded here as Mother and Son.

THE MONUMENTS OF THE NEW HEBRIDES

The two periods of settlement known to the inhabitants of the New Hebrides, are still differentiated in their myths, social organization, and monuments, in which a similarly matrilineal level of culture, especially important in Vao and the small islands to the north of Malekula, is associated with the erection of the dolmen. This, they explicitly state, represents both the Cave of the Dead[3] and the Table of Sacrifice,[4] exactly as it appears to do in Megalithic Europe. On some islands the name of the highest woman's rank, to be won in the Maki ceremonies presently to be described, is 'Stone Altar'.[5] The rites connected with the erection of the dolmen belong to the so-called Low Maki[6] (as it were, the Lesser Mysteries), for which the choosing, transportation and raising, of the stones may cover a number of years.

The later migration established a patrilineal system with historic records, represented in the monuments by the upright monoliths, which here, as in Indonesia, stand for the male principle.[7] These are ceremonially set up, again after prolonged preparation, to embody both the ancestral ghosts and the living initiates who share their spirit;[8] and may be arranged in Avenues (processional ways) and cromlechs (the circular boundaries of dancing grounds). Monolithic circles are also erected round ritually planted trees.[9]

A second type of monument belonging to this later stratum is the high stone platform or tower (pl. XXIa), a savage descendant, probably, of the Temple Tower of Mesopotamia, and

[1] Perry, op. cit., pp. 16–17. [2] Perry, op. cit., p. 46.
[3] Layard, op. cit., pp. 272–274. [4] Ibid., p. 700 ff.
[5] Ibid., p. 729, quoting Deacon and Rivers. [6] Ibid., chap. xiv.
[7] Ibid., p. 17. [8] Layard, loc. cit. [9] Layard, op. cit., p. 10.

serving, as we shall see, a similar purpose. It is included among Megalithic monuments because it conforms with Layard's definition,[1] being constructed communally for a religious end, of stones too heavy to be lifted by hand. Like the Near Eastern sacred pillar of the Bronze Age, it is ritually an extension of the upright monolith, being raised not only from the earth, but towards the sky; and is expressly stated to be associated with the idea of height, which is the aspiration of the Higher Maki. In these generation-long ceremonies, of which it forms the monumental culmination, one of the highest ranks, on a single island at least, is called 'The Ladder'.[2] This all points to the influence of the great Eastern civilisations with which, as we saw, the Megalithic Mediterranean seems to have been actually in contact. Its re-appearance on these distant islands is very striking.

THE DIVINITIES

Like its prototypes in the West, the dolmen, both as Cave and Altar, is associated with an Earth Spirit. This is the Guardian Ghost, dweller at the Cave entrance to the other world, and devourer of the dead unless propitiated by evidence of initiation, sacrifice, and, in the upper cultural level, by the intervention of a male deity. The Guardian Ghost, called on Vao 'Le-hev-hev', is the ultimate object of cult in this group of islands; the object of terror also, for the gentle traits of the Mother Goddess seem to have been left behind with the flocks and herds of the Asiatic continent, so that only her more lethal aspect remains. On the farther side of the Pacific, in Mexico, for example, the Earth Goddess herself became entirely ferocious, and there no animal was domesticated before the arrival of the Spaniards. In the New Hebrides, however, the tusked boar is bred; to be identified in the sacrifice both with the Guardian Ghost and the human initiate.[3] Through that sacrifice, as we shall see, the Devourer of the Dead does become Mother of Rebirth.

Le-hev-hev is usually conceived as sexless, but is recognised as female among the later, patrilineal, societies. The first

---

[1] Layard, op. cit., p. 19.   [2] See below, p. 169.

[3] Layard, op. cit., p. 257, note 2. The title Le-hev-hev is assumed by old men far advanced in Maki rank. See below, p. 162, and note 2.

syllable of the name is prefixed today to every woman's name among the small islands.[1]

She is sometimes imagined as a Rock, can be crab, spider, or megalopod,[2] but is chiefly a formless evil, like the Babylonian Tiamat—the chaos which Marduk caught in his net of ordered creation. Le-hev-hev represents, Layard says, the people's unconscious fears:[3] the past, that is to say, from which they are trying to rise. But in addition to the boar, she is also connected in the ceremonies with the hawk, which is carved at the end of the ridge-pole of lodges, and of huts built over the monuments and their ancestral ghosts (pl. XXI*a*), and over the place of retreat after ritual rebirth. The soaring of this hawk is mimed by initiates on their high platform at the critical moment of the sacrifice.[4] Le-hev-hev cannot therefore be completely dissociated from Taghar, a male deity who is the object of no cult, but only of aspiration. He 'represents their conscious striving', and is explicitly connected with the idea of height attained in Maki, and therefore with the temple-tower and its mythological counterpart, the fiery mountain of Ambrin, which, for devotees of the higher culture, lies beyond the Cave. Taghar, the people say, is the direct light of the sun and stars, and lives in the moon, though he is not himself the moon. He is the creator of all life.[5]

We have noted in Megalithic temples such as those at Carnac and Stonehenge, the signs of a later orientation made to conform with the apparent movements of the heavenly bodies,[6] suggesting some further transformation of the cults of the Earth and the dead, of a similar nature to this. The next chapter will show how such a development was accomplished in Egypt and Mesopotamia, reaching a peak of religious association of which these much later changes in the Far East and Far West may be reflections.

The myth in which the two powers play their part, is the basis of the long ceremonies upon which the history of the

[1] Layard, op. cit., p. 218.

[2] Layard, op. cit., pp. 220–222. Cf. the Scorpion Man and Woman who guard the Cave of Death in the Gilgamesh Epic.

[3] Layard, op. cit., p. 223.   [4] Layard, op. cit., p. 734.

[5] Layard, op. cit., p. 211 ff., quoting Jean Godefroy, S.M., *Une tribu tombée de la Lune*, 1933.

[6] See above, pp. 146 and 150.

community, and also that of the individual, is founded. *The Journey of the Dead*, as mimed in the ritual dances of Vao, bears the closest relation to the literary legends of our own civilisation, suggesting some common foundation in a universal ritual descended from the Stone Age of Europe and Asia. In Vao the newly-dead man is believed to arrive before the entrance to a cave on the seashore, where he encounters the dreaded Guardian Ghost. In front of the cave-mouth is a design called 'The Path', traced upon the sand by Le-hev-hev. At his approach she obliterates half the design, which the dead man must complete or be devoured. 'The Path' has of course been trodden in ceremonial dances during all his adult life, and knowledge of the whole pattern proves him to be an initiate of Maki. After completing the design, he must tread its mazes to the threshold of the cave, where he may now offer the tusked boar which was sacrificed in the mortuary rites performed during his burial. At this point the people of Vao believe that Taghar prevails with the Guardian to accept the surrogate in place of the dead man, who is thus free to join his departed kinsmen and friends gathered in the cavern depths.[1]

The earlier version of the myth ends within the cave, of which each small island has its representative grotto; but those who have taken the higher Maki rank, do not regard it as a final habitation. Beyond it the dead man finds himself on a lonely shore, where he kindles a beacon to summon a ferryman known as 'The Guide'. Having (in the Wala version) broken off a branch of weed[2] for the voyage and gnawn the bark of a 'milk-bearing' tree,[3] he is ferried safely to the island volcano 'Source of Fire', in whose flame some say that even Le-hev-hev may stand upright. Upon its summit, in certain accounts, the dead dance as skeletons all night long.[4] At every dawn their heads fall off, and the bones rest on the ground till sunset. The

---

[1] Layard, op. cit., p. 225 ff..

[2] Corresponding apparently with the bough or cane carried in the boat of the dead in so many legends of the Old World.

[3] J. Layard, in Essays presented to C. G. Seligman, 1934, pp. 126–127. This tree is comparable with the milk-yielding tree of the Egyptian and Mesopotamian underworlds described in the previous part, chap. ii, for babies whose mothers cannot suckle them are said to feed upon it. The dead man by gnawing it may be considered to be new-born; cf. figs. 59 and 60.

[4] Layard, op. cit., p. 226. The populations of Wala and Atchin believe this, but Vao denies it.

corresponding mortuary rites resemble the occasional Palæo-lithic practice of decapitating the corpse,[1] which is here buried at sundown, so that its owner may join the dance immediately after the required conditions have been fulfilled.[2] But we must now turn to the ritual by which this myth was made a familiar experience among the living.

THE SAND DRAWINGS OF VAO AND ATCHIN

These are patterns for dances, traced upon the ground, like the designs belonging to the Old Stone culture of Australia.[3] Layard says that they are based on the 'Labyrinth' mythology of South West Malekula, that is, on the story of the Guardian Ghost derived from the earlier stratum of culture.[4] He finds such dances to be:

1. Always related to death and rebirth.

2. Always connected with a cave and rarely with a con-structed dwelling also.

3. Where the ritual is preserved, the Labyrinth, danced or drawn, is always at the entrance.

4. The presiding personage is always a woman.[5]

Here, in fact, is the winding path of conditional entry, of which there were signs even in the narrow corridors and the scrawled 'macaroni' at the entrance to Palæolithic caves.[6] We should presumably add to the cave and dwelling of No. 2, the tomb which imitates a cave, remembering the engraved 'mazes' of the Western tombs, some of which so strangely resemble those which we are about to consider.[7]

---

[1] Above, p. 69.   [2] Layard, loc. cit.   [3] Above, p. 50.

[4] Layard, op. cit., p. 650 ff., quoting Deacon, 'Geometrical Drawings from Malekula and other islands of the New Hebrides,' *J.R.A.I.*, lxiv, Jan.–June, 1934, for corresponding symbolism in S. W. Malekula.

[5] Layard, 'Labyrinth Ritual in South India' (*Folk Lore*, vol. xlviii, June, 1937). Almost identical designs are drawn, he says, by living Hindu women before their thresholds in the month when the sun dies and is re-born. Their husbands then walk over the designs.

[6] Above, p. 16.

[7] Fig. 70 above. Layard considers the 'early' variety to be never stereo-typed, but intended to baffle and confuse those unfamiliar with its special plan. He believes the formal type (represented on the coins of Knossos) to have lost its original meaning. This seems unlikely, since the formalised symbol may emphasise crises by turns and crossings, as in a modern maze, without losing its illusory and deceptive functions.

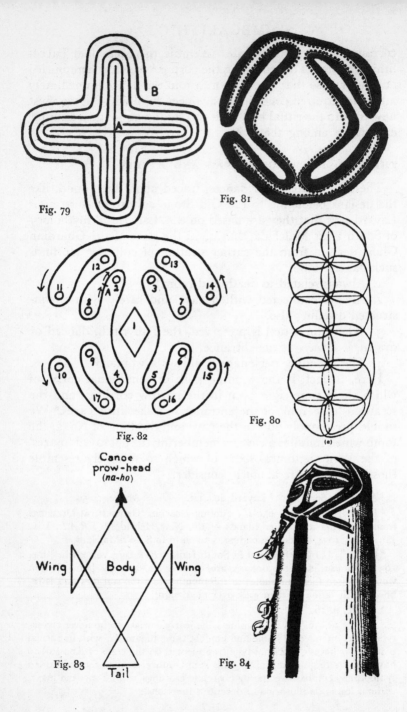

Fig. 79

Fig. 81

Fig. 82

Fig. 80

(a)

Canoe
prow-head
(na-ho)

Wing   Body   Wing

Tail

Fig. 83

Fig. 84

Layard finds in Malekula two types of design[1] in both of which the continuous line is an essential condition, because it marks the path trodden by the aspirant or initiate: (A) a figure in straight lines (i.e. a framework of walls and barriers), representing the Journey of the Dead; (B) a circular pattern representing the Guardian Ghost. Here the continuous line is without beginning or end, and the framework is composed of small circles. It will be remembered that the Australians interpret their ground drawings as depicting both the Journey of the animal ancestor, and also its body, and that the Palæolithic female figure from Mezin (pl. IIa) is in the parallel line technique used elsewhere to represent pathways.

Layard subdivides type A into (1) figures in parallel lines (fig. 79, p. 158), and (2) curvilinear figures (fig. 80, p. 158). For the purpose of this book, through which the Maze dance is trodden to the end, the differentiation is of secondary importance, since both varieties lay special emphasis, by the formation of 'knots'[2] and angles, on the sudden crises of the initiation ceremonies, such as marriage, death and rebirth. The European distinction between mæander and spiral (both types appearing in Palæolithic art (fig. 40, p. 32 and pl. Vg)) seems to be of a somewhat different character, for the spirals, for instance, on the thresholds of the inner shrines at the Hal Tarxien (pl. XVIb), emphasise no events, but the whole spring-like tension of conditional entry—the recoil to gather power. The concentric circles, too, of Western cromlechs, may be considered as shaped for a spiral dance, though it should also be remembered that the circles as well as spirals are interpreted by the artist or owner of Australian ground and churinga designs, as representing the passage between the worlds.[3]

Type B, the unbroken line depicting the body of Le-hev-hev, apparently in her crab or spider or megalopod form, is illustrated in figs. 81 and 82, p. 158. Its general resemblance to engravings on dolmenic stones in Brittany (fig. 70, p. 144) will be immediately apparent. The primitive conception of the divine body as the road travelled by itself and its seeker, will again be recalled in the Australians' interpretation of their ground drawings,[4] as will its possible origins in Palæolithic cave religion.[5]

---

[1] *Stone Men of Malekula*, I, p. 654 ff.

[2] See below, p. 248 and note 4.   [3] Above, pp. 47 and 50.

[4] Above, p. 50.   [5] Above, p. 64 and pl. iia.

THE DANCES

The mumming dances of Atchin and other small islands are 'consciously creative'.[1] There are tragedies, comedies, and formal figure dances with a chorus and individual rôles. The actors are masked or veiled, since they represent the ancestral dead.[2] Deacon's account[3] shows that the figure dances of Atchin describe at the same time: (*a*) a sacred marriage, (*b*) initiation, (*c*) the journey of the dead. In discussing the most primitive known initiations, we found that birth, marriage and death were not completely differentiated in the rites,[4] and such partial overlapping appears indeed to be integral to this ritual even in its later developments. The figure dances of Atchin are thus themselves to some extent mumming plays, illustrating the gradual initiation into the Maki mysteries. The processional and circular dances stir, Deacon says, the deepest emotion of all. Their focal points are sacrificial posts from which float the hawk-banners (fig. 83, p. 158): huge kites whose beaks are shaped like the prows of canoes—for the mythical Journey by Water never loses its significance as passage from state to state. The circular dance is performed at the height of the Maki ceremonies, and also during initiation.

THE GONGS

The gongs which provide the music for these figures (pl. XXI*d*) are hollowed trunks of trees whose upper ends are roughly carved to represent the heads of ancestral ghosts.[5] Their distribution coincides in the New Hebrides with the Maki rite and the monolith, to which they are ritually akin. Whole orchestras are played together in contrapuntal rhythm, the chief instrument being the Mother-Gong; the rest striking a different time-beat. They sound the approach signal for the processional dances, in which feet are brought down together to the blows of the upright, and the rattle of the horizontal, instruments.[6]

[1] Layard, op. cit., p. 336 ff.   [2] Ibid., p. 337.
[3] A. B. Deacon, op. cit.   [4] See p. 298 below.
[5] Layard, op. cit., pp. 13, 310.   [6] Ibid., op. cit., p. 310 ff.

(a)

(b)

(c)

(d)

Plate 21. MALEKULA

(a)

(b)

Plate 22. THE ZIGGURAT

MEGALITHIC

We come at last to the developed Megalithic ritual of which this music and dancing form a part. The rites, as we saw, are of two grades:

1. Low Maki, of which the central Megalithic ceremony is the erection of the dolmen, which represents the Cave of the Dead.

2. High Maki, culminating in the erection of the Stone Platform, identified with the island volcano Ambrin, upon which the dead dance in bliss.[1]

In both grades the ritual is based on rebirth. Four years are spent, in Low Maki, seven years in High Maki, in growing the tusks of the sacred boar and choosing and transporting the monumental stones, in preparation for the great sacrifice by which it is attained. The outward tokens of rebirth, repeated throughout at higher stages, are the taking of a new name and the lighting of a fire, upon which the first food of the reborn is cooked. After the event he lives in seclusion, in a hut guarded, as we saw, by the Hawk. After the new birth he acts as a child for thirty days. By its means he becomes one with all the ancestral dead who have previously followed the rites, and monoliths are accordingly set up to embody both living and dead. The chiefs of some villages, therefore, take the title 'Stone' as a suffix to their names.

The new fire is lit upon the stone platform of High Maki, and from this, as already noted, those of upper rank take brands for cooking the neophytes' food. On this platform, at the supreme moment of the sacrifice (in Atchin at least), the sacrificer spreads his arms to imitate a soaring hawk, and sings of the stars.[2]

The boars destined for immolation are tied to 200 monoliths which have been arranged in the figure of a sea-going canoe, and before the sacrificial screen, called 'birth enclosure', is shaken down, a song is chanted about a canoe which has at last reached land.[3]

[1] Layard, op. cit., chaps. xi to xv.   [2] Layard, op. cit., pp. 733–734.
[3] Layard, op. cit., pp. 427–429.

THE TUSKED BOAR OF VAO

The Sacrifice is the great mystery in which the identification is accomplished, of the beast, its slayer, and the being to whom it is immolated.[1] Mythologically the boar is the animal which is offered to Le-hev-hev before her cave through which the dead must pass. In the high Maki rite it is considered as given to man by Taghar, the god of heavenly light, both in defence against, and also in honour of, Le-hev-hev. Both objects are achieved, in the initiatory as in the mortuary rites, through atonement with Le-hev-hev in the sacrifice; the substitution of the pig at a man's death being only possible because the man has been in life identified with the pig.

But the sacred monument is also identified. Père Godefroy, who lived long in the islands, says of this ceremony: 'We have here, as forming a single entity, victim, altar, and sacrificer.'[1] He refers to the dolmen, and thus includes also the Guardian Ghost. The votary who has attained the highest rank of the whole Maki ceremonial is, indeed, addressed by a title philologically equivalent to her name.[2] In Vao, at least, such titles of Maki rank are at first bestowed upon the tusked boar only, the boar who was previously sanctified by the sacrifice of other pigs, and has thus acquired a 'soul'. Through the passage of the boar's 'soul' into the sacrificer, the latter attains the rank of his victim.

The boars are first prepared for consecration by the knocking out of the upper canine teeth. After the lower canines have pushed through to the upper jaw, they emerge in crescent form, which represents the first stage of holiness. When they have completed a full circle the next stage is reached. Some beasts acquire the distinction of a second and even a third circle, and are thereby destined for the highest sacrifice. The spiral tusks of the victim (pl. XXIc) are afterwards hung from the sacred monuments and from the jaws of the human-faced gongs, suggesting that both these embodiments of the ancestral dead are thought to take the boar-nature also[3] (fig, 84, p. 158). There seems no doubt that the tusks have replaced in these Pacific

---

[1] Layard, op. cit., p. 257, note 2.   [2] Layard, op. cit., pp. 220–221.

[3] Layard, op. cit., pp. 268–269, quoting F. Speiser on 'dæmonic' powers conferred by the attachment of the tusks.

islands the horns of bull and ram in the Old World, with the same significance as funnels or concentrations of the beast's ghostly power. In Vao, however, the artificially induced growth of the tusks has enabled the breeders to impose on them the spring-like tension of a spiral path, such as we see carved on the raised thresholds of the Maltese shrines. This represents a remarkable fusion of Stone Age conceptions, comparable with the Horned Altar and Horned Gate of Western Asia, Europe and Africa. The boars are also fertility symbols,[1] thrown alive into graves as pigs were thrown into the Greek 'megara' of classical times.[2] The axe of sacrifice (pl. XXIb) is

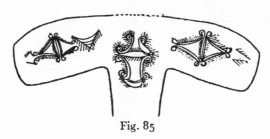

Fig. 85

sacred here as in the West. An illustration is also shown of the axe which is devoted to the rare and solemn human sacrifice which has not been described as it has no part in Maki ritual, though it is explicitly associated with rebirth. But the designs on this second axe exactly resemble the scrolled patterns on the door slabs of the Neolithic tombs of Castelluccio (fig. 85, above and p. 131, note 3).

On the night preceding the supreme Boar Sacrifice, there is a torchlight procession in which the Hawk banners floating from their staves are trampled down.[3] Next morning the Conch Shell trumpets are blown: shells which appear from archæological records to have played an important part in the Stone and Bronze Age rituals of Mediterranean lands,[4] where their spiral convolutions seem to have associated them with the Cave of rebirth. They are blown in the Maki rites to herald the slaughter of each of the four ranks of tusked boars. Layard calls the trumpet blast on the morning after the trampling of the hawk banners, a peal of victory over the Guardian Ghost,

[1] Layard, op. cit., p. 263. [2] See below, p. 293.
[3] Layard, op. cit., p. 424. [4] See fig. 114 below.

that is, over Death itself.[1] Later on that day, as we saw, the hawk soars in the moment of sacrifice above the high tower, in the persons of the chief initiates.

It has been necessary to go into some detail in the matter of these rites, because: (*a*) they supply all that was missing from the deserted monuments of the West; (*b*) they also form a logical development from earlier to latest Stone Age conceptions; (*c*) they show a profound relation with the systems elaborated out of those conceptions, which we find in certain later religions. Layard calls Père Godefroy 'the only white man on these islands to have appreciated the character of the Megalithic ritual, despite the great elaboration of its rites, and the many other uses to which it has been put, as essentially a mystery in the sense in which the Church receives this word. This point of view', he adds, 'agrees with my own conclusion that this ritual is comparable with the mysteries of Classical Antiquity.'[2]

The later chapters of this book may help to explain how such a relation could endure through time, because of the universal nature of the rites upon which it is based.

[1] Layard, op. cit., p. 265.   [2] Layard, op. cit., p. xx.

PART THREE

ZIGGURAT AND PYRAMID

CHAPTER I

CULMINATION

AGE OF INVENTIONS

At the end of the Chalcolithic phase of culture, there appeared among those Oriental states which had been moving along parallel lines, an acceleration in mental progress comparable in its effects with the speed of material development consequent upon the modern discovery of steam and electricity. In Egypt and Sumer, for instance, pictorial signs take a sudden movement towards phonetic combinations or a linear script, while the ideograms first found at a somewhat later stage in India, suggest a similar previous and contemporary development. Since this period is also distinguished by the construction of wheeled vehicles and the use of sails in navigation, the intercourse which had always been maintained by means of the caravan routes must have been greatly facilitated.[1] The use of copper to replace stone implements and weapons involved the exploration of distant lands, and the self-sufficiency of the Neolithic agricultural communities was thus permanently broken. The contrast, however, between the hieroglyphic and cuneiform scripts, shows clearly enough that though actual inventions were pooled, their application remained individual, as befitted nations in a creative epoch of their history.

In all these countries it is probable that the institution of city life, with its consequent specialisation, gave the priests (the first legible documents are religious)[2] the leisure for intellectual research, enabling them to develop to remarkable ends the gropings towards mathematical exactitude already displayed in Neolithic pottery and architecture.

[1] V. Gordon Childe, *Man Makes Himself*, 3rd impression, 1939, p. 139 ff.
[2] At Warka.

The earliest of such achievements, the rectification of the calendar, must have been carried to its conclusion at Heliopolis in Lower Egypt,[1] at a time when the chthonic powers still reigned, though it proclaimed for all the future the supremacy of the sun. For the year now began with the simultaneous rising of Sirius, Ra and the Nile, and Osiris as God of Vegetation was born on the first of the five intercalary days. From now onwards the cyclic changes would be ruled by predictable movements of the heavens, but their religious roots were laid in the ancient seasonal rites of earth's fertility.

The power dependent on this discovery must have assisted the concentration of government, while the religious prestige of the king, in Egypt as in Sumer, would have made great works possible by united effort, considered as reciprocal service to secure and preserve his divinity for the land in life or death. Thus in both countries the great monuments arose as intellectual and material expressions of national aspiration.

THE MONUMENTS

SUMER

The buildings by which this aspiration was perpetuated, kept in each centre of civilisation the individual character already visible in the Chalcolithic preoccupation with the two aspects of the Stone Age religion, with fertility and death. In Sumer the terraced enclosure with its Gate, round the primitive wattled hut, rose higher by stages of rough clay, reinforced, as at Warka, with pottery vessels and hollow cones to keep its sides at the maximum steepness;[2] to represent the lost ancestral mountain, the mythical Mt. Mashu, co-extensive with the earth, erected 'in the place of fertility' over a vast hollow, the primeval cave where the dead dwell.

The steep terraces of the Ziggurat were later constructed in a solid bulk of baked brick, eventually to the number of seven. We saw that they may have covered a cave or tomb,[3] the

---

[1] Because only in that region could the temporal and spatial positions have coincided. A. Moret, *The Nile*, p. 20.

[2] W. Andrae, 'The Story of Uruk,' *Antiquity*, x, 38 (June, 1936), p. 140.

[3] Above, p. 95.

resting place of the sun and fertility Gods, in their night or winter sleep 'within the Mountain'; but life appears in Mesopotamia to have prevailed over death. At Nippur the temple was called 'The House of the Mountain',[1] but also, as at Larsa and Sippar, the 'Bond of Heaven and Earth';[2] and because the king represented the God, his palace in Babylon was called 'The Bond'.[3]

But the Sumerian ruler Gudea calls his temple *dimgal* 'the Great Binding Post',[4] as if in memory of those tree-trunks which supported the wattle-hut, or flanked[5] the portal which symbolised the shrine in the art of his reign. This bond, like the tree-pillar, connected Heaven and Earth, and the Ziggurat was thus conceived as a kind of Jacob's ladder whose pathways were external, a stairway later mounting in a spiral from stage to stage; the Megalithic way of approach to the divine state here lifted towards the sky. Pl. XXII*b* shows at Samarra the only complete Ziggurat now existing and already half-way to the Minaret which replaced it in Islamic[6] lands, with its spiral circuit clearly visible. This change of dimension, prefigured farther West when the lintel stone was placed above the pillar, was the Chaldean fulfilment of the religion of the Stone Age. The formless plain had turned men's regard to the skies. The Egyptian hieroglyph for divinity, whether interpreted as axe or as standard for the totemic ensign, was in either case a Neolithic inheritance; but its Sumerian symbol was a star.

At first the invisible world was thought to be of one substance with the earth; but the calendar presupposes a distant field of causes intellectually perceived; and the Ziggurat creates a way of ascent by stages and a winding stair, which imposed its form

[1] E. Burrows, 'Some Cosmological Patterns in Babylonian Religion,' in S. H. Hooke, *The Labyrinth*, 1935, p. 50.

[2] Dur-an-ki. Burrows, op. cit., p. 46 and notes 1 and 2, p. 47, note 1. There is a possible connection with navel-string (49, note 1), and surely also with the looped door-post.

[3] Markas Sămē u irsiti used of the temple. Markas used of the Palace. Burrows, op. cit., p. 47.

[4] Burrows, op. cit., p. 47, quoting F. Thureau-Dangin, *Die sumerischen und akkadischen Königsinschriften*, 1907, p. 122.

[5] See pl. xi*b*.

[6] E. Herzfeld, *Samarra*, 1907, pl. 3.

Th. Dombart, *Der Sakralturm*, i, 1920, 'Zikkurrat,' pp. 29–31.

on the consciousness of Europe and Asia.[1] It was a true Tower of Babel, designed to reach the sky, 'coextensive with the earth' and founded upon the Abyss, for upon its summit was the booth or chapel in which the God communed with man. There, as we saw, the sacred marriage took place for the fertility of the land, and there the king yearly celebrated the festival of the year's renewal.[2] A text from Sippar calls the temple-tower, with its culminating shrine, 'heaven-high', in a double sense,[3] meaning also that it resembled the structure of the upper world. For the pattern of all temples was laid up in heaven; Gudea is shown in a dream the temple plan pricked out in stars,[4] and the king of Ur on the stele of Ur-Nammu,[5] himself bears the tools for the building of the Ziggurat, while the God in the upper register carries the measuring rod. A similar scene is frequently depicted on Early dynastic seals (pl. XXIIa). 'Except the Lord build the house, the builders labour in vain.'

A later text even states that on the day of creation men were moulded with Marduk's blood from clay in order that they might 'cause the Gods to abide in the dwellings of their delight'.[6] The king's duty therefore made possible God's sojourn on earth.

In Sumer as in Egypt the monarch bore the shepherd's crook; his title was Tenant-Farmer of God. When, however, the loose confederations of Sumerian city-states became united under the Semitic Akkadians into an empire, the God of earth's fertility had to fight for supremacy with the Sun. Early preoccupation with the skies had already set the latter in the Sumerian pantheon, as a minor deity, always shown on the seals as steering a barque whose prow becomes a crowned divinity, preceded

---

[1] Classical authors describe the stages of the Ziggurat of Babylon as coloured to represent the various Worlds. The Ziggurat of Borsippa was called the seven rounds of Heaven and each reappears for instance in Mithraism and in Dante's *Divina Commedia*. See Burrows, op. cit., p. 69, note 1 and p. 70.

[2] P. 104 above.

[3] Sidney Smith, 'A Babylonian Fertility Cult,' *J.R.A.S.*, 1928, pp. 849–850.

[4] Thureau-Dangin, *Die sum. und ak. Königsinschriften 110*, 19, 20 f.

[5] *Antiquaries' Journal*, v, pl. xlviii.

[6] C. J. Gadd, *History and Monuments of Ur*, 1929, p.3.

or accompanied by a man-headed lion and surmounted by a plough.[1] The Akkadian craftsmen also delight in the sun's boat, but even now it moves over no heavenly stream. The Earth-Goddess is present with her leafy sprays, such as Gilgamesh, and so many later heroes of legend, bear across the waters of death; the lion of the sun was first, as we saw, her funereal beast; the barge which the Egyptian dead must enter is also a deity;[2] and the plough and seed-bag, or jar, all point to chthonic ritual (pl. XXIIId). Again, the scene of pl. XXIIIb represents the God's liberation from his Mountain-grave, but this God is not Tammuz; he wears the Sun's rays and carries the saw by which the mountain is cleft for his heavenly rising. The Sun has gained the victory not by annihilating his predecessor, but, as in all divine conquest, by assimilation. This was a natural development; the older ritual for assisting the crises of seasonal change had enlarged its scope to comprise a similar cycle in the causal world. So the Sun-God's boat passes nightly underground as in Egypt. The text will be recalled in which the Tree of the Underworld was said to shadow both Shamash and Tammuz.[3]

But in two subjects on the Akkadian seals Shamash the Sun God does retain his specific character. The first is his Rising (pl. XXIIIa) between the heavenly portals lifted or swung back by attendant divinities, or between the two horns of the cleft mountain, which on early seals may even appear as two bulls, or bulls that are half mountain.[4] The second scene illustrates his administration of justice; the world-wide attribution of ethical principle to one who 'might not overstep his limits', here transferred to the earthly sovereign who by ritual identity maintained the punctual procession of the seasons.[5] The offender on the seals appears to be Kingu, who imprisoned Marduk in the mountain, and Marduk is that God depicted in pl. XXIIIb, who combines in one being the history, and therefore the perpetual functions, of Sun and vegetation Gods. Thus

[1] Frankfort, *Cylinder Seals*, 1939, pl. xv, *j*, has a good example, though the cutting of this impression makes the man-lion follow the boat.

[2] *Pyramid Texts*, 1201.

[3] See above, p. 120.

[4] *Rev. d'Ass.*, xxviii, 1931, 44, no. xi; H. Frankfort, op. cit., p. 72.

[5] See A. M. Hocart's valuable treatise on Kingship, 1927, especially the chapter 'Justice and the sun'.

on the beautiful seal from Ur (pl. XXIIIc) he duplicates the gesture of Shamash before his father Ea, enthroned in his chapel formed of the rising and falling waters of the Abyss, out of which the Fish once emerged to teach wisdom to the first barbaric king. But hcre Marduk springs, not from the twin peaks of sunrise, but from between the wings which represent the split body of Tiamat, of Chaos, whom he caught in his net of ordered being, and whom the texts compare to a dove flung down.[1] Marduk's battle on the day of creation against the powers of evil[2] was, of course, eternally repeated, since Gods are not killed; his defeat and resurrection from the heart of the mountain, and the judgment on his adversary, were yearly enacted in Babylon when the king renewed on the Ziggurat both his own reign and the life of the land. Then he made a circuit of the holy enclosure, to fortify the centre of national life for another season against the forces of destruction.

EGYPT

Here the story is strangely similar. We have seen how the king gathered into his royal name the emblems rooted in the communal vitality of the various peoples of his realm, under the protection of the Falcon Horus, whose child or incarnation he became by lustration on the day of his crowning.[3] The tombs of the earliest kings of united Egypt are at Abydos, where Osiris lay in his island grave, but they were crowned at the White Wall, built to command the Delta and the Valley. The coronation rites were repeated at intervals throughout the reign, when the king was said to 'renew his births' in the ancient ceremony, familiar onwards from the primitive initiations of death and rebirth, in the presence of animal-masked priests, and of cattle within their enclosure (fig. 86, p. 173). There he wore the winding sheet of Osiris and was mourned and reanimated, the Queen participating in the ritual. Next he set up the fallen Tree-Pillar of the God, while the people enacted

---

[1] See Frankfort in *Iraq I*, i, 'Gods and Myths on Sargonid Seals,' p. 26 and note 3, quoting Ebeling, *Tod und Leben*, 36.

[2] *Epic of Creation*. Transl. by H. Zimmern, in *Zweiter Beitrag zum Babylonischen Neujahrfest*, Leipzig, 1918.

[3] A. Moret and G. Davy, *From Tribe to Empire*, 1926, pp. 134-135.

the old warfare between North and South, symbolic of the battles of Horus and Seth.[1]

There was afterwards a procession round the White Wall, in order that the king's new sanctity might enclose it within a second defensive barrier.[2] These rites were once more repeated by the royal wife and son after his actual death. In the names of Isis and of Horus they enacted the search, the setting up of the new body or image, and the restoration to life.[3] In this body and this life the Pharaoh found the road to his divine ancestors after the old totemic manner, and reached the presence of Osiris, in whom he abode to watch over his successors.

Fig. 86

In the early dynasties only the king, who personified the whole community, could obtain this salvation on behalf of all, and thus the great monuments of Egypt's creative peak were not temples but royal tombs; an aggrandisement of the superstructure which enclosed a chapel above the grave, in which offerings could be laid and other rites performed, to keep enduring contact with the living, and to protect the body in which he was still the king to the end of time. At this period, by the gigantic efforts of engineers, builders and craftsmen, the Pyramid towered always nearer to the sky, but only the Gods might mount its sloping sides.[4] The

[1] A. Moret, *The Nile*, pp. 126–134, and fig. 37.

[2] Schäfer, *Ein Bruchstück altägyptischer Annalen*, 1902 (the Palermo Stone), p. 28, no. 8, fig. 35, shows him making this circuit clad in a winding sheet and preceded by ensigns.

[3] G. Maspéro, 'Le Rituel du sacrifice funéraire' in his *Bibliothèque Egypto-logique*, vo. i, 1893, p. 289.

[4] *Pyramid Texts*, paragraph 1659.

winding road of human passage led within, for even the king could only reach the other world through death; 'as far as the centre it is necessary first to fall.'[1] It should be noted that the labyrinthine galleries of approach, so elaborate and so secret or misleading, could not have been hollowed in the earth from fear of sacrilegious intrusion, since these were centuries of immunity from foreign invasion, and no subject would destroy the talisman of continued prosperity. These passages must represent the soul's wanderings, the familiar path of 'conditional entry'. For when victory in the grave came to depend on sacred texts rather than structural strength and altitude, the records on the walls of the tombs summed up the whole religious aspiration of the age of stone. They describe the journey by water, in the barque which is itself a Goddess; the entry through the Gates of rebirth—'the two hills are divided; the God comes into being'[2]— beyond which the newly dead is suckled by the Cow-Mother,[3] and his soul, purified in the Basin of Morning receives its immortal body.[4]

In one such chart of the passage within the Pyramid—for these texts play the same part as the cruder Megalithic 'labyrinths' and the savage ground-drawings—the Pharaoh Unas is said to hunt, lasso and devour each one of the Gods in turn, thus absorbing in totemic fashion their wisdom and power. But before reaching home he must first turn the furrow of the Neolithic mysteries.[5] His final triumph over mortality is thus described:

'Behold, their soul is with Unas, their shadows are with their companions. Unas is with these, who appear, appear, appear; are hidden, hidden. The evil-doers have no power over the

---

[1] Dante, *Inferno*, xvi, 61:

> Lascio lo fele, e vo per dolci pomi
> Promessi a me per lo verace duca;
> Ma fino al centro pria convien ch'io tomi.

[2] A. M. Blackman, 'Sacramental Ideas and usages in Ancient Egypt,' *Proc. of the Soc. of Biblical Archæology*, xl (March, 1918), p. 64 (*Pyramid Texts*, paras. 2063–2066).

[3] Pyr. Ut 337 in Breasted, *Development of Religion and Thought in Ancient Egypt*, 1912, p. 149.

[4] A. Moret, op. cit., p. 182.

[5] See p. 103, note 2, for ritual ploughing by the Chinese Emperor until recent times in Pekin.

ploughing of the earth. The seat of the heart of Unas is among
the living on this earth for ever and ever.'[1]

But this ultimate expression of the faith of the Stone Age was
yet to be raised to its final dimension. After Pepi I had founded
Memphis, on the site of the White Wall—Mennefer—to perpetuate the establishment of peace between North and South,
the ritual of the king's life and death became increasingly
associated with that locality, and always influenced by the
exploring intellects of Heliopolis. In the step-pyramid of Sak-
karah the Sun's disc already appears above the sign of Seth,
the Falcon's adversary and his counterpart;[2] by the twelfth
dynasty Horus wears the Sun as his crown.[3] So the living
'Pharaoh', whose title, Per-Aa, was to signify 'the Great House',
eventually became the mortal representative of the Sun-God
Ra, and upon his exact co-operation in each day's ritual, the
accomplishment of the divine task had come to depend.

In the daily service commemorating the death and resurrection of Osiris, the masked priests impersonated the Gods,[4] and
by such rites in course of time salvation became available to
all.[5] But the perpetual creative activity of Ra could be brought
into relation with human life only by the king, who broke every
morning the seal of the shrine which had been fixed for the
nightly sojourn below the earth, and opened 'the two doors
of the sky'[6] to renew the life of the God, and therefore his
own.

By the twelfth dynasty the central point of the day's ritual
was the setting of Maat, of Truth, the beloved daughter and
counsellor of Ra, at her father's side,[7] so that the administra-

---

[1] Pyramid Text of Unas in Maspéro, *Recueil*, vol. iv (1892), pp. 61–62,
partly revised from Faulkner's later translation in *J.E.A.*, x, p. 97 ff., which
is based on Sethe's text in *Die Altägyptischen Pyramidentexte*, Sprüche, 273–4
(= paras. 393–414). The translator and others believe this hymn, and the
almost identical one found in Pepi's pyramid, to refer to a past or present
practice of cannibalism, forgetting the animal forms of the Gods.

[2] Ra's sign over Nubti (Seth of Ombos).

[3] 'From now onwards the kings call themselves Horus Ra or Ra Horus.'
(Moret, 'Le Titre d'Horus d'or,' *Rev. Arch.*, xxiv, p. 23.)

[4] A. Moret, op. cit., p. 384.

[5] A. Moret, op. cit,, pp. 252–260. 'Every man, of every condition, took
the name of "Osiris justified" on his funeral monument' (p. 256).

[6] A. Moret, op. cit., p. 389.

[7] A. Moret, op. cit., p. 391, quoting the 'Teachings for Merikara'.

tion of justice was here, as in Sumer, the king's prerogative through his assimilation with the Sun.

Long before that time, indeed, the Pyramid texts show the dead Pharaoh to have acknowledged himself as responsible to Ra for his past government,[1] before rising as Osiris to share his father's dominion. He did, therefore, eventually ascend to the summit of the mountain, by way of the labyrinth and the cave, only when he had justified, on the pattern of the Sun's righteous course, his earthly acts before the Gods. So the polished apex of the pyramid of Amenemhat III bore the royal name. On the one face was the inscription 'Amenemhat has risen from the underworld', and upon the other, 'Amenemhat eternally beholds the glory of the Sun.'[2]

THE CROWNS

This chapter must end with a word concerning the royal headgear of Sumer and Egypt, since in each case it bears a relation to the monuments. It may in fact be considered as itself a little sanctuary, being considered, like the holy stones, alive and divine. The imposition of the Crown was not the creative act of the coronation ceremonies in Egypt and elsewhere. The actual communication of divinity was effected by lustration or anointing, by means of the fertilising property of water or oil,[3] as in the case of the sacred pillar or tree of stone-worship. And indeed a thunder-stone appears beneath the king's throne in the records of this ritual, between the entwined symbolic plants of South and North.[4] Only after his rebirth as God, by the ancient and universal rites, can the magic enclosure protect his head. The lofty cone of the Double Crown (fig. 87, p. 177) is definitely shown to be the cavern-form of the Mother Goddess who shelters him when new-born in death:

'This king Pepi knows his mother, he forgets not his mother; the White Crown shining and broad . . . and the bright Red

[1] A. Moret, op. cit., p. 186. The Justification of Unas 'by his deeds', *Pyramid Texts*, paragraphs 316 ff.

[2] H. Schäfer, in *Zeitschrift f. Aegyptische Sprache*, 41 (1904), pp. 84–85.

[3] See above, p. 124.

[4] See fig. 33 in Moret, op. cit. The stone of Scone still lies (1939) beneath the coronation chair of English kings, and the whole ritual is conducted on the ancient and universal pattern. See Hocart's *Kingship*.

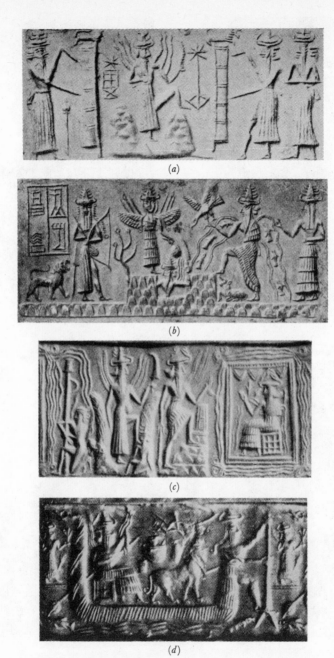

Plate 23. THE SUN GOD ON AKKADIAN SEALS

(a)

(b)

(c)

(d)

Plate 24. OLD EMPIRE. MAYA RELIEFS AND PYRAMID

Crown . . . O mother of this king Pepi, give thy breast to this king Pepi.'[1]

The crown is thus the tiny equivalent of the ascending Pyramid-tomb ('Thou art given to thy mother Nut (the sky) in her name of Sarcophagus').[2] At its base is the serpent of the Goddess; and there is even the spiral of entry, whether or not that descends from the Libyan head-feather.

So too the Sumerian horned crown, already worn by the prehistoric Mother Goddess (pl. XIc) as by later deities and kings, is shaped like a cone or peak rising from between the pair of horns, which spring as fountains of the earth's energy

Fig. 87

from its base, but are often repeated in successive zones to the summit. The crown thus resembles a Ziggurat in miniature,[3] founded upon chthonic power but pointing to the sky, and suggests the ascent of the great monument, being itself the vital summit of the divine form. In the Maltese temples also, planned like a human body, the holy of holies was, as we saw, situated in the head.[4] Only in a people intellectually awakened could the divine power be conceived as concentrated there, as the people's life was concentrated in the king; or the emblem of sovereignty be regarded as a temple of the brain. 'And they (my laws) shall be for frontlets between thine eyes. And thou shalt write them upon the doorposts of thy house, and upon thy gates.'[5]

[1] *Pyramid Texts*, 910–913 (Breasted, op. cit., p. 130).

[2] *Pyramid Texts*, paras. 609–621.

[3] See p. 101 above, for the horns on the Ziggurats.

[4] See p. 135 above, and pl. xv.

[5] Deuteronomy vi, 8. Here, too, the mental is assimilated to the architectural Gate.

CHAPTER II

PERVERSION

It may cause surprise that a description should be included here of the Neolithic and Chalcolithic civilisations of the Western hemisphere which had no part in the formation of European mentality. They are introduced because the conditions of their development, separated in the early Neolithic phase from an Asiatic past, caused them to reject certain aspects of their Palæolithic heritage which remained vital and enduring in the East. Whether or not sporadic influences from the Oriental empires, drifting across the sea, account for certain formal and intellectual resemblances in their culture, the very individual civilisations, which grew to maturity in and around Central America, are important for this investigation as a parallel evolution, already retrogressive before the arrival of the Spaniards, for lack of those particular elements.

Archæology and anthropology combine to show that the earliest tribes, other than the Eskimos, to reach America, entered the continent by the Northern land route from Siberia,[1] as totemic hunters with myths of a cave origin, organised into clans and phratries. They appear to have belonged to the Mongolian stock with an Alpine mixture, and their route seems to have covered a large area in North East Asia and North America where agriculture was never practised.[2] The migrations were probably prolonged through a vast period, extending to the era of possible reinforcements by sea, but the common Neolithic cultural inheritance, visible in their archæological remains, is sufficient to account for any Asiatic affinities acquired before they had taken root in the New World. If these included a knowledge of agriculture, they could put it to no

[1] H. J. Spinden, *The Ancient Civilisations of Mexico and Central America*, 1922, p. 47.

[2] Spinden, op. cit., p. 48.

178

use until the arid tropics were reached. Their cultivation of the wild maize, a feat which required hundreds of years for its perfection, can only, it is believed, have originated in Mexico and the surrounding regions,[1] where irrigation was necessary, exactly as in the beginnings of Egypt. In these first levels, inhabited wherever conditions were favourable to the digging of canals, clay figurines of a Mother Goddess of a curiously Asiatic aspect,[2] are everywhere to be found, their provenance extending, with stylistic modifications, right down to the earliest irrigated terraces of Peru.[3]

CITY STATES OF THE MAYA

After the specialised civilisations of this area had obliterated the prehistoric culture, the tribes on their borders retained and even developed it further into a homogeneous culture of fine craftsmanship and simple religion.[4]

Meanwhile the tilled fields spread far towards the temperate regions, where remains of pyramid mounds have been found,[5] but especially into the wet forest lands to the South. There the organisation required to keep in check the exuberance of the rich lowlands was the foundation upon which the Mayan civilisation arose. The Quiche myths of origin connected with the Jaguar, and those of the Tzental with the Serpent, suggest a double migration from the South East and South West,[6] for the Mayan Earth-Goddess wore this dual form. The presence, however, of transitional cultures on the borders of the Mayas'

---

[1] Spinden, op. cit., pp. 48–49 for the probable development of maize from the Mexican teoceutli. Thompson, in *Antiquity*, ii, p. 163, says that 2000 years would be required for its development, and remarks that no old-world plants existed on the continent till the Spanish occupation, after which they flourished exceedingly.

[2] Spinden, op. cit., p. 51, fig. 3.

[3] Spinden, op. cit., p. 54 and pl. ix.

[4] P. A. Means, *The Ancient Civilisation of the Andes*, 1931, passim; *L'Art pré-columbien*, A. Basler and E. Brummer, 1928.

[5] H. Beuchat, *Manuelle d'archéologie américaine*, 1912, chap. v, para. iii. The region of the pyramid mounds belongs chiefly to the Southern states.

[6] Beuchat, op. cit., pp. 410–412.

territory[1] points to the Atlantic seaboard as their starting point. Even if later voyagers penetrated the Westward mountain barrier, the Maya appear to have developed from native stock, and independently.

Judging by the modern Maya-speaking peoples of the region, their clans were still totemic, and were certainly exogamous. As everywhere in the New World, they were localised in divisions of four phratries, planted in families round the common land, with roads running to the cardinal points.[2] For the number four haunts this civilisation, and appears in the myths of origin of both Americas. In North and South alike, the first ancestors on emerging from the primeval cave 'stood on the hills and hurled their sling-stones to the corners of the earth'[3] to orient themselves in space. The world of Central American mythology is a cross, at whose extremities the four Bacabs support the sky, in the colours black, white, yellow and red; an allocation of colours to the cardinal points West, North, East and South, which is universal in Eastern Asia.[4]

The cities which rose so grandly above the areas of cultivation reclaimed from the forest, were religious centres of intellectual and ceremonial activity, the common dwellings being flimsy huts, which must move, with the constant shifting of tillage, to unworked soil. The builders brought with them that unique delight in the abstract properties of number of which their marvellous calendar was the result, but their mathematical explorations were only very partially extended to the monuments. They never learnt the formula for laying off a right angle; they never knew the true arch of Neolithic Asia, nor even the bonding of corners.[5]

Megaliths occur in Alaska, as on the neighbouring Asiatic coasts. They are absent down the length of North America. In

[1] Spinden, op. cit., p. 69. There are protohistoric monuments in North Guatemala (Beuchat, op. cit., p. 117).

[2] Diego de Landa, Relación de las cosas de Yucatan, 1864, p. 210.

[3] D. G. Brinton, Myths of the New World, 1868, p. 83.

[4] Brinton, op. cit., p. 80, and note 1, quoting Diego de Landa. He states that some Chinese cities, which have their gates orientated in this manner, are painted in a corresponding series of white, black, red and yellow.

[5] T. A. Joyce, Guide to the Maudslay Collection of Maya Sculptures, British Museum, 1938, p. 49, and note 1. He says that though this is true as a general statement, one or two isolated cases of bonding have been discovered.

the Southern States the foundations of pyramids and remains of chamber tombs appear to belong to the pre-Maya stratum.[1] It is possible that the Maya received a monumental tradition which they used and developed without full comprehension, because the underlying conceptions, not only intellectual, but religious also, as formulated in Asia and Northern Africa, were unknown. An earlier Megalithic substructure has been found within at least one of the pyramidal mounds of the customary stone-faced rubble.[2]

The acropolis of the Old Empire was usually a terrace or hill, upon which four Pyramids with temples on their summits, and a 'long-house' or 'palace', surrounded a central court.

All sacred buildings were raised upon an artificial platform, sometimes of great height, but were themselves of one storey, often ennobled by a pierced superstructure. The typical construction was of concrete or faced rubble, vaulted with a solid weight of concrete, usually sufficiently battened to allow a deep entablature to be utilised for sculptural embellishment of the façade. The inner chambers, roofed with a false arch, were of necessity very narrow. In early times the interior consisted of a single room, entered by a small door which allowed little light to enter. Later a second apartment was added, roofed with its own vault, and thus equally narrow and even more dark. This was the inner shrine, adorned with paintings and reliefs.[3] The waste of material involved in such a building may be seen in fig. 88, p. 182, the elevation of an early and extreme example with hollowed roof-comb from Tikal, and in fig. 89, p. 182, the plan and elevation of an exceptional three-roomed edifice from the same site. 'The impression produced from a study of the earliest Mayan architecture is that this people commenced by building caves.'[4] When the inner shrine became more elaborately protected by corridors, the outer chamber gradually developed into a portico, the façade being cut by doorways, till only pier-like sections remained; but during the Old Empire the interior kept its darkness,[5] though it might be adorned with such noble reliefs as those of Palenque or Menché (pl. XXIV*a* and

---

[1] Thompson in *Antiquity*, ii, p. 165.

[2] T. A. Joyce in *British Museum Quarterly*, vol. i (1926–1927), p. 61 ff. Excavations at Lubaantum.

[3] Spinden, op. cit., p. 74.   [4] Joyce, op. cit., p. 51.

[5] Thompson, op. cit., p. 164, quoting Spinden, *Mayan Art*.

b). The cave, by some strange distortion, is carried to the mountain-top.

For the quadrilateral, stepped Pyramid (pl. XXVI*a*) was not, as in Egypt, a self-sufficient structure, but like the Ziggurat the support or pedestal of a shrine (pl. XXIV*d*). The huge stairways, however, of typical Central American Pyramids were no pathways winding through a number of stages or planes to prepare the climber for communion with the God,

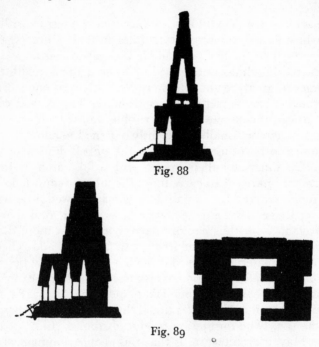

Fig. 88

Fig. 89

but brought him directly to the summit, from which in the later, degenerate days the body of the human victim was hurled. Here no labyrinth led to the divine threshold—an important divergence from developed Stone Age ritual, which is part of the deep cleavage between the service of the Central American powers of Nature, in whose honour the structurally insecure but marvellously embellished temples were shaped with stone tools, and of those divinities whose progress has been indicated in the previous chapters.

Since the pre-Columbian peoples of North and Central America never learned to domesticate animals, all those undertones of the pastures and the sheepfold were lacking, by which the Oriental peoples had united the protective aspect of the Mother Goddess with the deeply-remembered service of the hunted beasts. As to her function of fruitful Tree, the exuberance of vegetation was here a menace to be kept in check by united and unremitting toil for the salvation of the Maize-God. Therefore the Goddess whose image they had borne with them out of Asia kept only her voracious form, and in the great sculptures of the first Mayan civilisation, she is seen as Night or Death, and the sacrificial Altar. Because the Maya were divorced from their Palæolithic heritage, for all their cave-temples and clan emblems, the Neolithic preoccupation with recurrence and duality became the focus of their creative imagination. Their greatest achievements were made in its praise. None of the Gods of the Old Empire reached a human personality. Though partly animal by totemic assimilation, they appear to modern minds as natural energies held prisoner in time and space, engaged in ceaseless warfare to maintain their stations in equilibrium against the horror of infinity. Their expression, in an art of unsurpassed splendour, is formal and abstract, its elemental dynamism weakened neither by organic human synthesis (even where it is compound), nor by human thought and emotion.

The stone-wrought monoliths of Copan and Quiriguá are believed on the evidence of their inscribed signs and of later documents, to represent divisions of time, and to have been set up in the central square to mark the culmination of a cycle.[1] On the face of each, an anthropomorphic embodiment or ruler of the temporal period bears the ceremonial bar, sometimes in the form of a dragon with a head at either end, holding the sky in its jaws; sometimes rigid, and spaced with the glyphs of the heavenly bodies (pl. XXVc). The two-headed serpent is the Earth-Goddess herself, and for a time at Quiriguá the human

[1] Joyce, op. cit., p. 35: 'A survey of the monuments elicits the fact that whatever the chronological starting point of the inscription, the terminal date, in an overwhelming majority of cases, records the termination of a full Katun, the half of a Katun, or the quarter of a Katun. Now the Books of Chilan Balam show that it was the practice of the Maya of Yucatan to commemorate the passing of the Katun by the setting up of a "stone".' Andrae describes, in the central square of Assur, stelæ which appear to commemorate time periods. (W. Andrae, *Das Wiedererstandene Assur*, 1938, p. 103, and pl. 46.)

stelæ were replaced by animal monoliths (pl. XXV*a*), the huge stones being carved into the convolutions of this serpent, which bore the emblem of the young Maize-God within its coils. The monstrous heads, within whose jaws the sky or sun is seated, may portray the jaguar of the second totemic epiphany of the Goddess.[1] It is the ceremonial bar come to life. If the skull, embellished by solar emblems, at the rear of the monument, indeed represents the underworld sojourn of the Night Sun[2] already familiar in Egypt and Sumer, it is very significant that time should thus be recorded both in positive and negative rhythm; that Earth should triumph in her stability, as a writhing monster whose duality roots her to the dark. The serpent's convolutions indeed underlie the luxuriant yet strictly formal structure of all pictorial art among the Maya, not yet frozen into the cruel angularity by which their successors hid the terror of vacancy. For there may be noticed in these examples, and in pl. XXIV*a* and *b*, belonging to the same early period, a strangely Asiatic blending of calm simplicity in the human figures, with elaborate movement of the accessories, in a play of curves afterwards lost. This is again evident in the noble reliefs representing ceremonies (pl. XXIV*b* and *c*), where the inhuman composure of the priestly faces, and the abject mortification of the postulants, made terrible, in contrast with the early time-symbols, by the distortion of nose and lip, and the deformation of the brow intended to check their intellectual pride,[3] are surmounted and enclosed by the almost visible movement of the feathered head-dresses which express, even in the loss of the original hues, a vibration of colour and light comparable only with that evoked by flame and cloud round the holy persons of Far Eastern art[4] (pl. XXV*b*).

There was, however, another serpent whose undulations did not return on themselves, a serpent who developed the power not only to proceed but even to ascend, because his scales

---

[1] See above, p. 179.   [2] Joyce, op. cit., p. 36.

[3] This is given as the reason for the deformation of Inca foreheads by S. E. McMillin in the *National Geographical Magazine*, vol. li, no. 2, p. 256.

[4] The style of this early and greatest period of Mayan sculpture shows so many similarities with that of Eastern Asia, that it is difficult to believe that there was no intercourse. This would not of course detract from the striking individuality of the Mayan achievement, the expression of an original civilisation.

evolved into plumes; who already appears in the Old Empire upon door-lintels, or above the arched canopies of thrones.[1] In at least two cities of the later Mayan florescence he was actually to be represented by a tower with spiral stairway,[2] and at the last took over the function of the temple pillars (pl. XXVI*c*), but there his posture is once more head downward.

This was after the various sacred cities, at the height of their architectural exuberance, had been almost simultaneously abandoned to the forest for an unknown cause. There was a weak political revival in Yucatan,[3] soon reinforced by the powerful influence of Toltec tribes who had in like manner deserted their capital in Mexico.[4] These have left a record of their own religious decline, which combines with the concrete symbolism of the new and truly monumental architecture,[5] to suggest the reason why the Maya, the Athenians of the New World whom the Spaniards found already degenerate, did not, like Athens, achieve a spiritual victory over their conquerors.

MEXICO

Toltec remains have been discovered in Mexico immediately above the habitation levels of that primitive population[6] which made images of the Mother Goddess, and produced competent potters, practised agriculture, and perhaps raised pyramids. But the Toltecs before their arrival were in contact with the cultural ancestors of the Maya, for they brought with them a knowledge of the calendar, of hieroglyphic script, and of monumental building.[7] They had early acquaintance with metals, whose common use they appear to have introduced to the

---

[1] Spinden, op. cit., p. 86.

[2] The Round Tower or Caracol of Chichen Itza (Beuchat, op. cit., fig. 142, after E. Seler, *Quetzalcoatl-Kukulcan in Yukatan*). Landa mentions another at Mayapan.

[3] The League of Mayapan.   [4] See below, p. 187.

[5] Splendidly revealed by the excavation of Chichen Itza.

[6] In the stratified remains of Atzcapotzalco. See Spinden, op. cit., p. 44, and fig. 11.

[7] 'Toltec motives owe an obvious debt to the Mayan.' Spinden, op. cit., Beuchat, op. cit., p. 258.

Mayan New Empire,[1] together with their very formal, angular
and concrete, artistic style, their accomplished stone construction, and the general practice of human sacrifice. This rite was
not unknown to the Maya,[2] nor in fact to any of the pre-
Columbian peoples, but their carved and painted ceremonial
scenes show it to have been exceptional in the Old Empire, the
necessary offering of blood being represented by such mortifica-
tions as the passing through the tongue of a cord set with thorns
(pl. XXIV*c*). But now even the ball-game, whose courts were
erected in the new capital of Chichen Itza and elsewhere, is
shown on the magnificent sculptured frieze of pl. XXVI*d* as a
fertility rite, with death as the penalty of the vanquished. Here
the blood of the decapitated leader of the losing team springs
from his shoulders in the form of seven serpents before the skull-
head of the devouring Earth.

The Mexican ceremonies were of the familiar Chalcolithic
type, instituted to assist the seasonal functions of the natural
powers,[3] and it is reasonable to suppose that among the Maya,
so preoccupied with time, such rites had become an obsession,
and indeed the principal activity of the cities which overlooked
the cultivated plains. They were now independent of the
hunted beasts, and had no domestic animals for surrogates, and
the pitiless abstraction of their deities as types of natural
energy, precluded the self-identification of reciprocity. Nevertheless, they felt these powers as an overwhelming reality, and
were so far ennobled. The history of the northern rites shows
the human victims, at least before the institution of the mass-
sacrifice of war prisoners, to have been endowed with the attributes of the God.[4] The ritual was thus religious still, even the
loathsome investiture of human skin, and the cannibal feast
that followed, being descended from the totemic animal mim-
ing, and communal meal, of the Palæolithic hunting rites. But
when in the last centuries of degradation, amid the architectural
memorials of their vital days, the Gods became insatiable
monsters, to be propitiated by an unending banquet of human
hearts, only obtainable through ceaseless warfare, here was no
offering of 'himself to himself', no act of creation, but within

[1] Thompson in *Antiquity*, ii, op. cit., p. 195.
[2] It is represented, for instance, in the *Codex Tro-Cortesianus*.
[3] J. G. Frazer, *The Golden Bough*, abridged edition, 1923, p. 28.
[4] Frazer, op. cit., p. 587, quoting Acosta and Sahagun.

the framework of the ancient ritual, its purpose was bribery for a given end; it was magic, as the written chronicle has recorded.

The Toltecs had brought with them into Mexico their bird-snake ancestor whom the Maya knew, here identified with the bearded and white-skinned ruler Quetzalcoatl, who was said to have taught them civilisation, and may have been an actual teacher from across the sea. After his return to the ocean their capital Tula or Tollan became, on their own evidence, a prey to evil magic. 'The demons arrived', and in their wake, war, despotism, and the sacrifice of the nobility. After this 'the skin of slain warriors came to be worn'. Their assertion that the city which they abandoned, after their last king had disappeared, like his ancestor, into the sea, was destroyed by magic,[1] has therefore some foundation.

The deserted capital was later occupied by the Nahuan Chichimecs, who after leaving their primeval 'Seven Caves' had been joined by the Aztecs, bearing their clan ensigns from 'Aztlan'.[2]

The Chichimecs, according to their own traditions, were still cave dwellers when they arrived in Mexico, and had no knowledge of agriculture.[3] The focus of their religious life was a cavern in which a transparent stone was worshipped as the 'heart of the people',[4] but they must have acquired the hieratic civilisation of their predecessors, for at Cholula 'the place of flight of the Toltecs' they erected the Pyramid-temple of Quetzalcoatl, whom they too called their founder; and there the sacrifices to Tezkat (who among the Maya was the stormy sky), must have kept them continually in search of prisoners.

Finally the Aztecs left Tollan to found their empire a few centuries before the appearance of the Spaniards, who saw them settled in towns by phratries oriented to the four quarters like the Maya; living as a military democracy with land in common; nobility being acquired by religious discipline within the

[1] Spinden, op. cit., p. 155, from the *Annals of Quauhtitlan*.

[2] Beuchat, op. cit., pp. 263–264 (and fig. 96), quoting E. Seler, 'Wo lag Aztlan, die Heimath der Azteken?' *S.G.A.*, vol ii, pp. 31–48.

[3] Beuchat, op. cit., p. 271, quoting Ixtlilxochitl, *History of the Chichimecs*, chap. iv.

[4] Donald Mackenzie, *Myths of Pre-Columbian America*, p. 265, quoting Burgoa.

temple enclosures.[1] Such primitive totems as survived seem to have been individual possessions,[2] and therefore of the nature of fetishes. They had the symbolism of numbers of colours and spatial relations common to the peoples of the Western hemisphere, and seem to have shared the Mayan pre-occupation with time-cycles. Their most important divinities were the War God, yearly glutted with thousands of prisoners fattened in cages; the God of the Summer Sun, yearly renewing his vitality with the still-beating heart of his young human impersonator; Tlaloc, the Rain-God of fertility, whose weeping eye was reproduced in the tears of his child victims;[3] and lastly Quetzalcoatl, who is said to have forbidden human sacrifice in his own temple, and was worshipped here as patron of art and knowledge.

The Earth Goddess of Mexico was far more ferocious than her Mayan counterpart. Pl. XXVI*b* well shows the double dragon set in place of a head, the garland of severed hands and hearts, the death's head girdle, and the talons of a bird of prey. Her name was Eagle-Woman, and apart from her own terrible ritual, the altar upon which the human hearts were offered to the other Gods was called the Eagle Bowl.[4]

The many-breasted Mother in the Agave bush was only a minor deity.[5]

Apart from the mass-oblations to the increasingly hungry War-God, and the sacrifice of criminals, the sanctified, perhaps willing, victims of the other Aztec ceremonies went as Gods to the Gods,[6] and so far the inner meaning of Stone Age sacrifice was retained. The rest of the people, except for warriors killed in battle and women dead in childbirth,[7] crossed the ninefold river of death, to those caverns of the underworld from which

[1] Beuchat, op. cit., pp. 309–310, quoting Sahagun's *Nueva España*, pp. 197, 211, etc.

[2] Brinton, *Nagualism*, 1892. Beuchat, op. cit., pp. 313–314.

[3] See Joyce, 'The Weeping God' in *Esssays presented to Sir William Ridgeway*.

[4] Beuchat, op. cit., p. 320. She was apparently an ancient divinity of the Chichimecs.

[5] Beuchat, op. cit., p. 328.

[6] Frazer, op. cit., p. 589.

[7] Sahagun, op. cit., I, iii. The people had a temporary heaven with Tlaloc the Rain God, just like the Hindus' sojourn in Indra's heaven.

the race had first emerged,[1] wearing between their teeth green gems which were thought to hold the seeds of life, because, they said, all men had come from stones and must return to stones.[2]

But even in Mexico one emperor is said to have erected a temple of nine storeys, to represent the nine heavens (perhaps for him equivalent to the ninefold winding of Death's river), to the 'Lord of Duality', the 'Cause of All', a temple which was never to hold an image, nor be polluted with blood.[3] The other Gods remained insatiable, and perhaps it was well that the Spaniards came.

PERU

In the Southern continent there is evidence of the same racial and cultural substratum overlaid by a conquering civilisation, but possibly because there was no break there with Stone Age religious conceptions, since the indigenous inhabitants of the Peruvian empire had already reached or received an advanced Megalithic culture which the Incas did not wholly destroy, there is observable in the acts of daily life a sense of human happiness, a less burdensome preoccupation with religion. The conquerors were intellectually far less brilliantly endowed than the corresponding civilisations to the North. Compared with the Maya priesthood, the Incas were backward in astronomy, never acquired a written script, and left no sculpture in the grand style. Their magnificent architecture, founded on the solid achievements of their Megalithic predecessors,[4] was chiefly noteworthy for its scale and technical perfection. But their religious government, like that of Egypt in the Pyramid Age, which it so strangely resembles, must be counted a success. As in Egypt it gave scope for a steady and natural adaptation of Stone Age ideas to enlarged political conceptions, the more interesting by contrast with the restless history of the city states of Central America.

[1] Brinton, op. cit., pp. 248–249. The ninefold Styx of the Greeks will be remembered. Here is once more the spiral of entry between the worlds.

[2] Garcia, Or de los Indios, iv, 26, quoted by Brinton.

[3] Ixtlilxochitl is the authority who tells this of Nezahuatl of Tezcuco.

[4] Means, The Ancient Civilisation of the Andes, p. 524 ff.

There is striking evidence here, in all strata of the population, of totemic descent. Contemporary historians agree that the animal emblems of the conquered clans were no mere blazons. They report that these people refused to flee from a dangerous beast which embodied their totem, preferring to die rather than to put up a defence.[1] Several authors also record a belief that the edible beasts voluntarily offered themselves. The Sun worshipped by the victorious Incas was their totemic ancestor,[2] imposed upon the subordinate tribes, who preserved their own totemic names, and wore their ceremonial gear, at the state festivals held in the sacred capital of Cuzco.[3] Their masked dances form the subject of many vase paintings.[4] In the mountains they set up cairns for the worship of the Earth Goddess;[5] near the coast they had a sea-mother, and fish totems; erected pyramids, and mummified the dead. The Aymará of Bolivia said that the Creator raised up the peoples of that region, making each of clay endowed with soul, and ordered them to pass under the earth. Thus each nation emerged in the place ordained. The first-born from that spot was turned to stone. The lineal ancestors were changed to falcons, condors, or other animals or birds.[6] In one village a stone falcon was discovered, surrounded by four human mummies, who were called his sons, and the ancestors of that clan.[7]

It is in this region that the great Megalithic works remain, the first standing stones South of Alaska. It does appear exceedingly probable, therefore, that seafarers brought from the East the technical knowledge and underlying religious ideas of monolithic construction, though, since the dispositions are so simple, the possibility of a parallel discovery and development cannot be overlooked. Yet here are the menhirs, the dolmens with holed stones, the covered passage-ways, the 'labyrinths'

[1] Garcilasso de la Vega, *Commentarios Reales del Inca*, part 1, book i, chap. ix

[2] Beuchat, op. cit., pp. 604, 612 and 615. Also 615, note 1, where he quotes Cieza de Leon's assertion that their blazon was the rainbow, which was painted on the temple wall at Cuzco. This he considers a subordinate totem.

[3] Joyce, in *Man*, 1913. No. 65. The clan ancestor in animal form in Peru.

[4] Joyce, op. cit.

[5] Garcilasso, op. cit., part i, book i, chap x; Beuchat, op. cit., p. 612.

[6] Joyce, in *Man*, 1913, op.cit.

[7] Joyce, op. cit.

connected with tombs, and the concentric stone circles and alignments of the Old World, together with the huge rubble pyramidal foundations and sculptured monoliths characteristic of the Western hemisphere.

The noble monolithic Gateway, of dressed and sculptured stone, at Tiahuanacu (pl. XXVI*e*) was the Eastward entrance to a raised structure of upright menhirs, which may once have borne lintels, approached by a five-fold avenue, and a stairway flanked by two pillars.[1] The scene above the extant doorway probably represents Viracocha, the Creator and Storm God (who was 'ancestor' of the old population),[2] as the still centre towards which three ranks of winged figures, bearing similar rayed crowns and sceptres, speed from either side. The upper and lower rows are human-headed; the midmost wears the Condor's head and claws. The God's rays end in heads of the Jaguar, the totemic beast associated by the Maya with their Earth Goddess; the Condor being a Southern totem which bore the sun across the sky. The conflict between jaguar and condor depicted upon contemporary pottery of the region is said to symbolise the opposition of day and night.[3] The gateway, then, is intended to connect earth and sky, in the manner of the ceremonial bar and time-monoliths of Copan and Quirigua, and forms a wonderful illustration of Megalithic architectural symbolism.

The regularity of the masonry of this last period was preserved with copper clamps;[4] its perfection being due to a meticulous care for constructive detail. The long lines of the great Megalithic defence walls were imitated in the polygonal style of the Incas, a stage towards their unique achievement, 'the regular, austere and beautiful course-ashlar masonry of the latest reigns.'[5] It is possible that the Inca clan itself came from these people of the highlands, for its members spoke a language that was not Quichua and may have been Aymará,[6] and its hero-founder, the human ancestor of its kings, was said to have

---

[1] C. Wiener, *Pérou et Bolivie*, p. 428.

[2] Means, op. cit., pp. 130–132.

[3] *National Geographical Magazine*, Washington, vol. li, no. 2, p. 236.

[4] Means, op. cit., fig. 219, at Pumapuncu.

[5] Means, op. cit., p. 531.

[6] Beuchat, op. cit., p. 589, quoting Middendorf: *Die Sprachen Perus*, vol. iv, introduction.

emerged, with his sister, from Lake Titicaca on the Bolivian boundary.[1] In any case the ruling clan drew something more than architectural conceptions from the hill people, and it was this perhaps which gave their government its solidity. Nevertheless there could never have been the religious unity of the early dynasties in Egypt. The Inca sovereign was called 'Lord of the Four Quarters', but he did not bear among his titles the totemic ensigns of the early inhabitants.[2] The Sun-totem was forcibly set above these emblems and remained the prerogative of its direct descendants. Thus the Inca, as its child and incarnation, could not draw into himself the life of the totality of his subjects, but only of the double clan which inhabited the sacred capital.[3] As in Egypt four thousand years before, the Sun's animal embodiment was the falcon, and his royal descendants were endogamous from the need to protect the purity of their blood: the Sun quality, which the Inca received, together with the double feather, from the High Priest (his near relative) on his coronation.[4] None but he could pronounce the Sun's name, and none could approach himself without a symbolic offering. His words, as in Egypt, were acts of creation.[5]

He was considered not to die. The Sun called him to sleep. His funeral rites, like the Pharaoh's, were of the first importance to the whole empire, and his sepulchre was prepared during life. He alone returned to the Sun; his clan-kinsmen passed to the sky, and the rest of his subjects to the underworld.[6]

His mummy remained but a short time in the rock-cut tomb, and during that period the Queen, who personified the moon as sun's sister and spouse,[7] was immured with her handmaidens in an adjacent cave-chamber, being first made unconscious with drugs. When the Inca's mummy was borne to the Temple of the Sun, to be enthroned for ever with his predecessors before the golden image of the God, the Queen's body was embalmed, and placed in the adjoining chapel of

[1] Garcilasso, op. cit., bk. ii, p. 9; Beuchat, op. cit., p. 588.

[2] See p. 115 above.

[3] Beuchat, op. cit., pp. 603–604, quoting Garcilasso de la Vega.

[4] Balboa, *Hist. du Pérou*, chap. xiv.

[5] Garcilasso, op. cit., part i, book ii, chap. xix.

[6] Garcilasso, op. cit., book ii, chap. viii.

[7] Brehm, *Das Inka-Reich*, p. 121.

(a)   (b)

(c)

Plate 25. MAYA SCULPTURE OF THE OLD EMPIRE

Plate 26. NEW EMPIRE, MEXICO AND BOLIVIA

the moon.[1] Like the dead Pharaoh's, their immortality protected the land.[2]

The Inca's heir was always the son of his eldest sister, a conservation of primitive custom which was also commemorated in his annual leadership of the ritual hunt, in which the whole people took part, and afterwards consumed certain of the slain beasts.[3] This was contrary to the practice followed in the ceremony of animal sacrifice, when statue or pillar was anointed with blood after the Neolithic fashion.[4] The victims were commonly birds, but each morning a male llama was offered to the Sun. At the state festivals bloodless oblations were also customary, including the obligatory gift of first fruits.[5]

There was occasional human sacrifice. At the Inca's coronation, and at two or three seasonal celebrations, two children were immolated. Certain conquered peoples also paid tribute of their youth for this purpose, the victims being robed and drugged, and a passport fastened to their shoulders for reception among the Gods.[6] Compared with the ferocity of Mexican practice, all this was sufficiently humane.

At the greatest of the yearly ceremonies, adolescents were initiated into the Inca clan. Their ears were pierced for the familiar blood-offering, they ran races to the stone which represented the first ancestor, received their ensign and their totemic name, and finally partook, at the hands of the Inca[7] himself, of the communal bread baked by the Virgins of the Sun. These maidens were chosen in childhood from each class of the population, in order to tend in isolation the flame from which the ceremonial fires were lit, to bake this bread, and to weave the royal robes.[8] As in the case of the Roman vestals whom they so closely resemble, the people's welfare and the land's fertility were thought to depend on their chastity, violation of which

---

[1] Cieza de Leon, *Segunda parte de la Crónica del Peru*, chap. xxii.

[2] As presumably did the Queen's in the similar rites for the fertility of the kingdom at Ur and the Granada cave, pp. 105, 106 above.

[3] Beuchat, op. cit., p. 624.

[4] Velasco, *Historia del Reino de Quito*, book i, p. 133. This anointing of the pillar with the blood of the victim is a rite of Plato's Atlantis.

[5] Garcilasso and others, quoted by Beuchat, op. cit., p. 624.

[6] Cieza de Leon, op. cit., chap. xxviii.

[7] At the Festival of Capac Raymi. Garcilasso, op. cit., vii, 6.

[8] Garcilasso, op. cit., part i, book iv.

received the Roman penalty of living burial. They thus appear to impersonate the Mother Goddess of the Hearth, for in Peru the divinity of Earth is Pacha Mama,[1] the Mother of all life.

This deity also bears the following significant resemblance to the universal Goddess in the Stone Age of the old world:

When, after prolonged struggle, the religion of the ruling caste had been securely established, the Inca sovereigns incorporated into their sun worship Viracocha, the creator-God of their predecessors,[2] whom the 'giants from over the sea' had taught to build the Megalithic monuments. A temple for bloodless rites, and without an image, was raised in his honour. One emperor even speaks of Viracocha as the Supreme Being by whose command the ancestral sun performs his daily circuit,[3] and, in the single diagram that has survived of the Sun-Temple at Cuzco,[4] the central image is labelled Viracocha, with statues of the sun and moon to right and left. Above them is a cross of stars called 'the band of male animals', and below them the ladder, or litter, of the dead. But in this central shrine of the state religion in its final form, the female llama is placed among the heavenly bodies, as the Mother-Cow of Egypt is spangled with stars. This llama is elsewhere represented with her lamb.[5]

In the Peruvian synthesis of the religious evolution of the stone-builders with that of the hunting and pastoral clans, the dualistic complexity of the North is wholly absent, since totems, nature spirits, and unhewn stones, were all subordinated to a sovereign hierarchy. One submerged God appears to have risen, like the conquered divinities of prehistoric Greece, to spiritualise the state religion without destroying its coherence. In general the civilisation of the Incas seems much closer than those of Mexico and the central isthmus, to the cultures which produced Europe, and their records repeat the recurrent Western

---

[1] Balboa, *Hist. du Pérou*, ed. Ternaux Compans, p. 58; Garcilasso de la Vega, *Com. Real.*, part i, bk. ii, chap. v.

[2] Balboa, op. cit., p. 62.

[3] Acosta, *Hist. of the New World*, book v, chap. iv; book vi, chap. xix, Eng. Trans., 1704.

[4] Means, op. cit., fig. 168 (drawn by the Indian chronicler Santa Cruz, with additions by Father de Avila. After Lehmann Nitsche), and pp. 394–402.

[5] Means, op. cit., p. 399 and note. He quotes Father Cobo as saying that she should be accompanied by a llama lamb, accidentally omitted from the Santa-Cruz drawing.

legends of laws imported by a bearded teacher from across the sea. Yet Peru had no Osiris, through whose suffering an individual might receive salvation; reciprocity was expressed in the Emperor's person alone, and beyond the royal clan his totemic relationship was artificially imposed.

CHAPTER III

REVOLUTION

A point is reached, in the mutual development of God's image and the human soul, when the task of maintaining the equilibrium of seasonal recurrence, and the growth and renewal of man and beast, is no longer considered to depend upon the mutual effort of ritual; when the conception of deity becomes sufficiently detached to permit a corresponding individuality in a people regarded as a single being, and finally in every member of that people, for whom its solidarity is intact. As a result of this separation of the divine idea from its natural and animal affinities, the means of contact gradually becomes ethical.

The history of Asia is full of revolts against the Stone Age conception of unity, attained through embodiment in ritual, as an end in itself. India, Persia, China and Arabia, each created great and permanent religious systems dependent upon righteousness; but these had no direct part in the formation of European mentality. In the line of our inheritance itself, certain hymns of Egypt and Sumer reveal a sense of sin, of humility, a desire for service which is not merely ceremonial, and even a belief that right-doing is better than sacrifice, expressed almost in the words of the Hebrew prophets.[1] But in Palestine alone may be followed the history of a nation devoted from its beginning to a single purpose, to which it returns, after every variety of religious and political schism, to maintain intact, by faith and conduct, a direct relationship with its God.

The defenceless isolation entailed in the traditional flight of Abraham's clan from the sophisticated civilisation of Ur into the simplicity of pastoral nomadism, made cohesion a

---

[1] 'More acceptable in the sight of Ra is the nature of one just of heart, than the ox of one that doeth iniquity.' Alan Gardiner, New literary works from Ancient Egypt, *Journal of Egyptian Archæology*, i, 34 (Pap. Petersburg, p. 116).

prime necessity. Under such conditions the spiritual ancestor, who like the unifying divinity of all primitive human groups was both immanent and transcendent, had lost all animal attributes, and the communion at the unhewn altar of stone, with the ritual which the wanderers found established in the Canaan of Genesis, was well suited to their pure monotheism. There was as yet no danger from the seductions of alien Gods, but already the sense of destiny kept the clan apart, and drove them across the distant Euphrates, to seek their wives in that branch of the family that had halted halfway.[1] The first covenant[2] between Abraham and his God, extended this coherence to the posterity of the race—within which kinship was never to be a solely physical tie—binding them together through time, with the intensity of all primeval human groups who could find power only in union. Thus, although vestiges of totemism were later held in horror, as a barbarity which this conservative nation had never experienced, the half-religious, half-social cohesion, characteristic of the earliest known communities, was retained throughout the whole history of Israel, and became in fact the cause of its survival.

The second period of wandering in the naked wilderness, this time as fugitives from the mature civilisation of Egypt, was sufficiently prolonged to awaken a national character; to separate the people, now grouped into tribes, from this world in which they felt too much at home, and to narrow and intensify their religious life by forcing it upwards. Here, as the books relate, they developed the image of their solitary, dynamic God as a moral being, to be approached through the medium of the Law, whose inscribed stones were the token of his presence among them. In the records he is still the angry, generous, revengeful, compassionate spirit of the desert tribes. Treachery and violence are often overlooked, often indeed commanded, but disobedience is never forgiven, nor ritual omissions, nor the worship of neighbouring Gods, for these were sins against the essential bond by which alone the spiritual strength of Israel could grow.

The conquering tribesmen entered a Canaan now filled with

---

[1] So Abraham sent his servant to Harran, to bring back a wife for Isaac, 'from his own country', and Isaac charged Jacob to go to Padan-aram to find in his grandfather's house a wife from among his cousins.

[2] Genesis, xv.

intelligent and warlike races, who remained dangerous even in defeat, since most of them worshipped the Goddess of Western Asia, and her spouse the fertility God. Apart from the sensuality of its Syrian form, in regard to which the evidence of history and archæology partly justifies the denunciations of the prophets, and the occasional sacrifice of offspring which seems to have offered a widespread temptation at moments of national crisis, this religion was full of the emotionalism to which Semites easily responded. Henceforth the children of Israel were continually turning to the comfortable sacraments of earth's fertility, to the images of the beasts, to the consolation of the dying God, and the bounteous and pitiful Queen of Heaven.[1] For them, however, all luxury of feeling must become one-pointed, the vehicle of prophetic creation in their leaders, who drew upon the spirit of the race, and were therefore so far above its individual members, that it required the destitution of defeat, the political desert in which they saw themselves no longer a nation, before the spiritual bond could be extended to each one, in the final covenant where even ritual became meaningless: 'After those days . . . I will put my law in their inward parts, and write it in their hearts.'[2]

The visual arts had no place in a culture whose origins were pastoral. They were in fact to this people, as to the Arabs of Islam, an abomination arrogating the creative prerogative of God, since, as we saw, the form evoked the soul. So their monuments were not constructed with builder's tools. Their first and most characteristic sanctuary was a booth, hung round with curtains and skins—however splendid its interior furnishing—a glorified tent of the nomad,[3] and the erection of their temple, the centre of national life, was entrusted to foreign craftsmen.[4] No excavations have thrown any new light on their religion, but the poverty of native archæological remains is not solely due to the fact that their small strip of land was a highway for the passage of so many armies between Asia and Africa. With no racial totemic past, they did not imagine the archetypal form which sanctified artistic expression. Thus all

---

[1] For example, see p. 284 below (Ezekiel's vision).

[2] Jeremiah, xxxi, 33.   [3] Exodus, xxxv, xxxvi.

[4] I Kings, vii, 13 ff. The craftsman Hiram, who here replaces the king Hiram, is given a mother out of Naphtali. (In II Chronicles, ii, 14, out of Dan).

their faculty of formal creation was drawn into poetry, giving it a strength which was to carry it perpetually to men's lips, even through the medium of alien tongues, and the complexity of a partly antithetic civilisation.

To these records we must therefore turn, to discover more specifically what lay rooted in the primary religion, and what was the nature of Israel's revolt.

PATRIARCHAL

After the remnants of Sumerian tradition have vanished from the Biblical narrative with the Deluge,[1] we are at once swept into the simplicity of pastoral nomadism, with its sanctities of the family, of the tent-door, and of the symbolic relations of man with ram and ewe. The founder of the race, separating his immediate dependents from the remnant of his kindred who have travelled with him from Ur, is led by a vision to the Syrian hills.[2] As in most primitive foundation legends, he is in direct communion with the spiritual Father of the clan, and the tree sanctuaries of this land are accepted as natural points of contact where converse may be established, the local nature divinities being messengers of the parental word. The incoming clan, in fact, finds itself at home in a Stone Age environment.[3] It is more strange to discover the groups of two and three such manifestations, representing Abraham's one God, though these combinations, as we saw,[4] are characteristic of the region. Thus the three angels, who stand beneath the oak of Mamre to prophesy the birth of Isaac, are referred to sometimes in the singular, and at other times in the plural.[5] On departing, they turn towards Sodom, so that it appears to be the same messengers, now two in number, who rescue Lot from the doomed city.[6] Here the same change of pronoun takes place, but more

[1] The founding of the cities of Shinar and dispersal from Babel are set within the lists of Noah's descendants.

[2] Genesis, xii, 1–7.

[3] The writer of Genesis, that is to say, describes an earlier cultural stratum than his own.

[4] P. 126 above.   [5] Genesis, xviii, 1–21.

[6] Genesis, xix. Now two, because one stayed behind while Abraham pleaded for Sodom, xviii, 22–23.

explicitly, the plural being used when in the character of men they arrive to resist the Sodomites, the singular when they have brought Lot's family into the hills.[1]

Another form of sanctuary, later to be held in so much horror, is here a natural setting for worship: 'And Abraham planted a grove in Beersheba, and called there on the name of the Lord.'[2]

The stone altar, which he raises at spots where God has appeared,[3] would seem to be anointed with oil in the ancient fashion, for animal sacrifice is never recorded, excepting the ram-surrogate of Isaac, a burnt offering which takes us beyond the Stone Age, perhaps to the Phœnician coast—yet that ram too is caught in a tree.

The colourless personality of Isaac throws no light on contemporary beliefs, but the third generation sees the pillar-cult firmly established. When he too is a fugitive from home, Jacob receives his vocation in a dream upon a stone pillow, like those previously described;[4] he sets up that pillow as an altar, anointing it with oil to consecrate the spot for perpetuity, and calling it the House of God. It is also the Ladder by which he perceives the angels passing to and fro, already the Bond between earth and sky.[5] Rebekah's nurse was later buried there, beneath the oak which stood beside it in Megalithic contiguity,[6] after Jacob had deposited, in the earth below another oak, the small household images brought, with no sense of sin, out of Harran.[7]

For the covenant made with Laban on the homeward journey Jacob set up a pillar and a cairn as permanent habitations of the divinity invoked by their vows, which were confirmed by a communal meal partaken upon the stones.[8]

The pillar-altar of Bethel, at which the future race may be said to have been born, haunted Jacob's long and sorrowful life. In extreme old age, dying in the midst of a strange civilisation, he refers to the divine appearance at Luz, before bestowing, upon the twelve sons who are to be ancestors of the tribes, their emblematic names; names which are partly animal, like

---

[1] Especially xix, 17. And it came to pass, when *they* had brought them forth, that *he* said—

[2] Genesis, xxi, 33. [3] For example, Genesis, xii, 7.

[4] P. 153 above. [5] Genesis, xxvii, 12. Compare also pp. 154, 169.

[6] Genesis, xxxv, 7, 28. [7] Genesis, xxxv, 4. [8] Genesis, xxxi, 44–54.

clan ensigns. Only Joseph's life and fate are differently named.[1]
He is 'the fruitful bough' ('from thence is the shepherd, the
stone of Israel'), who receives not only the blessings of heaven
above, but 'blessings of the deep that lieth under, blessings of
the breasts and of the womb'[2]—words whose chthonic echoes
appear less strange when his history is remembered, which
shows him as a type of the Dying God of the Pastoral ritual,
child of Rachel the Ewe-Mother,[3] who 'was separate from his
brethren',[4] who in adolescence had gone down into the pit,
'the heart of the mountain', while his brothers displayed the
torn many-coloured robe of his feigned dismemberment; who,
brought to light after a second incarceration, was recognised as
bestower of corn in god-like bounty and wisdom.

Such a pattern suggests the weaving together of an underlying cult of the pastures—further implied by such a phrase as
'the Ashtaroth of the sheep'[5]—with new agricultural rites,
perhaps learnt in Egypt, both submerged under the intense
humanity of the characters and the morning freshness of their
hope in the future, which the later record has preserved un-
marred.

THE DESERT WANDERING

We saw that a spiritually ancestral relationship with their
God was the vital centre of the patriarchal generations, and the
object of their existence. This is what makes family ties so
sacred, and gives the recognition scenes at Harran and in
Egypt their startling poignancy.[6] The first covenant with
Abraham is necessarily direct and personal, but the second,
contracted with a whole people whose kinship is not directly
the bond of blood, requires the medium of a spiritual leader,
an individual in sharp contrast to their standardised solidarity,
who can materialise their tentative aspirations. Moses, like
Joseph, grew to maturity in Egypt; his floating cradle in the

---

[1] Genesis, xlix, especially 9–21.   [2] Genesis, xlix, 22, 24–25.

[3] רחל = ewe of God.   [4] Genesis, xlix, 26 and elsewhere.

[5] Deuteronomy, vii, 13. In the authorised version this is rendered 'The
flocks of thy sheep', in fear, presumably, of recording the hated names of
the Goddess in a blessing.

[6] Of the young Jacob with his cousin Rachel. Of the old Jacob with his
son Joseph, and of Joseph with his brothers.

reed-bed shares the ritual assimilations of other founders and lawgivers, being here related to the birth story of Horus.[1] But when he too is a fugitive in the pastoral landscape of the semi-desert, he sees a tree break into a flame which does not consume it, and there receives his mission.[2] Like Jacob remembering Bethel, he refers in later years to 'the good will of him that dwelt in the bush'.[3] We are back among the simplicities of stone and tree, amid which he was to rear his altar 'Jehovah-nissi', the Pillar-Jehovah.[4]

For the new covenant the tribes themselves became fugitive in the land of stone, for only in that emptiness could their reluctant hearts, craving the lost bondage, become sufficiently attuned. It is to the escape from Egypt that subsequent hymns of praise constantly return, rather than to the actual bestowal of the Law.[5] But even here is no direct communion; they had been slaves too long. Abraham's whole preoccupation was to preserve his relation with the God of the race to be. Moses is concerned for the people themselves. He often opposes Jehovah on their behalf, and always with success.[6] The disinterested humility of their leader is in complete contrast to their own fretful demands for release from the terrors of the wilderness.

---

[1] Cf. the birth-stories of Perseus and of Sargon, and the infancy of Horus in the papyrus-swamps.

[2] Exodus, iii. At Aphaca fire played in the tree-tops of the sacred grove during the annual feast of the Goddess, and between the Ambrosian Rocks at Tyre among the branches of the holy olive tree (Pietschmann, *Phoenizier*, p. 295, showing a coin of Gordian III); W. Robertson Smith, *Religion of the Semites*, 1914, p. 193, notes 2 and 3. See also part ii, p. 121, note 3, for mediæval and renaissance assimilations of Mary with the Burning Bush. To which may be added Chaucer's lovely invocation in the Prologue to the Prioress' Tale:

O moder mayde! O mayde moder free!
O bush unbrent brenninge in Moyses sighte.

There is also in recent times Rilke's poem of the Annunciation, in which the angel, forgetting the rest of his message, repeats again and again, 'Du aber bist der Baum.'

[3] Deuteronomy, xxxiii, 16.

[4] Exodus, xvii, 15. This is another example of a pillar set up to commemorate a covenant—'Because the Lord hath sworn . . .'

[5] W. Robertson Smith, *Prophets of Israel*, Lecture III.

[6] For instance, Exodus xxxii, 32: 'If thou wilt forgive their sin; and if not, blot me, I pray thee, out of thy book,' and Numbers, xiv, 20: ' I have pardoned them according to thy word.'

REVOLUTION

Between them moves the God's presence in a pillar of cloud or flame, the stone and tree come to life,[1] but when Moses alone on the Ziggurat-summit of the mountain receives the tablets engraved with the characters of the Law, the pall of darkness resting upon the peak is too bright for the people to bear, and even its reflection upon his face constrains him to hide it beneath a veil on his return among them.[2] So the new relationship with the 'nation of priests' must be established by ceremonial. For this treaty twelve monoliths were set up to represent the twelve tribes, and the blood of the sacrifice was sprinkled, in accordance with the old ritual, upon altar and people, to vitalise the bond.[3] They are now 'those that have made a covenant with me by sacrifice', as the psalm describes it.[4]

Their obligations consisted in preserving the integrity of their union by ritual and moral safeguards, by showing compassion towards strangers and the poor, and by a rejection, both of the dangerous Gods of the new peoples among whom they were soon to find themselves, and of the memories of the old.[5]

The altars set up in the desert had been constructed, according to command, of unhewn stone, in direct contact with the earth, or they were built up of earth itself;[6] but now it became necessary that the stones which were emblematic of the divine kinship of the tribes, should be guarded, as in the earliest ages, in a place hidden from all but the sanctified. Only the signs upon these were not symbols, but moral maxims. The setting is of the Stone Age, but the life is new.

While the children of Israel were still wanderers, therefore, the curtained tabernacle was erected, to veil like the face of Moses the too-great brightness of the written law in which the divine presence abode, as attested by the pillar of cloud stationary over the tent of the congregation.[7] When this moved, they struck the holy tent, and continued their march.[8]

[1] i.e. burning pillar = burning bush. [2] Exodus, xxxiv, 29–35.

[3] Exodus, xxiv, 4–6. [4] Psalm, l, 5.

[5] See Joshua, xxiv, 15. 'Choose ye this day whom ye will serve; Whether the gods which your fathers served that were on the other side of the flood, or the gods of the Amorites, in whose land ye dwell.'

[6] Exodus, xx, 24–26.

[7] Exodus, lx, 34. The Indo-Sumerian curtained booth will be recalled (pl. XII*e*).

[8] Exodus, lx, 36–37.

Before the inner sanctuary, where the tablets rested in the enclosure between the images of the cherubim (against whose carven forms there was consistently no prohibition), stood a Table of unfailing bread, and there too was its Tree—the seven-branched candlestick which budded into nuts and flower-heads of the almond[1]—the holy bush which burned and was unconsumed; the perpetual sacrifice of the fruits of the earth. Before these incense was offered.

In the outer chamber stood the horned altar of sacrifice, anointed with bull's blood in the Mediterranean tradition, and, after the consecrating oil had been poured upon Aaron's head (as it was dropped upon the heads of numinous pillars), ram's blood was laid upon the tips of the ears, thumbs and big toes of himself and of his sons, before they were clad in the fringed garments which had once been the skins of beasts, for entry to the shrine.[2] Whenever this occurred, Aaron suspended from his shoulders two onyx stones engraved with the names of the twelve tribes, and wore the breast-plate into which their individual stone emblems were set in four rows of three.[3] Thus stone met stone, in primeval fashion, when the people were renewed in the Law.

One lamb was to be sacrificed at morning, and one at evening, for ever: for the ritual maintenance of day and night in Egypt was not quite forgotten.[4] In general, the sacrifice of the pastoral animals entailed a communal meal; but the ritual slaughter of the wilder beasts and birds was piacular and taboo.[5] This distinction applied also to the domestic consumption of meat, which never lost its sacrificial meaning, since the blood must always be poured out upon the earth.[6] In the records of this period, the moral law and the ceremonies for renewal of communion are indivisible, but the first stages of the revolution are seen to be achieved.

[1] Exodus, xxv, 31–37.

[2] Exodus, xxix, 7, 12, 20. The fringes are ordained in Numbers, xv, 38, for all the congregation.

[3] Exodus, xxviii, 9–12, 17–21.

[4] Exodus, xxix, 39.

[5] W. Robertson Smith, *Religion of the Semites*, second edition, pp. 466–469. Additional note F.

[6] Robertson Smith, op. cit., p. 234.

PROPHETIC

The monarchy was always foreign to the descendants of the twelve tribes, since it was inaugurated for political ends, and the sovereign, though anointed, could therefore never usurp the functions of spiritual leadership. On these grounds Samuel opposes the election of the earliest king,[1] and after three reigns the history of the divided nation passes, dreamlike, through a confusion of wars and heresies, out of which, with a few exceptions, only the prophets emerge as living personalities. These individuals are unable, indeed unwilling, to save the kingdoms from final ruin, foreseeing that only by loss of their political existence can they return to God out of physical and spiritual exile.

Saul, drawn reluctantly into a destiny too high for him, so that his first conduct of theocratic warfare constituted an act of rebellion,[2] and the imposed spiritual power turned to magic and madness,[3] vanished with his heir like the first-fruits of sacrifice, at the battle of Gilboa—'the beauty of Israel is slain upon thy high places'.[4] Even David, the true leader, whose magnaminity and faith survived the corruptions of his long reign, did not, like the Pharaoh, represent the people in union with their God; his religion was personal, his rule political. Therefore the temple might not be built by him.[5] Solomon erected it, with inner spiral stairway,[6] and the numinous pillars before the door,[7] with its brazen bulls and lions cast by the craftsman of the Phœnician king;[8] and then he set up his altars, unchallenged, to the Goddess of the Zidonians and the neighbouring Baalim.[9] His groves and high places were fre-

---

[1] I Samuel, chap. viii.   [2] I Samuel, chap. xv.

[3] I Samuel, x, 6; xvi, 14; xxviii, 7.

[4] II Samuel, i, 19. If the literal translation rather than the metaphoric is retained, the 'gazelle' that is slain would be a piacular sacrifice, as Robertson Smith treats it, op. cit., p. 467.

[5] I Chronicles, xxii, 8–10. David, too, had gathered 'strangers' to prepare the materials of the temple which Solomon should build (xxii, 2).

[6] I Kings, vi, 8.   [7] I Kings, vii, 15–22.   [8] I Kings, vii, 23–29.

[9] I Kings, xi, 5, 8. Unchallenged by his people only.

quented until their destruction by Josiah.[1] Solomon was the last king of a united nation; the political cleavage that followed his reign was the outward aspect of a spiritual breach never to be healed while the kingdom remained.

Jeroboam raised his images of young bulls at Shechem, that his subjects might not go up to worship in Jerusalem, the seat of his rival.[2] But soon Judah too was installing high places and groves, and placing images and wooden posts 'on every high hill and under every green tree'.[3] The invading Syrians could say: 'Their Gods are Gods of the hills; let us fight in the plain'.[4] Elijah and Elishah took the golden calves to be natural symbols of Jehovah in the North.[5] Even Amos did not condemn them, for until Josiah's iconoclasm the Deuteronomic prohibition of the image was not yet clarified. But Hosea in his vision of a naked ethical relationship saw that the worship of these images was by its nature the worship of alien Gods.[6]

Thus until the dissolution of national life at the hands of Assyria and Babylon, the ritual from which the existence of Israel was a revolt, 'of the Gods which your fathers served beyond the flood in the old days . . . and of the Gods of the Amorites'[7] was never permanently rejected. This was the harlotry against which the prophets of the catastrophic years continually declaimed.[8] The return to the Syrian Goddess and her spouse, in order to awaken earth's fertility—'But since we left off to burn incense to the queen of heaven, and pour drink-offerings to her, we have wanted all things, being consumed by the sword and by the famine'[9]—was darkened, under the menace of invasion, by the terrible Phœnician offering of first fruits—'the passing of your children through the fire to Moloch,'[10] which becomes specifically 'slaying the children in the valleys under the clefts of the rocks'.[11]

At this period of crisis, when the weakening of earthly bonds

---

[1] W. Robertson Smith, *The Prophets of Israel*, Lecture III, citing II Kings, xxiii, 13.

[2] I Kings, xii, 28.   [3] I Kings, xiv, 23.   [4] I Kings, xx, 23.

[5] W. Robertson Smith, *Prophets of Israel*, Lecture IV.

[6] W. Robertson Smith, op. cit.

[7] See p. 203, note 5.   [8] Jeremiah, iii, 1.   [9] Jeremiah, xliv, 18.

[10] Jeremiah, xxxii, 35 (Melech = Moloch). See also Jeremiah, xix; Micah, vi, 7; Ezekiel, xxxiii, 39.

[11] Isaiah, lvii, 5.

gives the prophets their supreme moment of insight, the Stone Age ritual, in all its stages, rises up for final struggle and defeat. The vision of Ezekiel gives a curious insight into the aberrations of the age, which even includes a Palæolithic phase:

'And when I had digged in the wall, behold a door . . . , I went in and saw; and behold every form of creeping things, and abominable beasts, and all the idols of the house of Israel, pourtrayed upon the walls round about. . . . Hast thou seen what the ancients of the house of Israel do in the dark, every man in the chambers of his imagery? For they say . . . The Lord hath forsaken the earth.'[1]

The prophet is then shown 'greater abominations': 'Then he brought me to the door of the gate of the Lord's house which was toward the north; and, behold, there sat women weeping for Tammuz.'[2] As last and greatest horror, he sees men standing with their backs to the temple, and their faces to the East, worshipping the sun.[3] Jeremiah similarly fulminates against the primitive stone-worship which had become a vehicle of infidelity—'Saying to a stick, Thou art my father, and to a stone, Thou hast brought me forth.'[4] Yet he, like Isaiah[5] and Zechariah,[6] perceives the image of the future Redeemer as the Sacred Bough, the branch of the tree of David,[7] thus returning, after the destruction of the forms, to the perpetual archetype which shall take new life in the coming cycle of religious history.

The stages by which the prophets prepared the way, through the turmoil of these reigns, into the spiritual desert of defeat, where the last covenant might be concluded, when the pillars of the temple-door should be smitten like living men, to be no longer Bonds[8] between earth and sky; those stages may best be traced in the attitude to sacrifice, which had been the daily mode of communication with divinity from the building of the tabernacle.

In a Stone Age environment the victims were by their nature holy—God to God. Their blood was poured on pillar or earth as a physical bond of communion. When the altar became a hearth upon which their bodies were burnt for conveyance to

[1] Ezekiel, viii, 8–12. [2] Ezekiel, viii, 13–14. [3] Ib., 15–16.
[4] Jeremiah, ii, 27. [5] Isaiah, xi, 1.
[6] Zechariah, iii, 8. [7] Jeremiah, xxiii, 5.
[8] Amos, ix, 1 and 2. 'Though they dig into hell, thence shall my hand take them; though they climb up to heaven, thence will I bring them down.'

heaven, the offering was transformed into a gift, and the reciprocity of sacrifice, as the Biblical records clearly show, assumed the nature of a bargain.[1] The falseness of this relation is noted in the earliest reign, when Samuel rebukes Saul, as he bears to the altar the forbidden spoils of battle, with the words: 'To obey is better than sacrifice, and to hearken than the fat of rams';[2] and one of the psalms attributed to David throws scorn on the anomaly of the gift-offering: 'I will take no bullock out of thy house, nor he-goats out of thy folds, for every beast of the forest is mine, and the cattle upon a thousand hills.'[3] In these hymns, as in the prayers of other faithful kings, long life, prosperity, victory, children, are ardently desired. The Jehovah of the Psalms is yet a storm-God like the Syrian Baal,[4] causing the horns of the twin snow-peaks, Lebanon and Shirion, to leap like a young wild ox;[5] he is the sun rising in glory as on the Akkadian seals: 'Lift up your heads, O ye Gates; even lift them up, ye everlasting doors,'[6] and like Ea has his chapel in the abyss: 'his pavilions round about him were dark waters.'[7] But alike through the king's worldliness and the poet's vision of the holiness of all nature, there runs a single thread: the man's passionate longing for personal righteousness and fidelity. Jehovah is perceived as a spiritual being with whom the soul may have direct converse, in which the nation's elaborate ritual has no place.

The mission of the prophets, on the other hand, is to the people themselves, and Isaiah thus sees the bondage of ritual as an actual danger. He looks for a race freed from formal ties, finding the bare life behind them because only the inner unity is fundamental. For him the temple is already destroyed: 'The heaven is my throne, and the earth is my footstool: where is the house that ye build unto me? and where is the place of my

---

[1] W. Robertson Smith, *Religion of the Semites*, second edition, pp. 391–396.

[2] I Samuel, xv, 22.   [3] Psalm, l, 9–10.

[4] See T. H. Gaster in *Iraq*, vi, 2, p. 109 ff.: Baal is risen.

[5] Psalm xxix, 6. The beast is called a unicorn in Luther and the authorised version. E. Kautsch, *Die heilige Schrift*, 1923, p. 151, even makes him a buffalo, whose leaps are not easy to imagine. Since the unicorn is a creation of the mediæval fairyland, there remains some species of two-horned beast representing the two mountains separated by the valley of the Litány.

[6] Psalm xxiv, 9.   [7] Psalm xviii, 11, and pl. XXIII*c*.

(a)

(b)

Plate 27. MINOAN ART

(a)

(b)

(c)

(d)

Plate 28. THE HAGHIA TRIADA SARCOPHAGUS

rest? For all these things have been, but to this man will I look, even to him that is poor and of a contrite spirit.' 'He that killeth an ox is as if he slew a man . . . ; he that burneth incense, as if he blessed an idol.'[1]

The time-crises of ancient ceremonial are now attacked: 'Your new moons and your appointed feasts my soul hateth.'[2] Man must rely, when facing God, on his humanity alone.

It was in this period, when both Israel and Judah were to experience political destruction, that Jeremiah formulated the final Covenant: 'Behold, the days come that I will make a new covenant with the house of Israel, and with the house of Judah: Not according to the covenant that I made with their fathers in the day when I took them by the hand to bring them out of the land of Egypt; which my covenant they brake, although I was an husband unto them. . . . After those days I will put my law in their inward parts, and write it in their hearts; and will be their God, and they shall be my people.'[3]

This individual relation was even beginning to reach beyond nationality. The defeats of Israel and Judah were seen as the early stage of a wider catastrophe, in which Babylon was to fall as a Ziggurat which had mounted to heaven,[4] and Assyria as a sacred tree whose branches were swept into the valleys,[5] and Egypt as a river-beast, caught with a hook by the one God.[6] The return from exile became symbolic of the repentance and reunion which could once more become fruitful, though political independence was never wholly to return. The division into two kingdoms, formerly so catastrophic a testimony of moral disunion, would prove in the new cycle to be a source of strength. The Northern adherence to the nature-cults, strengthened by separation from Jerusalem, was reinforced after the captivity by settlements from Chaldæa. The gentler landscape of the North was thus a natural setting for the birth of Christianity; but because Judah's ideal of righteousness and faith had once

---

[1] Isaiah, lxvi, 2 and 3.   [2] Isaiah, i, 14.   [3] Jeremiah xxxi, 32–33.

[4] Jeremiah li, 25. 'Behold, I am against thee, O destroying mountain,' though Babylon, and Chaldæa in general, were obviously set on plains.

[5] Ezekiel, xxxi, 3 ff. 'Nor any tree in the Garden of God was like unto him for his beauty. . . . Because he hath shot up his top among the thick boughs . . , I have therefore delivered him into the hand of the mighty one among the heathen.'

[6] Ezekiel, xxix, 4.

become articulate, the religion of rebirth was henceforth inseparable from ethics, which are the purely human development of man. Its mystic elements were therefore no longer derived from the Syrian ritual, with its stains of sensuality and human sacrifice, but from the spiritual empire of Hellenism, the last permanent survival of Stone Age religion in the West.

PART FOUR

THE CITY-STATES OF THE ÆGEAN BRONZE AGE

CHAPTER I

THE RELIGION OF CRETE

At some period before the settlements along the irrigated banks of the Euphrates and the Nile had grouped themselves into towns, small bands of seafarers began to arrive upon the shores of Crete, and pushing into the uplands to establish themselves in caves and rock-shelters on various sites having access to the sea. They already knew how to build houses for the central village, and to pasture their flocks and herds, and some communication was always maintained with Egypt and Western Asia.[1] They buried their dead on the ledges of the caves, and made small clay images of a crouching Mother Goddess, with affinities in Northern Syria and Anatolia.[2]

At a certain point of time, probably before 3000 B.C., when a wave of creative unrest was communicated throughout Western Asia, and copper began to be used, a new population took possession of Eastern and Central Crete, issuing from Asia Minor and akin to the Neolithic islanders in cultural tradition and probably in blood.[3] There are signs at the same period of a Libyan colony in the South.[4] These two groups were the creators of the Minoan civilisation, comprising from the beginning a people of mixed affinities, and directly inspired by the now highly organised kingdoms of the East; so that the village capital of each community of cave-dwellers at once began to assume the architectural functions of a city.

[1] See J. D. S. Pendlebury, *The Archæology of Crete*, 1939, chap. ii, for a concise summary of the earliest conditions.

[2] A. J. Evans, *The Palace of Minos*, vol. i, 1921, pp. 45–49, and figs. 12 and 13. The resemblances with Western Asiatic types are even closer in the light of the recent finds in Northern Syria and North Iraq (fig. 43 of ii 2a above).

[3] H. Frankfort, Asia, Europe and the Ægean, *Royal Anthropological Inst. Occasional Papers, No. 8*, 1927, chap. iv; Evans, op. cit., i; Pendlebury, op. cit.

[4] Evans, op. cit., i, p. 66.

The states which thus arose seem to have been loosely united under the strongest of their number, and to have shared the advantages of a common culture while retaining their separate traditions.[1] Later legend gives them a dynasty of priest-kings; but since they were removed, through the greater part of their history, from the danger of invasion, and from the centralised compulsion necessary to win life from the great rivers, they developed a religion unusually detached from formal bonds, but emotionally binding in its constant endeavour to establish communion with the elemental powers.

Perhaps this was the reason why they never built temples, but performed their rites, through the most splendid epochs of their material achievement, on mountain peaks, in caves, in household chapels and rustic shrines. Their ritual remained primitive, preserving its relations with cavern, pillar, Goddess and tree, so that they could draw profoundly on the past, and bequeath something fundamental to their more intellectual successors. A survey of their contribution to the last phases of the Stone Age religion may appropriately begin with the cave.

CAVERNS AND MOUNTAIN SHRINES

The cave dwellings of the earliest immigrants continued to provide shelter for the living and the dead over a period of many centuries subsequent to the Minoan settlement of the island.[2] After their final abandonment, certain of the caves became the objects of a pilgrimage, uninterrupted in some instances by the rise and fall of several civilisations.

One of these is the grotto situated near the River Karteros outside Candia, which is probably Homer's Cave of Eileithyia, the Goddess of Birth, descended, there is reason to believe, from one personality of the Mother Goddess of the Minoans.[3] Its winding galleries lead the pilgrim to a vaulted chamber in the centre of which stands a nearly cylindrical stalagmite,

---

[1] Pendlebury, op. cit., p. 281.

[2] Martin P. Nilsson has collected the evidence relating to the use of caves in chap. i of *The Minoan-Mycenæan Religion*, 1927.

[3] Nilsson, op. cit., pp. 449–451, investigates the philological evidence for this connection.

within a square enclosure of little stones. An unhewn quadrangular rock lies in front, and all about the enclosure fragments of vessels have been found to bear evidence of a continuous cult, extending, it is said, from the Minoan down to the Roman occupation.[1]

This combined sanctity of pillar and cave receives further illustration in the cavern of Psychro on Mt. Dikte, which can probably be identified with the legendary birth-place of Zeus, though dedicated without doubt to a Minoan Goddess and yielding only Minoan remains.[2] In the upper grotto a sacrificial deposit, many feet deep, and composed of the ashes and bones of horned animals, was discovered beside a roughly built altar, round which lay the furniture of Minoan ritual—libation tables, columnar lamps, and fruit-stand vases. Into the stalactite columns of its lower chamber many double-axe blades had been thrust, as they are shown stuck into sacred pillars in late Minoan paintings.[3] Their fertilising, because sacrificial, potency will be described later; it is sufficient to note the resemblance of this lower chamber to the pillar-crypts invariably constructed beneath Minoan household shrines, and to remember that those pillars, too, bear the sign of the double axe.[4]

The peak-sanctuaries[5] were enclosed within their low boundary walls at the period when the caves first came to be frequented by worshippers. The offerings found on all these heights are of a type noted at Hal Saflieni, and common to later Greek oracular shrines, where healing was sought by communication through dreams; that is to say, they consist chiefly of the separate limbs or other portions of human or animal figures, modelled in clay and pierced for suspension.[6] On several of the sites a small building had been erected, and it does appear

---

[1] Hazzidakis in *Παρνασσός*, x, 1886–1887, p. 349; Nilsson, op. cit., p. 54.

[2] Evans, *Journal of Hellenic Studies*, 1897, p. 350 ff.; *Palace of Minos*, i, pp. 625–633; Orsi and Halbherr, 'Scoperti nell' antro di Psychro,' *Museo di ant.*, class ii, 1888, p. 905 ff.; Nilsson, op. cit., pp. 55–58.

[3] D. G. Hogarth, *Annual of the British School at Athens*, vi, p. 94 ff., on the Dictæan Cave.

[4] For example, Evans, *Tree and Pillar Cult*, pp. 12–13, and fig. 5, and *P. of M.*, i, pp. 218 and 425.

[5] Nilsson, op. cit., pp. 62–71; J. L. Myres, *B.S.A.*, ix, p. 356 ff.; Evans, *P. of M.*, i, p. 151 ff.

[6] See above, p. 136.

possible, in view of the restricted provenance of such offerings, that incubation was practised here also, to obtain the aid of that divinity who stands in the Knossian seal-impression upon a mountain peak between her guardian lions, like the Mountain-Mother of Asia Minor, which was probably the Minoan homeland.[1] Since the peak is here interchangeable with the column, and on some seals and gems receives the libations of ministering genii, which are elsewhere poured over the pillar,[2] it seems to have gathered round it some of those conceptions, belonging to both, which were discussed in Part III, and to which it is necessary now to return.

THE PILLAR

The pillar, it will be remembered,[3] was set up at some primitive stage of Middle Eastern culture as a focus of numinous energy, where contact might be established between the local divinity and his worshipper by pouring blood or other sacred liquid, at first upon the actual stone, and later upon pillar-altars like those yet standing at Mnaidra in Malta (pl. XVIc).

Within the elaborate palaces of the Cretan towns, and in many private houses, rooms are continually found to contain the bases of vanished wooden columns, before which this simple rite seems to have been performed. The rooms always rest upon the heavy pillars of a windowless crypt, and these pillars have trenches cut round them, or vats standing about them, as if for libations,[4] and occasionally the horns or bones of sacrifice, or a ritual vessel, lying nearby.[5] The symbol of the double axe was incised, as we have seen, upon the surface of the pillars, and

---

[1] See fig. 100.

[2] Evans, *The Mycenæan Tree and Pillar Cult*, 1901, p. 19; and fig. 12.

[3] See pp. 123, 124 above.

[4] For example, in the 'Royal Villa' (*Brit. Sch. Athens Annual*, ix, p. 149 and pl. i) there is a sunken channel round the central pillar. In the very old pillar room of the house to the North of the S.E. angle of the palace at Knossos, there was a circular pit (*B.S.A. Annual*, ix, p. 17 ff.).

[5] For example, Hogarth found in a house on the hill of Gypsades rows of inverted cups holding carbonised vegetable matter, placed round the central pillar in three rooms (*B.S.A. Annual*, vi, p. 76).

the fact that these signs must have been invisible, covered over with plaster or hidden under masonry or beams, in no way detracts from their religious virtue. Nor does their structural function, as supports of the upper storey; for a column complete with base, capital, and architrave is frequently to be found on seal-engravings, set between heraldic animals in the place of the Goddess herself,[1] not to mention the Lion-Gate at Mycenæ.[2]

It is also true that the columns of the upper chamber have never yet been found in position; they are represented, however, in models of shrines and in fresco-paintings, between the

Fig. 90

horns of consecration by which their sacred nature is confirmed. This suggests the worship of a divinity belonging both to the cave and to the upper air, and recalls the superimposed pillar-shrines of Malta[3], and Herodotus' description of the 'Labyrinth' of Hawara, whose subterranean chambers he was not allowed to enter.[4] A third level may indeed be indicated by the horned altars set above the roofs of holy places, and their alighting birds (fig. 90, above).

Thus the pillar of the Cretan Bronze Age came to be regarded dynamically, as raising itself from earth to sky,[5] as an architectural member, for the support of no visible roof, like Jachin and Boaz before the Temple of Solomon; and this quality

[1] See fig. 99.   [2] Below, pl. XXXa.   [3] pl. XVIc.
[4] Herodotus, II, 148.   [5] Cf. the Megalithic conception, p. 154 above.

naturally enforced the relation between pillar and holy tree. They are indeed interchangeable, here as elsewhere, in scenes of cult, and perhaps it is not merely for reasons of structural solidity that the pillar-chapels hold columns of wood superimposed upon stone. It was a connection of deep import for Minoan Crete, where vegetation cults developed aspects which were to affect the future of European religion. There are signs, as will be seen, that the tree, like the pillar and the Ziggurat,[1] stood between the three worlds, that it existed, as it did for Egypt and Babylon, in the land of the dead; that it was in fact an embodiment of the Mother Goddess.

THE GODDESS

We have come to the chief, and in some degree the only, anthropomorphic object of worship, among the Minoan people, as in the remote past among their ancestors in Africa and Asia; a being alive, as we have seen, in menhir or tree, and partly individualised, as the monuments bear witness, under three chief aspects:

THE EARTH MOTHER

In addition to the pillar chambers, a number of small domestic chapels occur in some area of all the great buildings, and in lesser structures scattered over the island. These contain ritual furniture and images, still found in position on their ledge against the wall, or laid away in depositories. Among them are figures, in clay and porcelain, of a Goddess with outstretched or uplifted arms, often encircled by snakes. She is more than once accompanied by a priestess, or double of herself, as in the deposit from the central shrine at Knossos,[2] or the far more primitive snake-girt images from Gournia,[3] together with libation tripods and models of birds, double axes, horns of consecration, shells, votive garments or knotted scarves.[4] In the Gournia shrine were also discovered the remains of five

[1] See pp. 169, 170 above.

[2] Evans, *Palace of Minos*, i, p. 500 ff., figs. 359–362.

[3] B. E. Williams, *Gournia*, pl. xi, p. 47 ff.; Nilsson, op. cit., pp 76, 77, fig. 3a.

[4] Evans, op. cit., fig. 377; *Gournia*, pl. xi; Nilsson, op. cit., p. 268, etc.

tubular vessels, down whose sides run handles which imitate a snake's undulations, and are in one case completed by representations of actual snakes.[1] These are connected in form with the Asiatic pierced censers or movable altars,[2] but are apparently constructed to pour libations into the earth. A large jar, found in the chamber of a private house at Knossos, contained a similar vessel with cups set at intervals down its length, together with a snake-table, fitted with grooves to allow four reptiles to drink at once out of a central cup, and lastly the

Fig. 91

model of a serpent coiling round a honeycomb.[3] In this room there was no anthropomorphic figure. It may represent a more primitive cult of the Goddess, whose cruder images are indeed of partly tubular form, even in the very late Shrine of the Double Axes at Knossos, as if half-emerged from a pillar.[4] The notched adder-scales depicted round the Knossian movable hearth, like those repainted at so many periods round the fixed hearth of the palace at Mycenæ,[5] suggest that the snake was here considered, as in classical and modern Greece,[6] to be

[1] *Gournia*, pl. xi; Nilsson, op. cit., fig. 33.

[2] For example, that found at Beisan, now in the Rockefeller Museum in Jerusalem. Alan Rowe, 'The Temples of Dagon and Ashtoreth at Beth-Shan' (*Univ. Pennsylvania Mus. Journ.*, xvii, 1926, p. 293 ff.); Evans, *Palace of Minos*, iv (i), fig. 129.

[3] Evans, *Palace of Minos*, iv (i), p. 138 ff.   [4] Evans, op. cit., ii (i), fig. 193.

[5] Evans, op. cit., iv (i), pp. 179–180.

[6] Nilsson, op. cit., pp. 279–280.

Fig. 94

Fig. 97

Fig. 96

Fig. 110

Fig. 93

Fig. 92

guardian of the house and its possessions, and emblematic, to judge by the Greek and Eastern parallels, of a chthonic power, the fertility of the underworld. It is noticeably absent, and its Goddess also, from the outdoor activities in which the seal-cutters took delight, but she does once appear, with lifted arms, gazing out of the opening of a clay hut-urn[1] (fig. 91, p. 219). She is the undoubted house-mother here.

Athena was one of the clearly defined personalities which the Greek Goddesses were partly to draw from the Earth Mother of this age. She kept the Mother's snake-emblem to become guardian of the city, combining it, as she had done, with a bird-emblem, her messenger in the upper air. Demeter, too, retained the serpent as nourisher of the dead and the reborn. She also had a companion in her daughter, who was her other self.

THE GODDESS OF VEGETATION

This aspect of the One Goddess appears most frequently on seals and signet rings as the object of, and partaker in, orgiastic dances. She stands above the spring meadows (fig. 92, p. 220), or descends from the air into the midst of her ecstatic votaries (fig. 93, p. 220), or, seated beneath her tree, receives offerings of lilies and poppy-heads, the first-fruits of her own bounty (fig. 94, p. 220).

The sacrificial appurtenances, double axe and horns of consecration, belong to this Goddess also, and so do the half-animal ministrants later to be described. She is very frequently the central figure between two child attendants (fig. 94, p. 220). and usually appears with that companion noticed among the images of the household shrines—a Daughter, perhaps, a kind of Kore, whose nakedness often contrasts with the luxuriant replication of her own attire. This figure is seen with the Goddess on the two great funeral rings, which depict the hopes of immortality that were centred round the Tree (pl. XXIX*b* and *c*).

It is possibly in this connection that the two deities seem to be occasionally associated in scenes of grief, perhaps for that very young male divinity who sometimes descends, armed with a shield, from the air or sky (figs. 94 and 95, pp. 220 and 222); the archetype of those earliest kouretes, who dance beside their

---

[1] Evans, *P. of M.*, ii (i), pp. 128–129, fig. 63.

shields to evoke the epiphany of the Goddess (fig. 93, p. 220).
This deity or his human representative may appear again in the
young ministrant of the Ring of Minos (pl. XXIX*c*), and of the
Mycenæan signet (fig. 96, p. 220), who draws the milk of the
Paradisal tree.[1] He is never of the stature of the Goddesses; in
fact these three may be not unreasonably considered, in the light
of later connections, as prototypes of the Fatherless Trinity at
Eleusis (pl. XXXII*b*).

Although this childish apparition is infrequent on the seals,
his personality is yet sufficiently marked to distinguish him
from the youthful consort of Asiatic cults. Yet no evidence of

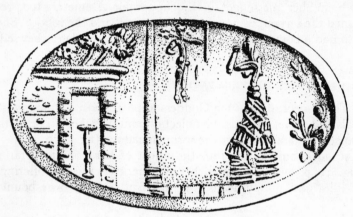

Fig. 95

his birth appears on any extant Minoan monument, a noteworthy fact in view of the later legends concerning Zeus and
Zagreus.[2] On a late mainland gem, with vestiges of Minoan
stylistic tradition, such a scene is indeed portrayed, and will be
described in a later chapter.[3] It appears likely that the Greek
world first laid emphasis on the Birth, in contrast to the pre-
occupation with the marriage or death of the young God prevalent in Asia; and to this conception the child-deity of Minoan
times must obviously have contributed.[4]

[1] Cf. pp. 120, 121 above, and figs. 59 and 60.

[2] See pp. 281–283 below.

[3] See pp. 257, note 3, and 267, chap. ii, concerning the doubts as to its
authenticity. It is illustrated in fig. 122 below.

[4] See Nilsson, op. cit., chap. xvi, on 'The Divine Child'.

THE RELIGION OF CRETE

THE MOUNTAIN MOTHER

This is that Britomartis or Diktynna whom the Greeks equated with Artemis,[1] whose figure appears only on gems, ranging the hillsides with bow or spear, or leading captive savage and fantastic beasts (fig. 97, p. 220) and the horned victims of sacrifice. In the later days of Minoan culture she is often seen standing between wild creatures subdued, the antagonist turned worshipper (fig. 98, below). These heraldic groups, a formal legacy from Western Asia,[2] include scenes in which mountain or pillar replaces the incarnate Goddess between rampant lions (fig. 99, p. 224), and the one seal impression from

Fig. 98

the Knossian palace shrine, where she herself is pedestalled upon her mountain (fig. 100, p. 224). Living lions were unknown in Crete, to judge by the seal cutters' maned lioness suckling her cub,[3] but in Asia Minor they regularly attended the Great Mother, and guarded her doorway to the other world (fig. 101, p. 224). Further East, Ishtar had her lions, and perhaps, before she armed for war, she too had been a huntress (though here again the Lion may be a chthonic inheritance; see p. 237 below). Nevertheless, the personality of this Cretan Mistress of the Wilds, the 'sweet Virgin' as the Greeks and Romans interpreted her name,[4]

---

[1] Hesychius, Βριτόμαρτις· ἐν Κρήτῃ ἡ Ἄρτεμις. For Diktynna, see Euripides, *Hippolytus*, v, 145, and more explicitly, *Iph. Taur.*, v, 127, ὦ παῖ τᾶς Λατοῦς, Δίκτυνν' οὐρεία.

[2] Frankfort, *Cylinder Seals*, p. 24, pls. iiia and b, iv, j.

[3] Evans, op. cit., iv, p. 559, fig. 522, a and b. Cf. also fig. 98 on this page.

[4] Hesychius, βριτύ· γλυκύ· Κρῆτες. Solinus, xi, 8, Britomartem gentiliter nominantes, quod sermone nostro sonat virginem dulcem. Nilsson, op. cit., p. 439, and Evans in *Journal of Hellenic Studies*, vol. 45, 1925, p. 21, note 53.

Fig. 100

Fig. 99

Fig. 113

Fig. 114

Fig. 101

Fig. 102

bore little resemblance to the Asiatic Goddesses of human fecundity. She is a creation of Minoan independence, and is occasionally replaced on the gems by a young male hunter wearing a peaked cap.[1] Once he is poised upon the horns of consecration;[2] it follows that he is divine, an earliest Apollo to this Artemis.

The Goddess, standing ritualistically between lions or the elegant griffins of Minoan fancy, sometimes bears above her head a triple emblem, possibly her bow (fig. 102, p. 224), which remained an attribute of the divinity who dominated the animal world after the disappearance of the Minoan civilisation.[3]

She and her male counterpart, her mountain or pillar, are occasionally supported, not by the heraldic animals, but by beings who partly share their nature, and also minister to the Goddess beneath the Tree.

THE GENII

These beings, who are often described as genii, came to hold an important place in Minoan religion and art, each mode of creation enriching the other.

They always appear as servants of the Goddess, bearing offerings in procession, or bringing home her slain or captive beasts (fig. 103, p. 226), in rare instances even replacing her between the heraldically opposed creatures, and rightly, since they represent a fusion of divinity and worshipper. Because of their half-animal nature they are more frequently seen in attendance upon the Mountain Goddess, but often, too, they pour libations upon pillar or cairn, or upon sacred boughs between the altar-horns—for like the Assyrian genii of later times they are much occupied with rain-making[4] (fig. 104, p. 226).

It is time to consider their form and nature more closely, for their lineage goes back through many millennia to the

[1] Seal impression from Haghia Triada, Nilsson, fig. 8-

[2] Evans, *P. of M.*, iv (ii), p. 467, fig. 392

[3] Nilsson, op. cit., fig. 94. Cf. the gold pendant from Ægina (*Catalogue of the Jewelry in the British Museum*, pl. vii, 762).

[4] Evans, 'The Ring of Nestor,' *Journal of Hellenic Studies*, vol. 45, 1925, fig. 22, and note 52.

Fig. 105

Fig. 103

Fig. 106

Fig. 104

Fig. 108

Fig. 107a

masked ceremonies of the Palæolithic caves, and forward to the Idæan Daktyls and Kouretes, the satyrs and half-human ministrants of the mystery Gods of Greece, and through them to the Drama. In cult as in art, here as in Mesopotamia, their development appears to be three-fold:

1. There are the animal-masked human priests or dancers, always portrayed in some ritualistic occupation. Such servers carry the pole upon which the sacrificial victims are borne in the seal stone (fig. 103, p. 226) and the Mycenæan fresco (fig. 105, p, 226), or the staves of the Phæstos shell-inlay (pl. XXX*b*); such dancers appear, goat-headed or bull-headed, with whirling human feet, upon the gems (fig. 106, p. 226), and may have created the later conception of the Minotaur. Their meaning and functions are too familiar at this point to need further elucidation.[1] The garment of hide with hanging tail, frequently worn in sacrificial scenes (pl. XXVIII*a* and *b*), would be a descendant of the animal skins of these masked performers.

2. Monstrous creations of the Minoan imagination, expressing the organic union of animal, human and divine natures, personified by the masked priests and dancers (pl. XXIX*a*). They maintain with solemnity their typical functions of guardians and servitors, always upright and girdled, and usually furnished with the human arms necessary for their tasks. Above the stylised skin-cloaks, ridged with hair, of the old animal-disguise, their heads are generally those of lions or asses (associated, it will be recalled, in Western Asia),[2] but their formal type was no doubt influenced by Egyptian representations of the Hippopotamus-Goddess bearing the crocodile upon her back.[3]

It is interesting to note in passing, that the shield or cymbal of the Iron Age found in the Idæan Cave, and depicting in Assyrian style the shield-dance of the Kouretes about the youthful Zeus, has given these dæmonic dancers the shapes of Assyrian Genii, whose functions so closely resemble those of Minoan Crete.[4]

3. Mere fantasies, suggested to the craftsman by the form

[1] Prof. A. B. Cook observed the Palæolithic connection as long ago as 1894 (*J.H.S.*, xiv, 'Animal Worship in the Mycenæan Age,' p. 81 ff).

[2] See pl. IX*c* and *d*.

[3] Evans, *Palace of Minos*, iv (ii), p. 431 ff.

[4] See A .B. Cook, *Zeus*, i, 1914, pl. xxxv, and p. 645.

only,[1] of various subjects from which he produced abnormalities without organic cohesion (figs. 107a and b, p. 226 and below). These but rarely attempted to function as Genii, having no reality in any world.

The Griffin and Sphinx, on the contrary, are true mythical entities, combining the natures of several sacred creatures. The Griffin in particular is a typical refinement of the Minoan artistic genius, the hawk imparting to the lion its own swiftness till they become one being[2] (pls. XXVIIa and XXVIIIc).

Fig. 107b

There is one late scene of a griffin's body borne through papyrus swamps,[3] but these two belong in Minoan art to a world beyond death, because unlike the genii they never had a physical existence. We turn from them to those animals whose sanctity was in their death.

THE SACRIFICE

The earlier parts of this investigation laid emphasis on the religious importance of horned beasts, especially of the Bull, whose vigour was communicated to god and worshipper by the shedding of his blood. Perhaps the wild bull was considered in

---

[1] Nearly all these were found on seal-impressions at Zakro. See Hogarth, 'Zakro Sealings,' *J.H.S.*, xxii, 1902, p. 76 ff.

[2] It was not a Minoan creation, having a long previous history in Asia. See Frankfort, 'Notes on the Cretan Griffin,' *B.S.A. Annual*, vol. xxxvii (dedicated to Sir John Myres), p. 106 ff.

[3] Evans, *P. of M.*, iv (ii), fig. 436.

Crete to be the reservoir of a yet more dynamic ebullition of energy, or possibly the bull-grappling, so frequently depicted, was a memorial of the older hunting days. But the struggle in any case reinforced the communication between worshippers and victim, especially the seizure of the horns,[1] which from Palæolithic times and in all countries have been regarded as vehicles of outflowing power. These bull-contests had an admittedly religious function, for emblems of the Mother Goddess, such as the sacral knot and the pillar shrine, are placed beside them on the frescoes and the gems,[2] and women, who play the most prominent rôle in priestly activities, share the perils of these games. On the analogy of Plato's *Critias*, which transports to his Atlantis so many half-forgotten elements of Minoan civilisation, it seems reasonable to consider the pursuit and grappling with the bull as the prelude to his sacrifice.[3]

There is no sign of bull-worship or of a bull-king. The bull-masked man appears to be of like nature with the goat-masked and other votaries. The bull was the embodiment of the fertility of the Earth, sacrificed to the Earth-Mother.

The sacred bull's skull and horns are painted on pottery as a motif, half decorative and half symbolic (fig. 108, p.226), which has, as we saw, a long previous history in North Syria.[4] The *horned altar* goes back to a sub-Neolithic level in Crete.[5] It is used in Minoan art to designate the sanctity of an enclosure or the neighbourhood of a shrine, like those set upon the roofs of buildings containing a household chapel (fig. 90, p. 217) and pillar crypt, or to denote the presence of a deity or ritual object. In Asia the head or skull is sometimes portrayed upon the altar itself;[6] as it was later depicted in Greece; and some African tribes still continue to preserve the skulls and horns of immolated bulls upon grave mounds, as a symbol of life out of

---

[1] A. B. Cook, op. cit., i, p. 499.

[2] Evans, *P. of M.*, iii, figs. 141, 142, and plate xvi. Also fig. 109 here.

[3] Plato, *Critias*, 119 d, e.

[4] See above, p. 93, and fig. 50a.

[5] Evans, *Palace of Minos*, i, p. 57, and fig. 16c (*Mochlos*, fig. 48), quoting Seager, *Mochlos*, p. 93.

[6] See Evans, *Mycenæan Tree and Pillar Cult*, fig. 20 from a stele found at Teima, in Arabia (Perrot and Chipiez, *L'Art dans l'Antiquité*, iv., p. 393). Nilsson, however, and Dussaud, throw doubt on the interpretation of this support as horned. And the drawing is certainly indefinite.

death.[1] The Bull thus became the altar of its own sacrifice, as the pillar had been its own altar in Stone Age ritual.

It has been suggested that the horned altar represents the Mother Goddess herself,[2] but unlike her Egyptian and Babylonian contemporaries the Minoan Goddess was never a cow. She neither wears horns, nor suckles a child, in any manifestation so far discovered, though offerings were sometimes made to her, as the Mother of all life, of modelled beasts nourishing their young.[3]

In the *Double Axe* again appears that instrument and emblem of sacrifice[4] which was blazoned upon the cavern wall of Niaux, and which, in the form of the polished celt, was laid in so many graves, memorial of reaped grain and hewn branches, the life-giving oblation of the vegetable world. Therefore it stands between the horns of consecration, above the bucrania on the painted jars (fig. 108, p. 226), and is set like a standard into the stepped pedestal of the household shrine,[5] or stuck into leafy stems or into the pillars of painted sanctuaries,[6] and even into the stalactite column of the Psychro cave.

It often appears as an emblem above the Goddess on gems;[7] once it is carried by herself or her priestess.[8] It has never so far been found in a man's hands, and has therefore a different part from the thunder-weapons of Western Asia.[9]

The occasional duplication of its blades, both in decoration and as actual cult furniture,[10] would seem to be directed to the increased potentiality of its cutting edge.

[1] See A. B. Cook, *Zeus*, i. p. 508 ff., on the survival of this custom among the Dinka negroes. Catlin gives a drawing (fig. 48) in *The N. American Indians*, vol. i, of such a burial mound among the Mandan Indians, upon which (according to invariable custom, he says) two horned skulls are set, male and female.

[2] By Miss B. E. Williams in *Gournia*, p. 48.

[3] Such as the lovely faience groups found among the objects of the central palace shrine, Evans, *Palace of Minos*, i, figs. 366, 367, 369.

[4] This is also Nilsson's view (op. cit., p. 192, quoting also Milchhöfer and Tsountas).

[5] Such a pedestal, for instance, was found in a deposit belonging to a pillar shrine of the Little Palace at Knossos. Evans, op. cit., p. 438.

[6] See pl. XXVIIIb, and Evans, *P. of M.*, i, fig. 319.

[7] For instance, in fig. 94.   [8] Evans, *P. of M.*, i, fig. 312a.

[9] As pointed out by Nilsson, op. cit., p. 192.

[10] R. B. Seager, *Pseira*, p. 31, fig. 12.

It is sometimes found in combination with another symbol, the *knot*, or twisted fillet, perhaps a variation of that fringed and cross-barred knotted scarf, suspended, it would appear, as a sign of the presence of the Goddess, like the earlier tied reed-bundle of Inanna which it closely resembles.[1] Examples occur in ivory and porcelain in a Mycenæan grave, and painted upon the wall of the sanctuary at Nirou Khani near Knossos.[2] In a fresco from the 'palace of Minos' it is worn behind the neck of a votary,[3] as in certain seal-engravings; here and on the mainland, it appears like small wings above the shoulders of the

Fig. 109

Goddess and her companion.[4] On late gems it is sometimes hung before bull-grappling scenes (fig. 109, above), perhaps as an aid to tenacity. Like Inanna's symbol, it is often found in pairs.[5]

In art, it is often hardly distinguishable from a votive garment, similarly suspended, or laid upon a sacred object as some aid to communication (fig. 110, p. 220). It is once worn over the ritual hide-garment (fig. 111, p. 232), again, most notably, on the Harvester vase (pl. XXVII*b*). In this procession it may well be that the bearded man who wears it personifies the barley, and that its fringe and scale pattern are a vegetable equivalent of the

[1] See pl. IX *f* and *g*.

[2] Evans, 'The Ring of Nestor,' *J.H.S.*, 1925, fig. 7.

[3] Evans, *P. of M.*, i, fig. 311.

[4] For instance, on the gold ring in the Ashmolean Museum, fig. 110.

[5] This may be the clue or key of Ariadne, a later name for the Goddess (see note 4, p. 248 below). For the vestiges of her cult see Nilsson, op. cit., pp. 451–456.

animal skins. Perhaps this ornamented robe was taken over from the knotted scarf, which would have held, like Inanna's, a content of fruitfulness.

Fig. 111

On late gems it is sometimes suspended beside the *shield* (fig. 112, below) From the Greek hymn found at Palaikastro,[1] it is evident that the shield-clashing dance of the Kouretes in the birth-cave of Zeus, was a fertility rite performed in spring to summon the young God from his winter sleep or death. The

Fig. 112

Minoan shield is of the shape used in historic Rome for the same purpose,[2] and its frequent appearance amid vegetation rites on the seals leads to the conclusion that here first it was made to clang in a springtime dance. At Knossos, as also at Tiryns, a frieze of these shields surrounded one of the palace-

[1] Below, p. 281, note 3, and fig. 122.
[2] See Evans, *P. of M.*, iii, pp. 314–315, and fig. 206, *a* and *b*. He considers the Roman Ancilia to have been struck 'to summon the God'. Cf. Neith's shield, above, p. 117.

chambers.[1] The marked dappling, visible upon these frescoes and coloured reliefs, shows them to have been, at least in their origin, the hides of bulls stretched over a raised wooden or metal framework, a fact which must largely have contributed to the efficacy of the rite. The Bulls of Sacrifice incarnated the fecundity of earth—on one signet trees actually spring from their backs (fig. 113, p. 224)—and it was the smitten earth that bellowed in the clang which controlled the rhythm of the dance. Perhaps even those bull-headed harps of Ur kept the memory of some such instrument.[2] On an island where scenes of warfare are almost never a subject for art, the frequent recurrence of these shields is very notable.

Somewhat close to them in function is the *Triton shell*, sounded, it seems, to summon the divinity to her pillar tree or shrine (fig. 114, p. 224). Such shells or their imitations are very numerous in domestic chapels and in tombs. They are frequently found, it will be remembered, in the Megalithic sepulchres of Italy and Sicily, and are sometimes sounded still.[3] Their great importance in Pacific island ritual will also be recalled.[4] Perhaps the spiral form keeps in Crete its significance of curbed tension. Other sea shells were strewn over the floors of the little chapels,[5] and sea-creatures such as the octopus and the nautilus, the flying-fish and the dolphin, so dear to the Minoan painter and metal-worker, may have been cherished also by that Goddess who steers her little craft with its sea-horse prow, and the sacred tree upon its deck, over the waters between the worlds (pl. XXIX*c* and fig. 115, p. 239). Whether or not that is true, the ritual use of the shell, as trumpet and otherwise, is one more link with the religious customs of the Stone Age.

[1] See Evans, op. cit., iii, fig. 197. A Restoration of Shield fresco at Tiryns, after Rodenwaldt, *Tiryns*, ii, pl. v; and plate xxiii for restoration of an almost identical fresco at Knossos.

[2] Woolley, *The Royal Cemetery*, pl. 169.

[3] A. Mosso, *The Dawn of Mediterranean Civilisation*, p. 363 ff.

[4] Above, part iii, 3, p. 163.

[5] Evans, op. cit., fig. 378. He quotes *Monumenti Antichi*, xix, 1908, p. 151 ff., for an account of such a deposit of shells found lying before a 'Mother Goddess' figure of the Neolithic period at Palaikastro. The Minoan shell-offerings in these shrines were not of the spiral type.

THE DEAD

There are three sources of evidence at present available with regard to Minoan beliefs concerning the after-life.

THE TOMBS

Throughout the period under consideration, from the early circular or rectangular ossuaries, to burials in chests and jars, within rock-cut and chamber tombs; through all this variety of custom, offerings were consistently made to, or on behalf of, the dead. Nevertheless the burials found in Crete bear no signs of the magnificence displayed on the Minoised mainland, and, even at the zenith of her cultural achievements, the rites of the dead remain simple and unobtrusive.

Offerings were laid in the annexes of the early vaulted tombs at Messara,[1] and upon the surface above the stone chamber of Isopata,[2] libations were poured within a special structure at Mallia,[3] but it is the Temple Tomb outside Knossos,[4] which brings this ritual into the sphere of religion.

It shows a construction exactly resembling that attributed by Diodorus to the legendary tomb of Minos in Sicily, that is to say, it consisted of a 'temple to the Goddess' (he calls her Aphrodite of the Dove),[5] 'above a sepulchral vault,' that is, a columnar shrine with horns of consecration above the familiar pillar crypt, inscribed with double-axe symbols, and leading to a rock-cut inner chamber—Diodorus' 'secret sepulchre of the double tomb'—whose central monolithic pillar was set within a sunken square for libations and sacrifice.[6] The body in its coffin had been removed through an opening in the rock, but close to the entrance was found a cupped block of stone for offerings, resembling the blocks used in predynastic Egypt.[7]

[1] See Xanthoudides, *The Vaulted Tombs of Mesara*, 1924, p. 6, etc.

[2] Evans, *P. of M.*, iv, 771 ff.   [3] Evans, op. cit., iv, 1, 78.

[4] Evans, *P. of M.*, iv (ii), p. 959 ff.

[5] Diodorus, I, ivc, 79, 3. He thus makes Minos a votary of the Goddess rather than of the Zeus of later legend, as Evans remarks.

[6] Evans, op. cit., p. 977, and fig. 937.

[7] Evans, op. cit., fig. 939 (from Temple Tomb), and 1940 (from Hierakonpolis).

The Tomb of the Double Axes, again, which is actually cut in the form of the sacred emblem, has a pillar sculptured in relief against its inner wall, before which lay at one time ritual vessels and models of the double axe.[1]

It seems therefore that, in certain cases at least, worship was paid to the Goddess herself for the sake of the Minoan dead, who might be considered, like their forefathers, to have returned to her keeping. Such discoveries elucidate the scenes painted upon the monument, which must now be described.

THE HAGHIA TRIADA SARCOPHAGUS[2]

The subjects which ornament the sides of the Haghia Triada Sarcophagus, a limestone coffin of late workmanship, are of exactly the double nature required by the above conditions (pl. XXVIII, *a*, *b*, and *d*).

One procession of men clothed in the ritual tailed skirt of hide or fleece marches forward with offerings, the leader bearing a model ship, and his followers the images of bulls, towards a motionless figure who stands or rises, with arms hidden in his long robe (the feet are missing), beside a cypress tree, and before the gateway of what is almost certainly his tomb, since it is furnished with a stepped platform upon which the offerings will be laid (pl. XXVIII*a*).

The remaining scene of this panel faces the other way. A priestess in the same tailed skirt pours blood into a jar between two leaf-wound poles into which double axes are set, and upon either axe perches a 'dove'. An attendant and musician wait behind her (pl. XXVIII*b*).

On the farther side of the sarcophagus, in front of a second procession of women led by a flute player, the dying bull lies on his table of sacrifice, shedding his blood into a vessel below. Beyond him a votary, perhaps wife to the dead man, offers libations at an altar set before a double-axe standard, upon which another bird is visible. Beyond that again an enclosure, with its horns of consecration, surrounds the sacred Tree.

Here are all the chief ritual emblems of the Goddess, and her very presence is to be presumed. Indeed upon one of the ends

[1] Evans, *Archæologia*, lxv, 1914, on The Tomb of the Double Axes, and *P. of M.*, ii, p. 279.

[2] Paribeni, 'Il sarcofago dipinto di Haghia Triada,' *Mon. ant.*, xix, p. 5 ff.

of the painted sepulchre she may perhaps be seen, arriving with her Companion in a horse-drawn chariot. But at the other end the work is accomplished. She drives the dead man, his face yet grey, in a car drawn by two of her Griffins to his Elysian home[1] (pl. XXVIII*d*).

Another coffin[2] shows the young God descending with his shield upon the waters, and another[3] has painted horns of consecration, bulls, bird and double-axe, yet further strengthening the impression of the tombs that service was paid to the Goddess for the departed, and offerings to himself; that the boat, the tree, libations, sacrifice, played their part here as in Egypt and Sumer, and that the rites in general followed the ancient course.

THE FUNERAL RINGS

The hoops of certain gold signet rings are too small even for dead fingers.[4] They must have been suspended as amulets, their bezels engraved, to judge by many of the known examples, with a kind of chart of the new country, which warrants a detailed description.

The presence of the trees which dominate the designs of this class, might be anticipated from the previous scenes of mourning, and from recollections of the lapis-fruited *kishkanu* of the Babylonian,[5] and the sycamore of the Egyptian underworld,[6] and lastly of the buried trees of Abydos and Deir el Bahri.[7] Perhaps this tree was conceived by them all as rising in spring through the body of its earthly counterpart, the abode of the Goddess.

---

[1] Nilsson, who thinks an apotheosis is represented (op. cit., pp. 378, 381), interprets the griffins as transporting him to heaven. But the Ring of Nestor shows them as guardians and denizens of the Realm of the Goddess in the Underworld. See below, p. 238.

[2] Evans, *Mycenæan Tree and Pillar Cult*, fig. 50.

[3] *Delt. arch.*, vi, 1921, app., p. 158, fig. 5; Nilsson, op. cit., fig. 107. The larnax from Palaikastro (*B.S.A.*, viii, pl. xviii) has horns of consecration and a double axe.

[4] Evans, 'Ring of Nestor,' p. 47.

[5] P. 120, pl. X*d*.   [6] Figs. 59 and 60.

[7] See *The Cenotaph of Seti I at Abydos*, 1933, i, p.11 (Frankfort, de Buck, and Battiscombe Gunn).

The most remarkable of the signets, the so-called *Ring of Nestor* (pl. XXIX*b*), though said to have been found in a tomb of the mainland,[1] may safely be held to represent Minoan beliefs, because its style is completely Cretan, and almost all its elements, apart from the actual scenes portrayed, have Minoan prototypes.

The order of the subjects will be read from the intaglio, not from its impression, for the engravings of hunters and warriors who are right-handed only on the signets, make it evident that their amuletic function required the correct version to be displayed upon the ring.[2]

A branching Tree, then, divides the surface into four quarters, showing a care for orientation usually foreign to Crete, for all the swastikas and wheel-motifs to be found in the decoration of its pottery. The beast who guards or devours the Tree's root has so far no Minoan analogies; a mythical representation of time seems quite out of character. But the scenes thus separated are peopled with one exception, by familiar types. The lion who guards the entrance, like one of the Great Mother's Phrygian lions, is not elsewhere found in this culture, with the possible exceptions of the early stone amulet[3] in which a lion crouches above a figure bent in the attitude of early burial, and a couchant gold lion from a Mycenæan grave.[4]

The Babylonian plaque, which shows lion-masked priests conducting funeral rites, and the encounter of the dead man below them with the lions of the threshold,[5] may safely be considered analogous here; only the chthonic aspect of the Goddess in Asia and Africa can explain the relation of lion to tomb. Above the recumbent beast, sprays of ivy spring from the tree trunk; ivy which was twisted round the columnar stone lamps in the cavernous gloom of the pillar crypts.[6] Its spiral growth

[1] Evans, 'Ring of Nestor,' part ii, in *J.H.S.*, 1925, pp. 43–75.

[2] The seal-cutters of Mesopotamia cut so as to make the hunters and fighters on the impression right-handed.

[3] Evans, *Palace of Minos*, i, p. 55, and fig. 26. An E. M. ivory seal from the tholos at Kalathiana.

[4] See H. Schliemann, Mycenæ, 1878, p. 361, No. 532.

[5] Bronze plaque in the Louvre; Clermont-Ganneau in *Revue Archéologique*, 1879, p. 337, pl. xxv; A. B. Cook in *J.H.S.*, xiv, pp. 118–119, and fig. 13.

[6] Evans, op. cit., i, fig. 249.

and evergreen nature perhaps account for its presence here, as in the Crete-derived mystery religions of Greece.

Beneath the lion a human couple kneel in terror and supplication, probably the same man and woman who meet so joyfully on the farther side of the tree, in the presence of two female forms, one of them naked—surely the Goddess and her companion. If the tiny objects above them are indeed butterflies emerging from the chrysalis (and both butterfly and chrysalis wrought in gold are common in Mycenæan graves),[1] they only seem to emphasise what the figures already imply. It appears, however, that the presence of divinity is not yet recognised; for that we must turn to the scene below. A griffin-headed apparition conducts the newcomers to the goal of their journey. Hand in hand, with dancing steps,[2] they pass to the last region encompassed by the Tree. A griffin-woman (on earth she would be griffin-masked; or rather falcon-masked, for human beings cannot bear the double nature)[3] turns to welcome them to a presence before which griffin-headed votaries stand with hands raised in an attitude of intercession or devotion. A winged griffin faces them, poised upon a platform or altar, the Lion-hawk of Earth and Sky.[4] Behind him in full panoply stands the Goddess.

It is unlikely that a special story is illustrated here, but the possibility exists because of the mainland provenance of the ring. As a presentation of religious belief, however, it is immaterial whether the subject is particular or general. That is true also of the *Ring of Minos* found on a hillside near to Knossos, close to the Temple Tomb,[5] from which it is therefore possibly derived (pl. XXIX*c*).

To eyes reading from the left of the intaglio as before, the Naked Goddess first appears before a small enclosure, bending the branches of the Sacred Tree, or possibly breaking off a

---

[1] Schliemann, op. cit., p. 176, nos. 256–260.

[2] Because it is a ceremony.

[3] Frankfort, in *B.S.A.*, vol. xxxvii, p. 120, distinguishes in this connection, the griffin from the griffin-dæmon, familiar in Syrian and especially Assyrian art.

[4] The griffin-drawn chariot of the dead on the Haghia Triada sarcophagus will be remembered.

[5] Evans, op. cit., iv (ii), pp. 962–963, describes how the existence of the ring caused him to search for the tomb.

bough—surely the 'Golden Bough' of legend. In the foreground the Goddess, wearing her flounced robe, steers across the waves a little barque which bears her two altars, its prow shaped like a sea-horse. One would call it a river-craft, if Crete had possessed navigable rivers, remembering those strangely similar dragon-headed skiffs upon which a like Goddess, with her leafy branch, is borne beside the Sun-God of Akkadian seals, across the waters of the underworld.[1]

On a gold signet of similar form from Mochlos (fig. 115, below), the same subject is portrayed, but in that example the naked Goddess[2] of our first scene guides the vessel, shaped as before,

Fig. 115

from the shrine at the sea's edge, and above her appear the sprouting corn-seeds, or bags of grain, familiar in the Akkadian examples. Upon the deck of this boat also, stand the two altars, which take us right back to the double altar of the Warka seal,[3] within a boat which approaches a gateway guarded by the emblems of the Goddess.

But the Mochlos signet shows the Tree itself, or its branches, above one altar, and confirms the impression of boughs rising from the higher altar on the Ring of Minos, half confused with the network of the omphalos-like mountain behind. There is yet another gold signet, attached to a similar narrow ring, on which a couple, hand in hand before the pillar of a shrine, welcome an approaching barge upon which the Goddess stands

[1] See pl. XXIIId.
[2] Persson sees signs of a robe in a protuberance on the thigh.
[3] Pl. XIa.

erect above a line of obscure figures (oarsmen perhaps), her
tree rising behind her (fig. 116, below). That too should be a
funeral ring.[1]

The Tree then, or a part of it, would here seem to be borne
like a 'Golden Bough' across the waters dividing the two worlds,
to the shore where the Goddess sits in full glory upon her
horned altar, reinforced by her second personality descending
through the air, and partaking of her own life in the fig-juice
of the Elysian tree, which the young ministrant collects for her
sustenance. Its lofty triple-pillared shrine stands within horns
of consecration, and piled about its base, as around the other
shrines, are great objects resembling the shields which play so

Fig. 116

large a part in the vegetation rites. Of course they may be
merely boulders, but the gold ring, shown in fig. 93, p. 220, to
illustrate the rites of the Vegetation Goddess, has again this
narrow-hooped form, and there the shields find place in a dance
of welcome to the Goddess, risen between youths and maidens
above the blossoming soil. The lovely example reproduced
beside it (fig. 92, p. 220), which was found in a chamber tomb at
Isopata,[2] shows a similar epiphany amid ecstatic worshippers
in a field of lilies. The Knossian signet, on which a young shield-
bearing divinity descends before a pillared tree-sanctuary
(fig. 95, p. 222), the great ring from the Mycenæan grave-circle
already described (fig. 96, p. 220), and that other relic of the
Vapheio tomb (fig. 110, p. 220), in which the votary bends the

[1] Evans, op. cit., ii, fig. 147*b*.
[2] Evans, *Tomb of the Double Axes*, fig. 16.

(a)

(b)

(c)

Plate 29. FUNERAL RINGS

(a)

(b)

Plate 30. RELIEFS

sacred bough in the presence of the Goddess, the shield with votive garment, the knot entwined about the double-axe, and lastly a chrysalis and two butterflies—all these examples belong to the class of funeral ring.

The prevalence of such subjects among amulets of this form, most of them actually found within, or in the neighbourhood of, graves, is clearly traceable to beliefs, previously investigated, which were seen to be held in common by Egypt and Sumer, and to have been already advanced at the period of emergence from the Stone Age. But in Crete and the Greek Peninsula a singularly close link must have been felt to exist between the burgeoning of earth and rebirth of the dead. It became indeed the central tenet in the mystery-religion of their successors.

CHAPTER II

MYTHICAL FOUNDATION
OF THE MAINLAND CITIES

THE SACRED DEFENCES

D uring the earlier centuries of Minoan civilisation, the
Greek peninsula appears to have been colonised by a
race having cultural affinities with Crete and the
islands, with the exception of Thessaly, into which a stream of
influence had penetrated from the Chalcolithic towns of the
Black Earth region.[1]

The place-names which link the Greek mainland with Crete
and Asia Minor do not occur on Neolithic sites;[2] a migration of
kindred stock, therefore, may be supposed to have introduced
the Bronze Age culture across the Ægean, making settlements
on the marshy plains, which were drained for their pastures
and cornfields.

Upon these settlements fresh irruptions seem to have in-
truded, streaming out of North Western Asia Minor. Whether
or not they were the first Ionians[3]—and only Ionians retained
myths of the heyday of Knossos—their migration seems to
have been set in motion by some disturbance in the East contemporary with the appearance of Indo-European names on
inscriptions in Northern Syria.[4] Since these wanderers appear
to have brought the tamed horse into Europe, together with
the rectangular dwelling with fixed hearth and portico, which

---

[1] V. G. Childe, *Dawn of European Civilisation*, pp. 65–74.

[2] Nilsson, *Homer and Mycenæ*, 1933, p. 67, in upholding Blegen's theory
(in 'The coming of the Greeks', *American Journ. of Archæology*, xxxii, 1928),
that the founders of the *nth* and *ss* civilisation brought the use of bronze.

[3] Nilsson, *The Minoan-Mycenæan Religion*, Introduction, p. 31 ff., quoting
Kretschmer on linguistic grounds.

[4] See below, p. 263.

is found fully developed in Greece at that period,[1] it seems reasonable to believe that the adventurers who built on the hill-tops their Cyclopean strongholds of Asiatic type,[2] into which they received the Minoan culture, were akin not only to the late comers, who continued to develop it after their own manner, but in part at least also to the race, bringing the iron weapons and the geometric pottery, which destroyed it.

But, arriving direct from contact with Asia Minor, these earliest forerunners of the Greeks would be prepared to accept superior achievements, based upon conceptions already familiar, so that, when ships began to pass to and fro, they offered so wholehearted a welcome to the art and religion of Crete, that their separate existence, even, is a matter of conjecture.[3] A Minoan colonisation, empire, or vassalage, have all been assumed to account for this sudden transplantation to the soil of Greece. The immediate cause is irrelevant here, since the spiritual dominion of Crete is unequivocally stated by the existing remains. But certain important aspects of their life, over which that dominion did not extend, point to a dissimilarity, not only of geographical and political conditions, but of actual character, and therefore of origin. They designate in fact a particular race, alive for us in the legends of a later epoch, which are localised round the Bronze Age citadels, roughly termed Mycenæan.

It will be well, then, first to glance through the objects of religious art, received or derived by the mainland townships from Crete, which illustrate in fragments the identity of cult, and exhibit also, during the early period at least, a general similarity of technique and even of material; and then to turn to the Mycenæan contribution to that peculiar conception of the city as a religious unit, which owed something to both peoples, and was to found the first truly European civilisation.

RELIGIOUS ART ON THE MAINLAND

The fortresses which Homer kept in memory, whose splendour excavation has revealed first at Mycenæ, Tiryns and Troy, and

[1] And in Anatolia and N. Syria. See Evans, *J.H.S.*, xlv, 1925, p. 46, n. 4*b*.

[2] V. Gordon Childe, *The Aryans*, 1926, p. 28.

[3] Sir A. Evans believes them to have themselves been of Cretan stock, *J.H.S.*, xxxii, 1912.

later on innumerable sites scattered over the Ægean world, embraced the chieftain's palace with all its adjuncts, and protected the dwellings of his subjects, grouped, to judge by their graveyards, in families or clans.[1] At Mycenæ no temples were found, but only the occasional furniture, such as the stepped base of a double-axe standard,[2] which had belonged to domestic sanctuaries, themselves obliterated under continuous reoccupation. From the graveyard of the Minoan period within the citadel, come little models in gold of the shrines familiar in Cretan representations, with their pillars on two levels between horns of consecration, and doves upon their roofs (see fig. 90 above); of bull's heads surmounted by the double-axe,[3] of a naked Goddess with 'doves',[4] of the fantastic griffins and sphinxes, of chrysalises and butterflies,[5] and the sea-creatures.[6] Among the large objects is a silver bull's head hollowed between the horns for the insertion of the double-axe,[7] and a gold cup, whose pillar-handles are surmounted by the birds which Homer calls doves,[8] and the representations in ivory and faience, already noted, of the sacred Knot (pl. IX, f and g).

Fresco fragments reveal both here and at Tiryns, Orchomenos and Thebes, the familiar bull-contests of youths and maidens, and the pillared shrines, with women in Minoan attire,[9] as well as lay scenes of hunting or war, in which the young men wear a form of Greek chiton, perhaps retaining it, as the fixed hearth may have been retained, where a difference of climate made Minoan costume impracticable. Men

[1] For instance, at Mycenæ. See Ch. Tsountas and J. I. Manatt, *The Mycenæan Age*, 1897, pp. 33 and 337.

[2] Nilsson, *Min.-Myc. Religion*, fig. 61.

[3] Schliemann, op. cit., p. 218, nos. 329, 330.

[4] Tsountas, op. cit., figs. 38, 39.

[5] Evans in *J.H.S.*, 1925, fig. 52.

[6] For Cuttle-fish, see Schliemann, op. cit., p. 268, no. 424; for Griffins, pp. 177, 182; for Sphinx, see p. 183, no. 277.

[7] Tsountas, op. cit., plate xiii, and p. 103.

[8] *Il.*, xi, 632, 5. The description of Nestor's cup is an obvious memory of the Minoan age.

[9] See Evans, *P. of M.*, iii, fig. 48e, from G. Rodenwaldt, *Der Fries des Megarons von Mykenai*.

and women also appear in the long stole-like garment of late Minoan times,[1] keeping their distinctive flesh colours of white or red.

The sacred half-rosettes of Cretan frescoes, reliefs and vase-paintings were set up at Tiryns above the door of a chamber with a sacrificial pit,[2] and over the antechamber of the Treasury of Atreus.[3] The ceremonial bull-catching may be traced, beaten in gold of the finest Minoan craftsmanship, round the cups from the Vapheio tomb near Sparta,[4] the octopus and nautilus over the golden bowl from inland Mideia;[5] and swords from the Mycenæan shaft-graves overlaid with various metals, show Minoan leaping beasts and the dappled Minoan shield.

The familiar signet-rings abound in Cretan scenes of ritual, with a predilection for the Mountain-Mother between heraldic beasts, which are here especially fantastic, and often winged.[6] Often too they guard a pillar or tree in the place of a divinity, and their unity of function is sometimes enforced by the representation of a single central head, which holds their bodies combined (fig. 117, p. 258).[7]

A golden signet from Tiryns shows the Minoan Genii, lion-headed, with skin-cloaks and girdles and hieratic forward thrust, bearing their ewers in procession before the Goddess (pl. XXIX*a*), and on the gold funeral ring from the Mycenæan Acropolis already portrayed (fig. 94, p. 220), the Goddess beneath her tree receives offerings of flowers and fruit, while the Young God descends with his shield. Some of the finest illustrations of the tree cult come in fact from the mainland, and among other funeral rings appears the Ring of Nestor, described above, from the probable site of Homer's Pylos (pl. XXIX*b*), and a second unique example from a grave at Mideia, on which the triple bow of the Mountain Mother

[1] As, for instance, in pl. XXVIII (The Haghia Triada Sarcophagus).

[2] Evans, *Palace of Minos*, iv (i), pp. 222–223, showing corresponding half rosettes from Knossos.

[3] Evans, op. cit., iv (i), fig. 171*c*, p. 222.

[4] Tsountas, op. cit., pl. xix.

[5] A. W. Persson, *The Royal Tombs at Dendra near Midea*, 1931, plates ix, x, xi, and Frontispiece.

[6] See fig. 71 in *P. of M.*, vol. iii.

[7] There is a similar gem to fig. 117, in which two winged rams share a head (Evans, *P. of M.*, iv, 2, fig. 576.

symbolises her presence between heraldic beasts on two levels (fig. 118, p. 258).

The animal-masked priests are seen on the fragment of fresco from Mycenæ illustrated above,[1] and the adder-notching round the palace hearth has already been described. Except for this last, no sign has survived of a snake cult in the vanished household chapels; otherwise the ritual paraphernalia of the Goddess is here complete. No male divinity appears beyond the young attendant or companion of the Goddess, but all the elements are present of the Bull-sacrifice, the Pillar-cult, and the Vegetation rites.

THE CITIES

The Shield, which occurs, as we have seen, in a frieze round the walls of a palace chamber at Tiryns,[2] is once borne by a female (i.e. white-skinned) figure between worshippers on a limestone panel from Mycenæ,[3] a change which may signify a new relation between the Goddess and the community.

For the column that was exalted by the later builders above the entrance-gate of Mycenæ, the architectural embodiment, with capital and the beam-ends of the architrave, of the deity of a mountain-citadel erect between the heraldic beasts (pl. XXX*a*), expresses something far beyond the tribal coherence of settled nomads. On a sealing from Cretan Zakro[4] there is a gate completely encircled by the bodies of lion guardians, but that is the doorway of a shrine, through which may be discerned the antithetic semicircles of frieze or altar (fig. 119, p. 258). A companion seal-impression depicts a cluster of little towers against which huge shields are piled,[5] symbols of the protective fecundity of the earth,[6] both functions appearing here in one (fig. 120, p. 258).

Since fortified towns, however, do not remain, or never

---

[1] See above, fig. 105.   [2] Above, p. 232.   [3] Tsountas, op. cit., pl. xx.

[4] See D. Hogarth, *Zakro Sealings*, *J.H.S.*, xxii, 1902, p. 76 ff.

[5] Hogarth, op. cit., figs. 29 and 30. In the drawing of fig. 120 one of the shields has been restored as a helmet, of which the impression (pl. x, 131) shows no sign. See previous chapter for the function of the shield in fertility rites.

[6] See above, pp. 232, 233.

existed, in Minoan Crete,[1] it cannot be determined whether any Cretan conception of religious unity bound the mainland settlements to their focal cities. That is of little consequence, since the sacred defences derived their profound significance from a source older than both—the protective magic of the Stone Age.[2] Their archetype was the labyrinth, even if that existed only as Homer's pathway marked by Dædalus for the convolutions of Ariadne's dance in Knossos,[3] the fertility dance of the shield-bearing men and the maidens of our Copenhagen signet,[4] with all its implications of search and the discovery or re-creation of life,[5] The name is now believed to connote galleries of stone,[6] and it is reasonable on the literary evidence to locate the most famous of all labyrinths in Crete, whether it was constructed or rock-cut like the Egyptian sacred defences, or the naturally twisting corridors of a cave, like the Palæolithic.[7]

Such maze-like dancing-grounds have remained in use all over Europe down to modern times.[8] They are still frequented in the North for a game or race in which the boys compete to rescue a girl from the centre of the maze.[9] In Crete, however,

---

[1] See A. W. Lawrence, *The Alleged Fortifications of Cnossus*, *J.H.S.*, lxii, 1942, pp. 84–85.

[2] W. F. J. Knight, in *Cumæan Gates*, passim.

[3] Homer, *Iliad*, xviii, 590 ff., comparing with it the dancing-ground depicted on Achilles' shield, where the boys were armed with sword and shield, and the girls bore flowers. He describes a spiral or circular movement ending in a meeting at the centre.

[4] Fig. 93.

[5] Muller, *Mnemosyne*, series iii, para. 2.

[6] Hermann Greutert, 'Labyrinth . . . *Sitzungsberichte der Heidelberger Akademie der Wissenschaften. Ph. hist. Kl. 1930–1931*, I. Abh., 4, 5, 6; F. Muller in *Mnemosyne*, op. cit., connects it also with the Attic Laurion.

[7] Herodotus names after it the structure at Hawara (ii 148). Pliny also describes it as a building like the Egyptian labyrinths in *Nat. Hist.*, xxxvi, 84–85; but there is a long list of late authors who call it a cave. These have been collected by Knight, after R. Eilmann, in *Cumæan Gates*, p. 134.

[8] See W. H. Matthews, *Mazes and Labyrinths*, 1922, for a comprehensive account of these structures.

[9] Matthews, op. cit., pp. 147–151, and figs. 124, 125 (from Finland), 126 (from Gothland). This last is called Tröjeburg. Most of those in Norway and Sweden have Troy names, an interesting exception being 'Steintanz.'

the tributary youths and maidens of Athenian legend encountered not the Goddess but her bull-masked ministrant, whom we have seen so wildly dancing upon Minoan gems.[1] Only Theseus penetrated to the centre, to 'discover' Ariadne (whose name, the 'Very Holy', was retained in Cyprus as an epithet of the Goddess Aphrodite),[2] with the help of her own clue,[3] her knot or Key of Life,[4] and lost her again, as such a Goddess is always lost, in the return to the outer world. But he set up her image in Delos, and taught the rescued boys and maidens to dance before its horned altar the inward and outward windings of the labyrinth, singing the story as they moved.[5]

That dance was performed again at the breaking of the defences of Troy by those who wound the ropes about the

[1] Fig. 106.

[2] Ἀριάγνη, a variant form of her name, is given its Greek meaning by Hesychius: ἀδνόν· ἀγνόν· Κρῆτες. For the linguistic examination of these forms, Nilsson refers to K. Brugmann, *Indogerm. Forschungen*, v, 1895, p. 379.

[3] That is, he discovered the Goddess at the centre, as she is shown on vase-paintings watching the contest (*Mnemosyne*, iii 2, pl. vii 2, pl. viii 1), since he afterwards instituted the dance of the 'inward and outward windings' before the image of Aphrodite brought from Crete (Plut., *Thes.*, 21). On the François vase, Theseus, playing the lyre, acts as leader of a dancing band who approach Ariadne (Evans, *Palace of Minos*, i, p. 2). Delian inscriptions mention Ἀγνὴ Ἀφροδίτη (*Bull. Corr. Hell.*, vi, 1882, p. 489, no. 1; vii, 1883, p. 367 ff., no. 17). See Nilsson, *Minoan-Mycenæan Religion*, p. 452, no. 2. The Cord as Path will be remembered in more primitive ritual (pl. iiic).

[4] For Inanna's rolled and tied bundle, as illustrated in the terracotta inlay from Warka (pl. ixe), which exactly resembles the Minoan and Mycenæan emblem of the Goddess, combines the knot with the spiral of entry or birth. In an Egyptian illustration to the Book of the Dead the knotted Ankh sign of life is set before the horned gate of the cloven mountain, guarded by the chthonic lions. A lead coffin found in Palestine in 1928, whose exterior was decorated with knots and vine-branches in relief, contained a skeleton whose mouth was filled with similar knots in gold leaf —the bread of life, it would seem. Indeed, the Syrian Christians bake rolls of exactly that shape to be eaten once a year on Easter morning. The cry 'A nut, a nut' of the English folk-dance, is probably the 'knot' of the Labyrinth. See J. E. Weston, *From Ritual to Romance*.

[5] Plutarch, *Theseus*, 21; Callimachus, *Hymns*, iv, 307 ff. The daughter of Minos appears to be the human representative or priestess of the Goddess who walked with him the sacred pathway, and this would fit Homer's description of her ὀρχηστρά.

Horse.[1] The name of Troy, in fact, became attached in many countries to maze-shaped dancing-grounds[2] (in mediæval Crete it was applied to the labyrinth itself!)[3] and it was such a maze track that Vergil's armed youths followed;[4] in a dance deliberately associated with the building of a 'second wall' of magic defence round the cities of Latium. They ride it round an Etruscan vase, on which the maze itself is depicted, with the inscription 'Truia', in combination with other fertility rites.[5]

It is this 'second wall' which binds the towns of heroic legend with the old religion, and gives to their tradition its enduring content. For this reason the literary testimony of the mythical foundation and destruction of the strongholds of the Ægean world must be combined with the archæological evidence, for they corroborate each other to explain the peculiar relation of their conquerors to the cities that were their gift to civilisation.

[1] Verg., *Aen.*, ii, vv, 238–240. For the rope dance of girls and boys, see A. B. Cook, *J.H.S.*, xiv, 1894, 101–102; and Knight, *Cumæan Gates*, p. 106. The Delian dance, compared by Tryphiodorus with that which escorted the Horse of Troy, was called The Crane Dance. Cf. E. A. Armstrong, 'The Crane Dance, in East and West,' *Antiquity*, June, 1943.

[2] In Scandinavia; see note 9, p. 247. In England at Somerton and Hillbury ('Troy Towns'). In Cumberland and Lincolnshire as 'The Walls of Troy'; as Caer Droia in Wales. The dance itself under the name of 'Trojan game' is performed on horseback by Ascanius and his companions round Anchises' grave, and said by Vergil to have been repeated at the founding of Alba Longa. See note 4 below.

[3] Matthews, op. cit., p. 156, quotes a manuscript in the British Museum recording a journey to Jerusalem made by the Seigneur de Caumont in 1418, in which the traveller, calling at Crete, speaks thus of the Labyrinth: 'Lequelle meson fut nommée Labarinte et aujourduy par moultz est vulguelmant appellé le cipté de Troie.'

[4] Verg., *Aen.*, v, 597. 'Longam muris cum cingeret Albam.' Concerning this and the armed dance of the Salii, see the material collected by Knight, op. cit., pp. 85–86. He quotes Inez Scott Regburg, *Transactions (and Proceedings) of the American Philological Soc.*, lxiii, lxiv, for evidence that the armed dance of the Salii was originally a fertility rite. Their shields were of Minoan form.

[5] G. Cl. Giglioli, *Studi Etruschi*, iii, 1929, 111–159. See fig. ii in W. F. J. Knight's *Cumæan Gates*, after Matthews, *Mazes and Labyrinths*, 1912, figs. 133–135, and F. Muller, Jun., *Mnemosyne*, iii, vol. ii, 1935, pl. iv. Dr. Muller, op. cit., 229, recognised the scene behind as a sacred marriage from its resemblance to the seal found at Tell Asmar (Eshnunna), Frankfort, *Iraq*, i 1, 1934, plate i (2).

The myths have come down to us in the Greek language, but the Greek Zeus is absent. They are the creation of a people who delighted in tales of adventure and war; yet these are all fast imbedded in the ritual of the Goddess, and it is a very noteworthy fact that at Olympia and Delphi, where no fortress-city had existed, the Greek Gods came into their own, replacing in both towns the former female divinity;[1] whereas a chief temple to the Mother Goddess in one of her later aspects, stood upon the former palace sites of Mycenæ, Tiryns, Ægina, Athens and Troy.[2]

Troy must be reckoned among these towns, though she had an Asiatic past, and never came directly under the influence of Minos, for her architecture and later culture betray kinship with the Mycenæan strongholds of the Greek peninsula, and her myths as well as her legends resemble those of Thebes.

The walls of both cities were built by music,[3] that is, there was a magic defence of the kind just described, controlled by the sound and movement of a dance, whose breaking by a similar ritual we have noted at Troy; and the foundation or destruction of each was bound up also with the prolonged endeavour to win back a lost woman, or Goddess—for Helen among the Dorians was a divinity of vegetation hanged from a tree,[4] and Europa borne across the sea to Crete by the God in bull-form, was presumably the cow who guided the search of

[1] The opening lines of the *Eumenides* of Æschylus give a well-known enumeration of the stages by which possession of the Delphic oracle passed from Earth Goddess to Apollo, an account now borne out by archæology: *Fouilles de Delphes*, v, p. 1 ff.

[2] For Mycenæ, see plan first published in Πρακτικά, 1886, pl. iv. See Nilsson, *Min.-Myc. Religion*, p. 405, for the temple of Athena upon the ruins of the former palace. At Tiryns the palace Megaron seems to have been rebuilt into the temple of Hera, and the old altar actually used. (*Athen. Mitt.*, xxx, 1905, p. 152. Nilsson, op. cit., pp. 406–410.) As to Ægina, inscriptions show the classical temple to have been dedicated to Aphaia, the Goddess identified by ancient authors with Britomartis. Mycenæan remains were thrown out in levelling the ground for the later temple (Nilsson, op. cit., pp. 404 and 441). For Athens, and the Mycenæan building below Dörpfeld's old temple of Athena on the Acropolis, see Kavvadias, *Die Ausgrabung der Akropolis*, p. 84, and Nilsson, op. cit., p. 406.

[3] Troy 'rose slowly, to a music slowly breathed' by Apollo's lyre; Callimachus, *Hymn Apol.*, 15; Thebes by Amphion's, Hesiod, fragm. 60.

[4] Helen δενδρῖτις at Rhodes. Pausanias, iii, 19, 10.

Kadmos, till she lay down to be sacrificed at the spot where Thebes was to rise.[1]

Before that sacrifice could be accomplished, the snake-men had leapt out of the earth to perform their internecine sword-dance which was to populate the future city, and, after due service, Kadmos wedded the daughter of the young fertility God who was later the War God, in a sacred marriage (for the Gods were present). When his bride resumed her serpent form, he too became a snake.[2]

The earth-stories also haunt the decline of Thebes; Œdipus, Antigone and Amphiaraos return alive into the ground,[3] but Troy on alien soil was especially the scene of the struggle with the new order. It is the Horse that leaps her sacred walls, after dragging her defender in contrary circuit around them.[4]

The snake, which in the Theban myth relates the foundation of the city with the divinities of earth, does, however, appear as emblem of the Mistress of another city (who was to take rank as the Protectress of Cities); of the crowning city among the later Greek states. The Goddess found in the humble domestic sanctuaries of Minoan Crete, possessed, it will be recalled, the snake and the bird as her emblems. The bird she shared with her other personalities, but the serpent symbolised her peculiar

[1] Euripides, *Phœnissæ*, 638 ff. Apollodorus relates that Ilus, the eponymous hero of Ilion, founded Troy in a similar manner by following a cow. He may have been using a general legend concerning sacred towns, since the Pharaoh of the Pyramid Texts is guided by a cow to the celestial city.

[2] Euripides, *Bacchæ*, 1332 ff.

[3] Sophocles, *Œdipus at Colonus*, 1661 ff.; Sophocles, *Antigone*, 774; Pindar, *Nem.*, ix, 24–25.

[4] For the horse as introduced by the Aryan Greeks, see below. For the 'unwinding' of the magic defence, see Knight, *Antiquity*, vi, 1932, pp. 454–457. The mythological, as opposed to the human, significance of Hector as Pillar of Troy, is constantly asserted by classical authors (e.g. Pindar, Ol. II, 81. Τροίας ἄμαχον ἀστραβῆ κίονα.); but his 'stone-cult' seems to have become overlaid by solar influences, connected by the new race, both East and West, with the wheel and the wheeled vehicle. (See A. B. Cook, *Zeus*, i, 197 ff.) This appears to have happened also to Hippolytus, once the young fertility God, brother or companion of the prototype of Artemis (Frazer, *The Golden Bough*, ii, 380; Cook, *Zeus*, 392 ff. Above, p. 225) who, like the would-be Sun God, Phaethon, was flung from his chariot. The invocation of Æneas: 'O lux Dardaniæ,' to the ghost of Hector 'torn by the chariot's sweep', when the enemy have broken the defences (Verg., *Aen.*, ii, 281 ff.), again suggests a solar association. That is only on the edge of this enquiry, but helps to show why it was a horse that leapt the wall.

relation with the earth, as the Cave-Mother, and Hut-Mother, guardian of stored wealth, and of the household dead.

Athena, reluctantly perhaps, retained the serpent with the bird whose wings she bears in archaic art,[1] just as her owl itself appears on early vases human-headed, spinning, or armed.[2] She is almost lifted above the ground, but her Libyan identifications show her to have once been a chaste fertility Goddess, to whom seasonal armed dances were performed,[3] before she leaped in the Greek imagination from her father's head, sounding a war cry, the Defence of the City.

Hers is the only temple mentioned by Homer in Troy. Perhaps the chamber found there in the Mycenæan citadel,[4] with its three pillars foreign to Trojan architecture, was the Asiatic counterpart of the palace sanctuaries of the Goddess, and contained the sole image of which the poet speaks, in that after-age of many Gods.[5] The Palladium described by later authors seems to have been her shield, kept under the old dispensation in a secret place, resembling the shield borne by the Goddess on a painted slab in Mycenæ,[6] life-bearing like her

---

[1] On a black-figured cup, *Coll. Faina. Rom. Mitt.*, 1897, xii, pl. 12, reproduced in J. E. Harrison's *Prolegomena to the Study of Greek Religion*, 1903, fig. 86. She mentions another vase published by A. de Ridder, *Cat. Bibl. Nat.*, no. 269, p. 173, fig. 23, where Athena flies over the sea. One prototype of Athena may be the Owl-Goddess (Lilith?) published in A. B. Cook, *Zeus*, iii, pl. lxi, dating to the Larsa period in Mesopotamia.

[2] Nilsson has shown in *Minoan-Mycenæan Religion*, pp. 421–422, that in early art, as in Homer, Athena's attribute or epiphany takes the form of many birds—sea-eagle, swallow, vulture and dove. A human-headed bird sometimes appears beside her on vase-paintings (M. Mayer in *Hermes*, xxvii, 1892, p. 481). But the above representations are mostly non-Attic. Nilsson cites a late red-figured jug in the Louvre on which the owl is armed with shield and spear, and a series of plaques in which an owl with human arms is spinning wool.

[3] See above, p. 117, for the dances to the Libyan Goddess identified by the Greeks with Athena.

[4] Excavated by Dörpfeld in 1893–1894. A temple to Apollo is once mentioned, in *Iliad*, v, 446.

[5] In *Iliad*, vi, 297 ff., where Hekabe brings her fairest robe as an offering to be laid on Athena's knees (like the dresses hung up in the Minoan Goddess's shrine).

[6] Ernest Gardner, in 'Palladia from Mycenæ', *J.H.S.*, xiii, 1893, p. 2 ff., relates the palladium to the Minoan shield. Evans in *P. of M.*, i, pp. 172–173, adds the Neith connection. Bates in the *Eastern Libyans*, p. 203 ff., discusses the assimilation by Herodotus of Neith to Athena.

ægis,[1] whose goatskin fringe (a link with her Lybian proto-type) became the snake-border of later art.[2]

She was hostile to Troy; therefore it was doomed. She could work evil upon it, while Zeus grieved, without avail, upon his throne.

But already in the Iliad she has her temple in Athens.[3] Her name is probably adjectival of the older population—the Athenian Lady—as the Mycenæan Lady may have personified Mycenæ. Once in the Odyssey indeed she returns to the 'strong house' in Athens, as if re-entering the palace shrine.[4]

In the later Athens, where her temple stood on the lofty site of the Mycenæan palace, the earth-binding snake is very evident, and all its earliest myths connect her with vegetation rites. She wins Athens as her portion by causing the olive tree to spring forth; she receives out of the Earth her foster-child Erichthonios (pl. XXXI*b* of Part V below); and her snakes guard him in the chest which will be opened by the Dew-sisters, daughters of the half-snake Kekrops.[5] In his temple, which alone stood beside hers on the Acropolis, the Tree and the Snake were tended with devotion through the age of sophisticated culture which was her creation.[6] At its close, her city's long walls fell to the sound of music and dancing,[7] according to the ancient rites.

Those cities of the Mycenæan age, which found no glorious successors to preserve the story of their origin, have left behind only their surprising monuments. This is the case with Pylos, Orchomenos, the huge walls of Mideia and the tiny, unidentified Gla. The Mycenæ of legend belongs to the heroic age, but the myths of its ruling dynasty have another provenance. Tiryns, built by the Cyclopes, has one story about the daughter of its founder. She and her fellow-priestesses of the Goddess,

---

[1] This is Nilsson's theory, and Rodenwaldt's in *Ath. Mitt.*, xxxvii, 1912, p. 137.

[2] O. Bates, *The Eastern Libyans*, p. 128.

[3] *Iliad*, ii, 546, where Erechtheus is the son of Earth, and foster child of Athena (Erechtheus = Erichthonios).

[4] *Odyssey*, vii, 80 ff.; Nilsson, *Min.-Myc. Religion*, p. 418. Homer once mentions a heroine named Mykene.

[5] As illustrated on the amphora, *B.M. Cat. E.*, 418; J. E. Harrison, *Myths and Monuments of Ancient Athens*, p. xxxii; Prolegomena, fig. 13.

[6] Herodotus, viii 41 and 55.   [7] Xenophon, Hellenica, ii 23.

who on Greek soil became Hera, imagined themselves to be cows, a reminder of the animal-dances.[1]

The legends of the Minyai of Thessaly group themselves round tribes rather than towns, their Southern connections being slight.[2] Nevertheless, it is as a constellation of cities, each with its individual history, that the Mycenæan civilisation is remembered and revealed. Even when held together under some chief city, they seem never to have formed a political whole, as Crete did on the pattern of her neighbours in Africa and Asia.

CULT OF THE DEAD

Apart from the great systems of fortification, there is another material achievement which differentiates the mainland culture from the island of its origin, and this again seems based on a difference of racial history and political outlook. It is the skill and splendour lavished upon the monuments of the dead.

In Crete, it will be remembered, signs of offerings appear beside the burials of every period and type, and in certain special cases there is evidence also of rites practised there to the Goddess.[3] From the scenes depicted upon the Ring of Nestor it may be accepted that Mycenæan expectations of the after-life resembled those of their religious source. The difference of attitude lies rather in their endeavour to perpetuate the glory of certain individuals and families—for the eyes at least of their immediate descendants, since the great tholoi seem only to have been re-opened on rare occasions for later burials or ceremonies.[4] These bee-hive tombs, found all over Greece, whether their origin is to be looked for in Crete, in Asia or elsewhere, constitute an individual architectural achievement, representing, in perfectly fitted masonry, a cavern-shaped (that is vaulted) dwelling within the earth, with a pillared gateway enclosing a door, whose use was symbolic, for it was blocked by earth when

[1] A. B. Cook, *Zeus*, i, p. 451 ff.

[2] They have a close legendary connection, however, with Pylos. See Nilsson, *The Mycenæan origin of Greek Mythology*, 1932, p. 142 ff.

[3] Above, p. 235.

[4] Tsountas, op. cit., gives the evidence for this on pp. 139–142.

the tomb was closed.[1] The two finest still existing, the Treasury
of Minyas at Orchomenos and the Treasury of Atreus at Mycenæ, have a side-chamber like the rock-cut 'secret sepulchre'
of the Temple-Tomb at Knossos, and, as in the Temple-Tomb,
there stood within the second chamber of the Treasury of
Atreus a single pillar, whose square base remained sunk into a
similar depression, as if for libations or sacrifice.[2] It may also
have supported the ceiling, like the Cretan sacred pillars, but
the side-chamber at Orchomenos had an upper storey cut from
above, to relieve the weight on its beautiful carved ceiling of
Minoan design,[3] as well as to perpetuate, perhaps, the two levels
of Cretan religious architecture. No sign of a pillar remains. The
great tholoi all had pits for sacrifice within or before the tombs,
or niches in the long corridors leading in from the surface of the
hillside. They were all found empty of their dead, first violated
perhaps in the Dorian invasion (to judge by remaining fragments of geometric pottery), with the exception of those opened
in recent years at Mideia, a town on the Argive plain little mentioned in legend, but with a tremendous wall-circuit, speaking
of forgotten importance. Here the bodies of the chieftain and
the women of his family were found amid their possessions
dating to the height of Minoan artistic achievement, and beside
them the remains of sacrifice.[4] In a neighbouring tomb, intact,
but without trace of any burial, were two blocks of stone shaped
like the menhirs of the Megalithic West, with cup-holes for
offerings, and rudimentary heads.[5] It has been suggested with
much reason that these represented the unburied dead, lost perhaps in battle or at sea,[6] a survival of very ancient beliefs concerning stones. Another menhir has been found in a tholos near the
Heraion at Argos.[7] They lent some support to the theory, now

---

[1] Tsountas, op. cit., pp. 139–140, describes how the filling of the dromos
with earth and stones before the door of the 'Tomb of Clytæmnestra' was
found to have been intentional.

[2] Tsountas, op. cit., p. 121.

[3] Tsountas, op. cit., p. 129.

[4] Persson, *The Royal Tombs of Dendra*, p. 18.

[5] Persson, op. cit., pp. 100, 110.

[6] Persson, op. cit., p. 113; Evans, *P. of M.*, iv (i), pp. 245–246. Cf.
Elpenor's request that Odysseus should set up a pillar for him when his
body was lost at sea.

[7] Evans, *P. of M.*, iv (i).

no longer tenable,[1] which related the beehive tombs of Mycenæ to the burials in the grave-circle which lies within the ramparts. The circle is composed of a double row of stone slabs with a gateway, enclosing five[2] pits roughly lined with Cyclopean masonry, all but one containing several burials, perhaps of families, half-seated and partly embalmed, some of them wearing masks, greaves and breastplates of gold, or splendid diadems, amid signets, amulets, and all manner of equipment, much of which goes back, as we have seen, to the Middle Minoan period. The remaining masks are those of broadfaced, sometimes bearded men, apparently of Northern type.[3] Above the rude shafts were stelæ rather barbarously carved with scenes of hunting and warfare, but bordered with decorative motifs, the spiral and similar convolutions, which belong to the Mediterranean ritual of the dead.[4] Among the stelæ stood an altar which had been hollowed for offerings to the underworld.

Each pit had been opened but once to receive its family, and the style of the funeral furniture betrays some divergence of date between the graves. The encircling ramparts of the citadel describe a wider curve where the pits lie; to enclose, it has been suggested, the sepulchres of chieftains once situated beyond them.[5]

For about the period of the fall of Knossos, a more definitely 'Achæan' element seems to have strengthened the fortifications of Mycenæ and occupied Tiryns, the people, it may be, of the Hittite and Egyptian records,[6] whose memory was kept alive by Homer; and perhaps at this warlike epoch the ravages of some enemy were feared. Perhaps also, with the waning of Minoan influence, their own attitude had changed towards the famous men of their race, and when the great fortifications were set up,

[1] For a summary of the new investigations, and their results, see A. J. B. Wace, 'The Treasury of Atreus,' in *Antiquity*, vol. xiv, 1940, p. 233 ff.

[2] The sixth is unconnected with these.

[3] Illustrated in Schliemann, op. cit. See Tsountas, op. cit., fig. 35, for a good example of the physical type.

[4] Figs. 189, 190, in *P. of M.*, iv (i).

[5] Tsountas, op. cit., p. 113; *B.S.A.*, xxv, p. 124.

[6] See H. R. Hall, 'Keftiu and the Peoples of the Sea,' *B.S.A.*, viii, p. 157, and *Cambridge Ancient History*, II, p. 275; E. Forrer, *Vorhomerische Griechen in den Keilschrifttexten von Boghazköi*; *Mitt. der deutschen Orientges.* no. 63, 1924; preliminary report. Nilsson, *Min.-Myc. Religion*, pp. 35-38.

(a)

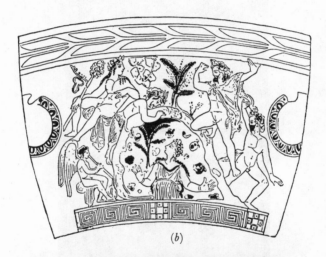

(b)

(c)

Plate 31. GREEK NATURE RELIGION

(a)

(b)

Plate 32. GREEK MYSTERIES

they desired, for the dead as well as for the living, the protection of the walls and of the holy gate.

The shaft graves, with their Minoized ornaments[1], suggest an ancestral rather than a hero-cult in the Greek sense, or perhaps more accurately something between the two, for the families of the ancient chiefs gathered thus within the city walls, must surely have been thought to take their part beside the living in its defence, whether rank or deeds conferred that right. Or both in one, for rank would require performance to confirm it among the occupiers of these hill-towns,[2] a fact abundantly illustrated in their art.

HEROIC SUBJECTS ON THE SEALS

For besides the scenes of Minoan ritual portrayed on ornaments found in these graves and on other scattered sites of the mainland, there are already many which bear, like the stelæ, subjects of purely physical struggle (fig. 121, p. 258). To the end there is never a sign of changed religion, only of changed attention, which becomes increasingly absorbed in the achievements of men. The best attested examples from a hoard of bead-seals and signet rings said to have been found at Thisbe, the port of Thebes, show from how varied a répertoire the subjects might now be chosen.[3] That these were still regarded as amulets may be inferred from the fact that here, as in the rarer Cretan examples, hunters and fighters are left-handed on the impression, so that only the intaglio would possess full efficacy. A

[1] See note p. 244, above, and J. L. (now Sir John) Myres, *Who were the Greeks?* 1930, pp. 282 ff., 381 ff., 574.

[2] See H. M. Chadwick, *The Heroic Age*, 1912, p. 381 ff., for dissolution among these warlike settlers of the religious bonds of kingship.

[3] See A. J. Evans, in *J.H.S.*, lxv, 1925, pp. 1–42. The mixture of sophistication and crudity in their style, and the unique subjects of many specimens, have given rise to serious doubts as to their authenticity. Sir Arthur's arguments, however, in the above article and later in *Palace of Minos*, iv, 452, n. 1, 515 and 17, n. 2, make it reasonable to suppose that their disconcerting peculiarities may be due to the development of a provincial style, influenced by memories of Minoan culture, and modified by the story-telling predilections of a 'heroic' age. The objections of some of the best authorities rest not on their curious style but on the completeness of their range of subject, which has been called 'too good to be true'. These objections suggest, therefore, that a number of false seals may have been introduced into a genuine hoard.

Fig. 117

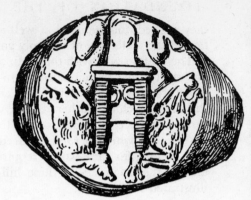

Fig. 119

Fig. 118

Fig. 121

Fig. 123

Fig. 120

left-handed action would have been as easily acquired by the engravers of Crete, as it had been in Sumer at a more primitive stage of technical development. The style of this hoard is a very far-off copy of Minoan forms. The power and speed of movement are missing; only details of dress and equipment are for the most part faithfully transferred. But the heavy treatment of individual figures is balanced by a vivid sense of drama, to which they rather clumsily and obviously adapt themselves. The memories of the dance, which gave the Minoan artist his peculiar grasp both of significant action and of rhythmic composition, are replaced by personal delight in telling a story, and in the actors themselves. It has been well said that if these signets do not illustrate actual legends of the later Greek world, they show the material out of which such legends took shape.[1] This is even true of the religious scenes. Wherever ritual is involved, the subjects of this hoard remain Minoan, but occasionally with modifications of form so prophetic of Greek conceptions as to offer some evidence of continuity (figs. 122, p. 267 and 123, p. 258).

A love of heroic deeds may be considered natural to a people so adventurous, who had left behind them, in generations of wandering, their national Gods, and must have sought their necessary ties in loyalty to chiefs rather than to kindred and ancestral graves.[2] In such circumstances individual prowess would come to matter intensely, but its imposition, within the organism of the Mycenæan city-states, upon a back-ground of mythic ritual, gives it the more universal character appropriate to legend. The spirit of these men was toughened and broken in many wars before they were called upon to face their Dorian kinsmen, but because of this dual association they left an enduring memory across centuries of disintegration.

THE WOODEN HORSE

The walls of Troy were not breached by the Dorian destroyers of the Mycenæan civilisation. The wars in which 'Zeus destroyed the generation of heroes' belong to an earlier period of conflict between the partly Hellenised Achæans and the strong-

---

[1] Nilsson, *Min.-Myc. Religion*, p. 44.
[2] Gilbert Murray, *Rise of the Greek Epic*, 3rd ed., pp. 71–72.

holds of the more ancient world. The likelihood, based upon archæological records, that some form of sovereignty, cultural or actual, had now been established over the islands, and that the tales of Troy or the voyage of the Argonauts recall further migrations of their restless spirit, is greatly strengthened by Egyptian stories of unsuccessful attacks upon the African coast[1] following settlements on the shores of Syria,[2] in which Homeric names occur.

But the legendary expedition against Troy, disastrous to both sides, may be taken as the type of these wars, which finally left the Achæans 'wasted in spirit', and a prey to barbaric swordsmen.

Homer, looking backwards upon the heroic age as historically suited to his great character-drawing, rejected its ritual background because he was concerned with a new order, but even to him, as to Hesiod,[3] the men who fought at Thebes and Troy had been a race apart. They and their fathers almost always bear the names of an older language, but their feebler sons usually receive a purely Greek nomenclature.[4] After their sons there is silence; the curtain of the dark age has fallen.

The Greeks who emerge are a new people. The 'Return of the sons of Herakles' is placed by the ancient historians at fifty years after the fall of Troy, but centuries may have passed before they succeeded in establishing their own communities upon the ashes of the fallen towns. Otherwise their intelligence could not have ignored, in tentative rebuilding, the technical knowledge and beauty that waited discovery below them. They had to initiate order after generations of constant flight and of piracy, after the peace of the seas had been lost in the general

---

[1] By the Aqaiwasha among others in the reign of Merneptah, 1221, B.C.; by the Pulesatha and Danauna, defeated by Rameses III about 1190, B.C. See H. R. Hall, 'Keftiu and the Peoples of the Sea,' *B.S.A.*, viii, p. 157 ff., and *Cambridge Anc. Hist.*, ii, p. 275. There are also the important though still disputed interpretations of E. Forrer; see, for instance, 'La découverte de la Grèce mycénéenne dans les textes cunéiformes de l'Empire hittite,' in *Rev. Et. grecques*, xliii, 1930, p. 279 ff.

[2] On the evidence of the Tell-el-Amarna letters.

[3] Hesiod, *Works and Days*, 156 ff., ἀνδρῶν ἡρώων θεῖον γένος, ἡμίθεοι.

[4] Nilsson, *The Mycenæan Origin of Greek Mythology*, p. 26 points out the usual -*eus* termination of the earlier generations, and the compound, purely Greek, names of their successors—Peleus—Achilleus—Neoptolemos; Atreus—Agamemnon; Tydeus—Diomedes; Odysseus—Telemachus; etc.

break-down of authority, cut off probably by all this destruction from the more advanced civilisations of the neighbouring coasts. For that reason, and because some loose cohesion of the cities, once necessary for the provision of expeditionary forces, was now broken, the new townships had to grow up in isolation and ignorance. The prolonged endeavour to create something upon those ruins toughened them for eventual success. They did establish their hierarchy of Gods and their patriarchal institutions above the terror-striking sanctuaries and graves of the dispossessed.[1] It has been finely suggested that the memory of that struggle at the beginning of their national life, gave the Hellenic peoples a distrust for the permanence of material things, and made their restless political life so great a contrast to the steady discipline of Rome, closely allied, as they were, in language and race.[2] It developed also a character fit to bear the fevers of artistic and intellectual creation at a later time, when the old ghosts no longer cried vainly out of the ground.

Their disillusion, as expressed by Homer, is a break with the faith based upon ritual participation in a divine life. It was like the change inaugurated by the Hebrew prophets, who looked forward across the catastrophe of their political world to an enduring empire of the spirit. Homer brought to birth the Greek nation, Europe itself, by exhibiting man's soul encompassed by all ruin, and betrayed by the Gods themselves, but not by Fate. He may himself have belonged to the older race, but the temper he describes was forged by men of a particular mentality under exacting conditions, 'estranged by beauty' through being thrown back into a remoter age. It would be well at this point to consider how they came to be fitted for the part.

THE 'ARYANS'

On the evidence of words common to many dialects of Indo-European, a language of great potentialities, the speakers of these dialects must have begun their divergent wanderings from a single locality, in which they had reached the Chalco-

---

[1] Murray, op. cit., p. 71, quoting Eur., *Troades*, 1083.
[2] Murray, op. cit., pp. 91–92.

lithic stage of culture,[1] living in pastoral communities in a steppe country, that knew snow and strong summer heat.[2] Their weapons were chiefly of stone, but they were acquainted with copper, and before they separated they had learned how to construct wheeled carts, and dwellings, with doors and pillars within fences, that were not yet grouped into towns.[3] They had no terminology for hunting nor fishing, and no word for the sea.[4] Agricultural terms are rare, but cattle appear to have constituted their standard of value.[5] Their peculiar contribution to material civilisation at this stage was the taming of the horse, probably the steppe-horse, since they called him 'the swift one'.[6] They worshipped as supreme God the Sky-Father, chief among a family of other elemental powers. They knew of the potentialities of sacrifice, but had lost sight of any earth-mother.[7] Their names for kindred point to an early patriarchal social system, and a common word for ruler makes it possible that their Father-God was also a king, on the pattern of human chieftains. Before the Indo-Iranian separation (it was this branch that called itself Aryan and remembered a common home), they had arrived at that conception of an abstract Divine Order, which perhaps constituted their peculiar spiritual gift.[8]

The scene of their earliest-known contact with the more advanced civilisations was Babylonia, where, in the eighteenth century B.C., a dynasty of Kassite invaders, from across the Zagros Mountains to the East, bore names inscribed in cuneiform which contain Indo-European elements, and seem to have replaced the wild-ass, long since tamed by the Sumerians, with

[1] Gordon Childe, *The Aryans*, pp. 82–85. The common words show them to have domesticated animals in the homeland. Two words for copper exist, though these appear to be borrowed from their 'neighbours'. Apparently they knew metal but not its working.

[2] Childe, op. cit., p. 89.   [3] Id. p. 86.

[4] Nor for amber, which, with the absence of these other terms, makes a North European origin very unlikely. An Asiatic word for fish is reproduced in the old High German name for salmon.

[5] Childe, op. cit., p. 83.

[6] Childe, op. cit., p. 88, quoting Duerst in Pumpelly, 'Explorations in Turkestan' (*Carnegie Pub.*, no. 73), ii, p. 431.

[7] Childe, op. cit., p. 81. 'No Earth Goddess is traceable in the language.'

[8] E. Meyer, *Sitzb. K. Preus. Akad. der Wiss.*, 1908, quoted by Childe, op. cit., p. 20.

the horse, whose Semitic name *susu* seems to be derived from their word *asua*.[1]

On the language test it would further appear that the dwellers in the original homeland, whether that was to be located to the north of the Caucasus or elsewhere,[2] must have early come into touch with Mesopotamia, for their words for ox, steer, axe, copper, and star are apparently of Sumero-Akkadian descent.[3] They may possibly therefore have learned from the neighbouring empire, together with stock-breeding and metallurgy, the conception of a celestial system which suggested their Divine Order.

Before the fourteenth century an Indo-European-speaking dynasty must have established itself in North Syria, for a treaty signed in 1360 between the Hittites and the Mitanni gives the names of four Indian Gods beside those of the local divinities.[4] In the Hittite capital a document on horse-breeding contains Indian numerals,[5] and at this period Indo-Iranian names occur in Syria and Palestine, among rulers who adopted the local Gods to supplement their own.[6]

One of the written languages of Cappadocia at this period was of the Western Indo-European type, allied with Phrygian, Greek and Latin.[7] Its syntax was un-'Aryan', and it has been suggested that a body of new words was taken over to express ideas at that time foreign to the country.[8]

---

[1] Childe, op. cit., pp. 17–18. The names have been collected in *Yale Oriental Series*, i (Clay).

[2] See Childe, op. cit., chapters v, vi, vii and viii, for various theories of origin.

[3] Ipsen, *Sumero-akkadische Lehnworter in Indogermanischen Forsch.*, Strasburg, xli, p. 417, quoted by Childe, op. cit., p. 87, note 2. See also his appendix at end of chap. iv.

[4] In the Archives of Tell el Amarna, H. Winkler in *Mitt. der deutschen Orient Gesellschaft*, Berlin, xxxv, p. 51, quoted by Childe, op. cit., p. 18.

[5] E. Forrer, in *Zeitschr. der deutschen Morgenlandgesellschaft*, Berlin, lxxvi, p. 250 ff., quoted by Childe, op. cit., p. 18.

[6] *Cambridge Ancient History*, ii, p. 331; Childe, op. cit., p. 19.

[7] Childe, op. cit., pp. 21–22, quoting Forrer and Friedrich in *Z.D.M.G.*, lxxvi.

[8] Childe, op. cit., p. 23, quoting A. H. Sayce in Anatolian Studies presented to Sir William Ramsay, p. 390 ff.; *Journ. of the American Oriental Soc.*, 1921, and Luckenbill in the *Journ. of the Royal Asiatic Soc., Centenary Vol.*, p. 58.

All this points to the incursion, between the eighteenth and fourteenth centuries B.C., of small bands strong enough to impose their rule among the kingdoms of Western Asia, and in close enough connection for the military architecture of the Hittites, and the worship of the Great Mother in Phrygia, to have become thoroughly familiar. In fact, everything fits them to be the Achæans who adopted Mycenæan civilisation, to whose rulers Hittite as well as Greek texts probably refer.[1]

But there seems to have been a similar Westward passage of Indo-European peoples, speaking, like these, the Western dialect of the common group of languages, who did not penetrate into Asia Minor, but kept a more Northerly course;[2] who must, after dispossessing the Chalcolithic peoples of the Black Earth Region, have remained for a long period in the Danubian or Balkan area, in a military organisation under chieftains whose graves have been found.[3] Here, no doubt in contact with the Northern and Eastern trade routes, they early learned to forge weapons of iron (a metal still considered precious in the latest Mycenæan graves), and to use the slashing sword, perhaps their own invention.[4] Here they bred their horses, and preserved the worship of their patriarchal Gods. It was a race of warriors who descended into the peninsulas of Italy and Greece, and overran the islands.

THE EPIC

The characters of Homer,[5] while reflecting of course the ideals of his own epoch, are separated from it by the need of a comparatively sophisticated age to find simplicity and nobility in the past. In this vision the milieu of the Northern tribesmen was partly confused with that of the Southern cities, while a faint glitter of Minoan brilliance rose at times from an age more deeply submerged—but not of Minoan inner life, which was

[1] See above, p. 256.

[2] On the evidence of the ochre graves. See Childe, *Dawn of European Civilisation*, chap. x, and *The Aryans*, chap. viii.

[3] Childe, *The Aryans*, pp. 196–197, and *Dawn*, p. 188.

[4] The use of this sword is considered by many to be the material cause of their victory over the peoples they dispossessed. See, for instance, Childe, *The Aryans*, p. 152, and fig. 25.

[5] It is still, of course, a matter of controversy whether the name Homer represented one or a number of poets.

inimical to the new order in course of creation. Homer forces out of sight all that is inherited from the Stone Age and therefore incompatible with his humanism.[1] His characters could not have existed in a setting of dæmonic participation.

The society discerned across the lapse of time was thus of the military type, and frequent references to quarrels between kin in the preceding generations point to a transition from the old close blood union of the clan to dependence upon a chief's personal prestige.[2] The tales of their near ancestors related by the Homeric heroes abound also in legends of the young prince who inherited a foreign kingdom by marriage with the king's daughter,[3] a memory of matriarchy, of the days, no doubt, when Minoan influence was still significant. The kings themselves are sharply separated from divinity, even where they may claim a divine ancestor. They do not incorporate any common life shared with their people and their land. The flame that plays round Achilles' hair upon the ramparts, burns not from his royal blood, but because of his heroic qualities.[4] There were legends of divine kings in all the greater cities founded under Minoan influence, but it is not Homer who speaks of Zeus-Agamemnon nor of Helen the Tree-Goddess, nor of the king's daughter sacrificed before the fleet could sail.[5]

Reflecting the social change is the epic vision of the other world as a vague and distant locality, shared (the burial rites once performed) by all the shadowy, unreturning company of the dead.[6] Along with their iron weapons the Northerners had

[1] For instance, in the epithets for Hera and Athena, as Gilbert Murray points out in *Rise of the Greek Epic*, p. 138, agreeing with A. B. Cook in *J.H.S.*, lxiv. 1924, that βοῶπις Ἥρη and γλαυκῶπιδα κούρην covered a cow mask and owl mask. (In which case incidentally, the owl would have an earlier association with Athena than the evidence of the vase paintings (note 2, p. 252) has led Prof. Nilsson to suppose. Cf. also the relief of an Owl Goddess of the Larsa period published in A. B. Cook, *Zeus*, iii, pl. lxi, note 1, p. 252.)

[2] See Chadwick, *The Heroic Age*, p. 443.

[3] For instance, in Glaukos' story of Bellerophon, *Iliad*, vi, 192–193.

[4] Cf. W. P. Ker, *Epic and Romance*, 1908, p. 39.

[5] Cf. H. L. Lorimer, 'Homer's use of the Past,' in *J.H.S.*, xlix, quoting Nilsson: 'The great cycles of myth spring from the great centres of Mycenæan culture.'

[6] The scene in *Od.*, xi, in which Odysseus first calls up the dead by ritual, and later is evidently among them in their own 'place', shows how negative were after-world conditions in Homer.

brought into Greece the practice of cremation, so that any emergence of a hero-cult, that may have begun to link the bones of warrior chiefs with local vegetation divinities or ancestral spirits, had been interrupted at this epoch.

Nevertheless it is to be noted that in funeral rites some older memories do seem to linger, such as the actual or magical embalming of the bodies of Patroclus and Hector before they were burned,[1] the circuit of Patroclus' tomb by Hector's trailing body until his ghost could be laid, the war-prisoners immolated for his satisfaction (a deed which the poet regards with horror), and the games performed to give him strength.

Probably such beliefs never died; but the moral ascendancy of the chiefs was in no way dependent upon them. The leaders must hold their men by their own powers of mind and body, excelling in those tasks with which all were familiar; that was the fundamental bond.[2]

To all this the religious setting, if such it must be called, bears a very strange relation. During some period of the dark age, the newcomers seem to have pedestalled their sky-God upon his mountain,[3] to become a king like the kings of the land, and, no doubt on the precedent of the princesses of the conquered race, the local Goddess of the oracular earth or tree, as at Dodona, or of the pastures, as in the Peloponnese, was made his queen.[4]

Other personalities of the ancient Goddess were drawn, as we have seen, into the hierarchy, to begin a long and great career, and the former fertility Gods, scarcely recognisable in their altered functions, became the sky-God's sons. His brothers, in some sort his reflections, were established as rulers of the other realms of nature. He was himself assimilated, by his

---

[1] See Tsountas, op. cit., pp. 95–96, pointing out that Homer several times uses ταρχύειν in the sense of 'to bury', the word being another form of ταριχεύειν = to embalm. The bodies of Patroclus and Hector are each kept fresh by ambrosia from the hands of a Goddess.

[2] Ker, op. cit., pp. 7–8. Epic, because divorced from ritual, can show its heroes delighting in the performance of everyday tasks in a manner impossible to tragedy, with its religious basis.

[3] Olympus and Ida being pre-Greek names for any mountain, where Zeus originally ruled alone. (Nilsson, *The Mycenæan Origin of Greek Mythology*, pp. 236–237, quoting C. Theander in *Eranos*, xv, 1916, p. 127 ff.)

[4] J. E. Harrison, *Themis*, p. 491.

birth-myth, with the Young God of Crete (fig. 122, below),[1] but beyond that the link was snapped, for he was never of the earth, and could not die. The Olympians were generally conceived to have been born in some vague past, in revolt from vast and uncouth parents, the elemental powers of a former cycle; and, as representative of the age then beginning, they were frozen into immortality while retaining their specifically human forms—and therefore natures.

So Homer, looking forward from that beginning, perceived in his divinities less dignity than in the mortals whom they were powerless to save. Yet he endowed them with physical perfec-

Fig. 122

tion, converting their former animal aspects into attributes, naming Hera with her cow-mask 'the ox-eyed Lady', and owl-faced Athene 'the maid with sea-grey eyes',[2] since he feared the greatness of the defeated religion more than he scorned the half-childish conceptions of the new era.

This changeless beauty was later used by the sculptors to make of the Olympians patterns of humanity, upon which the aspiring cities might build their race, tuning their inner lives to that outward majesty and calm (as the hunters of the Palæolithic caves sought fulfilment by communion with the animal splendour on the walls). That was after the almost complete disintegration of the family relationships of the Gods, which already in Homer betray their artificial origin. Where they touch most nearly upon the mystic realities of the old order, as in the 'sacred marriage' of Zeus and Hera in the Iliad, or

[1] See below, p. 281 and note 3, p. 257.   [2] Note 1, p. 265.

the taking of Aphrodite and Ares in the net, there is his laughter the more scathing.[1] The Gods of the Iliad are in fact extraneous, being supernatural but no longer dynamic, because their stations were never integral to the world order. They are brought in where 'all the world is brought in', to throw into relief the grandeur of its doomed and imperfect human lives.

The Odyssey, it is true, moves through an essentially mythical landscape, but there the story has a value above the persons, for it is only the aftermath of epic, and already falling back upon the ritual cycles.[2]

But the importance here of the earliest-known European literary composition lies in this very basis of personal character, as opposed to the later tragic drama, which used identical material in a ritual setting that compelled it to depend upon plot.[3] The chief antagonists in the Iliad are each superior to the fall of Troy. Achilles accepted the knowledge that he would not live to accomplish its downfall,[4] but Hector foreseeing death saw in it defeat also ('for well I understand in my heart and soul that holy Ilios will perish'),[5] and knew suddenly, as he

---

[1] *Il.*, xiv, vv 346 ff. Note how in spite of the too-human treatment of this scene, the earth blossoms as its result. *Odyssey*, viii, vv 266–366, and v 326: 'And quenchless laughter arose among the blessed Gods,' and the fact that all the other Goddesses remained at home for shame (v 324).

[2] The *Odyssey* consists of repeated experiences on islands which bear traces of a kindred ritual, the episode of Scheria being the most complete example. The hero, washed up naked and destitute, from the sea, is awakened from his swoon by a ball rolling beside him into a spiral eddy (*Od.*, vi, 116), and comes among the dancing maidens, holding a bough before him, to Nausicaa, whom he compares with a palm tree seen beside the altar at Delos. There follows a transformation and recognition, but after that he leaves the princess standing against a pillar (the usual preliminary failure, as Orpheus loses Eurydice and Theseus Ariadne, and all the heroes, Helen); and regains his own island, once more in sleep, beside a cave with two entries, just as Æneas returns from his other-world adventure by the ivory gate of false dreams, both having experienced not death, but a vision of death. The ship which bears Odysseus home is changed to stone on its return to Scheria, and a mountain is to be flung up to conceal the island from further intrusion (*Od.*, xiii 149 ff.). His homecoming is a successful repetition of his Phaeacian experience, again out of sleep, himself being once more disfigured and disgusied, only recognisable to his wife (who has meanwhile woven and unravelled her thread) when he describes the Tree round which their marriage chamber was built.

[3] See pp. 325–327 below   [4] *Il.*, xix, 420 ff.   [5] *Il.*, vi, vv 447 ff.

rushed to meet it, that this defeat could create the future.[1]

That truly Greek vision of man's existence as contained in Destiny, the origin of European individualism, and the abstract successor of the ceremonial organisation inherited from Stone Age beliefs, gave to Homer's Hector, when he knew himself abandoned by the Gods, an immediate sense of something indestructible. In like manner his one sentence defying the auguries, 'The best omen of all is to be fighting for one's country,'[2] cuts through the old bonds of ritual like David's 'a contrite heart is better than sacrifice'. It is the spirit of all later epic, expressed again by the defeated fighters of the Icelandic sagas,[3] and in the early English 'Song of Maldon', composed under conditions similar to those described above: 'Thought shall be the harder, heart the keener, mood shall be the more, as our might lessens.'[4] This is of deep import to religious history, as the utterance of a faith in ultimate values so profound that it challenges God direct: 'Honour was proudly to fling away the poor resources that we had, and dare Him empty-handed.'[5]

Because this defiance was not hurled in Satanic fashion against the world-order,[6] the Hellenic revolution, like the Hebrew, became creative. Securely orientated in this acceptance, the Greeks could later receive without harm the resurrected Minoan dances of ecstatic communion with the divinities of Nature, attuning them to a moral and intellectual discipline of great significance for religions yet unborn.

---

[1] *Il.*, xxii, vv 304–305.   [2] *Il.*, xii 243.

[3] As in the burning of Njal in Njala, *c.* 128, or the death of Eyjolf on the rock in Sturlunga, ii, pp. 312–347.

[4] Ker, op. cit., p. 55. Byrhtwold's speech to his deserted comrades fighting round the body of Byrhtnoth (A.D. 991).

[5] T. E. Lawrence, *Seven Pillars of Wisdom*, 1935, p. 412. Exhortation to the Serahin.

[6] L. Abercrombie, *The Epic: An Essay*, 1922, p. 100; M. Bodkin, *Archetypal Patterns in Poetry*, 1934, p. 241.

PART FIVE

RESURRECTION IN GREECE

CHAPTER I

THE GREEK MYSTERY CULTS

THE OLYMPIAN REVOLUTION

The Olympians, then, had set up on earthly models their constitutional monarchy, which was subject to Destiny, the embodiment of the cosmic order. The Sky-Father, while retaining dominion over the elements, had acquired a human personality and gathered into his paternal sphere the transfigured divinities of the Mycenæan world. Their immutability was only achieved after protracted wars, which the imagination of the growing states recorded as two-fold.

BATTLES WITH THE GIANTS

The lucid figures of the Gods had first to encounter, it will be remembered, the uncouth powers called into being by the emotional needs of a primitive epoch, the many-natured progeny of earth. In this warfare the Olympians, at first defeated, took refuge in animal forms,[1] but once their humanity was victorious, they possessed it for ever. Their animal bodies dwindled into emblems,[2] or into the elements of sacrifice;[3] very rarely they were recalled in the masks worn by priests.[4] They appear in the myths of a later epoch merely as the vehicles of contact with human kind.[5]

[1] Apollodorus, i 40–41; Ovid, *Metamorph*, v 321 ff.

[2] The eagle of Zeus, Athena's owl; sometimes they were remembered only as epithets derived from the masks. See note 1, p. 265 above.

[3] The stag which replaced Iphigeneia as oblation to Artemis; the cows offered to Hera.

[4] The priestesses at Dodona were called Doves (Herodotus, ii 55–57), the little girl ministrants of Brauronian Artemis, Bears. There are many other examples cited by A. B. Cook, *Zeus*, i, pp. 421–422. The bears are referred to by the scholiast on Aristophanes' *Lysistrata* as a 'mystery'.

[5] For example: in Zeus' many wooings of mortal women; Leda's swan, Europa's bull.

All of which seems to give a true picture of growth from a primitive religion.

The imposition of the Olympian order upon these monstrous existences, reflected the memory of mankind's earliest aspirations towards civilised life. It was a pre-Greek memory, applied to Gods who were to acquire their finished forms only in Greece, after one fateful contest more.[1]

BATTLES WITH THE TITANS

These much worthier foes were the children of Earth and Sky, engendered before the two primary powers of this and other cosmogonies had been torn asunder.[2] They belonged in fact to the world of dynamic elements, out of which the Olympian ruler himself had sprung, and his very station upon his mountain peak depended on their control. The peril lay in their double nature, which impelled them continually to aspire to Heaven.[3] Their sin was *Hubris*, that pride by which the angels fell, the unpardonable challenge to the Olympic order. Therefore in Hell Sisyphus forever rolls upward a stone which forever falls backwards into the Abyss, Phaethon is flung from the Sun's chariot, and Prometheus, once the ally of the Gods, is immobilised through a whole æon for the still more deadly sin of setting man himself on the first step towards divinity:

'Everlasting Zeus overcame the Titans.'

Historically this represented the fight for supremacy over the Mycenæan nature-divinities described in the last chapter, divinities who were the more dangerous because of their kinship with the Gods. The ancients themselves sometimes call the Titans 'descendants of the Idæan Daktyls',[4] those servants of the Cretan Goddess and the young God who stood in men's

---

[1] In this connection it is interesting to recall Herodotus' account (ii 51–53) of the religion of primitive Greece. In early times, he says, the Pelasgians prayed to the Gods, but had no names, shapes, or special functions for them.

[2] Euripides, *Fragt.*, 484 N; *ap. Diod. Sic.*, 1, 7; Apollonius Rhod., i 496; Diels, *Frag. d. Vors.*, ii, p. 479.

[3] J. E. Harrison, *Themis*, second edition, 1927, p. 454. 'They rebound like divine india-rubber balls.'

[4] Lucian, *De Salt.*, 21; also Plutarch as quoted by J. E. Harrison, op. cit., p. 453.

memories half-way between human and divine. The necessity for the early Greeks to create Gods in their own image, to look upon their own variety from without, would have rendered the pantheism of the Minoan deity an offence, and her shifts of function disastrous to their intellectual craving for definition, in spite of her numerous anthropomorphic epiphanies. These, therefore, like the Indo-European nature-divinities, had to become subordinate; at first, perhaps, even secret. They lived on among the tombs, making auspicious appearance in the snake-form of their earthly parent, a vehicle of beneficence for departed heroes.[1] They wielded powers of retribution.[2] They existed, too, as spirits of fountain or hill or tree, the human-bodied nymphs of the poet's dream.

WHAT WAS ACHIEVED

It has been noted that much survived. The votive offerings and sacrifices to Hera, and her myths, show her, the childless and embittered queen, to have once been mother of the pastures[3] like Hathor and Ninkhursag, and to have renewed her virginity yearly like the daughter Goddesses, by a ritual bathing in the Argive spring.[4] The unity, as we have seen, of the most civilised of cities, was incorporated in its Goddess, 'that astonishing ideal of the state as a statue,'[5] once an Earth-Divinity, 'our own Kore that is in the midst of us,' as Plato calls her still.[6] Being so far above the soil that she was born from her Father's head, she yet was foster-mother to the Earth's child, Erichthonios.[7] The solitary Artemis again betrays her descent from the Minoan Mistress of wild creatures,[8] while Aphrodite, dispenser of human fertility, retained much of the universal character of the oriental Goddess, and something that was alien to

---

[1] For example, Sosipolis at Olympia. Pausanias, vi 20, 3; cf. Verg., *Aen.*, v 95, quoted by J. E. Harrison, *Prolegomena to the study of Greek Religion*, 1903, p. 331.

[2] Euripides, *Orestes*, 256; *Iph. in Tauris*, 286; Æsch., *Eumenides*, 126.

[3] Cows were regularly sacrificed to Hera (Cook, op. cit., i, 451) and archaic clay images of cows and female 'idols' were found in great numbers below the wall of her temple at Tiryns (Frickenhaus, *Tiryns*, ii, p. 14).

[4] Pausanias, ii 38, 2: 'This story is of the Mysteries.'

[5] Spengler, *Decline of the West.*   [6] Plato, *Laws*, 796.

[7] *Iliad* ii. 547.   [8] See above, pp. 223, 224.

the Gods of the virile race which regarded the chastity of her sister divinities as a source of power. Thus her divine Son was rather a dynamic embodiment of her own functions than an individual; he was her Dove in human form.

If these daughters of the Olympian ruler show development rather than metamorphosis, we have seen that Hera, in her new position of wife and subordinate, has become quite another being.[1] Yet the legends give her one characteristic in common with Athena and occasionally with Artemis, which must owe something to the old relation between Goddess and young divinity. This is the peculiar position in which they stand towards some mortal hero—neither as mother nor lover, but as guide and inspirer to great deeds.[2] So Athena claimed service of Theseus and Perseus; so Hera, as ally to Jason, and as enemy to Herakles, tempted them both to glory.

Demeter is apart from these Goddesses. For all her Indo-European name, she only sits by courtesy in the Olympian Assembly, for she remains the Mycenæan Goddess of the fertility of earth, with her companion who rises to her side in spring. Her nursling is no single hero, but all who desire rebirth. When, therefore, the young vegetation divinity of the former world could safely return to Greece, she became the Mother of the Mysteries.

Those male deities of fertility, who were early adopted into the Olympic Pantheon as sons of Zeus, had, as we saw, a different history. Ares the Thracian War-God was once that Earth-spirit whose dragon-progeny became rulers of Thebes;[3] and one of the forerunners of Hermes, the Olympian messenger, had been a divinity of the flocks and herds.[4]

The King of the Gods had also absorbed certain chthonic personalities, and, though everlasting, had been born of the Great Mother in a Cretan cave, and suckled by a horned beast.[5]

---

[1] See above, p. 266.

[2] J. E. Harrison, *Prolegomena*, chap. vi, p. 273. 'It seems to halt somewhere between mother and lover, with a touch of the patron saint.'

[3] Above, p. 251. His Latin epiphany was also developed from a fertility God, reborn with the year (Harrison, *Themis*, fig. 50), and summoned by the clanging of shields. J. G. Frazer, *The Golden Bough*, vol. iii, p. 122 ff.

[4] His epithet, $\varkappa\rho\alpha\nu\alpha\iota\delta\varsigma$, for instance, is interpreted by Hesychius as 'shepherd'.

[5] Hesiod, *Theogony*, 480.

In Crete, he had also a grave.[1] Even his national festival at Olympia retained important traces of vegetation rites.[2]

The earthly associations, however, of all these Gods, were comparatively unimportant to their permanent character, and the Cloud-Compeller who had restrained the leaping phantasmata of the past, and ruled by Justice—that is, by keeping all things in their appointed stations—was sufficiently removed from the contagion of mystic participation. But that son who 'uttered his Word on earth',[3] whose every festival shows his descent—or ascent—from the young vegetation God,[4] brother of the Maiden of the Mountains who became Artemis—he it was who escaped most completely from his earthly origin. Legend relates the voyage of Apollo from Crete, and the birth at Delos connects him with Asia.[5] Whether or not he became fused with some divinity of the Northern immigrants, his character at least had assumed a Dorian colour when he established himself at Delphi within the mountain sanctuary of the old Earth-Oracle.[6] The ritual which commemorated his victory over the Serpent of Earth—always the victory of a deity of vegetation[7]—showed him bearing the laurel, his tree emblem, to the Delphic shrine; but at that festival it is to be noted that in later times at least, a pole was carried, round which revolved the globes which mimicked the heavenly bodies.[8] As in Egypt and Sumer, the God of the changing seasons easily effected the transition to a lordship of the punctual Sun. Apollo's succession to the Oracle, as Æschylus describes it,[9] seems to reflect a

[1] P. 283 below.

[2] F. M. Cornford, *The Origin of the Olympic Games*, chap. vii of *Themis*.

[3] Λοξιάς, Herod. I 91; Προφήτης Διός; Æsch, *Eumen.*, 19.

[4] L. Farnell, *Cults of the Greek States*, iv, pp. 291–295.

[5] Nilsson, *The Minoan-Mycenæan Religion*, p. 444, says that personal names compounded with Leto occur only in S.W. Asia Minor—her name being connected by philologists with the Carian *lada*, a woman. Mr. Jackson Knight reminds me here that a name resembling Apollo's occurs among Mitanni divine names in Asia Minor.

[6] See above, note 1, p. 250, for agreement of the archæological with the literary evidence.

[7] See G. R. Levy, *J.H.S.*, 1934, p. 40 ff., 'The Oriental Origin of Herakles.'

[8] Proclus quoted by Photius; Bibl. cod. 239, p. 321 ff.; J. E. Harrison, *Themis*, p. 438.

[9] Æschylus, *Eumenides*, vv 1–8. The Pythia's prologue.

double victory at Delphi over the Earth Goddess and over the
Titaness who personified the Moon; that transference of attention to the sky which was achieved in the New Stone Age.[1]
But Phœbus Apollo was never purely a Sun-God like the Titan
Helios. He was too human for that. Yet his solar functions, if
they did not impart, did at least develop his especially Hellenic
qualities of order, clarity, of purity through an intensity of
light, and of symmetry in poetry and music. Exempt from
the knowledge of sin, he was without compassion.[2]

This God most perfectly embodied the effulgence which had
thrown into shadow not only the gross forms of the earliest
savage tales, but those still vague shapes of the later order,
whose mystic significance was lost, but who had begotten, in
myth as in actuality, the rulers of Olympus. This the fallen
Titan[3] perceived in the clairvoyance of ruin:

> ' *So on our heels a fresh perfection treads,*
> *A power more strong in beauty, born of us*
> *And fated to excel us, as we pass*
> *In glory that old Darkness.*'

The Olympians conquered, indeed, because they had the
beauty of statues. The outward forms of harmony which became mathematical in their proportions, were, as we have seen,
the archetypes upon which their worshippers came to model
their inner lives. That is why changelessness was essential, the
'still point of the turning world' which the restless Hellenic
mind forever sought, to be organised for creation. Being so
vital, it could dare to rest upon this static ideal, which continually remoulded the mind to form it anew, as the Zeus of
Pheidias is said to have spiritualised the religion of all Greece.[4]
Because the Greeks were artists, they could presume thus to
re-create their Gods, and life, conversely, could be made to ir-

---

[1] See above, part ii 3, passim, especially p. 154.

[2] In his vengeance, for instance, on the children of Niobe who had compared herself with Leto, or in the flaying of Marsyas, who dared to compete
with him as musician. His cruelties were always the result of wounded
pride.

[3] Keats, *Hyperion*, book ii, vv 212–215.

[4] Quintilian, '. . . . whose beauty seems to have added something to the
received religion.' J. E. Harrison, *Studies in Greek Religion*, 1892, p. 219.

radiate every part of the human form as it does the animal bodies of Palæolithic art—not to brood over it, as in Egypt.

This was a tremendous achievement, but the intellectual resources of the Greeks could not long remain severed from their roots in the old order. Before their power flagged, it encountered an emotional impulse of great intensity; the outward ripple of a religious upheaval which in the eighth and seventh centuries B.C. was sending up teachers and prophets all over Asia.[1] It penetrated into every branch of the spiritual and intellectual activities of Greece, raising them into a wave which before it toppled had set the current of thought for the European cycle.

THE DIONYSIAN COUNTER-ATTACK

A movement solely from without could not so have shaken the Greek soul, now that it had found its orientation. This revolution was successful for two reasons: it provided an outlet for the pent-up energies of the buried Minoan religion, so long held under in fear and hatred, and it was brought by 'Orpheus'[2] within the Olympic discipline.

THE DÆMONS

The religious genius who worked the transformation did not even reject the monstrous existences of the early time, for his system embraced all known creation. He could join forces with the Titans because the dæmons had remained alive, first cherished, perhaps, by the conquered population here as elsewhere, from the time of man's struggle out of the regions of ice, but receiving from the earliest conquests of the Northern peoples a ritual appropriate to their character—the ritual of hero-worship. We have noted already in Mycenæ[3] the belief that certain of the dead, who in their lives had been a source of strength, conserved the powers of life for those who maintained

---

[1] Buddha in the 7th century. The date of Zoroaster may come within these limits, as do those of the Hebrew prophets.

[2] The name of Orpheus may possibly denote a succession of religious teachers.

[3] Pp. 254–257.

communication with them, as the ancestral spirits had formerly conserved them for all their kin. Herakles, whom literary and archæological evidence shows to have entered the Ægean world in the character of a divinity of vegetation,[1] and to have founded the Olympic Games to inaugurate the fertility of the year,[2] became in Greek minds the greatest of these mortal heroes who retained their contact with men; but every hero's tomb was the scene of rites, such as still belonged to the spirits of nature, and at an earlier time to the ancestors.[3]

The heroes were distinguished from nature-divinities by the individuality which memories of their deeds had conferred, but resembled them in forming a link between the two realms now sternly held apart. Because they were in some sort immortals who had once suffered death, they prepared men's minds to welcome in Dionysus the greatest of the dæmons, so great that he was eventually received into Olympus. But Plutarch's description is sufficient to show to what order of beings he belonged: 'These manifold changes, that Dionysus suffers, into winds and waters and earth and stars and the birth of plants and animals . . . are called Disappearances and New Births, and the songs sung to him are full of sufferings and wanderings.'[4]

His life story did not, therefore, recount an event in the past, like that of Zeus, but these sufferings and wanderings must be told here in so far as they appertain to his journey into Greece, that is to say, before the very changes, which Plutarch has described, became fixed by ritual in their Greek form. The tales themselves, of these births and deaths, are many and shifting, pointing to a fusion of several personalities. Their tangle must be unwound, before it can be understood what was woven into the enduring pattern at Eleusis.

[1] J. E. Harrison in *Themis*, pp. 364–370. Fresh evidence has now appeared on Akkadian seals. H. Frankfort, *Cylinder Seals*, pp. 121–122 and plates xx*e*, xxiii*j* and figs. 34–35; G. R. Levy, op. cit., passim; Stuart Piggott, *Antiquity*, xii, 1938, pp. 323–331: 'The Hercules Myth—Beginnings and Ends.'

[2] Cornford, op. cit., p. 235, quoting Pausanias, v 7, 6.

[3] Porphyry, *De antro nympharum*, 3. 'To the Olympian Gods they set up temples and images and altars, but to the Earth Goddess and to Heroes, *escharai*.'

[4] Plutarch, *On the Ei at Delphi*, ix; Harrison, *Prolegomena*, 441.

THE GREEK MYSTERY CULTS

JOURNEY OF DIONYSUS

Among those beads and signet rings, inscribed with scenes of legend and ritual, which are believed to have been recovered at Thisbe,[1] is one which startlingly illustrates, in all its provincial rendering of Minoan equipment and apparel, an event repeatedly sung by the Greek poets as initiating the Olympic cycle—the Birth of Zeus in the Cretan cave. In the savage myth, Rhea the Mother of the Gods saved her child from his father's devouring jaws by hiding him among the Kouretes, who clashed their shields round him to drown his cries. There were signs, it will be remembered, that such shield-dances awakened the spring in Minoan Crete,[2] and a Cretan hymn of late origin, though of very early material, shows that the human Kouretes of classical times must have summoned to the dance each spring the 'Greatest Kouros', 'whom as a babe the shielded nurturers bore away with noise of beating feet'[3]—the child given to others to rear, as in all ritual myths which recall the primitive initiations. On the signet under discussion (fig. 122, p. 267) the armed men, welcomed into the cave by the child on his Mother's knee, bear the Minoan bull-hide shields, and leaf-wound rods for striking them, which recall the rods so often used in other vegetation rites.[4] The cymbals of the Goddess are already raised, and the whole engraving exactly illustrates the scene invoked by the Mænads of Euripides:[5]

[1] See p. 267 above, and note 3 of p. 257 of iv 2, concerning their authenticity.

[2] Fig. 93.

[3] Found at Palaikastro. Fully discussed, with text restored by Prof. Gilbert Murray, in Harrison, *Themis*, chap. i.

[4] See Evans, *Palace of Minos*, iii, p. 473, for use of myrtle twigs connected with Adonis' Mother Myrrha, and of reeds in the rites of Attis.

[5] Euripides, *Bacchæ*, 119.

> ὦ θαλάμευμα Κουρή-
> των ζάθεοί τε Κρήτας
> Διογενέτορες ἔναυλοι
> τρικόρυθες ἔνθ᾽ ἐν ἄντροις
> βυρσότονον κύκλωμα τόδε
> μοὶ Κορύβαντες ηὖρον.

On the following page is Gilbert Murray's translation.

RESURRECTION IN GREECE

Hail thou, O nurse of Zeus, O caverned haunt,
Where fierce arms clanged to guard God's cradle rare,
For thee of old some crested Corybant
First woke in Cretan air
The wild orb of our orgies,
Our Cymbal.

The tale then, and the rite, seem to have existed in some form in Mycenæan times, but no rite celebrating the birth of Zeus was practised in Hellenic Greece. An Olympian could not become a helpless child, but poets and later prose-writers identify the Cretan child-Zeus with the hunter Zagreus who is the Orphic Dionysus.[1] As Clement says of Euripides, they 'divined as in a riddle that God and his Son are one'.[2] A reappearing divinity of seasonal change may rightly claim a dual, young-old, incarnation. Thus, below the Attic stage of later days, he, or his father, was carved as a grown man, seated between Kouretes clashing their shields.[3]

This is the first birth of our divinity, appropriately located in Crete; but, because Dionysus was the Son and not the Father, the Kouretes could not save him. The 'Titans' having lured him with toys, among them the old bull-roarer of the primitive initiations, tore and devoured him, and were lightning-smitten for their sin.[4] Mankind was created from their evil bodies, with something divine from the child's part in them.

The Titans, so-called, perhaps from the white clay with which, like many of the savage initiators they had painted their bodies, seem to have been assimilated to those Titans of the old dispensation who are sometimes called Idæan Daktyls.[5] They were, in fact, on all the older analogies, worshippers of the God whom they sacrificed; they were the Kouretes themselves.

[1] Euripides, *The Cretans* (fragment 475), in which the initiate declares himself a mystic of Idæan Zeus, who has experienced the thunders of Zagreus, and has become a Bakchos among the Kouretes. Harrison, *Prolegomena*, chap. xa. Also Plutarch, op. cit.: 'They call him Dionysus and Zagreus.'

[2] Eur., fr. 904; Clem., *Al. Strom*, v, p. 688, quoted by J. E. Harrison in *Themis*. 481.

[3] Harrison, op. cit., pp. 30–31; A. B. Cook, *Zeus*, i, p. 708 ff.

[4] Clem., *Al. Protr.*, ii 17, quoted by Harrison, *Prolegomena*, pp. 484–485.

[5] Harrison, op. cit., pp. 492–495.

This Orphic myth has many parallels in tales of the forming of man from a god or giant sacrificed at the foundation of the world,[1] and the Cretan 'Zeus' appears to have suffered a similar fate, for his tomb was shown on Mt. Ida in Crete down to Christian times. Thus a Nestorian commentator on St. Paul, Acts 17–28, quotes from a poem attributed to 'Minos':

> *The Cretans have fashioned a tomb for thee, O Holy and High!*
> *Liars, evil beasts, idle bellies.*
> *For thou diest not; for ever thou livest and standest,*
> *For in thee we live and move and have our being.*[2]

The Orphic votary tasted on initiation the raw flesh of a bull to commemorate the death of his God, after which no animal food ever passed his lips[3] (a variant of the ceremonial eating of the old totem-sacrifice), and the poem quoted above seems to refer to some such feast in honour of 'Zeus', unconsciously describing in the last line the aspiration of the celebrants in their communion. For Dionysus throughout his various personalities brought back into Greece the possibility of human participation in the divine life, with all its sacramental content.

The dismemberment was unknown to the Minoan seal-engravers; the bull-contests there apparently replace the savage rites, which may have been incorporated at a much later stage of the God's journey, as will presently be seen.

For the child's heart was saved, and he was born once again of Persephone, the Goddess from whom the dead are reborn in the mysteries,[4] but the living Dionysus disappears from Crete.

In Asia, where we next find him,[5] the divinity of the wild spring of the mountain glens has become the Wine-God, bestower of his own spirit in the grape, whose re-creative powers seem to have borrowed some deeper significance from the sacred soma-juice of the Indo-Iranians,[6] overlying, it may be,

[1] Marduk or Kingu in the Babylonian Epic of Creation. Purusha in Vedic hymns. Ymir in North European mythology.

[2] Cook, *Zeus*, i, p. 157, note 3, from the Gannat Busame, quoted by J. Rendel Harris in the *Expositor*, 1906, pp. 305–317.

[3] Euripides, frag. 475, *The Cretans*, and *Hippolytus*, v 592.

[4] Harrison, op. cit., p. 491.   [5] Euripides, *Bacchæ*, Prologue.

[6] In 'The Cretans' there is no mention of wine. The Prologue to the *Bacchæ* shows him passing over the plains of Central Asia on his journey to Greece.

Greek memories of that mystic fruit plucked by him in the Cretan paradise. The emotional ecstasy once portrayed by Minoan craftsmen, received along the Asiatic seaboard its stamp of excess, and something effeminate marred the God's personality henceforth. The thiasos, that essential band of followers, amid whose dances only could the dæmon manifest his spirit to the music of cymbal, pipe, flute and drum, was no longer composed of the armed youths who had protected his infancy in Crete, but of nursing nymphs, the maiden votaries who tended him as the Young God on the verge of manhood. The shield of hide was diminished to a timbrel.[1] In Western Asia the Young God was lover as well as Son, and here the phallic emblems may have been acquired, which are equally non-existent in Minoan and Olympic ritual. In Lydia he seems to have received his name of Bakchos.[2]

Entering Greece by the Northern route, as Euripides describes,[3] through Phrygia, which had kept intact from prehistoric times the worship of the Great Mother and her Son, he found in Thrace a new manifestation. Here too were tribes who had continued to venerate the divinities of Earth, unmoved by the Olympic victory. Here was a Mother and child— a very savage Mother, who probably dismembered that child;[4] whose outlandish name was yet to be retained in the humane and spiritualised ritual of Eleusis.[5] Here, in all probability, he attached to himself the wild creatures, satyrs and sileni, who were henceforth to remain always on the outskirts of his thiasos. They may, like the centaurs, have symbolised to the Greeks the wild tribesmen and wild landscape of those regions,[6] but were also without doubt the double-natured, animal-

---

[1] Pp. 232, 233 above.

[2] Farnell, *Cults of the Greek States*, v, p. 300, note 73; Cook, *Zeus*, i, p. 438, connects the name with Egypt and Libya, by way of Crete and Asia Minor, but the myths of Dionysus are all of Asia and Europe. Diodorus in a later age calls him son of Zeus and Io, giving the tale an Egyptian colour.

[3] Eur., *Bacchæ*, Prologue.

[4] For Brimo's Northern origin, see Harrison, *Prolegomena*, pp. 552–554.

[5] 'Holy Brimo has born a child Brimos,' see below, p. 298.

[6] The horse satyr is very common in early art, and often indistinguishable from the centaur of the North. On the François vase, a pair of horse-dæmons are inscribed *Silenoi*; Harrison, *Prolegomena*, fig. 166, and p. 388. See also below, p. 315.

masked dancers of the earth divinities,[1] who had become one being, animal and man, and were considered as immortal creatures because emblematic of the union with their deity in the dance. They represented the horned beasts of immemorial sacrifice; and their presence raised the irrational aspects, already noted in the train of the Asiatic Dionysus, to the pitch of frenzy; till the Nurses of the God, who had now become the Mænads, the Raving ones, entwined with serpents, ivy-wreathed and clad in fawn skins, would suckle the young of wild beasts in whom they recognised their child-divinity,[2] or rend them, perhaps in that preliminary Feast of Raw Flesh, which was here to be found in its most savage, possibly its original, form.[3] Even now drunkenness with actual wine seems to have played but little part in the endeavour towards union with Nature, and the licentiousness of the satyrs, often portrayed in art, is very seldom connected with these mountain dances, whether on account of Orphic influence or of some older ritual taboo.[4]

In Thebes Dionysus suffered yet another incarnation, and a second birth, once again from the Thunder-smitten. That victim was his mortal mother, blasted by the intolerable glory of Zeus, who caught up the untimely child to be born again in Heaven, 'him of the double door,' as the poets translated his epithet of Dithyramb.[5] In Thebes there was later enacted the martyrdom of the king who refused to recognise his divinity, and suffered the God's death by dismemberment at the hands of the Mænads, among them his own mother; a story underlying all tragic drama, which separates the sacrificial victim from his God.[6]

At Delphi Dionysus encountered that other Son of Zeus, the true Olympian, the lineaments of whose 'plummet-measured face'[7] held the terrible concentration of light, that could wither

---

[1] J. G. Frazer, *The Golden Bough*, i, pp. 326–328; ii, pp. 34–37.

[2] Euripides, *Bacchæ*, vv 699–702.

[3] ὠμοφάγον χάριν, Eur., *Bacch.*, 139.

[4] Its absence is strongly emphasised by Euripides in the *Bacchæ*; for instance vv 685–688.

[5] Especially Eurip., *Bacch.*, 526: "Ιθι, Διθύραμβ', ἐμὰν ἄρσενα τάνδε βᾶθι νηδύν.

[6] See chap. ii, below.

[7] See W. B. Yeats, 'The Statues.'

his own moist bloom. No history of that meeting survives;[1] only the tomb of Dionysus in Apollo's sanctuary,[2] the record of the three winter months, the 'year's conflagration', resigned to him, and the rite of his winter awakening,[3] as a child in the cradle, after a traditional dance performed by the Thyiades,[4] Attic 'nurses' whose moving torches the poet saw lighting the early snow under the twin peaks of Parnassos.[5] He is here the Night-Sun who leads the choral dance of the stars,[6] for in Greece he has met not Apollo only, but Orpheus, whose vision embraced the sky. Thus he had no need to spend the winter below-ground, like the vegetation-Gods of oriental imagination, though he did refuse to enter his Father's kingdom till he had brought from the underworld his mortal mother Semele.[7] This is a reversal of the great myths of Ishtar and Isis, but for the Greek world, as for the Minoan, it was nearly always a Goddess who rose from the earth in spring (under one of her many names), as she rises in vase paintings amid rejoicing satyrs (pl. XXXI*b*). Thus in Crete Dionysus had been Zagreus, son of Persephone, and in Thebes, Bromios the son of Semele; and Athens, under the sober guidance of Orpheus, was to set him, as the child Iacchos, in the lap of Demeter at Eleusis.[8]

---

[1] But see pl. xxxi*a*.

[2] See *Fouilles de Delphes*, ii 1, 69, fig. 61, for plan of Apollo's shrine as unearthed by excavation.

[3] Plutarch, *de Ei ap. Delph.* ix.

[4] Pausanias, x 42, on the 'fair dancing grounds' at Panopeus, says that the Attic Thyiades stopped to dance there and at certain other places every other year on their way to join the Delphic Thyiades for the rites of Dionysus on Parnassus.

[5] Sophocles, *Antigone*, vv 1125 ff.

[6] Id., v 1146–1147: ἰὼ πῦρ πνεόντων
χοράγ᾽ ἄστρων.

Macrobius actually calls him the Sun below Ground; Cook, *Zeus*, ii, p. 257.

[7] Apollodorus, iii 5, 3, 3.

[8] Sophocles, *Antigone*, 1119–1121: μέδεις δὲ
παγκοίνοις Ἐλευσινίας
Δῃοῦς ἐν κόλποις.

THE GREEK MYSTERY CULTS

ORPHEUS[1]

Several craftsmen have portrayed for us the reconciliation of Apollo with a resurrected Dionysus (pl. XXXI*a*). At Amyklai on the site of a prehistoric shrine near Sparta, the tomb of Hyakinthos, a vegetation deity of the Mycenæan Age, formed the pedestal of Apollo's image.[2] So might the sepulchre of Dionysus in the Delphic sanctuary have remained a grave indeed, had not those same river-gorges, which bred the barbarous Thracian Dionysus, nurtured also the humane musician, who, except in his pitiful humanity, seems the very incarnation of Apollo.

The religion of Orpheus was revolutionary,[3] for he took as its primary doctrine the Dionysiac faith in the attainment of divinity by man,[4] and he appears to have kept the many-named and many-natured Dionysus as the central figure of his rites. But, in making him the object of human aspiration, he endowed him with the one character which he could not have acquired unaided—the character of the Delphic God. Orpheus replaced the emotional ecstasy, which had been engendered in the thiasos through a realisation of unity with the dynamic energies of wild lives, by the rapture of the individual aspirant acquired through long discipline and purification, both ritual and moral, which conserved its vitality to face higher power; to know it, and therefore to be at one with it. To accomplish singly and permanently what the Dionysiac thiasos had attained at moments, was the Orphic way of redemption. The task entailed a journey through many lives, through all the 'disappearances and New Births and sufferings and wanderings' ascribed to Dionysus, which were therefore enacted in a ritual that included the votary with the God; the continual

---

[1] Here again it must be remembered that there is no direct historical evidence for the existence of a particular individual of this name. An examination of the question will be found in W. K. C. Guthrie's *Orpheus and Greek Religion*, 1935.

[2] Pausanias, iii 19, 3.

[3] G. Thomson in *Æschylus and Athens*, 1941, p. 153, will not allow that it was a revolution, because there was no social uprising, but Orphism was a religion of the individual, like early Christianity.

[4] See Orphic gold tablet from Petelia, Kaibel, *C.I.G.S.*, 638.

'climbings and fallings' of the Titans.[1] The doctrine has an Eastern, even an Indian, colouring, and it may well be that Orpheus incorporated foreign symbology, in his Wheel, for instance, of births and deaths. But the pattern was already implicit in the whole body of beliefs which we have seen to underlie the initiation ceremonies of quite primitive peoples, the seeds of which are even present in the rudimentary discipline of the Palæolithic caves, gradually unfolding as the heart and brain of man were enlarged to contain them.

The doctrine of the wholeness of all life, the need for communion and rebirth, which Dionysus had brought back to the Greek people, was now extended to embrace the world of intellectual imagination. By imparting to Dionysus Apollo's moral orientation, Orpheus made his dæmon a God; and later writers, perceiving this Apolline character in an elemental power, say that Orpheus was torn to pieces by the adherents of Dionysus for worshipping Helios, the ancient Sun-God of the Titans, in his stead.[2] For of course he suffered the death of his God. The legend appropriately shows his severed head still singing as it is swept down the mountain stream, and the Muses receiving on the seashore what the Mænads had flung away.[3]

The fragments of those songs became recurring themes alike in the Odes of the Apolline Pindar[4] and the choral hymns of longing chanted by the Bacchæ of Euripides.[5] They mingled with Aristophanes' clairvoyant ribaldry[6] as easily as they soothed the surgical probings of Socrates.[7]

Fragments only, for the salvation of the individual remained an unorthodox creed among a people whose unit was the city, and their Gods removed from the contamination of human mutability. At Eleusis alone, deeply rooted in Attic religious observance, did it come to receive a national character, and

---

[1] See above, p. 274.   [2] Eratosthenes, *Catast.*, xxiv.

[3] Eratosthenes, op. cit., 'But the Muses gathered (his limbs) together, and buried them in the place called Leibethra.' Lucian *Adv. Indoct.*, 11. 'The head they buried in the place where now they have a sanctuary of Bakchos.' Conon, *Narr.*, xlv. 'It was still singing,' Harrison, *Prolegomena*, p. 462 ff.

[4] Pindar, *Olymp.*, ii, vv 67.

[5] Especially in the chorus vv 370 ff., Ὀσία, πότνα θεῶν, with its crying for peace, and the Muses.

[6] Aristophanes, *Parabasis* of *The Birds*, for instance.

[7] For instance, *Phædo*, 69c.

only among the Greeks of Italy to inspire both the life and the philosophy of the Pythagorean order.

But the very nature of the ritual and moral discipline of Orpheus imposed a silence, the old silence of conditional knowledge, in which comprehension entailed a change of state. We are ignorant not only because the secrets have been kept; neither written dogma, nor a description of the rites, could have satisfactorily imparted all that was accomplished at these ceremonies, any more than an account of the animal dances of the savages can give us their experience of dæmonic participation. Something however may be learned of this climax of the religious exploration of the ancient European world, from sources of great variety, the most circumstantial being the hostile criticism of the Christian Fathers.

THE MYSTERIES

ORIGIN AND AFFINITIES

The Cretans, according to Diodorus, claimed to have imparted the Mysteries to the Greek peoples, saying that the ceremonies of initiation, performed at Eleusis, in Samothrace, and among the Thracians, were in those places a secret rite, but at Knossos had been an open festival from the earliest times.[1] Such revelation, in Crete as elsewhere, must naturally have remained conditional; the legend of the labyrinth itself bears witness to that, but it may well have taken place in a state ceremony like that of Eleusis, and have been open to all who were eligible.

Herodotus, it must be noted, refers in guarded language to the 'mysteries' of Osiris in Egypt as if those of Dionysus had been constituted on their pattern.[2] But the mythical history of the Greek divinity confines itself almost exclusively to the islands, the Northern peninsula and the Asiatic coast, so that it seems reasonable rather to consider the two cults, which must after all have diverged very greatly, to have each originated from a similar primitive source.

---

[1] Diodorus, v 77; J. E. Harrison, *Themis*, p. 54, note 7.
[2] See below, p. 322 and note 3.

The Phrygian mysteries of the Great Mother do seem to have retained an extremely close connection with the Greek,[1] but a similar connection was present, as we have seen, with Minoan Crete from the beginning of its history. The Cretan claim, therefore, to have established the ritual upon which the Greek secret cults were to be based, appears to have some foundation.

This would apply of course to the Mother equally with the young hero or foster child, for Homer already refers in the Odyssey to the marriage of Demeter with Iasion amid the thrice-ploughed furrows in Crete,[2] and this is described by Hesiod also,[3] while the Homeric Hymn declares in her name 'I am come from Crete over the wide sea'.[4] Iasion belongs also to Theban legend, and to Samothrace,[5] where the shield-bearing dances were performed. The triple ploughing likewise associated him with Triptolemos, child of the sacred furrows at Eleusis. Theocritus speaks of his Cretan marriage with Demeter as a mystery,[6] and it appears likely that such references preserve the actual route of the passage of the rites into Attica.

'Orpheus' is universally credited with this task, even by the Cretans. He took, as we have seen, the myth of the betrayed child as the starting point for his mystic discipline: 'They allege that the God (Zagreus) was born of Zeus and Persephone in Crete, and Orpheus in the mysteries represents him as torn to pieces by the Titans.'[7] He may, as we have seen, have brought the legend of dismemberment from Thrace. A fragment of Euripides' lost play 'The Cretans'[8] describes the commemorative feast of raw flesh, followed by future abstinence, and the 'thunder-cry' endured by the Idæan novices in the darkness (which recalls the terrifying bull-roarer of savage initiations); the 'blind' wanderings and the purifications, before the neophyte can be consecrated as a 'Bacchos of the armed priesthood'. There is also mention of the torches carried for the

---

[1] Strabo, x 3, p. 470. 'The orgies of Thrace, Phrygia and Crete are substantially the same.' *Philosophoumena*: 'And following the Phrygians, the Athenians, when they initiate at the Eleusinian rites. . . .'

[2] *Odyssey*, 125–127.   [3] Hesiod, *Theogony*, 969.

[4] Homeric Hymn to Demeter, vv 123–124: νῦν αὖτε Κρήτηθεν ἐπ' εὐρέα νῶτα θαλάσσης.

[5] Diodorus, v 45.   [6] Theocritus, *Id.*, iii 50.   [7] Diodorus, v 75, 4.

[8] See above, p. 282, note 1.

'Mountain Mother', a significant reference to the Cretan Goddess.

Another glimpse into this mountain ritual is given by Porphyry, in describing the initiation of Pythagoras among the Idæan Daktyls.[1] After the 'purification by thunder', and a sleep in the cave, he was allowed to look upon the empty throne of 'Zeus', draped with his garment only. This seems to indicate a preliminary stage to communion in which, as in the Attic Lesser Mysteries, only the outer form of the God was perceived.[2] What is known, however, of the Cretan ritual in general, shows primitive traits which seem to have become submerged in civilised Eleusis, but afford a very valuable link with the earlier phases of sacramental religion.

The thunder rite twice referred to, and prominent also in the similar Thracian mysteries in which 'bull-voices roar terribly from somewhere unseen, and from a drum an image as of thunder, is borne on the air heavy with dread',[3] has of course its mythical raison d'être in the thunder-blasting of the Titans, as well as in the smiting of Semele, the earth herself 'riven by love'.[4]

Epimenides too, who came from Crete to purify Athens, was called by his contemporaries the 'new Koures'.[5] His ministry had begun with a magic sleep in the Diktæan cave, 'where he had a dream for his teacher, and met with the Gods and divine intercourse, and Truth and Justice.'[6] He is said to have written a 'Birth of the Kouretes and Korybantes'[7]—the 'birth' of the worshippers, not the God.

That the Mailed Priests in historic times still hovered somewhere between human initiates and dæmons, is apparent from inscriptions which record oaths sworn in the names of the

---

[1] Porphyry, *Life of Pythagoras*, 17; J. E. Harrison, *Themis*, p. 56, note 3.

[2] P. 296 below.

[3] Æschylus, Fragment 57 of Nauck, quoted by J. E. Harrison, *Themis*, p. 61. The reader will recall the bull-hide shield of Minoan Crete.

[4] For Semele as the Earth, see Harrison, *Prolegomena*, pp. 404–405. 'Riven by love' of the earth that swallowed Œdipus: Sophocles, *Œd. Col.* v 1662: εὔνουν διαστὰν γῆς ἀλύπητον βάθρον.

[5] Plutarch, *Life of Solon*, XII; J. E. Harrison, *Themis*, p. 52, note 2.

[6] Maximus of Tyre, c. 22, p. 224 (Diels, *Fragmente*, ii, p. 494), and c. 28, p. 286; Diogenes Laertius, *Life of Epimenides*, 1, 109.

[7] Diog. Laert., op. cit., 1, 111.

Kouretes, Nymphs and Korybantes.[1] The bird-man Picus, described by Ovid as practising the arts of those 'called in Greece
the Idæan Daktyls' was buried in Crete with the inscription:
'Here lies the wood-pecker who is also Zeus.'[2] The masked
votary who is both animal and God had a long life in Crete,
but the Attic mysteries seem to have left him behind.

ATHENIAN AGRICULTURAL FESTIVALS

In the ritual of Dionysus the Son eclipsed the Mother. Of her
there remained only the nursing nymphs, and the dead Semele
evoked in spring. In Crete she was almost forgotten, but
Phrygia, as we saw, had remained faithful to the Great Goddess
from the time of the earliest records. We saw too that the 'bull-
voiced mimes' of Thrace paid devotion to a wild Mother,[3] but
the great predominance of the Goddess in the Mysteries of
Eleusis in Attica is due to the personality of Demeter, whose
worship, with that of her daughter, had been perpetuated in the
Athenian state festivals from prehistoric times, the ancients
themselves declaring that these agrarian rites had been taught
to the earlier population by the daughters of Danaos, and retained only among those communities who had never sub-
mitted to Dorian suzerainty.[4] The Danaides, Herodotus adds,
had learned them from the Egyptians. The tale of the wanderings of Isis has come down to us in too sophisticated a form
(and through an initiate into the Greek Mysteries), to afford
any certainty on that point.[5] The bereaved immortal Mother,
who eases her grief by suckling a human child, is common to
both, but the Greek form of the myth, as performed in Attic
ritual, and woven round the personalities of the Mother and
the Maid; this conception of the two phases of a single being,
one of whom descends into the underworld and emerges in
spring, while the other suffers no bodily change, but is broken
in spirit on her daughter's behalf, lends itself to an especially
intimate connection with the human passage from state to state.

Thus Orpheus contributed to the spiritual import of Eleusis
by transforming the personality of Dionysus, the divine Nurs-

---

[1] Blass in Collitz-Betchtel, 5039; J. E. Harrison, op. cit., p. 54, n. 4.

[2] Suidas s.v. Πῆκος; Harrison, op. cit., p. 109, note 2.

[3] Above, p. 284, and note 4.   [4] Herodotus, ii 171 ff.

[5] See Plutarch, de Iside et Osiride, for the whole tale.

ling, and through him the discipline of the human aspirant; but Athens, which had kept alive the memory of the Earth-Mother, in the dual form, it may be, that the Minoans had created, Athens, 'by establishing the Mysteries brought mankind from barbarism to civilisation', as a Delphic inscription declares.[1] It is necessary to consider for a moment those harvest festivals of Attica which contributed their peculiar quality to the secret rites.

The Thesmophoria.

'They fast in honour of Demeter at the season of sowing.'[2] These autumnal rites had already much of the character of a mystery. They were performed by women only, who lived apart for the three days of their duration. On the first of these was celebrated the Kathodos and Anodos: the Descent and the Uprising. They went down into cavities of the earth, after long and careful purifications, to bring back the decayed bodies of sacrificed sucking-pigs to be mixed with the year's seeds, leaving in their stead fertility-emblems of clay.[3] Pigs had originally been drawn into the chasm with Persephone, when she was rapt away from her flower-gathering by the king of the underworld. The pits were called *megara*, the word for palace or temple used here in its old Semitic meaning of cave.[4] On the second day the women fasted, seated on the ground, in memory of Demeter's mourning on the Stone of No Laughter, and prisoners were released.[5] The third day was called the Fair Born.

The ancient writers apply the epithet Thesmophoros to Demeter as 'Law-giver' because she had sent out her foster-child Triptolemos in his winged car to bring the civilising gift of corn to men.[6] It is interesting to observe that they sometimes

[1] *Bull. Corr. Hell.*, 1900, p. 96.

[2] Cornutus *de Theol.*, 28 (Harrison, *Prolegomena*, p. 121).

[3] Scholiast on Lucian, *Dial. Meretr.*, ii 1; Harrison, op. cit., p. 122; cf. the Malekulan custom in part ii, p. 163.

[4] Eustathius, para. 1387, says: Megara are the underground dwellings of the two Goddesses; Harrison, op. cit., pp. 125–126; Hebrew Meghara: a cave. The modern colloquial Arabic is Mughãra.

[5] Plutarch, *de Iside et Osiride*, lxix; Aristophanes, *Thesm.*, 80; Harrison, op. cit., pp. 127–128.

[6] L. Farnell, *Cults of the Greek States*, iii, p. 189. Porphyry writes: 'Triptolemos is said to have laid down laws for the Athenians.' Xenocrates relates that three of these were still in use at Athens.

confuse this festival with the *Skirophoria*, an agricultural rite held in honour of Athena,[1] who must here be the primitive Earth-Goddess, Athenaia Kore, the Maid of Athens.

The Haloa

The Haloa was sacred to Dionysus as well as Demeter, and here they appear together for the first time. It was a winter festival of the cutting of the Vine, in which dances were performed on the threshing-floors.[2] Bloodless sacrifices were offered and it was announced that Demeter had given men 'gentle food'—an Orphic touch.[3]

Eleusinia

Two days before the autumn full-moon, in the month preceding the consecration of seeds, the young citizens of Athens bore the sacred fertility emblems to the Eleusinion at the foot of the Acropolis.[4] On the fifteenth day of the month, the Hierophant, hereditary chief priest and spokesman of Eleusis, made proclamation to the candidates gathered in Athens for initiation, welcoming all who desired it without distinction of rank or sex, freedom or slavery, excepting only those with unclean hands or unintelligible speech.[5] Next day, the day named 'Mystics to the sea', the candidates bathed both themselves and the pig which was to be their oblation to the earth-divinities. It must have been an expiatory sacrifice, for this procession was called 'the banishing'.[6] Nor, throughout the ceremonies, was there any tasting of animal flesh. But on the night of the nineteenth of the month the procession of mystics, surrounding the image of Iacchos which was borne by the priestess of Demeter, was escorted to Eleusis by the same body of young Athenians who had performed the opening ceremony, and these, it is re-

[1] For instance, the scholiast on Aristophanes, *Thesmophoriazousæ*, 834, quoted in Harrison, op. cit., p. 134.

[2] Harrison, op. cit., quoting Schol. ad Lucian, *Dial. Meretr.*, vii 4, and Eustathius ad Il., ix 530, 772.

[3] Lucian, op. cit., vii; Harrison, op. cit., pp. 148–149.

[4] *C.I.A.*, iii 5. This is a Roman inscription, but it states that the enactments described are according to ancient usage; Harrison, op. cit., p. 151.

[5] Theon of Smyrna, p. 22: τὸ κήρυγμα τοῦτο κηρύττεται ὅστις τὰς χεῖρας μὴ καθαρός . . . ὅστις φωνὴν ἀσύνετος.

[6] *C.I.A.*, iv 385, d.l. 20: ἐπεμελήθησαν δε καὶ τῆς ἅλαδε ἐλάσεως.

corded, there took part in a bull-fight,[1] and offered the bulls in sacrifice—a strange instance of ritual continuity.

It was such a procession, as of 30,000 men, which was seen before the battle of Salamis to move across the Thriasian plain, with voices in the air singing the hymn to Iacchos,[2] whose name in the sea fight that followed was the Athenian rallying-cry. So, two generations later, when the battle of Naxos was fought on the sixteenth of the month, the war-cry through the line of ships was 'Mystics to the sea'.[3]

The moral prestige of Eleusis was still great enough in the later centuries of Roman supremacy, to enable its priests to refuse initiation to Nero. It is the Eleusis of that period alone of which any record of actual ceremonial remains, but in a ritual so conservative, little essential change is to be expected.

THE ELEUSINIAN MYSTERIES

A preliminary celebration was held at Agra in spring. It was a preparation for the Greater Mysteries, and seems to have centred round the *Anodos* or Rising of Persephone,[4] sometimes also referred to as the Birth of Aphrodite from the Sea.[5] On the analogy of rites such as the Thesmophoria a Descent would first have been enacted. Thus the painted tablet of Ninnion (pl. XXXIIa, below), in which the lower register seems to represent mythologically these Lesser Mysteries, shows the dancing candidate led by Dionysus as Torch-bearer into the presence of Persephone, Queen of the Underworld.[6] There is a

---

[1] Artemidorus, 1, 8: ταύροις ἐν᾽ Ἰωνίᾳ παῖδες Ἐφεσιῶν ἀγωνίζονται καὶ ἐν Ἀττικῇ παρὰ ταῖς θεαῖς ἐν Ἐλευσῖνι κοῦροι Ἀθηναῖοι περιτελλομένων ἐνιαυτῶν. Lobeck Agl. p. 206. C.I.A. II l. n. 471. ἤραντο δὲ καὶ τοὺς βοῦς το[ὺς] ἐν Ἐλευσῖνι τῇ θυσίᾳ καὶ τοῖς προηροσίοις καὶ τοῖς ἄλλοῖς ἱεροῖς καὶ γυμνασιόις.

[2] Herodotus, viii 65.

[3] Polyænus, *Strat.*, iii 11; Harrison, op. cit., p. 152.

[4] Schol. Aristophanes, *Plutus*, 845.

[5] Psellus, for instance, *Quænam sunt Græcorum opiniones de dæmonibus*, 3 (ed. Migne), quoted in Harrison, op. cit., p. 569, note 2, from Taylor's *Eleusinian Mysteries*. 'Aphrodite of the sea is represented as uprising.' He appears to be describing the Lesser Mysteries.

[6] This was Svoronos' view. Cook, *Zeus*, iii, pp. 222–224, inclines to accept it, but Nilsson in *Arch. f. Religionswissensch*, xxxii, p. 93 ff., considers the empty throne to indicate the absence of Persephone from the lower register, in which case the Lesser Mysteries could hardly be its subject.

tomb, and Demeter's empty throne, like the throne shown to Pythagoras before he could look upon the face of the God in Crete.

It is conjectured that this sojourn among the dead, followed by the uprising, was applied to the neophyte's personal life, and constituted a preliminary purification (pro-katharsis is the very word applied to it by the scholiast on Aristophanes),[1] such as Aristotle insists should be conveyed to the spectator of a drama.[2] It was not a true passage from state to state, because the Mystic was only a spectator of the divine life, beholding it 'through a glass darkly'. It is represented mythologically in all the legends of a journey to the other world, from which the hero returns empty-handed.

Ninnion on the pinax carries a vessel upon her head, into which three leafy branches are set, and holds a spray before her—the bough so frequently brought to Persephone in the lower world;[3] and Clement's list of the tokens borne by mystics[4] seem chiefly to refer to the Lesser Mysteries.[5] They relate to the old vegetation ritual bequeathed by the Ægean world. 'I have eaten from the timbrel,' once the bull's hide that gave forth his bellowing cry; 'I have drunk from the cymbal,' which must similarly have acted as a cup, perhaps for the wine of Dionysus; and lastly, 'I have carried the kernos,' the old composite vessel well known to pre-Hellenic ritual,[6] filled with various fruits and seeds, and in the midst a lamp, such as appears to be burning on Ninnion's head in the upper register,

[1] Previous note, and Harrison, op. cit., p. 560.

[2] Aristotle, *Poetics*, 1449*b*, 6.

[3] On a fragment of a vase which shows Orpheus in search of Eurydice in the lower world, and is illustrated in *Mon. Ant.* xvi, Tab. iii, the Bough appears planted before Persephone's palace, as Vergil's Æneas is bidden to plant it. Polygnotus' great wall painting of the world of the dead at Delphi showed Orpheus touching a willow tree and grasping its branch (Paus., x, xxx, 5).

[4] Clement, *Al. Protr.*, 1, 2, 13. He does not make it clear whether he is referring to Eleusinian as well as to Phrygian mysteries, but apparently considers them indistinguishable, like Strabo in note 1, p. 290 above.

[5] Because the Scholiast on Plato's *Gorgias*, p. 123, in quoting the same declarations, refers them to the Lesser Mysteries, and Psellus (note 5, p. 295 above) speaks of them in connection with the rites of Kore.

[6] Evans, *Palace of Minos*, i, p. 76 *a* and *b*; Nilsson, *Minoan-Myc. Religion*, pp. 112–118; Xanthoudides, Cretan Kernoi, *B.S.A.*, xii, p. 9 ff., etc.

which figuratively represents the later initiation.[1] The kernos is sometimes referred to as if identical with the liknon, which has been described at once as a basket of fruits, a winnowing fan and a cradle.[2] The liknon's place is definitely in the consummation of the Greater Mysteries.

The name Eleusis was believed by the ancients to mean a Way or Passage, and connected with Elysium.[3] Certainly the wanderings of Demeter were enacted at night on the sea-shore by the candidates in person. There are several references to 'blind marches',[4] and it is evident that a veiled maze-dance was performed on the threshold of the new condition. This is also attested by the description of these preliminaries attributed to Plutarch:

'At first there are wanderings and laborious circuits and journeyings through the dark, full of misgivings, where there is no consummation; then before the end come terrors of every kind, shivers and trembling and sweat and amazement. After this a wonderful light meets 'the wanderer; he is admitted to pure meadowlands, where are voices and dances and the majesty of holy sounds and sacred visions.'[5]

The meadow and the singing appear on the shore of the other world in the 'Frogs' and so does the difficult approach.[6] As to what was experienced, before the unveiled neophyte beheld the Goddess and was 'changed into the same image from glory to glory',[7] we know that there was a Marriage and a Birth, and they must here too have been preceded by a Death, a sacrifice experienced by the novice himself. There was no feast of raw flesh, but at a most solemn moment an ear of

---

[1] The Ionic column almost certainly indicates the Telesterion at Eleusis.

[2] Servius on Virgil, *Georg.*, i 165.

[3] Cook, *Zeus*, ii, p. 36 ff., quoting Hesychius, and also Porphyry, *de antro nymph.*, and Macrobius, as saying that this way lies between the Gates of the Sun. In this connection, too, he quotes an Orphic verse stating that the Path of the Gods passes between gold bull's horns. See also Nilsson, op. cit., p. 543, note 1, quoting L. Malten, 'Elysion und Rhadamanthys,' *Arch. Jahrb.*, xxviii, 1912, p. 35 ff., concerning the pre-Greek etymology of Eleusis, and its possible connection with Eileithyia, the Goddess of Birth.

[4] Lucian, *Catapl.*, xxii 644.

[5] Quoted by W. R. Halliday, *The Pagan Background of Early Christianity*, 1925, p. 237, and by M. Bodkin, *Archetypal Patterns in Poetry*, 1934, p. 125.

[6] Aristophanes, *Frogs*, 329 ff. Even Iacchos must use πολλὴν ὁδόν to reach it.   [7] *2 Corinthians*, iii 18.

corn was reaped in silence.[1] The instrument, if it was not a stone axe, seems to have carried on the memory of what the polished axe symbolised in so many Western graves of the New Stone Age.[2] That the act was sacrificial is apparent from the circumstances; the symbolism is used by Christ in speaking of his own death to Greeks, in the language that they could understand.[3]

'Was it a birth or a death?' asks Eliot's Magus who has witnessed the Nativity. In this ceremonial one phase passes into the other and cannot be entirely distinguished. In the Egyptian rites of the Passion of Osiris it was the Death that brought redemption; for the Ægean world, as we have seen, the Birth became especially significant. 'I have sunk beneath the bosom of Despoina' was a formula relating both to Death as return to the Earth-Mother, and birth as emergence also.[4] The nursling of the two Goddesses, whether he was called Triptolemos or Iacchos or another, represented every aspirant for initiation (pl. XXXII*b*). The corn-ear as symbolic of birth (again according to Jesus and Paul) is described by the author of the 'Philosophoumena':[5]

'And this ear of corn the Athenians hold to be the great and perfect light, from that which has no form, as the Hierophant himself, who is made a eunuch by means of hemlock and has renounced all carnal generation, by night at Eleusis, accomplishing by the light of a great torch the great and unutterable mysteries, cries in a loud voice "Holy Brimo has born a sacred child Brimos", that is, the Mighty has born the Mighty.'

Brimo was the old savage Mother Goddess of the Thracian rites,[6] and only her name remains, but the child appears on the vase painting (pl. XXXI*c*) lifted in the cornucopia out of the ground by the Earth-Mother, 'the first fruits of them that sleep.' This scene, which the presence of Triptolemos in his winged car shows to be taking place at Eleusis, explains the confusion of the Scholiast concerning the liknon, between basket of fruits and child's cradle, the cradle in which Dionysus

---

[1] Cruice, *Philosophoumena*, Paris, 1860, p. 170: ἐν σιωπῇ τεθερισμένον στάχυν; Harrison, op. cit., pp. 549–550.

[2] P. 142 above.   [3] St. John, xii 20–24.

[4] Compagno gold tablet, found in a grave near Sybaris. Kaibel, C.I.G.I.S. 641. Gilbert Murray in Appendix to J. E. Harrison, *Prolegomena*, p. 668.

[5] Cruice, *Philosophoumena*, op. cit..   [6] See p. 284 above.

Liknites was awakened for his winter reign at Delphi.[1] The fact
that in the Mysteries it was also called a winnowing-fan is expressly used to connect the New Birth with moral purification.[2]

It will be noted in the passage quoted above, that the Marriage of the Hierophant was symbolic only. The declaration of
the initiate: 'I have gone down into the marriage-chamber,' is
not distinctly related to Eleusis. The mystery was there performed on behalf of all, as the words of Asterius make very clear:[3]

'Is there not a descent into darkness and the holy congress
of Hierophant and priestess, of him alone and her alone, and
does not the great and vast multitude believe that what is done
in darkness is for their salvation?' Yet, as each candidate
emerged at the end of his initiation, he was greeted with the
words: 'Hail bridegroom, hail new light!'[4]

One archaic trait may be noticed in the use of the word
'descent' quoted above, implying that here as elsewhere the
rite was performed in a cave or crypt. Nevertheless it is as far
a cry from the consummation of the old Sacred Marriage as is
the cutting of the corn-ear from the bloodshed of the communal sacrifice. Yet dæmonic participation is obviously essential to the rite. The power of the sympathetic imagination has
at last replaced the sympathetic magic in which it had always
been present. In fact the outward paraphernalia of the old
vegetation ritual are almost absent; yet it is on that ritual that
these mysteries depend, and such preoccupation with the fertility of the soil on the part of a people who lived in cities and
had a considerable overseas trade, is very significant of the
essential conservatism of these beliefs. The local chthonic cults,
as we have seen, had never been entirely interrupted, and
firmly rooted in the soil, this intense religious revival, adapted
to the most intellectual as to the most ignorant aspirant after
holiness (each receiving according to his capacity), remained
alive as long as Greece lived, and made Christianity understood
and gave it its European form.

---

[1] See p. 286.

[2] Servius ad Verg. *Georg.* quoted above. He says that Vergil speaks of the
mystic winnowing-fan of Iacchos because the rites have reference to the
purification of the soul: Vannus est: quia ut diximus animas purgat.

[3] S. Asterius, *Amasen. Hom.*, x, in SS. Martyr., quoted by Harrison, op.
cit., p. 564.

[4] Firmicus Mat. *de Ev. Pr. Relig.*, p. 38c, quoted by Harrison, op. cit.,
p. 539.

CHAPTER II

THE INTELLECTUAL
DEVELOPMENT

It is time to consider in what manner the Hellenic religious
inheritance, now shaped to the needs of a people emotionally
mature, affected the intellectual creations which were so profoundly to modify the future of European thought.

In such an enquiry one astonishing fact is immediately apparent. The two paths of speculation along which the Greeks
most conspicuously diverged from their predecessors, the one
concerned with the causes of natural phenomena, and the other
with human destiny, were for all their novelty of method inseparably bound up with the older religion.

When the Ionians, for example, at the beginning of the sixth
century B.C. made the first fateful attempt to look at the cosmic
order without its Gods, they at once found themselves in the
world of pre-Olympic dynamism. This meant that they could
start their investigations from a single source, under whatever
aspect it was conceived—the one underlying life-force, whose
participation in material things was their concern.[1] As long as
this unity was affirmed, scientific enquiry moved in a metaphysical region.[2] The practical discoveries were its offshoots.

Attic drama, again, is the only art whose structure is wholly
conditioned by primitive ritual, its material being related by
this means, as in the Mysteries, to the pattern of human life.
Its inseparable limitations, in tragedy and comedy alike, made
speculation the more free.

[1] Gilbert, *Meteor. Theorien.*, 703. Der Stoff selbst, als der Grundstoff und
als die abgeleiteten Einzelstoffe, lebt und als lebend und persönlich
gedachtes Wesen bewegt er sich; der Stoff ist die Gottheit welche, in ihm
waltend, eins ist mit ihm. See F. M. Cornford, *From Religion to Philosophy*,
1912, p. 123; Gomperz, *Greek Thinkers*, p. 15. Greek philosophy began, as it
ended, with the search for what was abiding in the flux of things.

[2] Cf. F. M. Cornford in *J.H.S.*, lxii, p. 1 ff. 'Was Ionian philosophy
scientific?'

PHILOSOPHY

It was noted above that Philosophy grew to maturity from a religious basis; and that Ionian speculation was born of the desire to discover the cause or origin of the natural world. Not 'first cause' in a temporal sense; the old religion offered to the Greeks an ever-present and pervading dynamic force which they called Physis—nature or growth.[1] This involved no blasphemy against the Olympians, who were recognised by their worshippers as powers of a late dynasty, a particular phase of cosmic history. Speculative research, indeed, had no need to dethrone the Gods; it might in some respects be said to have established them more firmly by emphasising their functional and regional aspects at the expense of the human characters created by Homeric disillusion. The investigators of Miletus, however, were content to ignore them, being occupied in affirming the existence of a fundamental unity.

Thales, the earliest of these, found himself, therefore, in that dæmonic environment by which contact had been established with nature since Neolithic times. Miletus had been a Cretan colony, and Thales himself was said to belong to the pre-Hellenic stratum of society, being of Carian or 'Kadmeian' descent.[2]

Only three of his postulates survive, and these are sufficient to demonstrate not merely a discarding of polytheism, but the return to its predecessor. They are as follows:

(i) *There is one original soul-substance.* He calls it 'water', but has in mind something other than the physical element, for he continues: (ii) *The All is alive*—a confident declaration of the faith of the pre-Greek world, whether Asiatic or Ægean, which goes back, as we saw, to the beginning of all religion. The in-

---

[1] J. Dewey, in Baldwin's *Dictionary of Philosophy and Psychology*, s.v. 'Nature'. By the nature of a thing the Scholastics understood its essence 'considered as the active source (or principle) of the operations by which the being realised its end'. Quoted by F. M. Cornford, op. cit., para. 39. He groups it under the two heads of static and dynamic, but concedes (p. 73) that its derivation shows the latter to be its original connotation.

[2] Herodotus, i 46; Diog., 1, 22; H. Ritter and L. Preller, *Historia Philosophiæ Græcæ*, 8th edition, 1898, p. 8.

timate relation of (i) and (ii) is expressed by (iii) *The All is full of dæmons*, who are the agents of the activity of the one substance. This is of course a purely religious conception, as opposed to the 'scientific' term, water; which is thus shown to be that moving force, shared by all existence, which was already implicit in the ritual of the Palæolithic stage of culture, and emotionally perceived in the pre-Greek Ægean, but not till now, perhaps, isolated by thought. We have here, in fact, the first legibly written document of the pre-Hellenic religion, as deduced from its archæological remains and the beliefs of its neighbours. Thus Thales could offer with confidence his underlying substance as a fact of human experience common to dæmons and men, and once this was affirmed his successors differed chiefly in the particular attribute of the One, upon which their attention was to be concentrated: its mobility, its infinity, its divinity, its unity.

Anaximander, the great successor of Thales, more clearly differentiated the one principle, which he called 'nature', and 'the infinite', by refusing to include it as an element among the elements which it generates:[1] 'He did not ascribe the origin of things to any alteration in matter, but said that the oppositions in the substratum, which was a boundless body, were separated out.'[2]

This earliest 'scientific' attempt to relate the phenomenal universe to a single cause, uses that regional arrangement of space and time, previously found to be rooted in Neolithic imagination, as illustrated by its intense importance in the religious systems of the Far East and the Far West.[3] It was bound up, as we saw, with yet more primitive conditions—the opposition of the phratries and exogamy.[4]

But it will be remembered that in the Aryan homeland cosmic orientation had already received a moral significance,[5] and such is the framework of Anaximander's system as recorded in the utterance:[6]

---

[1] Aristotle, *Metaph.*, 1, 3, Z. 1, 215; *Physics*, iii 5, 204, 22; Ritter and Preller, op. cit., p. 15.

[2] Simplic., *Phys.*, 150, 20 D; Ritter and Preller, op. cit., p. 16.

[3] Above, p. 180.   [4] See also Cornford, op. cit., chap. i and ii.

[5] Above, p. 262.

[6] Theophrastus, *Physic. Opinion.*, fr. 2; ap. Simpl., *Phys.*, 24, 13, D (Dox. 476, 3); Ritter and Preller, pp. 13–14.

'Things perish into those things out of which they have their birth, as is ordained; for they give reparation to one another, and pay the penalty for their injustice, according to the disposition of time.'

This places the Greek fear of *Hubris* upon a fundamental basis; 'If any of the opposites were infinite, the rest would have ceased to be.'[1] In this first philosophic statement of order, natural law is the equivalent of moral law, as Homer had equated it in regard to human action. The reparations within the disposition of time, are similarly implicit in the ritual of the Dying God. In fact Anaximander made philosophy possible by taking over from religion a spatial and temporal rhythm in which thought could move.

The separation of opposites he held to be produced by the whirling motion of the one substance, *Diné*; the spiral movement whose long history, as pathway of the earliest divinities and of their human votaries, has been followed here from its source. This movement, he said, is eternal, and the cause of innumerable worlds within the Boundless, 'that becoming may not fail.'[2]

Anaximenes, 'who had been an associate of Anaximander, considered like him that the underlying substance was one and infinite . . . but he said it was determinate, for he called it Air.'[3] That is, he returned to an 'element' for his first cause, but, though he confused it with a physical substance, he did not regard it as such, any more than Thales had done. 'It is also our Soul'[4]—nature and man fundamentally inseparable. His great step was the introduction of quantity, as the mechanism of relationship between the One and its material expression. The other elements he considered to exist, and to be differentiated, according to the amount of 'breath' which they contain.[5] This rejection of qualitative values is a step towards the Numbers of Pythagoras, the seeds of Anaxagoras, and finally the

---

[1] Aristotle, *Physics*, v 5, 204*b*, 22; Burnet, *Early Greek Philosophers*, p. 55.

[2] Heidel, 'Qualitative change in Pre-Socratic Philosophy,' *Arch. f. Gesch. d. Philos.*, xix 313 ff.; Cornford, op. cit., p. 9, and note 3.

[3] Theophr., *Phys. opin.*, fr. 2 (ap. Simplic., *Phys.*, 24–25; Dox. 476, 16); Ritter and Preller, p. 20.

[4] Plac., i 3, 4; Dox. 278–279: οἷον ἡ ψυχή, φησίν, ἡ ἡμετέρα ἀὴρ οὖσα συγκρατεῖ ἡμᾶς.

[5] J. Burnet, *Early Greek Philosophers*, pp. 78–79.

atomism of Leukippos, which was the logical outcome of the sustained endeavour of the Milesians to isolate their material cause.[1] Here a mechanical change of position was made to take the place of conscious movement among the groups of physically indivisible, but substantially identical, existences. This farthest point of divergence from the religious source was accomplished after the progress of speculation in Miletus had been abruptly broken by the Persian advance to the Mediterranean. It was scientifically unassailable until recent times, when Anaximander's Diné has been found within the Atom itself, separating the opposite forces.

The exiles, who brought philosophy into Italy and Sicily, found themselves faced by an unexpected problem. They had at last to examine their position in relation to religion. And because Ionian science had its source in an environment of religious dynamism; and because the primary substance of its search had never yet received a physical connotation (though now on its way, as we have seen, to become a materialistic abstraction); and chiefly, perhaps, because Orphism had brought the dæmonic world once more into prominence, and having no local nor racial boundaries could meet it half-way; for these three reasons philosophy in the West became insolubly tied to religion, and the connection was equally intimate whether the religion was mystical or prophetic.

Ionian speculation had progressed by a series of steps, each investigator being dependent upon the work of his predecessors. It was in that respect scientific. Philosophy in the Italian cities, on the other hand, comprised a series of individual efforts to draw the physical world into relation with religious life and doctrine, always returning to Orphism as their source. Each of the following systems, therefore, resembles a work of art, of which its scientific discoveries are the by-products. Let us glance through them in turn.

Xenophanes. The Ionian conception of Nature, as the one underlying motive force, had always retained a spatial and temporal content, which it seems to have possessed even in primitive sensibility. Now, under the stimulus of the new environment, Xenophanes, 'the first partisan of the One' (as Aristotle calls him),[2] but a religious poet rather than a philo-

---

[1] G. Milhaud, *Les Philosophes géomètres de la Grèce*, 1900, p. 18 ff.

[2] Arist., *Met.*, A, 5, 986B.; R.P., p. 79.

sopher, effected the transference of the life, hitherto considered
to reside in the whole, to the one being of which all others were
passing forms.[1] This constituted the final break with Olympic
polytheism, no less than the turning of scientific attention from
preoccupation with the material cause.

Two lonely and prophetic figures followed in his wake.
Herakleitos of Ephesus, equally with Empedokles in Sicily, used
the Orphic cosmogony as the framework of their grandiose
dreams. The Orphic doctrine of cyclic experience will be recalled—man's fall into sin, and final escape from the Wheel of
births and deaths, through union with divine life.[2] This cycle,
as we saw, included the natural world. Souls returned into the
earth like seeds to be reborn, and the old animal kinship was
renewed, only now for that very reason the lives of the beasts
were respected in the sacrifice and at the feast. The sharing of
experience reached upwards also, and the God-like life must be
lived, before escape could be found. Dike, Justice, had personified such a returning movement from Homer onwards,[3] and
some part of these ideas, the moral part, had, as we saw,
already come into Europe with the Greeks. Possibly Orpheus,
and probably Pythagoras,[4] reinforced them from the developed
systems of India and Persia,[5] especially their conception of
world cycles, the 'Days and Nights of Brahma'.

The Fall from Heaven, on the other hand, goes far backwards to those humble beginnings in which the souls of the
primitive ancestors left the divine world to be born into the
human race. 'I am the child of Earth and starry Heaven,' says
the newly dead on one of the Orphic grave-tablets, 'but my
origin is of Heaven alone.[6]

Empedokles of Akragas, therefore, describes himself in his poem
as an exile and a wanderer,[7] led downwards by divine guardians

[1] Arist. op. cit. ἀλλ' εἰς τὸν ὅλον οὐρανὸν ἀποβλέψας τὸ ἕν εἶναι τὸν θεόν.
[2] Pp. 287, 288 above.
[3] *Od.*, xi 218: αὕτη δίκη ἐστι βροτῶν. See Cornford, op. cit., para. 97.
[4] Note 7, p. 307.
[5] See Cornford, op. cit., pp. 172–177. He observes in note 1 on p. 176 that
Plutarch, *de Is. et Osir.*, 370, translates Arta (The Aryan Divine Order) by
ἀλήθεια, truth.
[6] On the Petelia gold tablet now in the British Museum; Kaibel, *C.I.G.S.*,
no. 638.
[7] Empedocl. ap. Plut., *de Exilio.*; Hippol., vii 27; Plut., *de Is. et Osir.*, 26.

into 'this roofed-in-cave',[1] journeying for 30,000 seasons through mortal forms, the elements tossing him backwards and forwards, clothed in a garment of flesh (the Orphic 'chiton'), because he had sinned by 'putting his trust in strife'.[2]

He speaks with regret of the Golden Age, when there was no Ares nor Zeus nor Kronos nor Poseidon, but only the Goddess, Kypris the Queen[3]—a curious reminiscence of the pre-Greek world—to whom bloodless sacrifices were offered.

His speculative theology was like that of Xenophanes and also of Anaxagoras, for he speaks of God as a 'sacred and unutterable mind, flashing through the whole world with rapid thought'.[4]

In philosophy he moved towards the separation of life from matter.[5] He introduces the cause of motion as two-fold—Love and Strife. These are material soul-substances, by which the four indestructible elements are moved.[6] There is no coming into existence, only a change in what is mingled;[7] these two life-forces performing mechanically what Anaximander's Justice had done, during the four periods of a cycle. Our own world can only exist within two of these periods—neither when Love nor Strife is in absolute possession, but only when either is in process of ejecting the other.[8]

Herakleitos of Ephesus proclaimed a doctrine that was the embodiment of Dionysian dynamism.[9] He took away the moral stigma from Anaximander's Separation of the Many from the One, by making them co-exist. 'Men do not know that what is at variance agrees with itself. It is an attunement of opposite tensions, like the bow and the lyre.'[10] So he affirms that Rest is also Change; that we step, and do not step, into the same

---

[1] And 'Meadow of Calamity'. Frags., 119, 120, 121.

[2] Empedocl. ap. Plut., *de Exilio*; Hippol., vii 27; Plut., *de Iside.*, 26.

[3] Empedocl. ap. Porphyr., *de Abstin.*, ii 21 and 27; Athen. xii 510 D R. P., p. 150.

[4] Empedocl. ap. Ammon. in Arist., *de Interpret.*, 199 (Schol. Arist., 135, 25), R.P., p. 147.

[5] 'He takes a step beyond the Milesians in the direction of Atomism . . . and so has a place in the development of the scientific tradition.' Cornford, op. cit., pp. 150–151.

[6] Arist., *Met.*, A, 5.   [7] Plac. 1, 30 (Dox. 326); R.P., p. 128.

[8] Burnet, op. cit., pp. 270–271.   [9] Cornford, op. cit., p. 183.

[10] Frag. 45 (80) ap. Hippol., *Refut.*, ix 9; R.P., p. 27.

river,[1] and, because of the necessity for change, he glorifies strife.[2]

His religious vision is consistent with his philosophy, as perhaps that of Empedokles was not. He says that Wisdom is willing and unwilling to be called by the name of Zeus,[3] that Hades and Dionysus are one God,[4] that mortals and immortals 'live each other's death, and die each other's life'.[5] He describes the mutation of the elements in the same fashion. They have no special province.

He thus conceives of life as continually transformed by death, 'the ever-living Fire with measures kindling and with measures going out.'[6] This maintenance of proportion is to him Reason. It is a more primitive vision of the Pythagorean harmony.

Pythagoras. As Plato in later days was to found a philosophic system round the prophetic personality of Sokrates, so Pythagoras, another emigrant from the Ægean world,[7] brought philosophy into direct relationship with the religious creation of Orpheus. As the musician of legend had replaced the momentary union achieved in orgiastic ecstasy, by the lifelong, even the cyclic, endeavour after divine communion, so Pythagoras made the search for truth itself into a way of life, an intellectual redemption in which thought was re-created by experience. *Theoria*, contemplation,[8] which retained its mystic content of participation, was the inspiring force behind both. As Orpheus, again, had imparted an Apolline character to the figure of Dionysus,[9] so Pythagoras by a further step established as the God of his order, Apollo himself; but his was the Delian, the Ionian Apollo, who had kept his pre-Greek dæmonism.[10] In

---

[1] Frag. 26*a*; R.P. (i 81).   [2] Frag. 43.

[3] Frag. 65 (140) ap. Clem. Strom., v 14, p. 718. Ζηνός, not Διός, probably with a play on the word ζῆν. R.P., p. 32, note *a*.

[4] Frag. 127 (132) ap. Clem. Protr., 2, p. 30: 'ωυτὸς δε 'Αἴδης καὶ Διόνυσος.

[5] Frag. 67 (60) ap. Hippolyt., ix 10.

[6] Frag. 20 (46) ap. Clem. Strom., v 14, p. 711, P.

[7] The island of Samos. Ancient authors credited him with journeys to Egypt, Chaldæa and even India before he settled in Southern Italy. See R.P., p. 41, note *a*.

[8] Theoria: Cornford, op. cit., p. 200, relates this to the primitive sympathetic spectacle of the suffering God.

[9] See p. 288 above.

[10] Pythagoras and the Delian Apollo. See Iambl. *Vit. Pyth.*, v 22, vii 34, xxx 184.

his service the intellectual life could become an actual form of worship, a search for and practice of harmony, so that the music of Orpheus became for Pythagoras the plan of the structure of the world.

His discipline was still the 'Way of Death',[1] and his ritual, sacrifice; but now the animal victim existed only within the soul, a force to be liberated for creation, as the bull's blood had been poured out long ago. It did not involve a rejection of the life of the senses, but an absorption of power by their control, as it did for Plato after him.

The School was a legacy of the thiasos (Pythagoras is said to have even lectured to the animals, as Orpheus had played to them),[2] and was therefore communistic. Women, who, he said, had a natural gift for piety, resumed the importance which they had exercised in the pre-Greek religion, and from which Orpheus as well as the Olympians had degraded them. Their activity in intellectual research was a successful innovation, repeated in Plato's Academy.[3]

After the death of Pythagoras, no individual investigator among his followers might claim credit for any mathematical, astronomical or musical discovery, which was attributed to the continued presence of its founder.[4] This belief, inherited from the Dionysiac thiasos, of the One going forth into the Many, and the Many losing themselves within the One, seems to be the clue to that very doctrine of Numbers, which was the main contribution of the School to philosophy. Here the tetraktys (the ten in a triangle of four) was the nucleus of all material form. 'From this all numbers proceed, as the fountain and root of ever-springing nature.'[5] This procession is elucidated as follows by Aristotle, in commenting upon Plato's lectures: 'The self-animal is composed of the form of One, the first length two, breadth three, depth four.'[6] This fits the definition of the One as not in itself a numeral, being infinite. The 'One' among

---

[1] Cornford, op. cit., p. 200, quoting Plato, *Phædo.*, 64A.

[2] Iambl., op. cit., xiii; Porph., *Vit. Pyth.*, 24.

[3] 'In a common fellowship and mode of life.' Iambl., op. cit., 246.

[4] ἐκείνου τοῦ ἀνδρός. Iambl., op. cit., 88.

[5] The Oath of the Order οὐ μὰ τὸν ἁμετέρᾳ ψυχᾷ παραδόντα τετρακτύν, παγὰν ἀενάου φύσιος ῥίζωμα τ' ἔχουσαν. (Theon of Smyrna περὶ τετρακτύος. p. 154, Dupuis, 1892.)

[6] Arist., *de Anim.*, a, 2, 404b, 21.

Aristotle's dimensions described above is thus seen not to represent a point, but to constitute what we should call the Fourth Dimension; that is to say, it permeates the rest, and is the basis of that participation, by which Pythagoras and Plato after him, related his Forms to the physical world. To quote Aristotle again: 'The Pythagoreans say that things exist by representing numbers, Plato by participation—he merely changed the name.'[1]

Nor are the remaining numbers of the tetraktys mere groups of units; they have distinct properties, like the harmonic proportions in an octave. So the behaviour of numbers might be expressed by space and movement; and the formless darkness was conceived as being progressively conquered by light radiating from a central fire.[2] This was mythologically represented by Hestia, Goddess of the Hearth, and the Earth was thus for the first time removed from its position in men's minds as physical centre of the Universe; an interesting comment on the relation which at this period existed between religion and science.[3]

That the individual soul, a little cosmos built on the model of the 'Self-animal', was also conceived as a harmony, we know from Socrates' consideration and rejection of this argument before his execution, in attempting to convince his young Pythagorean disciples of his own immortality.[4] The conception, nevertheless, is in no way inconsistent with the Orphic Journey of the Soul, which from the nature of its transformations could never have been thought of as an indivisible unit like the atom. The uniting bond, as Socrates then proceeded to demonstrate, was Memory, of whose water the initiate soul partook, as the funeral tablets describe, in the Orphic underworld.[5]

But the philosophy of Pythagoras was not an endeavour to prove any religious doctrine, but rather to discover an intellectual truth as a painter of religious subjects might offer his art to God. Through Plato his discovery joined, for a moment, religion with science, before they were separated finally. We

[1] Arist., *Met.*, *a*, vi 987*b*, 9.

[2] Arist., *Met.*, n. 3, 1091A, 17, and Hippodamus, ap. Stob. Flor., 98, 71.

[3] Cornford, op. cit., p. 212.

[4] Plato, *Phædo*, 85E–86D.

[5] The Petelia Tablet, for instance (see note 6, p. 305), requires the soul of the dead to drink from the water of the Lake of Mnemosyne.

must pause here, however, to glance at one other great figure of the time.

Parmenides of Elea had been converted by the Pythagoreans to the philosophic life, and therefore used the method of argument rather than of prophecy. Nevertheless, his doctrine of reality is set as a revelation, within an Orphic myth of the soul's journey, before the opposite teaching is described. In this vision he is borne 'as far as his heart desires' on the renowned way of the Goddess. Beyond the Gates of Night and Day, opened for him by *Dike*, he is shown 'the unshaken heart of rounded Truth'.[1]

That is the Way of the One complete, immovable, and endless. The other, the method of Opinion, is of necessity illusory, for the One cannot evolve the Many; 'Dike does not loosen her fetters to let anything come into being or pass away.'[2]

The underlying principle which the Ionians had discovered, now drew all reality into its own nature, as the God of Xenophanes had drawn into himself the divinity of the living world.[3] Once this static conception is established, there can be no pairs of opposites, no sifting out, no everflowing fountain. So Aristotle calls Parmenides ἀφυσικός, a denier of *Phusis* or nature, because he does away with motion.[4]

For Parmenides, in his tremendous affirmation of the One, the negative is non-existent. Plato relates, as we have noted, the Many to the One by means of *Methexis*, participation, or sharing, but so impressive to his mind is the Parmenidean vision, that his abstract ideas are made inflexible. They are not reciprocally participant.

Plato in his youth had been inspired by Socrates with so burning a love of scientific integrity that he destroyed his poems and plays. Wherever his early religious proclivities may have lain, they too were overshadowed by his master's personality, for they have no place amid the ethical and political research of the early dialogues. Socrates belonged to the class of religious genius who preaches no doctrine, being concerned to impart to his pupils nothing beyond the reality upon which his life is founded. It is always the surviving disciples of such

---

[1] Parmenides, ap. Sext. Math., vii 111.

[2] Frag., 8, 13.   [3] See p. 305.

[4] Aristotle, ap. Sext. Math., x 46; Cornford, op. cit., p. 217.

men who establish schools of theology, for only after their death can the nature of their lives be understood.[1]

Plato could not have suddenly acquired the mystic temperament, and must have become early acquainted with the religious doctrines of the Pythagorean refugees from the Crotonian pogroms, now settled in Attica and Bœotia.[2] His constantly expressed contempt for degraded types of Orphism is of course by no means incompatible with that knowledge—on the contrary his quotation of the text, 'Many are the wand-bearers, few the Bacchoi,'[3] sufficiently indicates his discrimination. But in the disintegration of his own life which followed the execution of Socrates, he would have found among the surviving Pythagorean communities of South Italy, which had suffered a like catastrophe in the disruption of their order, a philosophic system by means of which the religious force implicit in the personality of Socrates could be formulated according to his own dialectic method. It was natural to make Socrates the mouthpiece of this new philosophy, as the Pythagorean discoveries had been attributed to the founder of their school—as Plato's own altar was to stand through future centuries within the Academy, which he set up in his maturity on Pythagorean models. His youthful study of tragedy may have imposed their dramatic form on these contests for truth, with Socrates as protagonist.

The discourse with the Pythagorean disciples in the prison shows the Plato of the *Phædo* for the first time concerned to uphold Orphic doctrines by reason. *Phusis* and the human soul here stand or fall together as in Miletus,[4] but in this dialogue, as in most of the later ones, the metaphysical argument is significantly reinforced by a myth. The tale here is of the true earth, of which this is an imperfect shadow, and the myths which haunt the later dialogues are in general of an Orphic or Pythagorean colour. There are the cosmic cycles, the harmony of the spheres, Necessity with her whirling spindle at the centre

---

[1] Such a life being an original composition only intelligible when complete, since they have 'absorbed the ritual' like the tragic heroes of the next section.

[2] There are accounts of these catastrophes in Iamblichus' *Life of Pythagoras*, 250; also in Polybius, ii 39 (R.P., 59).

[3] Plato, *Phædrus*, 253A.

[4] Cornford, op. cit., p. 243, and note 2, citing *Phædo*, 76, E.

of existence, the Judgement of the Dead, the Waters of Remembrance and Forgetfulness, and the soul's imprisonment in the Cave. In general, they describe the fall from, and return to, the divine life.

Plato's theory of Ideas constitutes a gigantic effort to establish the mystic doctrine upon an intellectual basis. The relation of created things to the 'pattern laid up in heaven' is, as we saw, that *methexis*, or participation, which Aristotle equated with *mimesis*, the 'imitation' by which the living world was built upon the Pythagorean numbers. Thus the relationship created by earliest man, and the means of his growth as already described; the vehicle of the first-known religion, is now made articulate. The wheel has come full-circle.

But it must be noted that Plato's Ideas are of two kinds, and both of the nature of the Soul.[1] Like the dæmons, some of whom are conceived as descending as watchers from higher spheres of being, and others as rising from the body or group, but infected by it, and so always drawn back into incarnation, the Ideas may be either transcendent, intellectual concepts, and therefore fundamental causes, or else potentially present in the lives which they inform.

The abstract Ideas, such as Truth or Beauty, are also the mythical objects of contemplation in the divine world.[2] Being thus perceptible, they are living forces, and able to impart their nature. But such transmission cannot be logically formulated; it is expressible only in metaphor. It seems therefore that participation can never be entirely defined by the discriminating intellect. It is the measure of Plato's greatness to have exposed the problem, and perhaps in doing so he took a step beyond Pythagoras.

The Idea that exists both within and beyond its physical counterparts is the concern of religion, but the abstract Idea henceforth becomes the subject of philosophy alone. The God of Aristotle moves the world as the object of love,[3] being himself unmoved. But the nature of religion is reciprocity. This is the parting of the ways.

---

[1] See Cornford, op. cit., p. 250 ff.

[2] In the myths of the *Phædrus, Symposium, Republic*.

[3] (The First Cause) κινεῖ δὴ ὡς ἐρώμενον, κινούμενα δὲ τἆλλα κινεῖ. Arist., *Met.*, 1072b, 3.

THE DRAMA

ORIGIN

Aristotle derives both Tragedy and Comedy from old fertility ritual, saying that Tragedy arose from the Leaders of the Dithyramb, and Comedy from the phallic processions.[1] Whatever may be the true meaning of the word Dithyramb, its earliest-known form was choral, with a leader who improvised a song which the rest took up as a refrain, as the women sang over Hector's body in the Iliad. Æschylus speaks of the Dithyramb as the appropriate hymn of Dionysus,[2] and both Euripides and Plato quote the popular connection of the name with the 'double door' of the God's birth.[3] A dithyrambic fragment of Pindar written for performance at Athens[4] invokes the spring and Semele, and the first of his compositions in that form is said to have made the word 'Dithyramb' echo the cry of Zeus at the second birth of Dionysus.[5] An inscription found at Delphi calls Dionysus *Dithyrambos* in an invocation for the return of spring.[6] In general, the dithyramb would seem to have celebrated the spring's awakening in the person of the infant God. Plutarch, however, says that in his day they sang to Dionysus at Delphi 'dithyrambic measures full of sufferings and transformations' during the months of 'conflagration' before Apollo's return,[7] a season to which Bacchylides also refers, in the few remaining words of a dithyramb contemporary with the rise of Attic drama.[8] It appears, therefore, that something more than the God's birth may have been celebrated in these hymns, and recent linguistic research has suggested a Phrygian origin for the name, deriving it from a dance performed before a tomb

---

[1] Aristotle, *Poetics*, 1449a, 9. [2] Æschylus, Fragm., 355.

[3] Euripides, *Bacchæ*, 526; Plato, *Laws*, iii 700b.

[4] Schroeder fragm., 75. 'It is plain that the Athenian dithyramb was a spring performance . . . and clearly Semele was one of its traditional themes.' A. W. Pickard-Cambridge in *Dithyramb, Tragedy and Comedy*, 1927, p. 33.

[5] Schol. Pind., *Olymp.*, xiii 25.

[6] H. Weil, *Bull. de Corr. Hell*, xix, p. 401.

[7] Plutarch, *de Ei ap. Delph.*, ix.   [8] Bacch. fragm. xv.

with double doors.[1] The Phrygian musical mode was indeed specially employed to accompany this form of poetry.

As we saw, the ritual of Mother and Young God in Asia Minor was not concerned with his birth,[2] but the Dionysiac myths of Greece and Crete show births and deaths so closely intertwined, that Navarre appears to be right in maintaining that the passion of Dionysus was the original subject of the dithyramb.[3] The confession of Archilochus of Paros, that he led the fair strain of Dionysus in the dithyramb, when thunder-struck with wine,[4] by no means limits it to a mere drinking song.

But at some unknown period people began to complain that certain songs composed or improvised for the dithyramb, 'had nothing to do with Dionysus,'[5] but described instead the labours and sufferings of heroes.

Similarly the earliest historical records of Athenian Drama reveal only a 'satyric' chorus trained by Thespis of Icaria in Attica, a locality (connected by its name with Minoan Crete), where mysteries were celebrated from very ancient times.[6] Mention is also made of a dance there, performed round a he-goat,[7] and an extant inscription gives to Thespis a goat for prize[8]—presumably for sacrifice, like the bull for Dionysus presented to the successful dramatist at the later Athenian festivals.[9] The goat-identification of Dionysus and his worshippers is indirectly referred to in the Bacchæ and on an Orphic mortuary tablet,[10] and the God wore a black goat-skin in the mumming dance performed in another Attic village with a presumably pre-Hellenic name:[11] Eleutheræ, the original home of the image of Dionysus Eleuthereus which was borne in procession to the

---

[1] W. M. Calder in *Class. Rev.*, xxxvi, p. 11 ff. The theory is discussed by Dr. Pickard-Cambridge, loc. cit., pp. 16–19.

[2] Above, p. 222.   [3] *Rev. Etud. Anc.*, 1911, p. 246.

[4] Archilochus fragm., 77, Pickard-Cambridge, op. cit., p. 5.

[5] Pickard-Cambridge, op. cit., p. 166 ff., οὐδὲν πρὸς τὸν Διόνυσον became a proverb. See also A. B. Cook, *Zeus*, i, p. 680.

[6] The locality is still called Dionysou by peasants of the district.

[7] Eratosthenes, ap. Hyg. poet. astr., 24; Cook, op. cit., p. 678; L. Farnell, *Cults of the Greek States*, v, pp. 234, 315. Pickard-Cambridge, op. cit., p. 102 ff., discusses the uncertainty of the ancient records.

[8] Parian Marble of about 534 B.C.; Pickard-Cambridge, op. cit., pp. 97–98.

[9] *C.I.A.*, ii 470.   [10] Kern, *Orphicorum Fragmenta*, 32 (C).

[11] M. P. Nilsson, *The Minoan-Mycenæan Religion*, 1927, p. 449 ff.

city Dionysia in the great days of Athenian drama. It appears likely, therefore, that the name Tragedy (Goat Song) comes from Attic choirs identified in the dance with Dionysus in goat form.

Yet those half-animal nature-spirits, who seem first to have joined the train of Dionysus among the Satræ of Thrace,[1] will not have been forgotten. Their familiar snub noses and pointed ears doubtless recalled, on vase-paintings or reliefs, the masks of those who represented them in ritual. The works of art often preserve the wild grace which identifies the worshipper with the God in animal form, as he was identified in the primitive ceremonies. But the Satyrs of the art contemporary with the rise of Attic drama, cannot have been represented in Thespis' 'goat chorus', since they are always shown with horses' tails. It is not until the vase-painting of the mid-fifth century that they appear, both in the thiasos of Dionysus and also as actors in satyric disguise, with goats' horns and tails.[2] It can only be asserted, therefore, that the 'goat dancers' and the mythical half-animal satyrs both contributed to the formation of the classic dramatic chorus. This is easily conceivable, since the origin and functions of each, human dancer in animal disguise, and half-animal dæmon, are associated in the age-long fertility ritual which is represented in the thiasos of Dionysus.[3]

The literary transformation of the chorus was achieved under the influence of the Doric dithyramb, which had been elaborated by Arion out of old folk-songs and applied to heroic subjects which required a solemn setting;[4] and the institution by Peisistratus, in the lifetime of Thespis, of public recitations of the Ionian Epic and especially of Homer, gave the founders of Athenian drama a rich storehouse of traditional material upon which to draw.[5] The sons of Peisistratus established the dithyramb as part of the city Dionysia; one of the two annual festivals in which dramatic contests were held, when the image of Dionysus Eleuthereus was carried in procession. The leader of the bands of singers was the poet who composed the songs and received the bull as a prize. This was presumably the bull known to have been sacrificed at the festival to Dionysus, and suggests that the leader was thought to personify the God.

[1] Above, pp. 284–285.　　[2] Pickard-Cambridge, op. cit., pp. 149, 152.
[3] Cf. above, pp. 225, 227.　　　　　　[4] Herodotus, i, 23.
[5] G. Thomson, Æschylus and Athens, 1941, p. 194.

Dioscorides, in fact, states that Thespis 'presented Dionysus as leader of the chorus'.[1] It has also been asserted that the name *hypokrites* (actor) which in Athens replaced that of *exarchon* (leader of the dithyramb), retained its Homeric sense of interpreter of dreams; that when the thiasos gave place to drama, what had been secret (that is, experienced only in dæmonic participation), required to be explained.[2] In time the two choirs of 'answerers' in the Athenian festival seem to have been replaced by the second and third actor. This taught the poet to orient the action between the actors and away from the chorus, so that the plot could be developed apart from its intervention.[3] It was still essential that the members of the choir should 'become what they sing', since the religious source of drama required the presence of an audience already sympathetically identified with the action. Thus the chorus eventually became the 'ideal spectator', removed from active participation in the conflict or ordeal which it had once created, and which had developed beyond it. As Nietzsche observes, Dionysus was at first only imagined in their midst; 'the scene was the setting of a choric dream.' That 'scene' was once the *skene*, the tent or booth, which did not display, but concealed, the death of a God, and when in later days it became a stage for the tragic actors, violent death, the focal point of a tragedy, was never shown there.[4] It was evoked for the spectators in the words of a messenger, as the chorus had once evoked it in their song.

The dancing-ground or *orchestra* of the Attic theatre was sand-strewn, so that the movements to be taken by the chorus could be defined according to their subject,[5] and the general pattern used in dramatic performances, was called 'square', in contrast with the circularity of the dithyrambic dances.[6] (As suggested

---

[1] *Anth. Pal.*, vii 410.   [2] Thomson, op. cit., p. 181 ff.   [3] Ibid., p. 178.

[4] The *Ajax* of Sophocles may be an exception to this rule, but there the hero's blow is self-delivered and his body, at least, appears to have fallen behind rocks or bushes, since Tecmessa and the chorus hunt for it on the stage.

[5] Hence called Konistra. See C. N. Deedes, *The Labyrinth*, in Hooke, op. cit., p. 32 ff.; Hesychius, γραμμοί· ἐν τῇ ὀρχήστρᾳ ἦσαν, ὡς τὸν χορὸν ἐν στοίχῳ ἵστασθαι. The importance of this figured dance before the stage (or booth) where the drama is enacted, should not be overlooked.

[6] For τετράγωνος χορός, v. κύκλιος χορός ; see A. B. Cook in *Class. Rev.*, ix 1895, p. 376. A good drawing of the squared mosaic in the theatre of Dionysus at Athens, can be found in A. B. Cook, *Zeus*, i, pl. xxix.

earlier, the square pattern would presumably emphasize dramatic crises[1]) Its still-existing late successor in the 'bare ruined
choir' of the theatre of Dionysus at Athens, is a square maze or
mæander laid out in mosaic.[2] It is interesting to observe that in
the heyday of Athenian culture, the dramatic chorus was chosen
not from professional performers but out of the full body of
citizens.[3] No doubt the music suffered from necessarily inten-
sive training, but 'participation' was the more closely maintained.

The long robes and high boots of the tragic actors perhaps
recalled the Asiatic dress of Dionysus and his train; they may
also have borrowed some splendour from the vestments of the
Hierophant and Torchbearer at Eleusis. In any case they
offered the necessary height and dignity required for the appearance of heroic personages in the open sunlight before an immense audience. The Mask, an evident and very important
survival of the animal choric dance, was made of linen and
covered the whole head,[4] as it does on Minoan gems.[5] In
Tragedy it enhanced, as it no doubt helped to create, the portrayal of types and suppression of personality, but so strong was
the influence of its ritual origin that even in the New Comedy,
where character became all-important, the grotesque type-
masks remained.[6]

The Village Festivals

Choric song and dance, whether satyric or dithyrambic, constituted only one of the factors which came to be incorporated
in the Athenian dramatic contests held in honour of Dionysus,
at first, perhaps, at the country festival, at the Lenæa only.
The Lenæ were the Mænads, and the festival itself seems to
have been a winter rite, like that of the Thyiades on Parnassus,

---

[1] See, for instance, p. 159 of II 3, above.

[2] A similar mosaic was apparently still to be seen in the 12th century on
the floor of the orchestra in the theatre at Taormina (Cook, op. cit., i, pp.
480–481, quoting D. Companetti, *Vergil in the Middle Ages*. Trans. E. F. M.
Benecke, 1895, p. 257 ff.).

[3] Haigh, op. cit., p. 60.   [4] Aul. Gell., v 7.

[5] See fig. 106 above.

[6] Pollux, iv 143. But even New Comedy plots closely adhered to the
ritual pattern. See Gilbert Murray in the *Classical Quarterly*, xxxvii 1943,
p. 46 ff.

for summoning the new-born child.[1] It is known that the Torch-bearer of the Mysteries shouted on this occasion 'Call ye the God', and that the people cried: 'Iacchos, child of Semele, giver of prosperity!'[2] But the hymn which they sang described the rending of Dionysus.[3]

This winter passion-play seems at some unknown period to have linked itself with the satyr dances. Thespis is reported by Suidas to have smeared his face with gypsum like the Titans,[4] and the same author enumerates the very suggestive titles of his plays—the Pentheus, the Young Men, the Priests, the Prizes of Pelias, all names apparently connected with ritual, and most of them with this particular type of ritual.[5] At the winter Lenæa in later times, tragedy took precedence; at the city Dionysia held in the spring, comedy was the more important.[6] It has been conjectured that the spring festival was originally a pure fertility rite (the Marriage of Zeus and Semele), and led to comedy, and that the Lenæa, which ten months later celebrated the birth and martyrdom, developed into tragedy.[7]

The Phallic songs, to which Aristotle refers, seem to have formed part of the usual village fertility rites. They were chanted by opposing companies of men, one of whom carried a phallos on a pole; the leaders improvising passages of invocation and abuse which were taken up by the remainder of the band.[8] Herodotus describes similar processions in Egypt in which marionettes were borne aloft.[9] The importance both of obscenity and invective as universal fertility charms will be remembered[10],

[1] Cook, op. cit., pp. 668–670.

[2] Schol. Aristoph. *Ran.*, 479; Cook, *Zeus*, i, pp. 670–671.

[3] Cook, op. cit., pp. 668–673, quoting the festival calendar of Mykonos and Clement on the 'Lenæan poets', and recital of sorrows turned into plays.

[4] Cook, op. cit., p. 678, quoting Suidas, s.v. Thespis = Eudok. *Viol.*, 471.

[5] Suidas, op. cit.; Cook, op. cit., p. 679.

[6] Cook, op. cit., p. 683. Haigh reverses this order.

[7] Cook, op. cit., p. 681 ff.

[8] F. M. Cornford, *The Origin of Attic Comedy*, second edition, 1934, chap. iii, passim.   [9] Herod., ii 49.

[10] For example, at the Thesmophoria in Attica, and the Jesting at the Bridge when the procession halted on the way to the celebration of the Greater Mysteries at Eleusis. Cornford, op. cit., p. 50, quotes St. Augustine's reference to Varro's description of the Liberalia: 'By such means the God Liber (=Bacchus) had to be placated for the success of the crops.'

and when personal and political satire came to replace the magic songs, the Parabasis of the old Comedy retained them both.[1]

Both Tragedy and Comedy must also have come to include village folk-plays, such as are still performed in Northern Greece at carnival time,[2] and have elsewhere retained to this day all their distinctive features, even in very remote localities.[3] In these as in the most primitive initiation legends the hero is always strangely born, taken from his mother, killed, and restored to life; a series of events which would equally fit a passion play of Dionysus. But these folk-plays contain further elements which relate them to another series of vegetation cults, such as a fight in which the hero is done to death, usually at his marriage feast, by a double, who often wears an animal skin or mask, or has a blackened face.[4] After the mourning and resurrection, his interrupted wedding is fulfilled amid general rejoicings followed by revelry. This type of play belongs to the rites which in Western Asia inaugurated the New Year;[5] its twofold character is therefore essential, and the structures of tragedy and comedy differ chiefly in their concentration upon

[1] The language even of tragedy was at the beginning 'rough and coarse'. See Aristotle, *Poetics*, op. cit.

[2] R. M. Dawkins, 'The Modern Carnival in Thrace and the Cult of Dionysus,' *J.H.S.*, xxvi (1906), p. 191 ff.; A. J. B. Wace, 'North Greek Festivals,' *Brit. School. Ann.*, xvi, p. 232 ff.

[3] See, for instance, Prof. H. Frankfort's account of a mimetic dance performed for rain-making in the remote foothills of the Iraq border-country *Iraq*, i 2, 1934. 'A Tammuz ritual in Kurdistan.' There the dancer who mimed the 'dying God', wore a black goatskin, across the lower part of his face, which was otherwise blackened. The part of the Goddess whose tears—augmented from the village water-jars—restored him to life, was taken by a man in woman's clothes. At one point in the 'satyric' dance which followed the resurrection, the 'God' whinnied like a horse and rode his staff strangely recalling the combination of horse and goat satyrs in Greek ritual representation. The musician who acted as chorus, sang, not the story which was enacted, but incantations for rain. He was in a state of ecstasy.

[4] Wace, op. cit.

[5] The New Year's Festival in Babylon went back to the middle of the third millennium B.C. The defeat of the God, the death of his antagonist, his resurrection and marriage, were here performed for the country's prosperity. See Frankfort, 'Gods and Myths on Cylinder Seals,' in *Iraq*, i, p. 2 ff. The hymns discovered on tablets at Ras Shamra suggest that similar dramatic performances were held in Syria during the annual festivals. See T. H. Gaster, *Antiquity*, xiii, p. 304, Ras Shamra, 1929–1939.

different parts of the story. Tragedy, as we saw, developed the earlier portion of this universal myth. Comedy uses the whole tale, down to its happy ending. Let us consider how this was achieved.

COMEDY

In the extant plays of Aristophanes, the ritual structure is usually well marked. It has been shown[1] to consist first of a contest, which determines the rest of the action, followed by a choral interlude, the *Parabasis*, of the kind already described, next a sacrifice and its feast, usually interrupted, and finally the triumphal departure of the hero with a mute and allegorically named bride.[2]

The Agon, equivalent of the duel of the White and the Black Man in the village mumming, is generally fought between a humble and middle-aged citizen, and a boaster or pretender, the embodiment of *Hubris*, and is often a battle of words, with invective as the weapon. It is taken up by the chorus divided into two bands on behalf of the opponents, and results in a reversal of the status of the protagonist, like the resurrection scene of the folk plays.[3] The Parabasis of the chorus, which here divides the play, provides the outlet for that stream of personal abuse whose essential function has been described, and is brilliantly employed to exhibit the allegorical and topical nature of the story.[4] Many of the existing dramas retain the old half-animal chorus which gives them their names—the Birds, the Frogs, the Wasps, and once a choir of nature-spirits, the Clouds. Vase paintings show these choric dancers wearing appropriate masks like those so familiar in primitive ritual.

The sacrifice and its feast generally involve, after the crushing of various pretenders, some kind of metamorphosis of the old or middle-aged hero to personify a new order.[5] In the Birds,

[1] Cornford, op. cit., chap. v and vi.

[2] The contention of Dr. Pickard-Cambridge, op. cit., p. 231 ff., that in some plays there was more than one 'silent bride', does not preclude their origin in fertility ritual.

[3] Cornford, op. cit., pp. 70, 75. The struggle with pretenders is presumably descended from, or of the same nature as, the initiatory illusions imposed in primitive societies.

[4] Cornford describes it as a kind of verbal battle-dance, op. cit., p. 128.

[5] Cornford, op. cit., p. 20 ff.

the Plutus, and the Clouds, he emerges as a new Zeus. In the Knights, Demos, personifying the Athenian people, recovers his youth by being boiled in a cauldron; the Birds, Plutus, and the two 'Women Plays' end in an overthrow of the existing political or social organisation, the Clouds in a breaking of intellectual tyranny, and the Frogs in the restoration of true literature, in the person of the resurrected Æschylus. The doubling or other distribution of the parts does not destroy the ritual link.

A strangely artificial element brings almost every one of these plays to a close. This is the important procession (Kōmos—the word from which Comedy takes its name), in which the victor leaves the stage amid ritual songs of triumph, accompanied by a woman who now appears for the first time. This ending is nearly as universal as in modern romantic comedy, but instead of being integral as in the modern instances, the love-interest in the rest of the plot has not even been episodic; it has been non-existent. The agon was fought for no lady's hand, but for some political or intellectual principle. The appearance of the silent and symbolically named partner (or partners), can only be attributed to the ritual, the Sacred Marriage which closed the fertility dramas.[1]

Thus the structure of the comedies includes the whole of the ritual plot; the true man is always triumphant over the braggart.[2] There could be no Falstaff to overshadow his conqueror. But because the story is invented, topical, allegorical, and peopled by the rich fantasy of its creator with characters rather than with types, its relation to the ritual is inorganic, and requires no more than a passing allusion, to throw into relief the structural integrity of tragedy.

TRAGEDY

The dithyramb appears in historic times as a stately piece of musical ritual, occasionally composed in celebration, not of the spring awakening, but of some heroic legend.[3] Thus Simonides wrote a dithyramb round the death of Memnon, one of

---

[1] In the *Birds*, for instance, she is Basileia The Queen. For all this, see Cornford, op. cit., chap. ii, The Exodos. See also note 2, p. 320 concerning instances of multiple partners.

[2] But after preliminary defeat, as in the folk plays.

[3] Haigh, *The Tragic Drama of the Greeks*, 1896, p. 23.

those mortal sons, such as Rhesus or Orpheus, whose lament by an immortal mother is an abiding theme of tragedy. The Doric mode was used, and the first choral songs which preserve its form have a sculptured calm reminiscent of Apollo rather than of Dionysus.[1] When the primitive Goat chorus of Thespis came to be relegated to the final play of a tetralogy;[2] to the dæmonic dance of resurrection which followed the human disaster, the solemn combination of poetry, music and movement upheld the heroic character of the main plot, which had been incorporated into the old rites. But the ritual can still be traced through the extant dramas. As we saw, tragedy was concentrated upon the first part of the story—that part which must have been enacted in the passion-play of Dionysus, where no 'happy ending' can be presumed—the 'reconciliation' of the known Æschylean trilogies, and the Euripidean *deus ex machina*, being beyond the human action.

Herodotus, in every mention of the ceremonies performed in Egypt round the death and burial of Osiris, avoids the utterance of his name: 'It is impious to say what they mourn.'[3] Yet these rites were quite openly performed, and, except in this connection, he constantly identifies Osiris with Dionysus. It seems likely, therefore, that in fifth century Greece the passion of Dionysus was a mystery—after all, their other Gods did not die—and this would explain the fact that in plays such as the Pentheus or the Bassarids of Æschylus (about the dismemberment of Orpheus), or the Bacchæ of Euripides, all of whose plots were directly based upon the ritual of Dionysus, it was a disguised antagonist who suffered the death of the God.[4] The profound relation which exists between the divinity and the worshipper who sacrifices him in some physical form, need not be recapitulated here, reaching backward as it does to the beginning of man's development.[5] In the old Comedy the doub-

---

[1] As, for instance, in the *Suppliants* of Æschylus.

[2] Pickard-Cambridge, op. cit., p. 124 ff., gives the arguments against interpreting Aristotle's διὰ τοῦ ἐκ σατυρικοῦ μεταβαλεῖν as implying the derivation of tragedy from the satyric drama as known on the Attic stage.

[3] Herod. ii 61.

[4] In the *Bacchæ*, for instance, there is the sinister scene in which Dionysus disguises Pentheus as one of his own votaries so that he can meet his fate amid their rites.

[5] And forward also, for Judas too was hanged upon a tree.

ling of the Young-Old, Summer-Winter deities in the persons of ordinary men, produced the victory of the true man over the impersonator, which is the subject of every one of Aristophanes' plays,[1] but Tragedy had learned from Epic that the mortal hero is ultimately pitted against an invisible foe.[2] In using heroic· themes Tragedy exhibits a duel no longer between equals but between man and a superior power. Therefore defeat is essential, for the real hero is the unseen God, who forces the protagonist to conform with his own fate, his Idea, in order to fulfil his destiny. Tragedy, in fact, at last reconciles the mystic with the heroic ideal—pre-Hellenic practice with new Hellenic thought. How the actions of its very imperfect legendary characters became thus glorified into archetypes, can be discovered by relating structure with material, since the story could never be fortuitous as in Comedy, nor even essentially varied by the fancy of the dramatist.

The internal *structure* of the tragic drama has been classified in the following manner as related to the unknown mystery play.[3]

(1) *Agon.* The Contest, no longer as we saw, between equals, for the hero of the trilogy, or separately complete play, is always greater than his human conqueror, on account of his relation with the God. Antigone's 'unwritten laws', which override Kreon's royal decrees,[4] express the general position.

(2) *Pathos.* The death of the Hero, often retaining vestiges of its sacrificial form. Agamemnon is thus spoken of as a bull, and as entangled in a net, and he is slain with a two-edged axe;[3] Hippolytus is torn,[5] and so is Orestes in his feigned death;[6] Orpheus and Pentheus are dismembered; and a number of lost

---

[1] See Cornford, op. cit., p. 118 ff., quoting Chambers, *The Mediæval Stage*, p. 187, and Frazer, *The Dying God*, 1911, p. 255.

[2] See above, p. 268.

[3] By Gilbert Murray, in J. E. Harrison, *Themis*, 'Excursus on the Ritual forms preserved in Greek Tragedy', following Dieterich, *Archiv. für Religions wissenschaft*, xi, pp. 163–196, Usener, ib., vii, pp. 303–313, as developed in Farnell, *Cults of the Greek States*, vol. v, p. 235, note A; Dawkins on the *Macedonian Mummer Plays*, and to some extent Ridgeway, while rejecting Ridgeway's tomb theory. Also Herodotus, book ii, especially his assertion (ii 48) that the yearly Festival of Osiris in Egypt was almost identical with the rites of Dionysus except that the Egyptians did not use a chorus.

[4] Soph., *Ant.*, vv 454–455.

[5] Æsch., *Agamemnon*, vv 1382, 1397, 1495.

[6] Eurip., *Hipp.*, vv 1153 ff.; Soph., *Electra*, vv 750–763.

plays had for their heroes Pelops or Pelias, both boiled in the cauldron of rebirth.[1] Herakles in the Trachiniæ suffers the ritual death of his Asiatic counterpart on the mountain-pyre.[2]

(3) A *Messenger*, as we saw, invariably relates the circumstances of the death, whose violence is never once portrayed[3] upon the stage. This consistent rejection of theatrical opportunity must be of religious origin. The Messenger (with one exception) is never individualised, because he is a technical adjunct.

(4) *Threnos*, the *Lamentation*, often divided between grief for the lost, and rejoicing for something attained. This usually closes the human drama, but at some point of nearly all the plays, or series of plays, occur:

(5) *A Recognition and a Transformation.* These are inseparably bound together because the dramatic climax, as in the primitive initiations discussed earlier in this book, follows the discovery of truth.[4] Œdipus' recognition of the truth turns him into a blind beggar, and the Furies of the Oresteia, upon their recognition of the New Law, become the 'Kindly Ones'.

The apparition of Artemis above the dying Hippolytus,[5] the suicide of Hæmon over Antigone's body in the cave, which she called her marriage chamber,[6] and the involuntary sin of Œdipus, may be reminiscent of the Sacred Marriage, which lies behind the happy ending of old Comedy, but is completely

---

[1] Cornford, 'The Origin of the Olympic Games,' in Harrison, *Themis*, p. 243 ff.

[2] Clem. *Recognit.*, x 24; Dion Chrysostom *Or.* 33, p. 23 f.

[3] With one doubtful exception. See note 4 of p. 316.

[4] C. M. Bowra, in pp. 362–364 of *Sophoclean Tragedy*, 1943, points out that in Sophocles the recognition takes place within the self, and that the transformation is no mere change from one state of things to another. Aristotle, he says, unduly limits the Sophoclean Reversal-Discovery, because he omits the part played by the Gods.

[5] Eurip., *Hipp.*, vv 1283 ff. In Roman times the resurrected Hippolytus was known as Diana's consort in Aricia.

[6] Soph., *Ant.*, vv 1240–1241, in which their deaths are actually called bridal rites; cf. Antigone's own invocation to the cave in which she is to be immured:

ὦ τύμβος, ὦ νυμφεῖον, ὦ κατασκαφῆς
οἴκησις ἀείφρουρος. . . .

'O tomb, o bridal-chamber, o dwelling hollowed from the rock, that will guard me for ever. . . .' Thomson, op. cit., p. 354, calls the peripeteia 'rudimentary' in Æschylus, yet it is the solution of all those trilogies whose plots are known.

absent from tragedy—it is that absence indeed that makes it tragedy; the purely human action being kept within the boundary of the Lesser Mysteries, that is, of self-deception and atonement. But the transformation in these plays often takes the form of a reconciliation, which is always effected by a God, and appears most clearly in Æschylus, whose intense faith in Divine justice (not always, however, in the persons of the Gods), resembles that of the Hebrew prophets. The Oresteia has such a close; and the Prometheia, extending through a whole æon in which Zeus himself must have suffered change,[1] and also the trilogy which contained the Suppliants, are each known to have been completed in this manner.[2] In Sophocles the change is more subjective. The knowledge acquired by his characters, which determines their final action, is of themselves in relation to the Gods. But in later tragedy the reconciliation was either left to the satyric resurrection drama which followed (the Alcestis, which took the place of a Satyr play, shows this resurrection for once within the structure of human events),[3] or effected by the epiphany, after the tragic close, of the Olympian deity to whom the heroic legend is related.[4]

The breaking off of the action on the note of human failure is a courageous expression of faith. The ritual purification of the audience through Aristotle's 'pity and fear', is thus made positive by the sharing of human experience in face of disaster. As has been seen, the failure was necessary to a plot which united mystic form with heroic substance. The importance of that *plot* is strongly emphasised by Aristotle, who places it in tragedy before character, comparing it to a living creature for whom

---

[1] Æschylus teaches that God, like man, is the product of evolution, the two phases being parallel. Thomson, op. cit., p. 240.

[2] A fragment of the *Suppliants* is preserved (Nauck., fr. 44) in which Aphrodite founds the institution of marriage; Murray, op. cit., p. 348. Professor. D. S. Robertson, in *Class. Rev.*, 38, suggests the founding of the Thesmophoria as the 'reconciliation' of the trilogy. In the case of the Prometheia, it is only known that the end was reconciliation. Thomson's reconstruction is interesting (op. cit., chap. xvii): 'An advance only rendered possible by an advance in society itself.'

[3] That is, Heracles brings Alcestis back from the dead.

[4] Such as the apparition of Artemis to the consciousness though not the sight, of the mortally wounded Hippolytus mentioned above; or of the God Dionysus, no longer a mere dæmon of the thiasos, after the martyrdom of his human imitator, in the *Bacchæ*.

completeness, fulfilment (τελεία), is essential. 'The end should be related to the beginning as a fruit to the seed.'[1] In such an organism those irrelevant incidents, which give vitality to Epic, could not exist, nor could any large element of surprise enliven the action of legends known to every spectator from childhood. Its reality depended upon the extent to which its relation to universal experience (the ritual) was united with its quality of heroism (the legend). So, in the greatest known plays, the protagonist, becoming absorbed within the action, came in turn to absorb it, as the greatest Shakespearian characters do. So he won his inward victory over Dionysus to whom the individual is the enemy. So Œdipus as king pulls his own world down (paying the price of involuntary deception), in order that Œdipus as wandering beggar shall achieve the power to curse or bless. The one necessity is that the hero should bring about his own defeat, whether as self-chosen victim like Prometheus or Antigone; as an actor foreseeing the consequences, like Medea or Orestes or Hippolytus; as involuntary victim of his or her own actions like Œdipus or Deianeira, or even as passive sufferer, like Hecuba in The Trojan Women.

Because defeat is essential, the action is decided before the beginning of the play, sometimes by a divine decree in the prologue,[2] but more often by placing the period of the drama after the decisive course has already been taken, when only its inevitable consequences remain to be experienced.[3]

Such limitation of the plot constrained the characters to find enrichment in depth alone; that is why Aristotle, while insisting on their imperfection, insists also upon their nobility.[4] The protagonist may be maleficent like Medea, or diminished by self-division like the Æschylean Orestes, but he must not be too weak to sustain the grandeur of the organic structure.[5] This

[1] Aristotle, *Poetics*, 7.

[2] As in the *Hippolytus*, where Aphrodite herself describes her coming vengeance.

[3] As in *King Œdipus*, where the hero's gradual enlightenment about the past forms the plot of the drama.

[4] Aristotle, op. cit.

[5] Cf. Bowra, op. cit., pp. 366 and 372. He contends that the characters of Sophocles are superior beings (the men in manly worth [ἀρετή], the women in love) because of the self-knowledge acquired in their defeat by the God. 'The wound is inflicted at the very centre of honour and affection,' but their greatness depends on their acceptance of the truth.

necessity to create types which could fulfil certain functions, rather than persons living their own lives, was made possible to the great dramatists by the adaptability of their *material*. This, as we saw, is almost purely heroic, since certain profound causes, already noted, made the legends of the Greek heroes the perfect subjects for drama. These causes may now be classified as follows:

(1) The Hero-cults.

(2) The previous fusion of Greek heroic legend with memories of the pre-Hellenic religious epoch.

(3) The Homeric challenge to destiny.

Hero-worship, as we have seen,[1] gave to the famous dead the functions of fertility dæmons. The ground was thus prepared for the assumption, by a human protagonist of sufficient quality, of the rôle of Dionysus, and the heroic subjects of the Doric dithyramb would have assisted the transformation. Thus the God's altar, standing in the midst of the orchestra, could if necessary be regarded as a tomb.[2]

The legends themselves are another matter. These tales of adventure belonging to the centuries of conquest and migration, and probably drawing much material from actual events, are infinitely involved in the ancient ritual, and especially that part of it which came to be included, on Attic soil, in the Lesser Mysteries. That is to say, they are tales of an estranged childhood, recognition, a journey, trials, a princess, then failure —a lost bride, a kinsman slain. Through all their variety of incident this pattern is never obscured; in the stories of Theseus and Jason it is complete. The poets concentrated on the adventurous deeds, the tragedians on the final disaster. Odysseus' adventures on the island of Scheria 'between a sleep and a sleep' are of this nature;[3] and so we find them to be the subject of a lost play of Sophocles.

But there is one type of legend which must have had its actual source in the former religion. In the tragic cycles of Orestes and Œdipus the battle for the New Year, and the New King, descended from the early days of the great kingdoms in

---

[1] Above, pp. 279, 280.

[2] This Ridgeway considered to be the Origin of Tragedy.

[3] Above, p. 268, note 2. It is noteworthy that subjects taken directly from the *Iliad* do not occur in the extant plays.

the East,[1] and mimed then, as now in the crude folk-plays, itself provides the plot. It was used long afterwards for one more masterpiece, Shakespeare's Hamlet, whose origin has been traced to similar rites.[2] The ageless emotion engendered by these yearly dedications of successive peoples to the powers of life and death in the person of their king, reverberates in each re-creation of this tale.[3] In all three instances the old king is dead before the hero's drama begins, and he himself returns to, and from, banishment, disfigured, black-robed, and feigning madness or death, like the black 'winter' fighter of the folk-plays who struggles for supremacy with his bright double.[4] In each case the subject of the drama is the inward battle of the protagonist; the tragedy lies in the horror of 'guilt'.[5] The plot was so firmly established in human memory, that the vacillations of Hamlet and Orestes, and the spiritually blinding ignorance of Œdipus, followed by his physically blinding knowledge, became more important than the very horrible action. It is interesting to note that in the Greek examples, where the shedding of kindred blood retained so much of its primitive pollution, the hero's moral innocence won him redemption at the end of the dreadful tale by the intercession of the Gods, and that even the dying Hamlet suddenly perceived felicity. These plays founded upon seasonal rebirth, thus represent, like the Prometheia, a reversal of a former dispensation. When, therefore, the daughters of ancient Night, who had claimed Orestes with their fearful enchantments, were finally conducted in peace and goodwill to their cave beneath the Acropolis upon which Athena's temple stood,[6] the fusion of the chthonic powers of seasonal fertility, of human endeavour and divine

---

[1] See pp. 170 ff.

[2] Sir I. Gollancz, *Hamlet in Iceland*. Saxo Grammaticus in his History of the Danes (12th century) mentions Hamlet as son of Teut, God of the Spring. There is also an Icelandic reference to Amlothi in 980 A.D. See Gilbert Murray, 'Hamlet and Orestes,' *A.S.L.*, 1914.

[3] 'How far into the past this stream may reach back, I dare not even surmise,' Murray, op. cit.

[4] *Œdipus*, first lame, afterwards blind also, and exiled; Orestes disfigured, disguised, then mad.

[5] 'Hamlet, though on the side of right against wrong, is no triumphant slayer. He is clad in black, he rages alone, he is the bitter Fool who must slay the king,' Gilbert Murray, op. cit., 23.

[6] Æsch., *Eumenides*, vv 916 to the end.

intercession, was established in its proper harmony, as it was again established when the self-cursed Œdipus, to the salute, in one prayer, of the Gods above and below,[1] descended alive into the earth 'riven by love',[2] now visible as the goal of his 'blind marches'.

That was one consummation. There remains Homer, and the hero's naked challenge to Fate, the challenge of Prometheus or Antigone, and the expression in art of the Herakleitan definition: 'A man's character is his destiny.'[3]

The fifth century Athenian can hardly have conceived of the death of the year as punishment for summer's pride.[4] He would rather have agreed that 'Ripeness is all'. Neither was the cyclic succession of the old ritual the result of *Hubris*, of the overstepping of natural boundaries, but rather of their retention, since in these rites all existence was considered as one. So the consistently moral poise of Tragedy chiefly, and the Old Comedy entirely, stood outside the ritual structure.[5] Nevertheless Anaximander's 'payment of retribution in the appointed time' is somewhat analogous in the type of plays discussed above, where human endeavour is a part of the ritual plan. This is especially evident in the creations of Æschylus, who saw all life held together in the Justice of 'Zeus, whoever He may be'. Yet he imagined Prometheus. Like Milton's, his faith was great enough to take as hero the Adversary in person and make him spiritually superior to defeat; only he went beyond Milton and Shelley in formulating a reconciliation 'within the disposition of time', because of the ritual relation of that Adversary to his God.

The rebellion of Antigone is a similar example, on the human plane, of martyrdom for a spiritual principle at the hands of the existing order. Here is no need even for a future trans-

---

[1] Soph., *Œd. Col.*, vv 1654–1655.

[2] W. B. Yeats, *Collected Plays*, 1934, p. 573. The ritual moment is, of course, the return to the Mother of Rebirth.

[3] Herakleitos frag., 121 (Burnet's numbering, after Bywater). ἦθος ἀνθρώπῳ δαίμων.

[4] 'Each year arrives, waxes great, commits the sin of Hubris, and is slain.' Gilbert Murray, *Four Stages of Greek Religion*, 1912, p. 47.

[5] Cf. H. Kuhn, *Harvard Studies in Classical Philology*, LIII, p. 63: 'The act does not impinge upon some single limitation, but shows human greatness outgrowing the world of limitation.'

formation. For Sophocles the heroic life was enough, as for Shakespeare and Homer. The tremendous catastrophe of King Œdipus or King Lear, if incommensurate with their deeds, is their 'offering to the grandeur of humanity'.[1] Euripides, involved in the disillusion of Athenian decline, often detached his characters from their heroic legend. They became persons, and their fitting within the ritual structure was consequently a little artificial, as in Comedy. But the heroes of the greatest three plays of all tragedians include their legend. They emerge from the gigantic background of their past to confront their Antagonist in the puny person of a Kreon or Ægisthus or Jason. The human opponents of the Iliad were comparatively equally matched,[2] but tragedy has isolated the protagonist by turning the combat inward, so that the hero in his crisis incorporates both divinity and victim in the ritual relation which lies at the dramatic source.[3]

That is why Aristotle assigns such importance to the maintenance of the plot from seed to fruition. The close of each of the more successful tragedies or trilogies reveals a step taken in spiritual progress by means of its physical disaster, a step that carries the protagonist beyond the cycle of seasonal drama, since it forces the barriers of a former social discipline. Each hero, as he emerges, brings with him a past world, for recreation by a divinity whose nature has been recast during their mutual struggle. By this time the other characters have fallen away. The whole previous action takes shape as an imaginative experience. Orestes and Œdipus face the Gods alone.

[1] 'Æschylus has made Apollo the instigator of Orestes' deed. In Sophocles' *Electra* his interpretation of the God's command is thrown upon Orestes himself. So the issue is entirely human.' Electra herself presents 'that contradiction which is the essence of tragedy. There is no way out'. Thomson, op. cit., p. 355.

[2] Compare R. Despaloff, Sur l'Iliade, *Fontaine*, 33, Algiers, 1944, 302: 'La poésie découvre, au delà des conflits, la prédestination mystérieuse qui rend dignes l'un de l'autre les adversaires appelés à une rencontre inexorable.'

[3] The isolation of the tragic hero is beautifully linked by Kuhn, op. cit., p. 84, with a passage in F. Saxl's *Mithras*, pp. 48–49, Berlin, 1931, concerning the focus of Greek classical sculpture on man alone: 'the Emancipation of the Individual.' He points out that the metopes of the Parthenon which depict the conflict of man with sub-man, not as heraldically opposed, but as organically involved, are perfect symbols of this imaginative attainment.

INDEX OF AUTHORITIES

INDEX OF AUTHORITIES

INDEX OF AUTHORITIES

GENERAL INDEX

Aaron, symbolic attire, 204

Abraham, 126, 196, 199 f., 202

Abri-Murat, 59

Achæan element at Mycenæ, 256; migrations, 264

Aeschylus, 325, 329. *See also* Index of Authorities

Agon, in Comedy, 320, 321; in Tragedy, 333

Agriculture, basis of Egyptian union, 111; earliest, in Sumer, 96; unknown to American immigrants, 178; agric. festivals; Athenian, 293 ff. *See also* Fertility rite

Altamira, 14, 15, 21, 22, 43, 44

Al 'Ubaid culture, 89 f., 92, 94, 96, 97

Altar, anointing of, 200, 204; double, 239; for burnt offerings, 207 f.; horned, 100, 204, 217, 229, 230, 248; moveable, 219; of Stonehenge, 151; unhewn stone, 197, 203; waisted, 127. *See also* Horns, Pillar

Amenemhat III, pyramid-inscription of, 176

America, Central, *see* Maya, Mexico; North, earliest immigrants into, 178; South, *see* Peru

Amulets, 99, 124; animal, 27, 109; axe-, 94, 132, 136; hut-, 98; rings as, 221, 225

Anaxagoras, 306

Anaximander, 302 f., 329

Anaximenes, 303 f.

Ancestors, primal, 36, 39, 46 f., 180. *See also* Stones

Angels, 199

Animals, carved on Palæolithic weapons, 25, 27; cave-paintings of, 18, 19 ff.; conception of human

relation to, 20, 23, 24; heraldic, 137, 223, 245; Neolithic domestication of, 73; on ivory knife-handles, 110; totemic, 34 f., 44; animal forms of Olympian deities, 273; animal masks of Egyptian gods, 112 f.; of Minoan genii, 227; of priests, 246; animal dances, 43, 285; animal orchestra, 90; chorus, 320

Ankh-sign, 248 n. 4

Antigone, 323, 324, 326, 329 f.

Aphrodite, 248, 268; institutes marriage, 325 n. 2; of the Dove, 234; oriental character of, 275; son of; Dove of, 276

Apollo, earliest, 225; cruelty of, 278; origin as vegetation-god, 277; and Dionysus, 286, 287; in Pythagorean system, 307 f.

Arabia, stone-worship in, 123

Architecture, first appearance of, 84, 92; Megalithic, *see* s.v.; Neolithic, 128; relation to pillar-worship, 127; of Mycenaean tholoi, 254 f.

Ares, once Earth-spirit, 276

Ariadne, 248

Aristophanes, ritual structure of plays, 320

Aristotle, 308, 310, 325, 326, 330

Arpachiyeh, 78, 128; domed buildings, 92; figurines, 78, 93; pottery, 78, 92

Art, first indication of, 6; function in religion, 35, 39, 83; Greek mainland religious, 243 ff.; magic intent, 19, 20, 41; Neolithic, abstract character of, 85

Artemis, 275; Britomartis equated with, 225; Goddess of the Gate, 120

HARPER TORCHBOOKS / The University Library

HARPER TORCHBOOKS / The Academy Library

[Selected Titles]

HARPER TORCHBOOKS / The Bollingen Library

C. G. Jung	PSYCHOLOGICAL REFLECTIONS. Edited by Jolande Jacobi TB/2001
C. G. Jung	SYMBOLS OF TRANSFORMATION. Illustrated. *Vol. I*, TB/2009; *Vol. II*, TB/2010
C. G. Jung & Carl Kerényi	ESSAYS ON A SCIENCE OF MYTHOLOGY: *The Myth of the Divine Child and the Divine Maiden*. Illus. TB/2014
Erich Neumann	AMOR AND PSYCHE: *A Commentary on the Tale by Apuleius* TB/2012
Erich Neumann	ORIGINS AND HISTORY OF CONSCIOUSNESS. *Vol. I*, illus. TB/2007; *Vol. II*, TB/2008
St.-John Perse	SEAMARKS. Translated by Wallace Fowlie TB/2002
A. Piankoff	THE SHRINES OF TUT-ANKH-AMON. Ed. by N. Rambova. Illus. TB/2011
Jean Seznec	SURVIVAL OF THE PAGAN GODS. Illus. TB/2004
Heinrich Zimmer	MYTHS AND SYMBOLS IN INDIAN ART AND CIVILIZATION. Illus. TB/2005

HARPER TORCHBOOKS / The Cloister Library

[Selected Titles]

W. F. Albright	THE BIBLICAL PERIOD FROM ABRAHAM TO EZRA TB/102
C. K. Barrett, *Ed.*	THE NEW TESTAMENT BACKGROUND: *Selected Documents* TB/86
Karl Barth	CHURCH DOGMATICS: *A Selection*. Edited by G. W. Bromiley TB/95
Martin Buber	ECLIPSE OF GOD: *The Relation Between Religion and Philosophy* TB/12
R. Bultmann	HISTORY AND ESCHATOLOGY: *The Presence of Eternity* TB/91
Jacob Burckhardt	THE CIVILIZATION OF THE RENAISSANCE IN ITALY. Illustrated Edition. Introduction by B. Nelson and C. Trinkaus. *Vol. I*, TB/40; *Vol. II*, TB/41
Edward Conze	BUDDHISM: *Its Essence and Development*. Foreword by Arthur Waley TB/58
Frederick Copleston	MEDIEVAL PHILOSOPHY TB/76
Mircea Eliade	COSMOS AND HISTORY: *The Myth of the Eternal Return* TB/50
Sigmund Freud	ON CREATIVITY AND THE UNCONSCIOUS: *Papers on the Psychology of Art, Literature, Love, Religion*. Edited by Benjamin Nelson TB/45
F. H. Heinemann	EXISTENTIALISM AND THE MODERN PREDICAMENT TB/28
Winthrop Hudson	THE GREAT TRADITION OF THE AMERICAN CHURCHES TB/98
Johan Huizinga	ERASMUS AND THE AGE OF REFORMATION. Illustrated TB/19
Søren Kierkegaard	THE PRESENT AGE. Intro. by W. Kaufmann TB/94
Søren Kierkegaard	PURITY OF HEART TB/4
Kenneth B. Murdock	LITERATURE AND THEOLOGY IN COLONIAL NEW ENGLAND TB/99
H. Richard Niebuhr	CHRIST AND CULTURE TB/3
P. Teilhard de Chardin	THE PHENOMENON OF MAN TB/83
D. W. Thomas, *Ed.*	DOCUMENTS FROM OLD TESTAMENT TIMES TB/85
Paul Tillich	DYNAMICS OF FAITH TB/42
Ernst Troeltsch	SOCIAL TEACHING OF CHRISTIAN CHURCHES. *Vol. I*, TB/71; *Vol. II*, TB/72
G. van der Leeuw	RELIGION IN ESSENCE AND MANIFESTATION: *A Study in Phenomenology*. Appendices by Hans H. Penner. *Vol. I*, TB/100; *Vol. II*, TB/101
Wilhelm Windelband	A HISTORY OF PHILOSOPHY I: *Greek, Roman, Medieval* TB/38
Wilhelm Windelband	A HISTORY OF PHILOSOPHY II: *Renaissance, Enlightenment, Modern* TB/39

HARPER TORCHBOOKS / The Science Library

[Selected Titles]

Harold F. Blum	TIME'S ARROW AND EVOLUTION. Illustrated TB/555
R. B. Braithwaite	SCIENTIFIC EXPLANATION TB/515
Louis de Broglie	PHYSICS AND MICROPHYSICS. Foreword by Albert Einstein TB/514
J. Bronowski	SCIENCE AND HUMAN VALUES TB/505
W. E. Le Gros Clark	ANTECEDENTS OF MAN: *Intro. to Evolution of Primates*. Illus. TB/559
R. E. Coker	THIS GREAT AND WIDE SEA: *Oceanography & Marine Biology*. Illus. TB/551
A. C. Crombie, *Ed.*	TURNING POINTS IN PHYSICS TB/535
W. C. Dampier, *Ed.*	READINGS IN THE LITERATURE OF SCIENCE. Illustrated TB/512
C. V. Durell	READABLE RELATIVITY. Foreword by Freeman J. Dyson. Illus. TB/530
F. K. Hare	THE RESTLESS ATMOSPHERE. Illus. TB/560
Werner Heisenberg	PHYSICS AND PHILOSOPHY: *The Revolution in Modern Science*. Intro. by F. S. C. Northrop TB/549
Max Jammer	CONCEPTS OF FORCE: *A Study in the Foundations of Dynamics* TB/550
J. M. Keynes	A TREATISE ON PROBABILITY. Foreword by N. R. Hanson TB/557
S. Körner	THE PHILOSOPHY OF MATHEMATICS: *An Introduction* TB/547
J. R. Partington	A SHORT HISTORY OF CHEMISTRY. Illustrated TB/522
H. T. Pledge	SCIENCE SINCE 1500: *A Short History of Mathematics, Physics, Chemistry, and Biology*. Illustrated TB/506
Paul A. Schilpp, *Ed.*	ALBERT EINSTEIN: *Philosopher-Scientist*. *Vol. I*, TB/502; *Vol. II*, TB/503